GOING
DEEPER

Foreword by Corey Russell

GOING DEEPER

40-Week Discipleship Guide to Encountering Jesus

JEFF MOOTZ

EQUIP PRESS

Colorado Springs

GOING
DEEPER

Published by Equip Press, Colorado Springs, CO.

First Edition: 2022
Going Deeper / Jeff Mootz
Paperback ISBN: 978-1-951304-88-1
eBook ISBN: 978-1-951304-89-8
Library of Congress Control Number: 2022904855

EQUIP PRESS
Colorado Springs

DEDICATION

I dedicate this book to my friends and leaders at the International House of Prayer in Kansas City. I am forever grateful for your zealous commitment to 24/7 ministry to God and equipping myself and others in prayer and the knowledge of God's heart. Your friendship and exemplary discipleship formed my life in God and still inspire me to this day.

Video Course Discount

Email us for a 50% off promo code!
-80+ Demonstration and Teaching videos
-Going Deeper Ebook Included
-7-Day FREE TRIAL

Email us for access to the *Going Deeper Student Facebook Group*. support@prayerdiscipleship.com

www.prayerdiscipleship.com

CONTENTS

Acknowledgments   11
Foreword   13
Introduction   15
Who This Is For   21
How To Implement   25

Module 1
Spiritual Planning

Module Introduction   44
Assignment Overview   45
Spiritual Pursuits   47
1. Called To Go Deeper   **49**
Consecration Assignment   61
Discipleship Meeting Guide   65
2. Intentional Spiritual Living   **67**
Discipleship Meeting Guide   79
3. Challenges With Intentionality   **81**
Discipleship Meeting Guide   94
4. Prayer List   **96**
Discipleship Meeting Guide   102

Module 2
Friendship With God

Module Introduction   106
Assignment Overview   107
Spiritual Pursuits   109
5. Designed For Encounter   **111**
**6. Jesus' Longing For A
Companion**   **125**
Discipleship Meeting Guide   140
7. The Happy God   **142**
8. Enjoyed By God   **153**
Discipleship Meeting Guide   169

Module 3

Meditation

Module Introduction	172
Assignment Overview	174
Spiritual Pursuits	178
9. Biblical Meditation	**180**
10. Five Ways To Interact With God	**191**
Discipleship Meeting Guide	205
11. Ten Practicals Part One	**207**
12. Ten Practicals Part Two	**215**
Discipleship Meeting Guide	223
13. Seven Heart Progressions	**225**
Meditation Observations	234
Meditation Observations	235
Discipleship Meeting Guide	236
14. Quieting The Mind	**238**
Meditation Observations	250
Meditation Observations	251
Discipleship Meeting Guide	252

Module 4

Praying In The Spirit

Module Introduction	256
Assignment Overview	257
Spiritual Pursuits	260
15. Receiving The Holy Spirit	**262**
16. Praying From Our Spirit-Man	**279**
Discipleship Meeting Guide	292
17. Communing With God In Tongues	**294**
18. Praying With Groups	**306**
Discipleship Meeting Guide	318
19. Different Uses For Tongues	**320**

Module 5

Deliverance

Module Introduction	332
Assignment Overview	334
Spiritual Pursuits	336
20. Demonic Strongholds	**338**
Discipleship Meeting Guide	353
21. Deliverance Guide	**355**
Leaders Deliverance Guide	370
22. Walking Out Freedom: Prayer	**375**
23. Walking Out Freedom: Church Family	**384**

Module 6

Bible Study

Module Introduction 392

Assignment Overview 393

Spiritual Pursuits 395

24. Bible Study Approaches **397**

Discipleship Meeting Guide 409

25. Book Study Part One **411**

26. Book Study Part Two **423**

Discipleship Meeting Guide 437

27. Word Studies & Interpretation **439**

Discipleship Meeting Guide 452

Module 7

Throne Room

Module Introduction 456

Assignment Overview 458

Spiritual Pursuits 460

28. Seated In God's Temple **462**

29. God's Throne & Glorious Colors **472**

Discipleship Meeting Guide 485

30. God's Glory Storm **487**

31. Around God's Throne **499**

Discipleship Meeting Guide 512

Module 8

Fasting

Module Introduction 516

Assignment Overview 518

Spiritual Pursuits 521

32. Lovesick Fasting **523**

33. Weekly Fasting Part One **535**

Discipleship Meeting Guide 548

34. Weekly Fasting Part Two **550**

35. Weekly Fasting Part Three **562**

Discipleship Meeting Guide 575

36. Transition Week **577**

Transition Assignment 582

Discipleship Meeting Guide 586

ENDORSEMENTS

I remember when I finally confessed that I didn't enjoy praying or reading the Bible. My "devotions" were nothing more than a religious ritual. Then, a friend helped me realize that a season of discipline could launch me into a relationship with God that was actually enjoyable. It was so effective that I now teach this life-transforming message to thousands of people around the world. Jeff Mootz has now taken this same teaching and made it accessible to everyone. *Going Deeper* is a simple, hands on, and Biblical guide to the kind of enjoyable friendship with Jesus you have always wanted. It's time to turn duty into delight. This is your way forward. Don't delay!

Murray Hiebert

Director - OneEleven Global

Jeff Mootz has a rich history of personally loving Jesus and encountering Jesus' heart that has encouraged and provoked me over our 15 years of friendship. He has taken from that history and written one of the clearest, most inspiring books on encountering Jesus that I've ever read. *Going Deeper* is a clarion call to cultivating a lifestyle of encounter that many desire but few have clarity to intentionally pursue. Jeff does not stay in the theoretical, ethereal realm of vision alone—though does present a high vision of experiential encounters with God—

but offers practical tools and discipleship structures to equip believers for breakthrough in their hearts and in their relationship with Jesus. This guided journey is a gift to the body of Christ globally that will play a pivotal role in preparing communities of believers to grow continually in love for Jesus until He returns.

Daniel Grenz

International Missionary – Firestarters Academy

As we get closer to the return of Jesus, the earth will experience great shaking and great revival. God is raising up a company of messengers who have invested the time to go deep in their relationship with Jesus to catch His heart, understand His Word, and proclaim His message with great authority. Jeff and Bethany Mootz are two of these messengers. They have invested years of their lives going deep with God and discipling a company of these messengers at the Underground House of Prayer in Sioux Falls, South Dakota. I highly recommend his book *Going Deeper* and encourage you to invest the time to gather a few friends and go through this 40-week journey together. The book is laid out in such a way that it will help you to develop lifestyle rhythms of prayer that will help you encounter God deeply, continually grow in your relationship with God, and bear much fruit for His glory!

Jeff Mann

Author of *Relentless Passion: Encounter God and burn with passion for Jesus* and *God's Eternal Plan for People and the Earth*

It's hard for me to think of people who enjoy their relationship with God more than Jeff Mootz. Consequently, when he talks about discipleship and how to build a friendship with Jesus through disciplines like prayer, fasting and Bible study… I listen. I'm thrilled to have Jeff's book as a companion for my personal growth, but also excited to offer it as a helpful tool to our congregation as well.

David Sinkgraven

Senior Pastor: Life Church - Sioux Falls, South Dakota

Jeff Mootz and the *Underground House of Prayer* have been a Godsend for our high school & middle school campus ministry. Jeff's calling to be an intercessor has blessed many people, and it has been a covering for the entire Sioux Falls region. Prayer & Missions are working together. Jeff has great wisdom and experience in battling through prayer to see breakthrough and revival. I am personally grateful and know that this book will help people dive deeper into communication and fascination with our Savior. May Jesus fill you and burn a fire in your soul as you spend time praising Him and hearing Him speak to you.

John Glasser

Founder – Collision Ministry

ACKNOWLEDGMENTS

Thank you to my wife Bethany for non-stop encouragement, affirmation, ideas, editing, and strategy meetings about the content and flow of this curriculum. The substance of your personal life in God and your zeal for discipleship are all over these pages.

Thank you, Susan Blosser, for reading every single page of this book through every phase of writing. I could never repay you for all the hours of work you put in. Your daily encouragement and detailed corrections helped make the book what it is!

Thank you to my friends at Encounter Church (Jerry Mootz, Brandon and Tammy Smith, Bethany and Francis John, and Aubrey Anderson) who have tested this curriculum, given feedback, and labored to see people experience the beauty and love of Jesus.

Francis John, thank you for your encouragement and labors in setting up the online curriculum.

David Stokes, thank you for pouring over these pages in the editing process and bringing your expertise in writing and pastoring.

Mom and Dad, thank you for your overwhelming support, celebration of victories, and life-long display of what it looks like to love Jesus in every season. Dad, the greatest privilege a son could have is to minister and pray with a fiery dad every day of the week as his full-time occupation. Because of you, I have a long-term vision to be wholehearted, joyful, and to love my family.

FOREWORD

I've read many books on prayer, been to many conferences on prayer, and heard many messages on prayer, yet I've rarely been around many of the same people who actually pray. It's sad to say that there are few people whose very presence carries the fragrance of heaven on their life, whose words release power and conviction, and whose actions point to a living faith in God.

I've recently been struck by Jesus and His discipleship model in Luke 11. After spending 3 1/2 years with the Son of God, the disciples asked Jesus one thing: "Teach us to Pray." They watched Him pray, heard Him pray. They witnessed the countless times when He woke up early and withdrew into the wilderness and prayed. I believe this left the greatest impact on the disciples.

I've given my life to the place of prayer over the past 20 years, and there have only been a handful of people I've consistently witnessed who've stayed true to prayer, fasting, and ministry to God—Jeff Mootz is one of these few. He and his wife, Bethany, graduated from our Bible school at IHOP-KC and ran close with me during their last two years. Their faithfulness, humility, hunger, and purity constantly provoked me and called me higher in God.

Since 2014, Jeff and Bethany have taken the DNA and lifestyle of the house of prayer in Kansas City and established a praying church that hosts city-wide prayer hours a day. This book isn't simply good messages but has been tried and tested in doing it versus talking about it. They have walked through the failures, successes, victories, and setbacks involved in continually calling people to God.

Going Deeper is a prophetic call to the Body of Christ to connect with our original design for intimacy with God through daily prayer with brothers and sisters in community. Friend, you were made by God and for God, and you will never be satisfied until you live out of that fellowship with God. God longs for friendship and intimacy with you and He enjoys the process and journey of relating to you. Jeff calls us to push past the barriers of our culture and even our own souls into a deeper place of encounter with God and His heart. He also highlights the barriers that stand in the way and how we can practically get through them.

I wholeheartedly endorse this man and this message, and I am excited to see this material get out and touch this generation. Again, there are few people whose life of prayer is greater than the message they preach. Jeff Mootz is one of these people, and I pray that God multiplies him and this message across the earth.

—Corey Russell
Author and Speaker

INTRODUCTION

FIRST ENCOUNTER WITH JESUS

"It's the first day of my new life!" This was the declaration I wrote in my Bible on February 25th, 2003 (in college) when my relationship with Jesus was radically changed. For a month leading up to this day, I was sucked into a deep depression with tormenting thoughts that drove me to sleep as much as possible as an escape. I had given my life to Jesus a year prior with minimal follow-through, but during that tormenting month, I committed to following Jesus by obeying His commands and engaging in prayer and the Bible for the first time. Having no idea what to do in my prayer times, I read the Bible and a men's devotional book and tried my best to talk to God.

Out of sheer desperation, I went from spending no time with God to spending two hours a day with Him. My prayer times weren't earth-shattering, and the Bible and prayer seemed foreign to me, but I found a momentary peace that I didn't have at other times of the day. However, on February 25th, everything changed. I turned to a verse in Ezekiel that was referenced in my devotional book. As I read it, the words became alive to my heart by the power of the Holy Spirit. It was as if God was speaking the words directly to me in the most intimate and personal way possible. He felt so real and close. My heart melted. I began weeping uncontrollably as God breathed hope and healing into me. After a while, the weeping turned into an indescribable joy and peace as I felt my emotions restored. I literally felt the broken pieces of my heart being brought back together. In that one encounter with the Living God, I became a new person and began a new season.

It was the "first day of my new life" because the depression and torment stopped with that one encounter. Later that day, friends even said my countenance was different and brighter and that it was like I had come back from the dead. I entered a new experience of freedom that made me feel like I had a new life. Not only that, but I was also joyful and had a new vision to experience intimacy with God. The new life of expecting intimacy with God caused me to begin orienting my daily life around Him. Without that holy moment, I wouldn't have known it was possible to experience freedom or such realms of pleasure in God.

DEVELOPING AN ENCOUNTER LIFESTYLE

My life has been transformed and fueled by encountering God in my daily times and yours can be transformed, too. God created you to encounter Him in intimate ways and to overflow in your heart and life. In the place of encounter, He desires to fascinate you, satisfy your longings, heal your thoughts and emotions, and empower you in your calling.

The heartbeat of this discipleship curriculum is to inspire and equip you to encounter Jesus by growing in prayer and spending one or two hours a day with Him for 40 weeks. Initially, this may sound like a lot of daily time with God, but it won't seem like enough after you're done.

From my experience, a good amount of prayer time is necessary because it gives your soul time to dial down and hear and receive from God in intimate ways.

It wasn't a coincidence that I experienced God for the first time after spending close to two hours a day with Him for a month. God responded to my hunger in that season, my heart was tenderized by the daily time with Him, both of which led to my climactic encounter and a new season of intimacy. Spiritual hunger and quality time with God are the necessary ingredients to going deeper in God.

When I was a kid, there were workout videos that promised perfect abs in only eight minutes a day. The idea was promising but not realistic. Similarly, I would say Christians promise each other deeper relationships with God through quick and convenient means such as fifteen-minute devotionals and short models of guided prayer. However, I'm not convinced they're leading anyone to a consistent and intimate experience of Jesus' heart and a transformed life. In fact, I think they're leaving Christians disillusioned and frustrated with their lack of true connection to God while thinking they're doing what they're supposed to. The fruit of this quick approach to prayer is a bored, broken, barren, and compromising Church in many places.

There is no other method to spiritual growth and freedom besides prioritizing encountering Jesus and overflowing from there. In almost twenty years of discipling, walking people into freedom from addictions and depression, equipping leaders, counseling marriages, and coaching parents, there has never been another option in helping them than first calling them into the supernatural life source of encountering Jesus in prayer.

Without exaggeration, experiential intimacy with Jesus is the foundation for everything in life. He is the power outlet, and daily prayer is the way we plug into Him and receive life. In my life, those who have pursued God in a serious way have encountered Him consistently and have seen ongoing transformation. Those who haven't pursued Him haven't encountered Him as much and have ended up staying in their same broken cycles.

Because of this, I believe it's most helpful to be honest and call you to shift all your priorities and schedule to spend more time with God. Now is the time to go deep into God's heart at the expense of any life changes and challenges. You need a lifestyle change and a clear focus on spending more time with Jesus. If you say yes, God will set your heart on fire with desire for Him and change your life. Whether you're a high school student, young-adult, stay-at-home parent, working full-time, or in full-time ministry, a fiery heart is your portion. One or two hours of daily time with God is possible in your life right now. Don't believe the lie that you're too busy or that you have to wait for another season because the next season will probably be just as challenging.

Your longings will only be met in Him, and your broken cycles will only be healed by encountering Him. Are you desperate to break out of spiritual boredom? Are you desperate to experience God more often? Are you desperate to break the sin patterns and emotional cycles? Are you desperate for God to overflow in your heart and life with others? Despite my spiritual dullness, lack of spiritual understanding, and depression, God took my desperation to find Him and brought me into a lifestyle of friendship with Him. In the same way, God will take you with all your weaknesses and bring you into a deeper friendship.

There is something powerful about the number 40. It's the number of *transition* and *testing* in the Bible. God sent rain on the earth for 40 days. Goliath mocked Israel for 40 days before David challenged him. Moses was in the wilderness for 40 years before His commissioning to deliver Israel. More than once, he spent 40 days fasting on Mount Sinai in God's presence. Israel was in the wilderness for 40 years before she entered the Promised Land. Saul, David, and Solomon were each kings for 40 years. Jesus fasted for 40 days to gain victory over Satan and come out of the wilderness in the power of the Spirit.

I hate exaggerated promises and hype, but if you approach this 40-week journey wholeheartedly, I'm confident it will help transition you into a lifestyle of intimacy with Jesus, one that will act as a spiritual foundation for the rest of your life. Like Israel in the wilderness, God wants to take you on a journey to ground you in the reality that you don't live by bread alone but by the precious words that come from His mouth. Intimacy with God and prayer take time, and this 40-week journey will carve out that necessary time for you to learn and grow slowly. With the help of others—and a clear structure—you will develop a strong rhythm in prayer.

Are you ready to step into a transition season with God and others?

—Jeff Mootz

WHO THIS IS FOR

In discipling people in prayer in general, and in using this specific curriculum with people for the past few years, I've found that certain heart postures and belief systems to be more fruitful than others. The answer to the question about who will benefit the most from this curriculum is that it's for believers who are spiritually hungry, teachable, and open to the work of the Holy Spirit. It's for people at all stages of spiritual development, and it can be used in various discipleship contexts (church program, small group, 1-on-1, peer accountability groups).

SPIRITUALLY HUNGRY

I'm not a salesman, so I'll be straightforward. This curriculum isn't for everyone. It's not for the Christian who is passive, content, or casual about spiritual growth. It's not for the Christian who's disinterested in a lifestyle change or the idea of daily prayer. This curriculum is for those who know there has to be more intimacy with God available to them. It's for those who are hungry to experience intimacy with God and are willing to pursue daily prayer for 40 weeks. This is for the person who wants to be called into deeper prayer, is moldable, and is searching for a lifestyle that expresses their wholehearted love for God. This is for you if you've been saying, "I want to go deeper!"

OPEN TO STRUCTURE AND DAILY PRAYER

The purpose of these 40 weeks is to inspire and equip you to encounter Jesus through daily prayer. To be able to live this out, you will need a commitment to fighting through all the challenges—practical and spiritual—to spend daily time with God and letting others help you by holding you accountable. To get a strong rhythm and depth in daily prayer through these 40 weeks, you will be asked to design and follow a simple weekly prayer schedule. Your schedule will consist of written down prayer times each day, a basic focus for each day (Bible study or meditation), and short-term direction in the Bible. This curriculum will not work for you if you are not committed to growing in daily prayer or open to learning how structure can flow with spontaneity in your prayer life. However, if you are open to both of these values, you will be enriched by this course.

OPEN TO DISCIPLESHIP

At the core of this curriculum is the strength of having one person pour into another in a discipleship relationship (or peer to peer). In saying that, the blessing of encouragement, prayer, challenge, and correction can only come to the degree that a student is willing to be transparent and teachable. If you are saying yes to this curriculum, you are saying yes to humbling yourself and receiving from another weak and broken person. This is how your spiritual growth will be multiplied and accelerated.

FOR NEW AND MATURE BELIEVERS

As long as there is hunger, a willingness to pursue more daily prayer time, and an embracing of mentorship, this curriculum will benefit believers who are newer or mature, undisciplined or disciplined. It works for newer or undisciplined believers because the structure, content, and mentorship provide the needed strength and step-by-step training to grow. If you're struggling to read the Bible and pray, but hungry to grow, you can use this curriculum and grow. I call it the beginners guide to prayer because it can take you from no prayer life to the beginnings of a deep prayer life in a very clear step-by-step process.

The lifestyle changes might be hard initially, but you can do it, and your heart will be set on fire. This is what you're wanting anyway, and it will be easier than doing it by yourself in another season. If I was able to jump into a lifestyle of prayer in a dark season with no past experience, so can you.

This curriculum will also be fruitful for mature and disciplined believers for five reasons. First, many of the topics will probably be newer or go deeper than they're used to and will stretch them. Second, the assignments will be newer and will help anyone go deeper in the prayer expressions. Third, the curriculum is mostly personalized to the individual's spiritual journey. Students will focus on pursuing truths in the Word that God highlights to them, pursuing healing from sins and lies, and pursuing calling. The components and structure of this curriculum will empower them to pursue each of these with more focus, time, tools, and encouragement.

Fourth, all the assignments can be adjusted in length of time and frequency to grow anyone in their prayer life. For example, if praying one or two hours daily isn't stretching someone, the amount can be increased to any amount they desire. Or if they are really experienced in one of the module prayer topics, they can increase the frequency and amount of time spent in those prayer assignments.

Finally, everyone goes further with a coach. Even the best athletes in the world have coaches and trainers to push them further than they can go by themselves.

No matter the maturity or experience (even pastors and prayer leaders), we all go further in our spiritual lives or in any area of life when someone is there to push, encourage, and process with us in a focused way. Because an emphasis of the program is pursuing freedom from heart issues, mature believers will be greatly helped by someone walking them through to victory.

OPEN TO THE HOLY SPIRIT

This curriculum is for those who are open to studying the topic of the Holy Spirit's ministry to believers. The modules on praying in the Spirit and deliverance have the most emphasis on the gifts of the Spirit (praying in tongues, hearing God's voice, casting out demons). But all the modules will emphasize the role of the Spirit in revealing the deep things of God's heart, experiencing God's manifest presence, and hearing His voice. There is time, space, discussion, and freedom within the curriculum to study the Holy Spirit topics to see what the Bible says, so if you are open to learning more (not necessarily agreeing with everything), this curriculum will work for you, and you will be blessed.

GROUP OR INDIVIDUAL USE

The structure and content of this curriculum allows it to be used in almost any ministry context. It can be used as an annual discipleship program within a ministry. Our church uses this and is building the ministry around it. Small groups could walk through it one time with the option of using the focus and structure of the curriculum (daily prayer, Bible pursuits, lies to pursue freedom from) as an accountability piece in the group moving forward. Mentors could use this whenever they disciple someone one-on-one. It can also be used by individuals to walk through on their own.

HOW TO IMPLEMENT

CURRICULUM PURPOSE

*G*oing Deeper is a comprehensive, personalized curriculum that will inspire and equip believers to encounter Jesus by establishing a lifestyle of deep daily prayer (1-2 hours or more). Students will practice different foundational prayer expressions each month and add them to their weekly spiritual rhythm as each module progresses. By the end of the 40 weeks, students will have:

1. *A higher vision for experiencing Jesus*
2. *Personal testimonies of intimacy with God*
3. *Increased spiritual hunger*
4. *Clarity on how to make weekly prayer schedules with clear direction in the Bible and prayer*
5. *Depth and rhythm in core prayer expressions*
6. *Biblical clarity on how to receive freedom from heart issues (sins, lies, and negative emotional patterns)*
7. *Clear pathways and empowerment to pursue giftings and calling*
8. *The ability to confidently disciple others into an encounter lifestyle*
9. *A life-giving vision and structure to use with future accountability groups*

ENCOUNTER LIFESTYLE

This curriculum is built on the perspective that our greatest eternal calling is to know and tangibly experience God's heart. From this place alone, God has designed us to receive from Him and overflow in our lives. In essence, God is the electrical outlet, we are the machine needing power, and we need to plug into Him to work properly.

This encounter lifestyle of experiencing God's presence, thoughts, and emotions overflows into many areas. It satisfies our God-given longings for intimacy, beauty, purpose, and fascination. It heals and fuels our thoughts and emotions. Lastly, an encounter lifestyle fills us with life and love in our relationships, and it gives us clarity and empowerment to function in our callings.

DAILY PRAYER: THE PATHWAY TO ENCOUNTER

The way you grow in friendship with God and experience Him more isn't a mystery. All you have to do is spend quality daily time with Him and let His presence awaken and tenderize your heart. As you do this, you will experience His heart in tangible ways in your thoughts and emotions.

This curriculum is built on spending one to two focused hours a day with God. This amount of time might seem like a lot, but it's doable and it quickly becomes enjoyable because God is beautiful and joyful. I believe it's a necessary amount of daily time to experience God in satisfying ways. Time with God doesn't earn intimacy with Him; it is a relational principle that time is required in any friendship. Practically, one to two hours allows you to enter into a deeper and more focused place of prayer, meditation, and study than fifteen or thirty minutes allows.

EQUIPPING FOR DAILY PRAYER

The natural question after being called to daily prayer is, "What do I do during this time?" This curriculum answers that question by equipping you with what to do in your daily prayer times. Each module covers prayer expressions that are foundational to daily prayer times. The chapters give biblical understanding and practical instruction to help you grow. The weekly assignments help implement the prayer expressions in your daily prayer times. The modules are four-eight weeks long to allow you to practice the prayer expressions, get a rhythm in them, and hopefully experience God in them before moving on.

OVERVIEW AND STRUCTURE

The goal of the discipleship curriculum is to help people form prayer lifestyles that lead to encounters with Jesus. Every part of the 40 weeks is set up to slowly and methodically establish that encounter lifestyle, at least to a foundational level. There are many practical and spiritual challenges to growing in prayer, so 40 weeks with a mentor, community, and a clear prayer pursuit is a gift to spiritual growth.

I liken this slow and methodical approach to the process of pouring concrete and allowing it to solidify. When cement is poured for a sidewalk, it's runny and needs wooden forms to keep it in place until it can harden. The prayer topics, assignments, other components, and the community aspect are like the wooden forms, and your daily prayer times are like the cement. Given time with training and community, your daily prayer rhythm and experience of intimacy with God will have time to form and become more solidified.

FOUR LIFESTYLE PURSUITS

The 40 weeks are structured around learning, practicing, and finding a rhythm in foundational prayer expressions, hearing the Holy Spirit for direction, pursuing freedom, and pursuing calling. Long-term, the goal is for students to make these pursuits the foundation of their spiritual lifestyle with prayer partners and as they disciple others.

1. *Foundational prayer expressions* - Students will pursue growth in one prayer expression at a time and add them to their prayer lifestyle with each new module. These prayer expressions will help them connect with God daily.

2. *Hearing the Holy Spirit* - Students will ask the Holy Spirit for direction in their spiritual life. This includes discerning one heart issue (sin, lie, negative emotional pattern) that God is highlighting and discerning direction for Bible reading and meditation.

3. *Pursuing freedom* - Students will intentionally pursue freedom from one heart issue at a time by studying and meditating on Bible verses that speak into their issue, praying for freedom weekly, processing and being accountable with their Discipleship Mentor, and receiving deliverance prayer at different times. By the end, students will feel more confident in God's power to transform their lives and have more clarity on what tools they can use in partnering with Him.

4. *Pursuing growth* - Students will intentionally pursue growth in one area of gifting or calling at a time by acknowledging what they want to grow in and making a simple action plan to walk it out. Depending on the student's needs in the curriculum, this pursuit may be minimal until they feel like they can do more than their prayer schedule.

The purpose of centering conversations and plans around what God is highlighting is to train believers in a lifestyle of asking God for direction and transformation. These are questions we believe are valuable for every believer to be asking throughout their lives. This Holy Spirit-centered approach allows God to create a strategic plan for each person, which is a more effective and relational form of discipleship.

STRUCTURAL COMPONENTS

Below is a list of components that make up this Going Deeper discipleship curriculum. The first four items will apply to any discipleship context, but the last four will be unique to those using the curriculum in a group setting.

1. ***Spiritual Pursuits Document*** - At the beginning of each module, students will fill out a document that helps guide their spiritual life. The questions on the document will help students pray and think through what God is highlighting to pursue in Bible reading, meditation, heart issues, and gifting/calling for a month or longer. Working through the questions will give clarity for each month's pursuits, but it will also exercise the muscle of hearing God and living intentionally as a long-term lifestyle.

2. ***Prayer Schedule*** - The first module is focused on establishing a basic prayer schedule, which includes when to engage with God in a focused way in prayer and the Bible. Since the focus of the curriculum is encountering Jesus through daily prayer, the prayer schedule will be a discussion point in *every* discipleship meeting.

3. ***Module Structure*** - The curriculum focuses on one prayer topic for four-eight weeks at a time, which is called a module. There are a total of eight modules. Within each module, there are weekly chapter readings and

prayer assignments focused on developing the one prayer expression. The benefit of this structure is that there is more time to learn about a topic and to practice it enough to experience God in it—getting a rhythm in it before moving on to another module.

4. *Assignments* - Every week, there will be an assignment based on the chapter reading. A few of the assignments are journal responses about the chapter content, while most are practical assignments that apply the content to the prayer life of the student. The majority of assignments are not meant to be on top of the student's prayer life. Their purpose is to guide what the student would already be doing in their prayer times.

5. *Bi-Weekly Discipleship Meetings (1 hour – 1 ½ hours)* - If the mentorship component is utilized, students will meet with their Discipleship Mentor every two weeks. The meetings will consist of processing chapter content and assignments, reviewing prayer schedules, hearing how prayer times are going, and praying through heart issues. Module One (Spiritual Planning) and Five (Deliverance) are different and require meeting every week. These meetings and this discipleship relationship are an important part of the "form" used to keep the "wet cement" of the student's prayer life in place until it solidifies.

We have you meeting with a Discipleship Mentor to encourage you in your life in God and to establish you in a lifestyle of accountability. Accountability relationships are a part of walking out freedom because they bring you out of secrecy, shame, and levels of passivity while pursuing God. Secrecy is the soil in which demons plant their seeds of accusation and sin, but, in contrast, transparency and honesty bring things to light to expose and uproot those seeds.

There is something powerful about confessing sins and lies out loud and being forgiven and sharing godly personal dreams and plans with another person and receiving affirmation. When done before God alone, you can dismiss or belittle them, but they feel tangible before another person. Accountability relationships are also helpful because they help you feel known by others for who you really are when it comes to your strengths, weaknesses, and heart-felt dreams.

6. *Discipleship Meeting Guides* - There are discussion guide documents for Discipleship Mentors to use for every scheduled discipleship meeting. These guides have intentionally crafted discussion questions to process the heart of each chapter. Each discussion has three parts: prayer schedule review, book questions, and praying through heart issues.

7. *Group Gatherings* (*1-2 hours*) - At the beginning of each module, there should be a group time for students and Discipleship Mentors to gather. During these times, everyone can share what God did in them during the previous module, and then a leader can present the topics and assignments for the next module. These group meetings build unity and help everyone feel like they're running with each other in the prayer topics. Corporate sharing times add unique strength and focus to those growing in prayer. *For those who have extra time, consider adding one-two hours of group prayer time before some of the gatherings.*

8. *Corporate Prayer Room Times* - Students and Discipleship Mentors are asked to spend at least one prayer time a week in a corporate prayer room. This time can be spent reading and meditating with a personal focus, or it can be used to worship, meditate, or intercede for something together.

9. ***Extended Group Prayer Days*** - There are three group prayer days scheduled (Module Three, Six, and Eight). I suggest scheduling two to four hours of prayer for these days. Some people may want to pray even longer, and that's great. The purpose of these extended prayer days is to allow individuals to taste and see the benefits of longer times in prayer, which can act as a catalyst launching them into more prayer moving forward. Longer times in prayer give ample time for hearts to quiet down and receive greater intimacy with God. This sense of intimacy is what drives people to spend more time in prayer. Sometimes people even experience a breakthrough with their heart issue during these times. People will be shocked at how quickly the time passes and how much they enjoy God's presence.

10. ***Deliverance Prayer*** - To aid in pursuing freedom from sins and lies, students will learn about deliverance in Module Five and experience deliverance prayer each week. The principles of the deliverance module and prayer guide will be encouraged in Modules Six through Eight to continue the pursuit of freedom.

PERSONALIZED TO EACH INDIVIDUAL

The combination of the four *Lifestyle Pursuits* and *Structural Components* creates a curriculum that is both structured and tailored to fit each individual, which is why it is effective for people in all stages of their walk with Jesus. Every pursuit and every part of the structure is personalized to where individuals are in their understanding and rhythm in the prayer expressions. Most of the assignments will be in line with what God is doing in an individual's life and can be increased in time and intensity based on each person's capacity. Examples of this include: Bible study and meditation direction, lie and character issue from which to pursue freedom, and the intensity and duration of daily prayer times and prayer assignments.

WEEKLY TIME COMMITMENT

In summary, the weekly time commitment consists of a *chapter reading* (30-60 minutes), a *prayer assignment* (15-30 minutes), and a *discipleship meeting* (every other week for 1-1 ½ hours). As a side note, many of the *prayer assignments* simply involve applying the chapter ideas in your daily prayer times. On a *discipleship meeting* week, this would average out to be a two and a half-hour time commitment. These commitments are on top of the daily time commitment to prayer.

CORPORATE PRAYER ROOM VALUE

In considering how you want to use this curriculum, I highly recommend creating a corporate prayer room at your church or participating at a local prayer room. My prayer life was formed and strengthened in a prayer room in my early days and helped me stay consistent and pray longer than I could have alone at my house. I'm so convinced of the power of corporate prayer rooms that I spend much of my time with God at my local prayer room each week and plan to do so throughout my life.

In whom the whole building; being fitted together, grows into a holy temple in the Lord, in whom you also are being built together for a dwelling place of God in the Spirit.—Ephesians 2:21-22

You also, as living stones, are being built up a spiritual house.—1 Peter 2:5

I believe God wants to revive and reclaim corporate rooms across this nation where each person's incense and offerings are mingled together as one before Him. Individually, we are temples of the Holy Spirit, but God is calling forth corporate dwelling places for His Spirit where individuals are "being fitted and built together" into a holy temple in the Lord.

ATMOSPHERE FOR DISCIPLESHIP

Spending time with God in the same room with others is the ideal place to be discipled and to disciple others in prayer. Prayer is learned and encouraged by doing it with seasoned leaders, not just being taught about it. Prayer rooms facilitate this natural discipleship process, and this is why the local prayer room is a major part of my method of discipling others. I help others grow in prayer by cultivating an atmosphere of prayer in a room where people can spend time with God together, be encouraged by one another, and see prayer modeled.

PRAYER ROOM BENEFITS

Corporate prayer rooms have anointed atmospheres. When a group of people consecrate themselves and pursue the Lord together, rooms and buildings can be filled with more of God's presence.[1] These atmospheres are primed and make it easier for other people to engage with the Lord in a sustained and enjoyable way. I've seen many people pray for long periods of time and encounter God in our prayer room, while before they struggled to pray at all. This sacred atmosphere is

---

1   Ephesians 2:22; 1 Peter 2:4.

available to you at your local church as you pursue God as peers and alongside a Discipleship Mentor in intentional relationships.

When people pray together, individuals can get momentary breakthroughs in God's presence that then ushers in a corporate breakthrough for others in the room. When somebody touches God in a prayer room, it releases God's presence to others in the room at the same time. We can easily pursue more in God together and spiritual atmospheres can shift when two or three are gathered. People can pray for each other, or with each other, at different times, and life is imparted in those times to keep engaging with the Lord.

On a practical level, when I see others pursuing the Lord on a given day when I feel tired or bored, it inspires me because they are physical reminders that continuing in prayer is worth it. In our houses, we have many distractions to attend to during our prayer times, and we have our beds as options when we get tired. But in a prayer room with others, we have a grace-filled atmosphere with fewer distractions and no bed to go to in moments of weakness. We utilize the inspiring power of doing things with others when we work at coffee shops, collaborate in offices, or work out at gyms—so why not utilize it for our prayer lives?

Lastly, praying in the same room together is part of God's process of growing us in friendship with one another. When we engage with God together, it naturally brings us into His heart. I truly believe that the unity of the Spirit we're called to pursue only happens if we engage the Holy Spirit together.[2] There are many intangible benefits to praying in the same room, but the two I'll highlight are having consistent shared spiritual experiences with others and experiencing a deep sense of camaraderie in prayer.

---

2 Ephesians 4:3.

STARTING A PRAYER ROOM

Starting a prayer room at your church can be as easy as opening the sanctuary for scheduled times each week that work for those going through the curriculum. Ask everyone to commit to coming or hosting at least one of the prayer room times. During the scheduled times, have worship recordings playing (www.ihopkc. org has live worship 24/7, or turn on various *YouTube* worship sets), or have one or more people play live worship. As a group you can decide what times are meant for personal prayer in the room and which times, if any, are meant to intentionally worship, meditate, or intercede together.

 # HOW TO IMPLEMENT

The optimal way to use this curriculum is to incorporate the bi-weekly one-on-one discipleship meetings and corporate prayer room requirement. Having said that, the curriculum can be used for each of the options below with adaptations. If you're willing to be creative with your approach and your schedule, I believe you can utilize most of the *Structural Components* and see much fruit after the 40 weeks.

DISCIPLESHIP PROGRAM (ANNUAL PROGRAM OR ONE-TIME USE)

At our church, we use this curriculum every year beginning in the fall. A new round of people goes through it every year with the goal of having most of them becoming equipped Discipleship Mentors for someone else the following year. Using this curriculum annually helps Discipleship Mentors continue their own journey in prayer as they lead others, and it creates a shared experience and shared value for deep prayer for all those going through it. We're building our church by making Discipleship Mentors with this curriculum—and by having a corporate prayer room.

To implement a yearly program (similar for one-time use), either disciple your leaders through it for a year before bringing others into it or prepare the leaders well beforehand and have them disciple others the first time through the curriculum. Once you have decided your number of Discipleship Mentors, you can invite people into a 40-week journey into prayer with the goal of having them leading others in the future. Establish your start date, end date, and when each *Group Gathering* would begin (beginning of each module), and what *Structural Components* you are going to utilize. When inviting people into the curriculum, make sure they know what the expectations are because they will have to be wholehearted in their decision (1-2 hours of daily prayer, having a prayer schedule, meetings, etc.). Communicating the expectations can be done by sharing the details of the program and by having people fill out an application that clearly states what they'll be asked to do during the 40 weeks.

Also, decide and communicate what your standard is for someone to pass the curriculum. For example, for someone to pass at our church, they must read every chapter and fulfill every assignment and be very consistent in their daily prayer times by the middle of module three. Also, decide and communicate what your standard is for people to become Discipleship Mentors after the program. For example, we require people to pass the curriculum, to have some rhythm and personal conviction about each module topic, and to allow the leadership team to pray about if they're ready.

SMALL GROUPS

For small group use, there are two clear ways to implement the curriculum. Option number one is to utilize all the Structural Components but to group people in pairs that meet up in place of the Discipleship Meetings. One other adaptation could be to discuss the chapter content and assignments in every small group and to save the heart issue and weekly prayer schedule questions for the one-on-one meetings. Option number two is to not have one-on-one meetings and to only meet as a small group every week. You could discuss the chapter readings and assignments every week but only have half the group share about their heart issue and personal prayer schedule every other week, rotating which half shares each week. If there is a small group leader, they could meet up with individuals outside of group times on a rotation.

ONE-ON-ONE MENTORING (NO GROUP)

To disciple one person with this curriculum, utilize all the Structural Components except the group gatherings. The curriculum is set up for bi-weekly Discipleship meetings, but you could meet weekly to go deeper into the prayer topics and heart issues. If you're the one wanting to be discipled, find someone at your church to walk you through this curriculum.

INDIVIDUALS

Using this curriculum by yourself is going to be a challenge, but you can still grow a lot by using it! The challenge is that you won't have a Discipleship Mentor encouraging and challenging you to go farther than you can by yourself (in prayer and in your heart issues), and you won't have the camaraderie of a group that is pursuing prayer together. To use this curriculum well, you must commit to following the 40-week flow of chapter readings, assignments, and somehow finding ways to process what you're learning and ways to pursue freedom from your heart issues. If possible, try to find a prayer room in your community, or start a prayer room at your church.

DISCIPLESHIP MENTORS

The role of the Discipleship Mentor is critical. I firmly believe everyone benefits from having another person in their life to encourage, challenge, and keep them in focus. For those preparing to use this curriculum as Discipleship Mentors, the important things to be aware of are the following:

1. *Curriculum overview and structure* – Review the curriculum so you understand it well enough to help your student navigate through it and own the purpose of each module topic and assignment. You will sense more purpose in the details if you see how everything fits together—and this will transfer to your student.

2. *Module assignments* – At the beginning of each new module, review every assignment for the month. At the end of each one-on-one meeting, you will review the next two weeks of assignments that need to be completed before your next meeting.

3. *Discipleship Meeting Guides* – The meeting guides are thought through to bring out the most relevant discussions for each chapter reading and assignment. They are also planned with the 40-weeks in mind so that things are addressed at certain points. For example, some weeks are more focused on the *Spiritual Pursuits Document*, others on the chapter reading, and later weeks on talking through heart issues. The discussion guide is laid out in the order of importance, which can change on some weeks. The way to work within the structure of the meeting guide document is to decide on which questions to spend the most time and add in your own follow-up questions beforehand or during the meeting.

4. *Preparing and facilitating meetings* – Prepare for your meetings by praying and reviewing the *Discipleship Meeting Guide* for fifteen to thirty

minutes. During this time, circle the topics you want to highlight, and write down your own questions to ask, follow-up questions based on your ongoing conversations, or encouragements to bless them. Facilitating meetings is mostly about asking good questions that help them process, being a good listener, challenging them to walk out prayer, and encouraging them abundantly.

5. ***Prayer room involvement*** – If possible, try to arrange your schedule so that you can be in the prayer room at the same time as your student. If this isn't possible, be consistent to pray together in your meetings, and briefly practice the prayer expression of the current module.

6. ***Pray for them*** – Spend time praying for your student according to the things that they are pursuing.[3] Your prayers will release God's power on their hearts, and God will fill you with His thoughts, emotions, and plans for the student.

TRANSITIONING OUT

After students complete the curriculum, the goal is for them to continue living out the rhythms and approaches they learned and practiced during the 40 weeks. The topic of the final week will be how to transition out of the program while still maintaining and growing in this rhythm and value system with others. Practical options will be to do the curriculum again, lead someone else through it, or form a group of prayer partners who meet to strengthen each other's prayer lives around the *Spiritual Pursuits* structure.

---

3 Colossians 4:12.

WEBSITE RESOURCE

As a supplemental resource, you can purchase access to videos and documents on my website (www.jeffandbethanymootz.com) that support the content of this book. The book is set up to be substantial enough to use by itself, but the resources may be helpful for those wanting extra guidance and encouragement, or for those who prefer visual learning. There are resources for leaders, such as how to set up and implement the curriculum, and how to pastor people who are growing in prayer. For students, the resources include introduction videos for each module, teaching videos for each chapter, and videos or documents about extra topics within the focus of each module.

MODULE 1

SPIRITUAL PLANNING

MODULE INTRODUCTION

Welcome to the first module of this discipleship program. You are on the first leg of a journey towards a deeper relationship with Jesus. If I may be so bold, you will not regret the lifestyle changes you are about to make over the next weeks and months.

Within this first module, you will wrestle with what it looks like to live with clear direction in your spiritual life. Just to warn you, you will probably both love and hate this topic because it challenges personalities, belief systems, and lifestyles. Because of these challenges, and because this topic is critical to building a foundation of prayer, this first month is entirely focused on praying and processing through every *hindrance* to building a prayer schedule.

You must work through the hindrances—otherwise, the rest of the program will be frustrating and won't impact you as much. Freely process with your Discipleship Mentor and take your prayer times seriously so you can get a foundation of clarity that will benefit you for the rest of your life. Those who are intentional in their relationship with God grow so much more quickly than those who aren't.

The tangible goals of this module are to develop a weekly prayer schedule, create a prayer list, and decide your direction in Bible study and meditation. You will also identify lies and sin issues God wants to heal during this season. The clarity and the basic plan you develop during this month will become the foundation for your long-term prayer life.

Are you ready to jump in?

ASSIGNMENT OVERVIEW
MODULE 1 – SPIRITUAL PLANNING

Week One Assignments:
(To be completed before your first Discipleship meeting)

❏ Read Chapter 1 – "*Called to Go Deeper.*" Journal your thoughts and questions about the chapter.

❏ Come prepared to share your life story and *why* you want to grow in God in this season.

❏ Complete the Consecration Assignment and discuss at your discipleship meeting.

❏ *Meet with your Discipleship Mentor.*

Week Two Assignments:

❏ Read Chapter 2 – "*Intentional Spiritual Living.*" Journal your thoughts and questions about the chapter.

❏ Fill out the *Spiritual Pursuits Document* with rough draft answers (direction, simple plans, and a prayer schedule).

❏ Write down your three main questions from Chapter two for this week's discipleship meeting.

❏ *Meet with your Discipleship Mentor.*

Week Three Assignments:

❑ Read Chapter 3 – "***Challenges with Intentionality.***" Journal your thoughts and questions about the chapter.

❑ After reading the chapter, identify and write down challenges you have with completing or having a prayer schedule. Take time to process these challenges with God this week.

❑ Continue working on the *Spiritual Pursuits Document* as needed.

❑ ***Meet with your Discipleship Mentor.***

Week Four Assignments:

❑ Read Chapter 4 – "***Prayer List.***" Journal your thoughts and questions about the chapter.

❑ Bring your completed prayer list to this week's discipleship meeting.

❑ Finalize the *Spiritual Pursuits Document* if you haven't already.

❑ Continue following your weekly prayer schedule.

❑ ***Meet with your Discipleship Mentor.***

SPIRITUAL PURSUITS   *DATE:* _____

1. **Bible reading direction and plan**
   (Write down what you will read and when you will read it):

2. **Meditation verse** (Choose a verse that speaks truth into your heart issue):

3. **Sin/character issue from which to get freedom:**

4. **Lie from which to pursue deliverance:**

5. **Gifting to pursue** (Include simple ways you can pursue it):

6. **Weekly Prayer Schedule**—Write down your plan for the *specific times* you are committed to spending with God each day, and *what specifically you plan to do during those times*. Include what your study or meditation focus will be. Refer to the example schedule in Chapter Two. (e.g., Monday 6-6:30 am—Tongues, 6:30-7:30 am—Meditation on Song of Solomon 1:2)

Monday

Tuesday

Wednesday

Thursday

Friday

Saturday

Sunday

1

CALLED TO GO DEEPER

NO SETTLING

As you begin this 40-week journey with God, I want to call you to go deeper in an intentional and committed way without looking back to your old life rhythms and experience of God. Your decision to go after God is holy and precious, and you will never be disappointed by the results. It may not seem practical or wise to those around you to give more time, energy, and focus to God, but in the end, pursuing Him is the only thing that makes sense. He is why you exist, and He created you to have a deep friendship with Him. You can't function right without having a deep friendship with the One who fashioned you.

Too many Christians are settling for the status quo when it comes to their relationship with God. All the while, they're struggling to find purpose and true satisfaction in life. They're experiencing depression, boredom, confusion, and anxiety, and wasting life pursuing entertainment. They also wrestle with a multitude of small addictions. In reality, having an unsatisfied and spiritually bored heart is the thing that isn't practical. The failure to solve the heart's most significant needs can lead to a thousand other life issues that will only fester until dealt with.

Demons lie to us and say that if we pursue God and live counter to the world or status quo Christianity we're going to miss out on life. Friend, this is such a lie. Life is only lived if we experience God because He is the source of all life. Jesus promised to satisfy and give abundant life.[1]

Pursuing more of God will cause you to live differently and, as a result, change your current relationships and experiences. But the greater perspective is that what you're trading in for more of God is nothing compared to what you will get with God. Giving Him more isn't a sacrifice; it's laying down momentary and inferior pleasures for endless and superior pleasures. Every other pleasure and source of life that we have ever known pales in comparison to experiencing the daily closeness of God.

God is the highest spiritual, emotional, and physical pleasure we can possibly experience. In experiencing Him, we are filled with His life and receive supernatural transformation. Over time, His presence heals, satisfies, fascinates, gives us purpose and empowerment in our callings, and causes us to walk in wholeness towards those around us.

NOURISHED VS. MALNOURISHED

Ironically, many people are afraid of missing out on a life with which they're not even happy. A good analogy compares people's needs for food and water with their spiritual need for God. It would be foolish for them to see that they're thirsty for water, starving for food, and malnourished, yet at the same time be

---

1 John 7:37, 10:10.

unwilling to change their lifestyle to get the nutrition they so desperately need. In the same way, it would be foolish for us to partake of little to no spiritual food, live spiritually malnourished, yet be unwilling to leave empty lifestyles to satisfy our God-given spiritual needs. Many people live like this—unhappy and spiritually malnourished—but are unwilling to come to God to receive His life.

People hold on to little pleasures and comforts as if they were crumbs in their hands while Jesus has a banqueting table of encounters behind them. If they'll drop the crumbs and turn around, they can partake of what He's laid out for them. I have a question for you. What crumbs are you holding that are so amazing you won't let go of them to experience more of God?

Is it food, comfort, entertainment, video games, social media, immorality, shopping, or shallow friendships? Is the Tempter getting you to believe that what you're holding will satisfy more than God? If so, confess it to God right now and declare that it is nothing compared to experiencing Him. Lay it down at Jesus' feet so He can fill you up with something eternal.

 ## A HIGH VISION FOR ENCOUNTERING GOD

Encountering God is the ultimate source of life and the greatest pleasure God can offer the human heart. God is beautiful, joyful, and filled with life, and His priority for you is that you would encounter Him. He wants you to discover Him, be fascinated and captivated, and then overflow in love back to Him. There is no greater pleasure in this life or in eternity that will compare to experiencing God. In fact, Jesus defined eternal life as intimately knowing the Father and the Son, which means we can step into our eternal calling and experience the life of God now by pursuing the revelation of God.

And <u>this is eternal life, that they may know You</u>, the only true God, and Jesus Christ whom You have sent.—John 17:3

HE DESIRES TO ENCOUNTER

Father, I desire that they also whom You gave Me may be with Me where I am, that they may behold My glory which You have given Me.—John 17:24

Not only has God made intimacy with Him available to us, but He goes further and pursues us to encounter us. God wants to encounter us more than we want to be encountered. Jesus' prayer before the cross was that we would see His glory, which means His heart is burning with desire to reveal Himself to you. God so desired to reveal Himself to humanity that He sent His exact image to the earth to declare the knowledge of God.[2] He is not distant, and He is not hiding.

Because of a lack of experience, it's easy to resist the truth that God is zealous to reveal Himself. But He isn't silent or distant; He is singing and shouting over us all the time. The issue is that many people's hearts are dull, and ears are full of other things. Because of this, they aren't hearing or perceiving Him, yet. But they will if they give Him time.

PRESS PAST UNBELIEF

God made your heart to experience deep friendship with Him. Don't settle for your current experience or the level of expectation you see in Christians around you. God has more for you in this season if you'll position yourself before Him by

---

2   John 1:14, 17:26; Hebrews 1:3.

giving Him more time. Take this year to ask God for a higher vision for encounters. Can you believe for more than your current experience of God in prayer? Can you press through the levels of spiritual boredom that you may be experiencing in your life until truth strikes your heart?

DEFINING ENCOUNTER

You were made to encounter God in life-giving ways, so what does encounter mean? *I define encounter as supernaturally perceiving a truth of God in our thoughts and emotions by the power of the Holy Spirit.* Encounter is when an idea becomes a living reality on the inside of us. It's when an idea becomes a tangible experience, a living interaction with God as a Person for a moment of time. Encountering God is supernatural, experiential, and happens in different measures.

SUPERNATURAL

Encounters are supernatural in the sense that it takes the Holy Spirit to reveal something to us. There is nothing normal or natural about this process. It's a supernatural work for the Holy Spirit to reveal God, who is uncreated, immortal, and infinite, to human beings who are created, mortal, and finite. Our natural minds cannot receive from God by themselves—they must receive understanding from the Holy Spirit.[3]

The Spirit must awaken the eyes and ears of our hearts in the same way as the men on the road to Emmaus had theirs opened.[4] They walked and talked

---

3   1 Corinthians 2:9-14; 1 John 2:27.

4   Luke 24:16, 31.

with Jesus for a few miles, but the eyes of their hearts were blind until Jesus opened them supernaturally. In the end, God opened their eyes to see Jesus. They recognized that their hearts were burning with the Spirit's revelation during their time with Jesus.

EXPERIENTIAL

Encountering God is experiential, meaning our thoughts, emotions, and bodies feel something tangible from God. Our minds can experience God as a person. Our emotions can feel God's emotions towards us, and our bodies can feel His physical presence. In the same way that we can experience love and other powerful emotions from and towards our friends and family, we can experience God.

Reading about meals on a menu and eating the food are two completely different things. One is just an idea or a theory, while the other one is an experience that involves all the senses. When reading the menu, you only have ideas and pictures of the food, but it's not yet experienced. But when the food comes, you see it, smell it, touch it, taste it, and savor it in real time. Encountering God's heart is a tangible experience in contrast to just knowing about God as an abstract idea.

Biblical knowledge is supernaturally understood in the mind and experienced in the heart. In many of Paul's prayers, he used the specific phrase "the knowledge of God" and other words that communicate an intimate experience with God. Many times, the Greek word for "knowledge" means an intimate first-hand knowledge that comes through relationship.[5] Paul's prayers should give us confidence that we can ask for and expect to experience God.

---

5 Strong's Greek #1922 - Romans 10:2; Ephesians 4:13; Philippians 1:9; Colossians 1:9, 3:10. https://biblehub.com/greek/1922.htm

Attaining to all riches of the full assurance of understanding, <u>to the knowledge of the mystery of God</u>, both of the Father and of Christ, in whom are hidden <u>all the treasures of wisdom and knowledge.</u>—Colossians 2:2-3

Grace and peace be multiplied to you <u>in the knowledge of God and of Jesus Christ</u>.—2 Peter 1:2

That the God of our Lord Jesus Christ, the Father of glory, <u>may give to you the spirit of wisdom and revelation in the knowledge of Him</u>.—Ephesians 1:17

In Ephesians 1, Paul asked the Father to give the spirit of wisdom and revelation to believers to open their spiritual eyes to the knowledge of Jesus. This was a prayer for believers to experience God's personality and heart by revelation—not just for them to have head knowledge. In Ephesians 3, he asked for the hearts of believers to know the fullness of the love of Jesus in a way that surpassed knowledge. Surpassing knowledge means His love is so vast that our minds can't fully comprehend it, and it means our mental study alone can't achieve the knowledge of His love.

Paul prayed for their minds to perceive God's vast affections supernaturally and for their emotions to experience and feel them. He experienced God relationally and intimately, and he prayed for his churches to experience the same thing. The main point is that God is more than an idea to be understood—He is a person to be known and experienced.

That Christ may dwell in your hearts through faith; that you, being rooted and grounded in love, may be able to comprehend with all the saints what is the width and length and depth and height – <u>to know the love of Christ</u>

which passes knowledge; that you may be filled with all the fullness of God.
—Ephesians 3:17-19

Be anxious for nothing, but in everything by prayer and supplication, with thanksgiving, let your requests be made known to God; and the peace of God, which surpasses all understanding, will guard your hearts and minds through Christ Jesus.—Philippians 4:6-7

MEASURES

Finally, encounters come in different measures. There are faint impression-level experiences that last for a few minutes, longer-lasting experiences, emotional experiences, and experiences everywhere in the middle. Every level of encounter is an authentic encounter with God. We don't want to neglect or minimize the impression level encounters, but at the same time, we don't want to lose vision for the more intense emotional encounters.

Whether an experience is faint or strong, short or long, it's a supernatural encounter with God. It's something we were all created for and should rightly desire. Many sincere Christians love God and long for more of Him but only have the vision to glean biblical principles from the Word and be inspired by a Sunday sermon. Encountering Him is more than reading a devotional on the love of Jesus or having good ideas and language about Him. It's about having tangible experiences with the love of Jesus in our emotions and having a current reality of feeling near Him.

WHOLEHEARTED PURSUIT OF JESUS

If God is the greatest thing you can experience and the only answer for your deepest questions and needs, why wouldn't you give Him everything? Don't hold anything back in your relationship with God. If you know you're compromising with a specific sin, confess it to God, and repent of it right now. If you know there are specific things or relationships in your life that are causing you to be dull or putting out your spiritual fire, get rid of them.

Get around people who are seriously going after God and spend time with Him in prayer and the Word as your highest priority. Give Him the best part of your day and carve out as much time for Him in your schedule as you can. Pursue Him as you would seek a great treasure, and you will experience an incredible source of life.

This book will inspire and equip you to experience a greater friendship with God, but you have to choose to be wholehearted. Every Christian must fight against the spiritual currents of busyness, apathy, lethargy, boredom, and accusation until they experience a spiritual breakthrough. A wholehearted approach to God will cause you to get those breakthroughs more quickly, and it will allow you to maintain them long-term as you build upon them with even greater breakthroughs. God is looking for a fully-given response that says, "I'm going to sit before You and believe Your Word until I feel You and get awakened at another level. I'm going to wage a spiritual war against everything that's getting in the way."

JESUS IS PULLING YOU CLOSER

NEW NORMAL

I believe Jesus is strategically drawing you away into a season of encounter that's going to reorient your heart and life around the vision of experiencing Him more. You're saying, "I want to go deeper," because God is putting that cry in your heart right now. There are seasons in our lives when Jesus takes the initiative to draw us into a deeper experience of Him to give us a "new normal" in our lives from which we then live. As we experience more of Him, we end up changing our lives accordingly. Before we know it, we have a "new normal" way of living to meet our "new normal" expectations for encounters.

God prepares us for these encounter seasons by stirring us with hunger so that we pursue Him more intentionally. Then He meets our hunger with encounter. This is His process. Hunger escorts us into the deeper things of His heart. Your hunger is proof that He is pursuing a greater relationship with you because He's taking the initiative in the relationship and stirring you. You're simply responding to His wooing.

HE DESIRES YOU

God wants you to know that He longs for more of you. We always say that we want more of God, but God also wants more of us. There is something in Him that moves when He thinks about you. He is strategizing ways to win your heart at deeper levels, and He is planning the days when He is going to encounter you. God is knocking on the door of your heart because He wants to love on you. But

He is also knocking because He wants to enter into a more intimate experience of your heart.

You may be feeling a lack of satisfaction with the things in your life. The things that once brought you life don't anymore, and you feel unsettled on the inside. Maybe it's certain relationships, sources of entertainment, jobs, or ministry opportunities that make you feel valued and important. Perhaps it's just an overall unsettledness. Either way, all these unsettled feelings are God's gift to awaken you to a more fervent pursuit of His heart. He is making you unsatisfied with your current life experience so that you'll pursue the greater pleasure and satisfaction that is within Him.

I believe God is saying this to you right now, *"Come closer to Me! I want all your heart, and I want you to experience all My heart. I want you to experience a deeper friendship with Me. I'm drawing near you this season, and I'm breathing on the little fire in your heart to make it a bonfire of love for Me. Keep responding to what I'm stirring in you. I have so much more for you if you'll come closer. I want to be your greatest pleasure, your daydream, and your source of life."*

REVELATION IS THE FOUNDATION

Encountering God and growing in friendship with Him is the end goal of being a Christian, and it's the starting point of transformation. The foundation of every heart issue is the lack of experiential knowledge of God's heart. Without learning how to plug into Jesus as the power source, you will continue to be dominated by sins, lies, and spiritual boredom. But in the place of experiencing the knowledge of God, your thoughts, emotions, and desires will be healed, and the building blocks for darkness will be dismantled. The famous preacher A.W. Tozer said it this way:

"The man who comes to a right belief about God is relieved of ten thousand temporal problems."[6]

▌WEEKLY ASSIGNMENT

This week, take time in prayer to talk to God about your Consecration assignment. These consecration questions will help you get God's vision for the 40 weeks and lay down any hindrances. They will help you set your heart to walk in a new lifestyle from the outset. I encourage you to take these questions and your prayer time seriously, because they will set you on a new trajectory in your walk with God. This week you will have your first discipleship meeting, in which you will spend time sharing and praying together over these consecrations.

---

6   A.W. Tozer, *The Knowledge of the Holy*, (New York: HarperCollins Publishers, 1961), 2.

CONSECRATION ASSIGNMENT

The purpose of this first assignment is for you to intentionally consecrate yourself to the Lord for the next 40 weeks. To consecrate means to set your heart and life apart from the world and from the normal standards in the church and to be devoted to seeking God in a unique way. It's a posture of dedication and commitment to God alone, as well as a commitment to hearing and responding to His words in this season.

Set aside a specific prayer time (one to two hours is suggested) before your first meeting with your Discipleship Mentor to pray about and write down a paragraph response to each of the questions that follow. After writing down each paragraph, take time to respond to God in prayer based on what you wrote. This could be repentance, asking for grace, giving thanks, or expressing commitment in your heart to what He revealed, or what you're desiring.

As you write down your thoughts and prayers, remember this document is primarily between you and God as a consecration, not for you to turn in for a grade. You will only be asked to share the main points of each answer with your Discipleship Mentor. Feel free to write your answers in your journal instead of here.

1. *In your relationship with God, what are you wanting to grow in concerning your heart connection with Him over the course of this program?*

2. *Write down the overarching reasons why you want to go through this program and what you want to be like afterward, spiritually and practically.*

3. *Ask God these questions and write down His answers. "What do You want to do in me during the next 40 weeks? How do You feel about my desire to do this program, and what are You thinking about me right now?"*

4. *Write down ways you've been sensing God stirring you with desire for Him recently and ask Him why He has been stirring you (reference "Jesus Is Pulling You Closer" section in Chapter One).*

5. *What is your current experience of God on a day-to-day basis (feeling His presence, His love, your heart moving in the Word, etc.), and what are you asking to experience of Him moving forward? Pray for God to stir your hunger for more of Him.*

6. *Ask God what areas of your life He is asking you to change or repent of in order to experience more of Him? Have you been pursuing and obeying Him with all your heart, or are there areas you know your obedience hasn't been wholehearted?*

7. *Bring your desires to pray daily to the Lord and consecrate your life schedule to Him. Surrender your time to Him, give Him permission to reorient your life around prayer, and commit to the one-two hours a day of prayer as the beginning point. If you have any fears about this commitment, tell God and process those with Him. Ask Him to satisfy you to the point that you would long for more time with Him within the 40 weeks and beyond.*

DISCIPLESHIP MEETING GUIDE
MODULE 1: SPIRITUAL PLANNING – CHAPTER 1

MEETING FOCUS:

The purpose of this meeting is for the Discipleship Mentor to get to know the student more and to discuss the Consecration Assignment.

DISCUSSION QUESTIONS (IN ORDER OF IMPORTANCE):

1. *Prioritize the Consecration Assignment* - Discuss the Consecration Assignment questions and answers from your prayer time. Were any questions highlighted more than others? Did God speak anything to you? Pray together to consecrate these areas to God.

2. Briefly share a few significant pieces of your spiritual journey (10-15 minutes) or share your heart for wanting to grow in God in this season. If you would like to share more of your story, you can set up another extra meeting this month

3. If there is time, discuss what heart issues you want to pursue freedom from.

4. *Chapter Questions:*
   a. Have you had a high vision for encountering God in your past? After reading the chapter, what is your understanding of the spirit of revelation and encounter? What are your thoughts on the definition of encounter as presented in the chapter?

5. Briefly review next week's homework together.

MEETING NOTES:

_____

_____

_____

_____

_____

_____

_____

_____

_____

_____

2

INTENTIONAL SPIRITUAL LIVING

INTENTIONALITY DEFINED

What does it mean to be intentional about your spiritual life? It means getting some sense of clarity concerning what God is highlighting in your spiritual life for growth and then creating a simple plan for how you're going to pursue that weekly. This directs what you read and meditate on from the Bible during your personal times, but it also directs books you read, what you pray about, and what you do with parts of your calling.

The basic idea is to form your weekly times with God around what He specifically wants to do in your heart in any given season of life. I call it breakthrough discipleship because it's focused on equipping people to hear the Holy Spirit's direction for spiritual growth, encounter God as a lifestyle, and receive supernatural breakthroughs in heart issues. Breakthrough discipleship focuses on getting victory over lies and sin patterns by intentionally feeding on biblical truths through study and meditation.

WHY INTENTIONALITY?

Why is having direction and a plan in your spiritual life critical to growing closer to God? God has specific things He wants to say and do in this season to bring you into the deeper things of His heart. He's wise, strategic, and pastoral—and He knows what truths you need right now that will act as building blocks for future truths.

Also, spiritual breakthrough requires focused investment over time in order to bear fruit. If you're unfocused in what you're doing in your prayer and Bible times, you'll end up not going as deep as if you had stayed on one topic or in one direction for weeks or months. It takes significant time in one truth to come into true revelation and transformation.

I'm guessing that many Christians read the *One-Year Bible*, a morning devotional, or read random verses for their times with God and are not feeling deeply connected to Him. Drawing near to God in these ways can be edifying, but they probably lack the kind of spiritual depth that intentionality offers. If this describes your past approach to spiritual living, take courage, there is a greater place of intimacy with God to experience through a more focused pursuit of God's truths.

SPIRITUAL MOMENTUM

Having direction and a plan will help you feel spiritual momentum. Momentum will help you stay consistent in your daily time with God. When you feel purpose in what you're reading and meditating on, and if you're hungry for the Bible verses you're studying, supernatural desire for more time with God will grow in your heart.

Staying with a passage of scripture long enough will get you deep into its storyline. This will hook you with a holy curiosity and a desire for greater understanding. Being hooked by the Bible means an intense interest grows in you for greater insight into the things you're reading. When you're hooked, questions about the things you're reading start flowing from your heart. Once that happens, your hunger will grow to search out questions. This will continue to grow until you're thinking about Bible verses throughout the day, passionately talking to others about them, and adjusting your schedule to get even more time with God.

Being hooked on the Bible and feeling spiritual momentum could be compared to what you feel when watching a really good television series or reading a good book. If you're really into the storyline, you want to know what's going to happen next, and you end up wanting to watch the next episode or read the next chapter. Some people even binge-finish the book or series in one sitting. If a book or a television series can capture your heart, how much more can the Word of God when it's anointed by the Spirit? You can get hooked on the Word of God in this way if you go deep enough in the biblical storyline.

I know my heart is hooked on a section of the Bible when I randomly have fifteen minutes to myself, and my automatic response is to study my Bible verses and read commentaries. Another sign is that I stay awake longer at night to read the Bible, or I wake up early with anticipation for what I'll discover during my time with the Lord. I think about the verses throughout the day, talk about them with friends, buy books about their subject, and wrestle with the truths until I understand and experience them. In a positive way, being hooked is disruptive to normal life because it demands satisfaction and moves you to reorient your life around discovering the truth.

STEP ONE – GET DIRECTION

Discerning direction from God and designing a plan should be a simple process. Start by asking yourself and God the questions listed below. As you answer these, you will feel purpose in what you're doing and feel like you're stewarding what God wants to do in you. These questions help determine your direction for Bible study, meditation, and prayer.

If you're not familiar with hearing God's voice, don't be intimidated. Get a notepad and your Bible and think about each question. As you do, write down your own thoughts, and then picture Jesus in front of you and ask Him the same question. You may have thoughts, a picture comes to your mind, or just experience deeper conviction about what He may be saying to you about direction. Many times, your own desires—or awareness of what you need spiritually—will be comparable to what you sense God is saying to you. So your own thoughts are totally valid. You can even ask one of your spiritual leaders who knows you well enough to give you a perspective on each one of these questions.

BIBLE READING DIRECTION

What are one or two Bible truths that you want to pursue right now, and why do they interest you?

What do you think you need to receive from these truths?

These could include Bible topics, specific Biblical passages, or specific books of the Bible. Then pray and ask God to bring to mind a truth or an area of the Bible to focus on in order to grow in these truths. These are the two most important questions you can ask yourself and God in discerning direction for your spiritual life because what you study and meditate on in the Bible will be the thing that makes the greatest long-term impact on your heart.

AREA OF TRANSFORMATION

What lie or character issue do you want freedom from and what biblical truth could help set you free in that area?

Ask yourself these questions and then picture Jesus in front of you and ask Him to bring to mind a lie or sin pattern from which He wants to free you during this season. Choose one Bible verse that has the truth that will oppose the lie or sin issue to meditate on. Meditation on this truth will become the doorway to transformation.

Experiencing freedom is foundational to being a follower of Jesus, so why not target the primary issues in your life that hinder you from experiencing God and walking in fullness? What if you were intentional about pursuing freedom from one area of sin or from the biggest lie that daily holds you back? What if you got supernatural freedom from fears, anxieties, depression, anger, unforgiveness, insecurities, addictions, various lusts, and lies about God and yourself by attacking them with truth during each season? Most people are aware of their issues but don't consistently attack them with the truth. You, however, can attack them by forming some or all your spiritual life around truths that will set you free.

AREA OF GIFTING/CALLING

What spiritual gift or part of your calling do you want to pursue in this season?

This could include gifts of the Spirit, ministry gifts that you see in your life, or aspects of your calling that you've identified. For me, this has included topics such as prophecy, healing, deliverance, preaching, and being a husband and a father. I give time to studying the Bible and other books in order to grow in those areas of my calling because I know this is one way to partner with God in these areas.

STEP TWO – MAKE A PLAN

After getting some sense of direction, the next critical step is to make a simple plan to fulfill your spiritual desires. Plans put feet to your desires. The process of thinking a plan through will excite you and give you faith because you will feel empowered to walk out real desires.

These plans will help you to be focused on what God wants to do in you. My suggestion is to stay focused on what you're reading and meditating on for at least one to two months, but you could easily stay on them for a few months in order to go deeper into the truths. Below are the main areas for planning in your spiritual life.

PICK A BOOK OF THE BIBLE

Choose a book of the Bible, a section (New Testament, certain Psalms, Gospels, etc.), or several verses that have the truth you're wanting to pursue. Make that your Bible reading focus for one or two months. My overall value with Bible study is to go deep into a small section of scripture as opposed to reading through the entire Bible in a year.

MEDITATE ON ONE VERSE

Meditate on a single verse for one or two months or until your heart is burning with its truth. I suggest scheduling meditation times every other day of the week. The truth of the verse will act as a spiritual hammer progressively knocking down the walls in your heart.

MAKE A SIMPLE PRAYER LIST

Write down five to ten things you want to pray for in your life. As a part of your prayer list, put the truth/lie or character issue toward the top of the list until you see a breakthrough.

READ A BIBLE-BASED BOOK

Purchase Bible-based books or listen to a teaching series that will help you understand what you're studying in the Bible—or one that will help you grow in a part of your calling.

JOIN A CORPORATE PRAYER TIME

Schedule an extra prayer time or one of your personal prayer times at your church. This corporate time could have worship, meditation, or intercession as the focus.

STEP THREE – MAKE A SCHEDULE

FIGHT FOR DAILY PRAYER

Prayer schedules are crucial to actually growing in prayer. I'm convinced that the greatest spiritual warfare from Satan is over our daily time with God. Our daily time with God is where we plug into the divine outlet and receive power for the day. If Satan can get you unplugged from the divine power source, he can quickly get you off course with spiritual dullness, sinful desires, and deception. Spiritual warfare begins by resisting the flesh and the Devil and by fighting for daily time with God. Fighting for daily prayer will be very hard at first, but you will connect to God more, and you'll develop spiritual momentum.

Scheduling times with God is an expression of loving and prioritizing Him. It's very easy to let needs, distractions, the flesh, and other people's priorities define our schedules, but we must take the initiative with our schedules. Your prayer schedule shows where God is on your priority list in the same way that your budget tells you what your financial priorities are.

PRAYER SCHEDULE

Think through each day of the week and pick the best times to spend focused on God. I suggest picking times where you can focus on prayer and your Bible without distraction. You can always pray while exercising or working, but these scheduled prayer times are meant to be set apart from other activities.

Write down the exact times you want to spend with the Lord and what your plan is for each day based on your answers to the guided questions in step one. I have my sacred times with God written out in my personal journal, and I have certain things I focus on for each day. I reference my schedule most days to remind myself about what I've already planned to do.

Focus on one or two things each day (study, meditation, prayer list, etc.) so that you don't feel rushed in your prayer time. For me, some days are more focused on Bible meditation and others are more focused on Bible *study* and praying through my prayer list. Give yourself plenty of time to go deep into something and don't feel the pressure to do everything every day. Try a prayer plan and then adjust it every week as you learn what helps you. Be flexible to adjusting your weekly schedule to better fit your prayer schedule.

It takes time to dial down our hearts and receive a true encounter with God. Because of this, I suggest scheduling one or two hours a day with the Lord as a starting length of time, then to grow from there. If you already have a strong rhythm of time with God and are hungry, try scheduling two hours or more a day with the Lord. Also, look at your days off and see if you can get a longer prayer day once a week. If you already fast or are ready to fast on a weekly basis, plan your fasting days and prioritize more time with God on those days.

MORNING PRAYER

Consider scheduling your prayer times for early morning before school, work, or family responsibilities. I see three practical benefits to early morning prayer. The first benefit is that your mind is fresh and uncluttered. Second, if you pray first, you'll do it for sure. If prayer is saved for later, things could come up that get in the way of your prayer time, or you just might not feel like doing it. Third, if you connect with God during the first part of your day, you will be more likely to overflow with His life for the rest of the day. In the same way that eating food in the morning gives you energy, morning prayer will fuel you for the day.

Waking up early can be challenging for a lot of people, but don't dismiss the option. Much of the challenge is because people don't give it a fair chance and don't set up a full life rhythm that allows them to wake up early while feeling fully rested. From my experience, it takes around two weeks of going to bed at the same time to be able to set my body clock to comfortably wake up early the next morning.

SCHEDULE SUGGESTION

A simple schedule might be to alternate between Bible reading and meditation every day. Then pick which day—or days—you want to pray through your prayer list, pray in tongues, or simply worship. At the end of this chapter there is an example of a simple prayer schedule that alternates between Bible reading and meditation, has an hour and a half of scheduled prayer each day, a fasting day, one long morning of prayer, and a weekly corporate prayer time.

EXAMPLE PRAYER SCHEDULE

Monday (5:30 am-7:00 am)
Pray in Tongues (5:30 am-6:00 am)
Bible Reading – Ephesians Chapters 1-3 (6:00 am-7:00 am)

Tuesday/Fasting Day (5:30 am-7:00 am, 12:00 pm-12:30 pm, 8:00 pm-8:30 pm)
Pray in Tongues (5:30 am-6:00 am)
Bible Meditation - Psalm 149:4 (6:00 am-7:00 am and 8:00 pm-8:30 pm)
Prayer List (12:00 pm-12:30 pm)

Wednesday (5:30 am-7:00 am, 12:00 pm-12:30 pm)
Church Prayer Meeting for my city (5:30 am-7:00 am)
Bible Reading – Ephesians Chapters 1-3 (12:00 pm-12:30 pm)

Thursday (5:30 am-7:00 am)
Pray in Tongues (5:30 am-6:00 am)
Bible Meditation – Psalm 149:4 (6:00 am-7:00 am)

Friday (5:30 am-7:00 am)
Pray in Tongues (5:30 am-6:00 am)
Bible Reading – Ephesians Chapters 1-3 (6:00 am-7:00 am)

Saturday/Longer Prayer Day (5:30 am-8:30 am and 8:30 pm-9:00 pm)
Pray in Tongues (5:30 am-6:00 am)
Bible Meditation – Psalm 149:4 (6:00 am-7:30 am)
Bible Reading – Reading through New Testament (7:30 am-8:30 am)
Spiritual Book – Parenting Book (8:30 pm-9:00 pm)

Sunday (5:30 am-7:30 am)
Pray in Tongues (5:30 am-6:00 am)
Prayer List (6:00 am-6:30 am)
Bible Reading – Reading through New Testament (6:30 am-7:30 am)

WEEKLY ASSIGNMENT

This week, your assignment is to follow the three steps outlined in this chapter to make a rough draft prayer schedule. This includes answering each question on the *Spiritual Pursuits Document* and creating a daily prayer schedule. After meeting with your Discipleship Mentor, you will have another two weeks to finalize the *Spiritual Pursuits Document*. This prayer schedule will become your reference point throughout the 40 weeks. Be intentional with it but know you will probably change it in small ways each month as you grow and learn. Also, write down your three main practical questions from this chapter to discuss in your discipleship meeting.

DISCIPLESHIP MEETING GUIDE
MODULE 1: SPIRITUAL PLANNING – CHAPTER 2

MEETING FOCUS:

The purpose of this week's meeting is to discuss the value of scheduling times with God and to talk through the rough draft of your *Spiritual Pursuits Document.*

DISCUSSION QUESTIONS (IN ORDER OF IMPORTANCE):

1. ***Chapter Questions:***
   a. What are your three main questions from this chapter?
   b. Do you understand the value of being intentional? What excites and challenges you about having an intentional approach to your times with God? Are there parts of this chapter you initially disagree with and want to discuss?

2. ***Spiritual Pursuits Document:***
   a. Talk through what you've written down on your *Spiritual Pursuits Document.* Ask any directional or practical questions you need that would help you better answer the document questions over the next two weeks. Do you feel clear on what you want to pursue in the Bible, heart issues, gifting, and how to pursue them?
   b. Are there other times in the day you can get more prayer time? Are there any days you can get more than one or two hours of prayer? What lifestyle changes do you need to make to prioritize your prayer times?
   c. Starting tomorrow, try to follow your rough draft prayer schedule.

3. ***Heart Issue:*** If you have time, start or continue the discussion about what you want to pursue freedom from. With heart issue discuss, process, confess, encourage, and pray together for God to release transformation.

4. Briefly review next week's homework together.

MEETING NOTES:

_____

_____

_____

_____

_____

_____

_____

_____

_____

_____

3
CHALLENGES WITH INTENTIONALITY

INTRODUCTION

This chapter addresses the most common struggles I've observed in myself and others for years in the area of intentional spiritual living. I believe the struggles and lack of clarity about this topic are keys to Satan's assault to rob people of powerful daily connections with God, connections that are meant to launch them toward their God-given destinies. By identifying these challenges and exposing the lies, you will grow in wisdom and feel more free to embrace structure in your spiritual life.

Some people gravitate towards schedules and plans and others avoid them, consciously or unconsciously. But both approaches come with potential challenges. As you dive into the challenges in this chapter, please know that the fruitfulness of intentional spiritual living is worth overcoming any obstacles in your heart.

CHALLENGE ONE – FEELING OVERWHELMED

NEW RHYTHMS

Feelings of being overwhelmed and stretched by thinking about developing spiritual direction and plans and walking them out may sound odd, at first. But some of these feelings are good because they signal that this new approach is challenging a casual and unfocused approach to spiritual living. Shifting from one life rhythm to another will always produce this feeling, but the experience becomes easier if you slowly bring plans and desires into place over the course of several weeks. Similar to entering into a new exercise lifestyle, start by putting one thing in place in your spiritual life at a time, such as committing to spend time with God when you've scheduled it. Let the spiritual "muscle" of focus and consistency grow and give room for spiritual desire to increase. Then add other components at your own pace (Bible plan, meditation verse, prayer list, praying in tongues, etc.).

ADDRESS HEART ISSUES

When you recognize the feeling of being overwhelmed, ask God why you're feeling that way. Talk to Him about it rather than giving up or deciding that living focused isn't for you. You will develop new spiritual muscles in this process, so the growing pain should be an expected part of the process.

KEEP IT SIMPLE

Sometimes, people are overwhelmed because they imagine planning is more complicated than it really is. Your Bible direction should be very simple, and your plan can be straightforward and easy to memorize—so keep it basic for now. If needed, ask a more mature friend or spiritual leader for direction in what you should read and meditate on based on your growth goal.

CHALLENGE TWO – FEELS RELIGIOUS AND NON-RELATIONAL

SATAN'S STRATEGY

One of Satan's strategies is to make believers passive in their pursuit of God by causing them to feel religious in doing spiritual disciplines altogether—or doing them with intensity. If he can make you feel "religious" when reading the Bible, praying, fasting, or obeying, he can get you to draw back from doing them aggressively. If he can get you to draw back from pursuing God like the hidden treasure that He is, then he wins by disconnecting you from God as your daily source of life.

Think about this for a minute. You need daily quality time with God to grow. To get that daily rhythm, you have to consistently fight your flesh and circumstances. If Satan can convince you that fighting your flesh and circumstances is religious, you'll back off and give way to the normal current of life. You'll still pursue God, but you'll be apprehensive about pursuing Him with all your heart because you feel religious. The result will be less and less quality time with God. The more disconnected you are from God, the greater the religious accusations will be, and the smaller your desire for God will become. If you struggle with these kinds of thoughts, confess to your Discipleship Mentor and rebuke the demonic confusion.

NOT LED BY DESIRE

The first religious struggle people confess is, "I feel mechanical, and I don't feel led by desire when I have a prayer schedule." My usual response is that plans don't make someone feel religious; they bring the once hidden religious mindset to the surface. The instinct is to throw out the schedule because of the negative feelings, but in this situation, I think it's best to address the heart issue through repentance. Rather than throwing out the thing that is exposing and has the power to heal the religious mindset, let it help you encounter the truth in Jesus.

Scheduled prayer times don't have to feel fake and mechanical. They can be led by desire. Making and prioritizing your schedule is an act of desire for God. Following through on it, whether you feel like it or not in the moment, is being led by desire because you made your schedule out of a sincere longing to be with God each day. Even in friendships, there is the need to schedule time together to make sure it happens. We schedule time with them out of love, whether we feel it or not at the actual time.

Being "led by desire" often means being led by our unsanctified flesh. Schedules are a good thing because they show us how often we don't "feel" like talking to God. If we were led by the Spirit at every point of the day, wouldn't we feel a desire for God during our scheduled prayer times? Not feeling desire for God in the moment probably means we're operating out of our broken flesh instead of our spirit-man. Why give in to what our flesh is feeling in those moments if our flesh is at war with the Holy Spirit within us?[1]

This is like the tensions we feel when we want to eat right and exercise but struggle to walk them out. We get excited about healthy eating, so we buy wholesome

---

1   Galatians 5:17.

food. We get excited about working out, so we make up an exercise routine. But when meal and workout times come, we may not "feel" like doing what is healthy. The problem in this scenario is not the health plan, it's the weakness of our flesh to follow through with the initial healthy desires. Your flesh is getting in the way of following your spiritual plan so that you can be spiritually healthy. So, wage war against it and know that it's an expression of your love for God.

What people mean by feeling mechanical and fake during prayer times is that their emotions don't feel what their mouths are speaking and singing to God. They don't feel like they are being authentic when their heart doesn't feel the truth of their words. This fake feeling is part of the normal process of being tenderized by God. It might not feel authentic for a while, but when people start to spend consistent time with God, their hearts will start to move and feel more authentic.

EARNING AND DISAPPOINTING

The second religious struggle people confess is, "I feel religious with schedules because I feel like I'm earning God's love when I fulfill them and disappointing Him when I don't." This is a common hurdle for many people to overcome when growing in prayer because they don't yet understand the extravagance of His free love. If you feel this way, know that you're not alone and that this motivation will change as you encounter God's love more and more. It's fruitful to wrestle with this for a season because there's a significant revelation of God's heart throughout the process.

The main answer to this challenge is that God's heart doesn't change towards us whether we do or don't follow our prayer schedule. Instead, our hearts are impacted and tenderized to feel Him more when we spend time with Him. His presence and affections towards us are always there for us to experience. But those who touch His presence, are the ones who say yes to that open door day after day.

Some people wrongly use the words "legalistic, works, and religious" regarding anything spiritual that requires time, effort, and resisting the flesh. They probably assume that anything to do with God will be easy or that God completely determines the quality of our relationship experience, because to say otherwise means you're earning something from God. The biblical truth is that we have to deny our flesh, pursue God with energy and focus, and sow in the Spirit to reap of the Spirit.[2] They praise people for their diligence and faithfulness in doing other life things consistently, but they prefer to call these same people legalistic and religious if they're as zealous about their times with God.

Being intentional about spending time with God involves a relational principle that governs all friendships. The principle is that relationships require focused times together to talk, and also require heart responses from both parties. When we spend time with Him, there is a natural growth in the relationship. When we don't do our part—giving Him focused time consistently— there is a natural decrease in our tenderness and sensitivity to His friendship.

That negative experience is painful—and is revealing. We have to resist the lie that we're disappointing Him, but the pain of spiritual dullness is good because the pain is a sign that love is moving in our hearts. It's a sign that we are longing for intimacy with Him and we realize it is lacking. I even dare to say that such pain is the beginning of repentance turning the heart toward God.

Wrong motives and feelings of disappointing God are broken as we stumble in our sincere, but weak, pursuit of God and continue to experience His free love. My first experience with this was during my first month at IHOP. I was excited to

---

2   Matthew 7:14; James 4:8; Titus 2:12; Galatians 6:7-9.

try praying for hours a day and had a fresh vision to encounter God. At the end of one day, I was fasting and sitting in the prayer room feeling so weak in my pursuit of God, and not "feeling led by desire." I was doing what I knew to do, fasting, praying, and reading the Bible that day, but in the moment, I became so aware of how little I had to offer God. I was weak in my pursuit of Him, and my heart didn't feel much love for Him.

My pursuit was real and meaningful, but it became clear to me that His affection was towards me unrelated to my level of pursuit. I began to weep as He spoke to me about His love for me in the midst of my weak love and my weak pursuit of Him. I truly felt the reality of Psalm 40:17, *"But I am poor and needy; yet the LORD thinks upon me."* That experience shifted my heart because it made me more confident in His free love for me despite my weak pursuit. This actually increased my desire and pursuit of Him.

To get free of the lies and wrong motivations, acknowledge them to God any time that you're aware of them. Repent of them out loud to God by saying you are choosing to not be led by those lies or wrong motivations. Then keep praying and reading the Bible as normal, trusting that He will wash away those motives day by day in His presence. Ask Him to wash you with His presence that day and renew longing in your heart for Him.

TANGIBLE MEASUREMENTS

Schedules and plans make us aware of how we're doing in our pursuit of God. They create some level of expectation or standard that we naturally want to meet. This is beneficial because it makes us aware of how much we are actually praying— or not praying. If we're a little blind or willfully ignorant to how much we're not praying, the reality check can awaken desperation within us and help us get on track.

When we have a schedule, expectations, and accountability, we quickly become aware if we don't pray for several days in a row. When this happens, we can examine our hearts and confront the underlying issues that have always kept us from consistent prayer. Again, there is good pain in the reality check—it's the revelation of our hearts and repentance.

There is a potential negative related to tangible measurements for *perfectionists*. They have a sense of earning God's love and presence if they fulfill the plans, and conversely, they feel like a failure if they don't. I believe feelings of earning God's love or disappointing God were already happening in the person's heart before the schedule was created—it just wasn't as clear to them. Those motivations and feelings were subtle. They were there with many other things in life and caused negative patterns in relation to God.

Praise God for the schedule that brings these things to the surface. Now the hidden motives and feelings can be addressed and healed. Any day that you become aware of these motivations or feelings, acknowledge them and repent before God. As you spend daily time with God and talk to Him about these heart challenges, trust that He will free you from them.

CHALLENGE THREE – "I PRAY ALL DAY"

Some people say, "I pray all day, so I don't need to schedule focused times with God." When people tell me this, I think they are either lying to get out of praying or they really are unaware of how much they don't talk to God. They think they pray while they run, drive, and work, but at its best, it's superficial and distracted prayer. Either they don't have a vision for more experience of God, or they want distracted prayer, because it keeps them unaware of their spiritual dullness.

I've never yet met the person who has proven to me with spiritual fruit that their prayer lifestyle of no scheduled times actually works. The fruit I would like to see from these people is a growing hunger for God, a tender heart that weeps when they read the Bible, spiritual clarity and understanding when they share about Bible verses, and to hear God's voice clearly, particularly in the areas of personal conviction and prophecy.

I truly believe we all need focused quality times with God each day to experience Him in deeper ways. These focused times, in turn, cause our hearts to overflow in prayer throughout the day. If you are wrestling with the idea of praying all day versus having scheduled prayer times, ask yourself these three questions. What is your vision for experiencing God, and is that happening with your approach? Are you avoiding the deeper things of God in prayer by engaging in distracted prayer throughout the day? Are there legitimate reasons why you can't schedule undistracted times with God?

CHALLENGE FOUR – FLEXIBILITY WITH PLANS

Many people ask, "How flexible should I be with my schedule and plans?" It's okay to be flexible with committed prayer times occasionally, but not to the point of losing spiritual momentum. I say fight to keep your plans the same as what's written down. If you've made a prayer schedule, you've thought through your life enough to know that these are the times you want to consecrate to prayer. My prayer times get interrupted by sleeping in or by my kids waking up early, so my wife and I talk through how to prevent those things from happening or how to get us prayer that day if they do happen. If you sleep in, or something comes up, try to rearrange your schedule that day to get in your prayer time.

Being flexible *within* your prayer time is a little different. First, I always want to be responsive to what I sense God doing in my heart in the moment. If I'm praying through my prayer list, and God is clearly doing something in me, I don't stop. I keep praying for the thing on my prayer list that moves my heart until I'm ready to move on to the next thing in my schedule. If He's speaking to me through my meditation time, or I'm flowing in worship, I stay with it as long as I want that day. If I need to shift my focus for a few days to allow for the expression that God is touching in me, I do that.

Scheduling long amounts of time for each thing I want to do during my prayer time helps remove this tension because I don't usually feel rushed to go on to the next thing. Also, pushing for more prayer time every day removes the tension. The second value is that I always want to be aware of what I have spent my prayer times on each week. For example, this awareness helps me know if I need to change my plans to make sure I get more Bible meditation if that seems to be lacking due to going long in other prayer-related things that week.

If I feel like reading or meditating on something other than my main verses on a certain day, I do that. Normally, I just write down the verses to do at another time. If I'm unusually stirred and excited to read or meditate on something other than my verses, I change my plans for a couple of days—or even a week—until I receive clarity on the topic.

Recently, I was listening to a sermon, and it sparked a hunger in me to search out a few verses that had not been on my radar. I wound up reading a book by the same pastor, and I processed a lot of the information for a couple of weeks. After I felt closure from chasing the Bible bunny trail, I went right back to my original Bible reading direction.

CHALLENGE FIVE – STRUCTURE AND SPONTANEITY

Is it possible to be led by the Spirit and have a prayer schedule? Yes, it is possible to have both because they flow together naturally. The Holy Spirit is the One who will help you decide your direction for Bible reading, meditation, and prayer times as you create your prayer schedule. If He's the one helping with that initial process, then your plans are led by the Spirit overall, so you don't have to wonder if He's directing you somewhere different every day. You can have confidence that God is leading you from the start and that He wants you to be consistent with your plan so you can go deep into the truths.

Some people feel confused about this and wonder if they are supposed to be spontaneous in everything related to the Bible and prayer, as if that is what being led by the Spirit means. The Holy Spirit knows that it takes time to get revelation in truth, so He's not going to distract you or have you investing in different things in the Bible every day. He's the wisest teacher in the universe. Wise teachers slowly and intentionally build on truths each day instead of speaking about random things each day.

As a general rule, being led by the Spirit while having a plan means responding to His presence, truth, conviction, and direction within the things He's called you to in the Word. For example, as you read and meditate, you will feel the Spirit prompt you to repent of lies and sins that are contrary to the truth you're reading. Another example is when you feel an increase of God's presence in meditation or worship. When this happens, be sensitive and steward His presence in the ways you feel led as opposed to moving on too quickly without regard for what He's doing.

CHALLENGE SIX – DISCOURAGED ABOUT INCONSISTENCY

It's normal to get discouraged by your inability to meet your committed prayer times. I don't know all the reasons why it's easier for some people to fulfill their prayer commitments than others. What I do know is that you'll grow in consistency when your longing for God increases, and that only happens as you spend time with Him. Your ability to spend time with Him should not fully depend on your discipline over your entire life. It's a choice and a discipline to begin with, but, as your heart grows, it should be fueled by desire and personal encounters with God.

Also, being aware of your weakness is a good thing. Seeing your lack of spiritual hunger and follow-through will cause you to come to God with fresh desperation for His empowering grace. This initial humbling will probably help deliver you from any thoughts that you're earning God's love by doing your prayer schedule.

CORPORATE PRAYER ROOMS

The best suggestion I have for you to normalize your prayer schedule is to establish or participate in a corporate prayer room. You don't have to grow in prayer alone! A major part of this discipleship program is growing with others by doing the curriculum together and by praying and reading your Bibles in the same room. The program strongly encourages a prayer room because there are many practical and spiritual dynamics and graces that are released when people set their hearts to seek the Lord together in the place. (Refer to the prayer room value section in the "How to Implement" chapter of the book for more perspective on this.)

My ability to maintain my prayer schedule for the past fifteen years has been deeply connected to my involvement with corporate prayer rooms. Because of these prayer rooms, I was strengthened to grow during my early years, I've been able to be more consistent, pray for longer times, and grow in friendship with those around me. I encourage you to make the extra effort to participate in a prayer room as many days a week as you need, even if it's every day for some weeks. It's good to lean on the body of Christ for strength in the place of prayer and the Word.

WEEKLY ASSIGNMENT

There are two assignments for this week. For the first one, write down any challenges you're becoming aware of with the value of having a prayer schedule or challenges you're having with walking it out so far. Include any comments or disagreements you have with the ideas in this chapter. Take one prayer time to bring the challenges or questions to God and ask Him for wisdom and truth. If you're willing to be honest and wrestle with your challenges, you will find freedom.

Your second assignment is to finalize the answers on your *Spiritual Pursuits Document*. This includes having direction and a growth plan in the Bible, heart issues, giftings, and then a detailed prayer schedule. The next chapter will help you write a personal prayer list, so be sure to include a time in your weekly schedule for praying through this list. You will fill the *Spiritual Pursuits Document* out at the beginning of every module to refresh your focus on what you're pursuing and to get a rhythm in asking these intentional questions of the Lord.

DISCIPLESHIP MEETING GUIDE
MODULE 1: SPIRITUAL PLANNING – CHAPTER 3

MEETING FOCUS:

The purpose of this week's meeting is to talk through any challenges you are aware of with having a prayer schedule and discuss your *Spiritual Pursuits Document*.

DISCUSSION QUESTIONS (IN ORDER OF IMPORTANCE):

1. ***Chapter Questions:***
   a. Discuss any practical or heart challenges you've noticed with having a prayer schedule and walking it out. Discuss any heart challenges you have with filling out the *Spiritual Pursuits Document*.
   b. What challenges did you most relate to in this chapter? Pray together concerning each challenge. Repent where you know you're believing a lie and ask for wisdom with the ideas you're not sure about.

2. ***Spiritual Pursuits Document:***
   a. Practically, how has your prayer schedule been going? Did the times of day you picked work well? How many days were you able to complete your prayer times? Do you need to make any changes to your schedule?
   b. How did your prayer times go spiritually? Were they difficult or enjoyable? Did anything impact you?
   c. Share and discuss any updates you made to your *Spiritual Pursuits Document*. Talk through each question and finalize plans for each area of the document.
   d. Continue to follow your updated prayer schedule each day and make note of what you need to change after trying it another week.

3. Briefly review next week's homework together.

MEETING NOTES:

4

PRAYER LIST

PRAYER LIST VALUE

t is foundational for your weekly prayer schedule to include a Bible reading plan, a meditation verse, corporate prayer times, and a written-out prayer list. It is important to have a prayer list so that you can be clear, thoughtful, and intentional in your prayers. A prayer list should include praying for yourself and praying for others and specific topics. The Bible highlights different prayers that you could pray for yourself and highlights what God values. It is worth the time to think through and lean into how you want to invest your prayers. Review the rough draft of your prayer schedule, and experiment with times and days to pray through it. Try scheduling one morning a week to pray through a list, but you could also pray parts of it over several days—according to your preference.

VALUE OF PRAYING FOR YOURSELF

Having a prayer list reminds you to pray for yourself as a value. Just to be clear, it is godly and biblical to pray for yourself. Purposeful prayer for the needs of others or praying in groups for your city at other times is very important. But it's equally important to pray for yourself. It isn't selfish to be focused on what you need from God in your heart or life and to spend time in that kind of prayer. It is holy to partner with God in praying His destiny (heart and calling) over your life. God has ordained prayer as the primary way we partner with Him to release His kingdom. By praying for yourself, you will see God answer and increase His presence, revelation, wisdom, provision, and power.

Not only is praying the way to see His plans manifested in our lives, it's also a powerful way to reconnect with His heart. I find that, in the place of prayer, God fills me with zeal and details for the things I'm praying about. When you pray His prayers for your life, it will refresh your vision and passion for those topics. You'll be reminded of them each time, which helps with intentionality. Through prayer, God will fill you with faith and courage in His promises. These refreshing times will give you the clarity to repent and re-align in any ways you have strayed from the truths you're praying about.

VALUE OF REMEMBERING

One practical value in writing a prayer list is that it will be a constant reminder of what you are wanting to pursue in God. If I didn't have a prayer list, I would forget the things that I was so excited to pray about. The more you pray over your list, the more the list will be rooted in your heart—but the reminder is always helpful. Also, reading and praying through what I've written before aligns me to a longer-term vision for where I want to go in God for the next decades.

VALUE OF RECORDING

Having a written prayer list—with some space to journal thoughts in between each prayer point—allows you to record things that stir you while praying for specific things. When you write down your stirrings, you can pray further into them the next time you pray through your list. The act of journaling is helpful to your heart, and it helps you remember it for the future. By recording and praying into the things that develop each week, you receive more from God in so many ways.

PRAYER POINTS

When you're making your prayer list, I recommend keeping it simple and limiting it to about ten different prayer points. As you begin, keeping it shorter will make it less intimidating, less of a task list, and easier to focus on the main prayer values. As you go on, you will discover your rhythm and know if you can add more points to the list.

There are no wrong ways to make a prayer list, so make it look however you want. Put any prayer points you want on there and change them whenever you want. You'll find a groove in the core things you want on your list long-term. Then you can change other points around at different times. Start by making a rough draft list of Biblical values, Biblical pursuits, personal circumstances, and promises that you want to consider praying over yourself. After brainstorming, pick the ideas you want to start with and make a physical copy of your list.

Here are examples of what you could include in your rough draft list: intimacy with God, the revelation of God, insight into the Word, wisdom, increased holiness, humility, fear of the Lord, hearing God's voice in dreams and visions, walking in the power of the Spirit, the fruit of the Spirit, personal promises from God (prophecies, desires, dreams), and personal circumstances (relationships, finances, responsibilities).

For one of your prayer points, I encourage you to pray for the heart issue (e.g., sin, lie, negative emotional pattern) you're pursuing freedom from. Along with meditation, living in a spiritual community, and deliverance sessions, praying over this area of your heart is one of the things God will use to deliver you. This sounds so simple, but it's fruitful. When praying through my heart issue, I pray for truth, repent where needed, ask God to protect and deliver me from the enemy, and for divine transformation.

FLOWING HEART VS. TASK LIST

As with any other prayer expression, the end goal of praying through your list is to connect with God. Therefore, take your time and connect with Him on each prayer point. Feel free to pray for a long time on one thing and not much time on another—and skip any points you want. There are no rules, and there is no pressure to thoroughly pray through your entire list every time.

Sometimes a prayer really moves me, and I only stay on one topic during my entire prayer time. At other times, I feel a little life on a few prayer points and end up praying through half my list. I feel God's heart for the prayer points, and the prayer time allows my heart to be strengthened and aligned by Him. To not feel rushed and to promote this deeper connection, I schedule one day's entire prayer time just to pray through my prayer list. Other people I know take their time in praying for one or two prayer points every day on top of whatever they have planned for Bible study or meditation.

Your prayer list is not a task list, or mission to accomplish. If that is your view, it will become an intimidating spiritual chore that might drain you. I used to make long detailed lists with the goal of making it through the entire list, which included myself, circumstances, family, friends, and things in the nation. I dreaded that list, but I thought it was the best thing to do. The task list mentality drained me, causing me not to connect to God in the process. Since changing to an intimacy approach, I look forward to my prayer list times, and I leave my prayer times invigorated—not exhausted.

EXAMPLE PRAYER LIST

Again, design your list however you want, but I suggest leaving space between every prayer point so you can write down things that come to you while praying over those points. In that space, I write verses that connect to the prayer point, further Biblical language on my prayers, more direction in how to pray the prayer point, commitments to walk out the prayers, or promises and insights God speaks during the prayer times. I have space to pray for my wife and children, so I write down anything prophetic I feel about them.

Currently, I have my handwritten list in a notebook, and I have a page open for each prayer point. I include verse references or written out verses next to most prayer points so that I can grow in praying God's language back to Him. Below is an example of things I would include in my list. I'm able to have a short prayer list because I pray for my extended family and my nation at other times with my wife and friends.

BIBLICAL VALUES AND PURSUITS

#1 - Revelation of God's Heart (Ephesians 1:17-19; 1 Corinthians 2:10)

#2 - Experience God's Love and pleasure for me (Ephesians 3:16-19; Psalm 16:11)

#3 - Walk in God's Power - Gifts of the Spirit, deliverance power, dreams and visions (1 Corinthians 12:8-10; Acts 1:8; Acts 2:17-19)

#4 - Increased Righteousness—current heart issue God is highlighting (sin/lie/negative emotional pattern), other Biblical pursuits (speech, thoughts, attitudes, actions, anger/bitterness, etc.) (Philippians 1:9-11; Matthew 6:13)

#5 - Increased Fear of the Lord (Psalm 86:11)

#6 - Strength and Might of the Spirit (Colossians 1:11)

#7 - Humility and a Servant Heart (Matthew 11:28-30)

PERSONAL ROLES AND CIRCUMSTANCES

#8 - Grace and Wisdom to Lead as a Pastor (2 Timothy 2:23-25; John 10:11-13)

#9 - Grace and Wisdom to Lead as a Husband and Father (Eph. 5:25-26; Ps. 139)

#10 - Prayers and Promises for My Wife

#11 - Prayers and Promises for Child #1

#12 - Prayers and Promises for Child #2

#13 - Prayers and Promises for Child #3

WEEKLY ASSIGNMENT

This week's assignment is to create a prayer list and finalize your *Spiritual Pursuits Document*. In your discipleship meeting, you'll have time to finalize either of these. Observe how your prayer schedule works for you and make changes as needed.

DISCIPLESHIP MEETING GUIDE
MODULE 1: SPIRITUAL PLANNING – CHAPTER 4

MEETING FOCUS:

The purpose of this meeting is to talk through and finalize how to make a prayer list and the benefits of praying it. Discuss anything else that needs to be finalized with your *Spiritual Pursuits Document* and prayer schedule.

DISCUSSION QUESTIONS (IN ORDER OF IMPORTANCE):

1. *Prayer Schedule:*
    a. How is your prayer schedule going spiritually? What has God been doing in your heart in your prayer times (Bible reading, meditation, etc.)? Have you had any heart challenges to following through on your schedule?
    b. How is your schedule going, practically? How many days were you able to follow through in prayer? Are there any changes you need to make to the schedule?
2. *Spiritual Pursuits:*
    a. Discuss anything needed to finalize your *Spiritual Pursuits Document.*
3. *Prayer List:*
    a. Read and discuss the different prayer points you have on your initial prayer list. When can you put your prayer list into your weekly prayer schedule? Pray through some of the prayer points together.
4. *Heart Issue:*
    a. Share how your heart issues have been this past week. With heart issue discussions, process, confess, encourage, and pray together for God to transform you.
5. Briefly review the assignments for the next two weeks together. This is not necessary if you are having a group gathering to introduce the next module topic.

MEETING NOTES:

_____

_____

_____

_____

_____

_____

_____

_____

_____

_____

_____

MODULE 2

FRIENDSHIP WITH GOD

MODULE INTRODUCTION

The purpose of this module is to ground you in the revelation that you were designed by God to encounter His beautiful and joyful heart, and for you to be filled with His pleasures. The foundation for growing in relationship with God in prayer is enjoying Him—and being enjoyed by Him. The main issue isn't about having more discipline—although that helps—it's about cultivating a revelation of His heart, so you will want to be around Him more. When your heart begins to enjoy Him more, you will begin to drop your guard and receive His love and life. When this happens, everything changes! Your heart gets satisfied in God, your emotions get healed, sin patterns get transformed, and you receive empowerment to walk out your calling.

These next four chapters are drawn from the creation story of Genesis 1-2, with the focal points being our unique design as God's image-bearers and God's extravagant heart as Father and Husband. These chapters are put in a strategic order to expose lies you likely believe about God's heart and to progressively unlock your heart to His overwhelming goodness. The assignments focus on meditating on key aspects of the creation story and praying through the things that hinder you from receiving from Him, things like self-hatred, unworthiness, rejection, and wrong beliefs about God's personality (His intense longings and infinite happiness). I urge you to come to these assignments with an open heart and to not assume you're totally free from these issues.

ASSIGNMENT OVERVIEW
MODULE 2 – FRIENDSHIP WITH GOD

Week Five Assignments:

❑ Read Chapter 5 – "***Designed for Encounter***." Journal your thoughts about the chapter, including the specific truths you sense God highlighting.

❑ Meditate and journal on Genesis 1:26 at least one day this week. During meditation, ask God what emotions He was feeling when He spoke Genesis 1:26 out loud, and ask Him why He made you in His image.

❑ Continue following your daily prayer schedule and your *Spiritual Pursuits*.

Week Six Assignments:

❑ Read Chapter 6 – "***Jesus' Longing for a Companion***." Journal your thoughts and questions about the chapter.

❑ Meditate on Genesis 2:7 at least one day this week. Ask God what He was feeling when He was forming Adam and when Adam first opened his eyes.

❑ Continue following your daily prayer schedule and your *Spiritual Pursuits*.

❑ ***Meet with your Discipleship Mentor.***

Week Seven Assignments:

❑ Read Chapter 7 – "*The Happy God*." Journal your thoughts and questions about the chapter.

❑ Continue your meditation on Genesis 2:7 and add in the perspective of God's happiness from Proverbs 8:30-31.

❑ Continue following your daily prayer schedule and your *Spiritual Pursuits*.

Week Eight Assignments:

❑ Read Chapter 8 – "*Enjoyed by God*." Journal your thoughts and questions about the chapter.

❑ Meditate on Psalm 149:4 at least one day this week.

❑ Answer the three probing questions and take one prayer time this week to ask God where you feel shame or unworthy of being 100% enjoyed by Him.

❑ Continue following your daily prayer schedule and your *Spiritual Pursuits*.

❑ *Meet with your Discipleship Mentor.*

SPIRITUAL PURSUITS *DATE:* _____

1. **Bible reading direction and plan**
   (Write down what you will read and when you will read it):

2. **Meditation verse** (Choose a verse that speaks truth into your heart issue):

3. **Sin/character issue from which to get freedom:**

4. **Lie from which to pursue deliverance:**

5. **Gifting to pursue** (Include simple ways you can pursue it):

6. **Weekly Prayer Schedule**—Write down your plan for the *specific times* you are committed to spending with God each day, and *what specifically you plan to do during those times*. Include what your study or meditation focus will be. Refer to the example schedule in Chapter Two. (e.g., Monday 6-6:30 am—Tongues, 6:30-7:30 am—Meditation on Song of Solomon 1:2)

Monday

Tuesday

Wednesday

Thursday

Friday

Saturday

Sunday

5

DESIGNED FOR ENCOUNTER

INTRODUCTION

The vision to experience God comes from understanding His original purpose for creating us, part of which is reflected in the way He designed the breathtaking facets of our human make-up. Therefore, getting a revelation of God's heart in the creation story is essential to our spiritual lives. It helps to define our vision for encountering God, and it opens the door to higher expectations of what God wants us to experience in Him.

Genesis 1-2 give us incredible insight into God's eternal desires and intentions in relationship to humanity. God's original motivation was to design one creature in His image, someone He could relate to in deep friendship, rule creation with, and reveal Himself to for all eternity. We were handcrafted by God with the internal and external capacity to experience Him. This tells us that God wants to encounter us.

MY TESTIMONY

The creation story changed my life and became a spiritual milestone during my fourth year of Bible school. I had an assignment to write sermons on the subject of the Bridegroom Heart of God. I decided to meditate on the creation story to see how God had revealed Himself. During the following weeks, God confronted several flawed mindsets that were limiting my ability to receive more of His love. The perspectives suggested that He was distant, emotionally disconnected, discouraged by my repeated failures, and that He was mad, sad, boring, and even lacking life within Himself.

After spending weeks journaling, singing, and praying through verses that highlight God's passion for humanity, something surprising happened—I broke down and began to weep. For weeks, I experienced God's free love and overwhelming desire for friendship with me. At times, I wept out of gratitude and love for God. At other times I was filled with supernatural joy and laughter as I rejoiced because of His heart. The weeks leading up to the encounters, and those encounters themselves were life-changing, forming the DNA of this module.

THE CREATION STORY: GOD'S INTENTIONS REVEALED

WEDDING NARRATIVE

The first two chapters of the Bible are mainly about Jesus' desire for a bride and the Father's desire for His Son to have an eternal companion who would love Him wholeheartedly. From beginning to end, the central narrative of the Bible is God's desire for a bride. It begins with the creation of the bride and a wedding in

Genesis, and it ends with the marriage supper of the Lamb and His bride in the Book of Revelation. Even the New Jerusalem, where Jesus and His bride will live together forever, is called the bride.[1]

For we are members of His body, of His flesh and of His bones, 'For this reason a man shall leave his father and mother and be joined to his wife, and the two shall become one flesh.' <u>This is a great mystery, but I speak concerning Christ and the Church</u>.—Ephesians 5:30-32

The New Testament declares that Adam and Eve's story was literal, but it was also *poetic* and *prophetic*. Their creation and marriage foreshadowed a greater fulfillment in Jesus' marriage to the Church. In Genesis, the prophetic picture of Jesus and the Church is the foundation for the entire Bible.

THE CENTER PIECE: THE BRIDE

In partnership with the Father, Jesus created for six days and rested on the seventh day.[2] Jesus took His time to create and set things in place day after day like a wise builder. After the heavens, the seas, the plants, and animals were all in their proper places, Jesus made His bride. The events of that week dramatically build toward, and climax at, God's proclamation that He desired a bride in His image. In the drama of the ages, God set forth the scene of creation largely to highlight the formation of the only being He would make in His likeness.

---

1 Revelation 19:7-9, 21:2.

2 John 1:1-3; Ephesians 3:9; Hebrews 1:2-3.

Then God said, "<u>Let Us make man in Our image, according to Our likeness;</u> let them have dominion over the fish of the sea, over the birds of the air, and over every creeping thing that creeps on the earth." <u>So God created man in His image,</u> in the image of God He created him; male and female He created them.—Genesis 1:26-27

In Genesis 1:26-27, I believe there was a holy conversation between the Father, Son, and Spirit on the fifth day in anticipation of Adam's (the bride) creation. I believe the Father, in an infinitely joyful burst of emotion, spoke out, "Now is the time! Let Us make man in Our image. Let's make one creature who can experience Our deep love and give wholehearted love back to Us. Let Us make a bride for Jesus and sons and daughters for My family."

IMAGE BEARERS: CAPACITY TO EXPERIENCE GOD

In the beginning, God revealed His desire for one creature to be made in His image. Being an image-bearer means that we are the one creature who can, because of our design and position, deeply relate to God, understand Him, give love back to Him, and display His glory to all of creation. We were fashioned, in a detailed way, with the longing and capacity to experience God. No angel or living creature around God's throne has the internal capacity to know and love God to the level that humans can.

We are relating to God and experiencing communion with Him all the time—potentially—without even recognizing it. We may be so accustomed to the idea of relating to God that we easily forget how glorious and supernatural it is. At any moment, we can close our eyes and see an impression of Jesus, hear His voice, and feel His emotions. This is only possible because of *how* God made us.

"FORMED" BY GOD

And the <u>LORD God formed man of the dust</u> of the ground, and <u>breathed into his nostrils the breath of life</u>; and <u>man became a living being</u>.—Genesis 2:7

For five days, Jesus created every object in the universe by speaking out words, but He did something different with His Bride. He "formed" Adam from the dust. Jesus stood at a distance to speak the galaxies into existence, but with the image-bearer, He came down low to give a personal touch. Jesus made a billion burning suns and vast galaxies with gravitational pulls that keep them all together in a rhythm light-years away. But He took the time to form one creature in His image. *Let that sink in for a minute.* I imagine Jesus saying, "This is the most precious thing I am going to make all week. This is the centerpiece of it all. I'm going to take My time with this one."

What was the scene like when Jesus formed Adam? What were the sights, the sounds, and even the smells? What was Jesus thinking and feeling in that moment, and how long did it take to form Adam? Was there a whirlwind of dust spinning in the air with Adam's DNA within it? Or did Jesus take His time to scoop up the dust, make it moist, form it in His hands, and then begin to craft the perfect image like a sculptor would a clay statue?

In fact, the Hebrew word for "formed" is the same word that was used for potters crafting clay pots with meticulous detail at the spinning wheel.[3] Like a potter with his fingers on the spinning clay, Jesus slowly formed you with laser-beam attention to the details of every cell in your being. His eyes were on you, and no part of your design is flawed, incidental, or accidental. Did you know that you

---

3   Strong's Hebrew #03335 - https://www.studylight.org/lexicons/eng/hebrew/03335.html

have Jesus' fingerprints on your spirit, soul, and body? The great architect of the universe crafted your frame and your design—and He wants you all to Himself.

What kind of wisdom and strategy did it take from Jesus to form that one creature? Our human makeup is more complex than any other object in the universe. King David was filled with fascination and worship as he reflected on the revelation of human design, "*I will praise You, for I am fearfully and wonderfully made; marvelous are Your works, and that my soul knows very well.*"[4] We have been fearfully and wonderfully made. This means that God took our human design seriously, that our very existence is holy before God.

MADE IN GOD'S IMAGE—SPIRIT, SOUL, AND BODY

To be made in God's image means He designed our frames in such a way that we could relate to Him as friends. God has made us spiritual beings that have a soul and a body. These three aspects of our being reflect God's desire for us to experience Him. This is the case because they all indicate that we are *sensory* beings, which means God has made us to receive from Him, experience Him, and respond to Him in love and worship.

THE HUMAN SPIRIT

At the core of our beings, we are a spirit. God is Spirit. He dwells in the spirit realm, and He made us so that we could relate to Him spirit-to-Spirit.[5] Our spiritual essence is a complex idea to understand because we can't fully define what our spirit looks or feels like outside of the Bible's details. However,

---

4   Psalm 139:14

5   John 4:24; 1 Corinthians 2:9-12, 6:17, 14:14.

it is a Biblical truth that we are spiritual beings with a soul that functions within a physical body.

Jesus formed Adam from the dust and then breathed into him. Adam only became a living being *after* God's breath was given to him, which I believe was when God created Adam's soul and spirit and put the Holy Spirit in him. The spirit of a man is what brings life to the body, *"For as the body without the spirit is dead, so faith without works is dead also."*[6]

And the LORD God formed man of the dust of the ground, and <u>breathed into his nostrils the breath of life</u>; and <u>man became a living being</u>.—Genesis 2:7

The original Hebrew word for "breath" is *Neshama*, which refers to God's Spirit, power, and activity.[7] Adam was the only creature to receive the breath of God, which makes him unique as the image bearer. Jesus modeled this giving of life again when He breathed the Holy Spirit on His disciples after His resurrection.[8]

Jesus answered, "Most assuredly, I say to you, <u>unless one is born of water and the Spirit, he cannot enter the kingdom of God</u>. That which is born of the flesh is flesh, and <u>that which is born of the Spirit is spirit</u>".—John 3:5-6

---

6   James 2:26.

7   Strong's Hebrew #5397 - Job 4:9; 26:4; 27:3; 32:8; 33:4; 34:14; Psalm 18:15; Isaiah 30:33. http://biblehub.com/hebrew/strongs_5397.htm

8   John 20:22.

The gospel deals first with our spirit's condition.[9] Adam and Eve's spirits were profoundly affected by their sin, and they lost their direct connection to the Holy Spirit because of it. But because of Jesus' finished work of salvation, the Spirit of God fills us once again. He renews our spirit and joins it to His. Now we have the capacity to experience the same union and intimacy with God that Adam and Eve knew.

Jesus designed our spirit in such a way that God could live in it and be one with us. This union between our spirit and God's Spirit gives us continual access into the deepest places of His thoughts and emotions. *"But God has revealed them to us through His Spirit. For the Spirit searches all things, yes, the deep things of God. For what man knows the things of a man except the spirit of the man which is in him? Even so, no one knows the things of God except the Spirit of God. Now we have received, not the spirit of the world, but the Spirit who is from God, that we might know the things that have been freely given to us by God."*[10]

Our spirit can commune with God and perceive eternity. Just as the body has senses to interact with the physical realm, our spirit was designed with senses to interact with God in the spiritual realm. We can only perceive His whispers, thoughts, and emotions, and understand God because of our spirit's design and our direct connection to Him.

OUR SOUL—MIND, EMOTIONS, LONGINGS

Jesus designed Adam's spirit and then his soul—which can be defined as the mind, will, and emotions. In this section, I'm commenting on longings instead of

---

9 John 3:5-6; Titus 3:5; 1 Corinthians 3:16, 6:17.

10 1 Corinthians 2:10-12.

the human will. As you read this section and consider the purpose of the human soul, remember that every detail of our minds, emotions, and longings were thought-through by Jesus the wise builder. The One who planned the design of the galaxies, with all their complexity, devised the intricate design of our souls, and they point to our eternal purpose of encountering Him.

OUR MIND

The mind is the central operating system within the body. It determines everything we think, feel, and do. The mind is connected to more than 60,000 miles of nerves running through the body. These nerves gather sensory information from every location, including the sensory organs of the eyes, ears, nose, mouth, and skin. The nerves then bring the information to the mind to process it, experience it, and ultimately respond to it—both physically and emotionally.[11] What this tells us is that our bodies and emotions can only interact with God and the outside environment because the mind directs and processes all the activities.

Jesus designed our mind to encounter Him by searching Him out, processing Him, evaluating Him, memorizing Him, and interacting with Him. Computers have a hard time matching the dynamic processing speeds, memory space, and ability to search things out like the human mind. If we're impressed by what technology can do, think about what the human mind can do, particularly when it comes to searching out and relating to God.

God calls us to set our minds on Him because that is the pathway to transformation, as well as the doorway to encountering Him.[12] As we search out

---

11 Rita Carter, *The Human Brain Book 2nd Edition* (New York, NY: DK Publishing, 2014), 78.

12 Romans 12:2.

and consider the truths of God's Word with our minds, doors are opened for those truths to touch and renew our emotions by the Spirit. We set our minds on spiritual things to experience spiritual things and have them become our reality.[13]

OUR EMOTIONS

God has given us an incredible capacity for feelings—which we call *emotions*. In the natural realm, we experience positive and negative emotions every day, things like joy, happiness, love, peace, excitement, compassion, anger, sadness, and fear. Whether right or wrong, when someone asks how we are doing, we usually refer to what emotions we've been experiencing. Emotions are central to our human experience.

We have emotions because God has emotions, and we were made in His image. These emotions are holy containers for us to experience His feelings towards us. We get to "feel" God's emotions towards us in our emotions as an intimate experience and express our heart to Him through our own emotions. Emotional moments with the Lord give us a real sense of intimacy with Him in the same way that emotions connect us with others in our human relationships.

When restored and influenced by the Spirit, emotions are meant to be powerful and beautiful. God is emotional and He designed us to be the same. We get to feel joy and can rejoice with our whole hearts in worship. We get to experience love and weep as God's love and delight touch us. Hope and excitement fill us with anticipation of what God is going to do in our circumstances. Overwhelming peace becomes our experience as we see God on His throne over our lives. We get to feel God's compassion for a friend's difficult situation and partner with Him in intercession. These—and more—are available to us in our emotions.

---

13 Colossians 3:1-2.

OUR LONGINGS

Jesus fashioned Adam's inner being with longings and desires that could only be satisfied in Him. Our longings are one of the greatest proofs that God wants to encounter us because the deepest things within us are meant to draw us to Him more and more. Every human longs for pleasure, intimacy, fascination, and beauty. As Adam was being formed, I imagine the loving Potter putting His hand into Adam's heart and designing intricate longings while thinking, "Adam, these are going to draw you to Me in love." Jesus hard-wired Adam with intense desires on the inside as an invisible work of art.

We all have these cravings inside of us, and whether we are aware of it or not, we spend most of our days trying to satisfy them. The gnawing feelings of unsatisfied longings are the most significant driving force to us going deeper in God. These longings completely drive unbelievers, and they try to repress or numb them because they are tired of not being satisfied.

One thing I have desired of the LORD, that will I seek: That I may dwell in the house of the LORD all the days of my life to behold the beauty of the LORD, and to inquire in His temple.—Psalm 27:4

We long for pleasure, intimacy, fascination, and beauty, and God wants to satisfy us. Longings are like cups that God has given us so that He can fill them. For example, take a minute and think about the idea that we want to be beautiful, as well as to see beauty. We have an inherent knowledge and definition of what is beautiful. There is something in us that longs for beauty because God enjoys beauty. He is beautiful and wants to show us His beauty. God put the longing for beauty, as well as the other longings, in us to draw us to Himself as the greatest source of satisfaction. King David experienced God's beauty in prayer, and it became the chief goal of his entire life.

Jesus takes pleasure in beholding beauty, and He wants to encounter us with His beauty. Jesus isn't just practical—He loves to look at beautiful things and show us beautiful things. He loves it when our hearts are thrilled with the pleasure of seeing His beauty in worship or seeing His beauty in nature. The reality that God wants to satisfy our God-given longings may be a new paradigm for some, but God wants to expand our understanding to see Him as the God of encounter and satisfaction. Our human design declares that God didn't just make us workers for His kingdom. Instead, He made us to gaze on Him in all His beauty and overflow in pleasure-filled worship.

OUR BODIES

God made our bodies to take in and experience His life and then respond to Him in love and worship. Our bodies are perfectly designed to interact with and experience the natural realm in ways that are supposed to bring us godly pleasure and joy. From the beginning, God's plan was for us to dwell in a paradise that was the full union of the natural and spiritual realms.

The LORD God planted a garden eastward in Eden, and there He put the man whom He had formed, and out of the ground the LORD God made every tree grow that is pleasant to the sight and good for food. The Tree of Life was also in the midst of the garden, and the tree of the knowledge of good and evil.—Genesis 2:8-9

God first placed Adam within the garden called Eden, which literally means *paradise*, because He wanted Adam to enjoy the physical surroundings. Then God promised believers that they would live forever in a paradise called the New Jerusalem. God bookends the storyline of history with a wedding and a physical paradise to reveal His original intentions for us to enjoy His creation with our physical bodies.[14] The fullest experience of this will come when we have our resurrected physical bodies and can fully interact with both the natural and spiritual realms.

Adam had all his physical and spiritual senses alive in the garden to take in the things that were "pleasant to the sight" and "good for food." Just like us, Adam had over 60,000 miles of nerves running through his body to react to every sensation creation had to offer. He had eyes to see beauty, ears to hear every kind of sound, and a mouth to taste flavorful foods. He had hands to touch the textures of creation, and he had skin to feel the atmosphere around him. Adam's human design was built around godly stimulation and pleasure.

Isn't it interesting that Jesus didn't pick a barren desert as the place to cultivate friendship with Adam? Instead, He personally designed a beautiful garden that was filled with physical pleasures to be their place of communion and fellowship. Jesus wanted a place for them to spend time together, time that would bring Adam pleasure. That paradise is where we're going to live for all eternity. There is tension in this age as to how much physical pleasure we should pursue and within what godly boundaries it should be sought. But in the next age, we will have a perfect and holistic experience of pleasure in both the spiritual and natural realms.

---

14 2 Corinthians 12:2; Revelation 2:7.

SUMMARY

As an image-bearer, God has designed you with the desire and the capacity to encounter Him, and He wants to encounter you. Your eternal calling and divine design are to know God in His deep places and be known by God in your deep places. The beautiful God who is fully satisfied with pleasure wants you to experience beauty and pleasure in the Spirit as you draw near. Deep satisfaction and fascination *in* God are what your heart has been yearning for since He formed you in the womb. This is the season to believe for Him to satisfy longings and for you to reach for an encounter lifestyle. It's not too far off, and it's not reserved for elite Christians.

WEEKLY ASSIGNMENT

For this week's assignment, journal your thoughts about this chapter. Include what parts you feel God is highlighting for you. Also, meditate (picture God, write down your thoughts, speak and sing the truths) on Genesis 1:26 at least one day this week during your scheduled prayer times. Meditate on the truth of being an image-bearer and meditate on what emotions God was feeling when He spoke this verse out loud. Take time to picture God's face and ask Him what His emotions were and why He made you in His image. Your meditation times on this passage will begin to tenderize your heart in preparation for the truths and verses in the following chapters, so come to this expecting what God might do in you.

6

JESUS' LONGING FOR A COMPANION

GOD DESIRES FRIENDSHIP

A foundational revelation of God's heart, one that takes us deeper in prayer, is knowing He desires deep friendship with us, even to the point of *longing*. God isn't content to know about us in His omniscience, or for us to know about Him in our heads. He wants an authentic relationship where He knows us experientially, and we know Him the same way. God wants an ongoing, ever-deepening experiential relationship with us where we both share the deepest places of our hearts.[1]

The revelation of God's love for us is what sets our hearts on fire with love for Him. Our longings for Him will grow to the degree we experience His thoughts, emotions, and longings for us.

---

1   1 Corinthians 2:10.

Let's continue our study of the creation account through the lens of Jesus' longing for a bride.

OVERVIEW OF ADAM AND EVE'S STORY

The entire creation story is summarized in Genesis 1 with a quick mention of the image-bearer at the end. In Genesis 2, God tells the story again, but zooms in on the centerpiece of the storyline—the formation of the image-bearers and their marriage relationship with the Creator.[2] Genesis 2 is an expansion of what God was thinking, feeling, and doing in Genesis 1:26 when He said, "*Let Us make man in Our image.*"

Ephesians 5 gives us insight into Adam's wedding story and declares that Adam represented Jesus and Eve represented the church. The apostle Paul connected the literal story of Adam and Eve to Jesus' future desire for a bride. This means that we can look back on the creation storyline with a greater perspective and see how Jesus, as represented by Adam, longed for His bride.

An interesting poetic change occurs in Genesis 2 that signifies a shift in God's relationship with humanity. In Genesis 1, God is given the title *Elohim*, which refers to His creative power and eternal nature. In Genesis 2, His only title is *Yahweh-Elohim*, which is God's covenant name paired with His creator name. In this holy chapter, God connects these two names to purposefully reveal Himself as the Creator who desires covenantal friendship.[3]

---

2 Matthews, Kenneth. *Genesis 1-11:26*. The New American Commentary (Nashville: Broadman & Holman Publishers, 1996), 189.

3 Matthews, *Genesis 1-11:26*. 192.

ADAM NEEDS A COMPANION

And the LORD God formed man of the dust of the ground, and breathed into his nostrils the breath of life; and man became a living being. The LORD God planted a garden eastward in Eden, and there He put the man whom He had formed.—Genesis 2:7-8

At the beginning of this story, God set the context for friendship with humanity. Adam was formed out of the dust and set in an enclosed garden within Eden. Jesus then gave him the job of cultivating and maintaining the garden as his home and place of fellowship with Him.

After Adam was placed in the garden, God said something unusual that purposefully takes us into the prophetic storyline of Adam and Eve, *"It is not good that man should be alone; I will make him a helper comparable to him."*[4] This statement is unusual because Adam lived in an environment of paradise before sin and brokenness ever entered the created order. He had full access to God's presence and the tree of life, yet in God's perspective, he still needed a companion. In this story, God deliberately waited to make the bride to get Adam's attention—and ours.

The statement about being alone without a helper was about Adam, but it was also about Jesus' desire for a companion. In this statement to Adam, we see the Father speaking prophetically over Jesus. The Father's heart was for Jesus to have an eternal companion in His likeness with whom He could rule the nations.[5]

---

4 Genesis 2:18.

5 Matthew 22:2; Psalm 2:7; Ephesians 1:18; Revelation 19:7-9; John 17:24.

LOOKING FOR A COMPANION

Out of the ground the LORD formed every beast of the field and every bird of the air, and brought them to Adam to see what he would call them.....
So Adam gave names to all cattle, to the birds of the air, and to every beast of the field. But for Adam there was not found a helper comparable to him.
—Genesis 2:19-20

After telling Adam He was going to make him a bride and that it wasn't good to be alone, Jesus brought him animals to name. Again, it seems out of place for the Lord to tell Adam he needed a companion in his image and then immediately bring animals to him to be named. But the animals are not a deviation from the bride topic. We know Jesus was doing something specific with the animals because the end statement is that Adam didn't find a creature like him. The naming process was twofold: it was about Adam expressing dominion with God in naming creatures, and it was about finding Adam a partner in his likeness.

Jesus used the naming process to awaken Adam's desires for a companion in his exact likeness. Adam got to see all the animals, and he got to take time to consider their make-up and their purpose before naming them. He was able to see that every animal had a counterpart, but he was alone and didn't have a counterpart. It's as if his desire and hope for the one in his likeness grew every time a new animal approached him, "Will this be the one made for me?" I imagine Jesus standing next to Adam asking how he felt as he saw each animal and helping him identify his longings for a companion. "Adam, you don't have anybody to relate to deeply. They don't have the capacity or the make-up to be friends with you—but one is coming soon."

EACH ONE ACCORDING TO ITS KIND

In Genesis 1, there's a pattern of God making everything according to its kind and blessing them to be fruitful.[6] Something new was created every day, and everything had a creature in its image to relate to and with which to be fruitful. After all the plants and animals were formed, God said, *"Let Us make man in Our image."* At the climax of creation, God essentially says, "Let's make a companion suitable for Us and let Us bear fruit and multiply together."

Two storylines are unfolding. It is a *literal story* about Adam, but it is also a *prophetic story* about Jesus. Adam was longing for the companion that God promised Him, and prophetically speaking, Jesus was longing for a companion. The rest of chapter two describes the literal and prophetic story of how God would make the bride.

THE BRIDE FASHIONED

And the LORD God caused a deep sleep to fall on Adam, and he slept; and He took one of his ribs and closed up the flesh in its place. Then the rib which the LORD God had taken from man He made into a woman, and He brought her to the man.—Genesis 2:21-22

After Adam finished naming the animals, Jesus brought him into a supernatural encounter to make him a bride with his DNA. This part of the story is so dramatic. This deep sleep was the same kind of visionary encounter that Abraham experienced when God made a covenant with him.[7] As with Abraham's experience, Adam was probably able to see God taking out his rib and forming it into a woman.

---

6   Genesis 1:11-12, 21-22, 24.

7   Genesis 15:12-17.

The deep sleep and the rib are a prophetic picture of Jesus being put to death on the cross by the Father so that a bride could come forth from His side.[8] Adam was put to sleep by God so that he could give life to a bride in the same way that Jesus was put to sleep on the cross to give life to a bride. In other words, the cross was necessary to bring forth the bride of Christ.[9]

THE BRIDE PRESENTED TO THE HUSBAND

God took Adam's rib and hand-crafted another living being in direct relation to the man. This is a massive statement because Eve was the only creature not directly made from the dust. She was specifically made from Adam's DNA to be in his image and then presented to him in a marriage ceremony. In the same way, the Father will present Jesus with a wholehearted bride at the marriage supper of the Lamb.[10]

BONE OF MY BONES

In that visionary encounter, Adam saw Eve and declared, *"Bone of my bones and flesh of my flesh. She shall be called woman because she was taken out of Man."*[11] Eve literally came from Adam's flesh. They were of the exact same DNA. Adam was saying bone of my bones and flesh of my flesh because she was in his exact same likeness and had the ability to be his companion in every way.

---

8   John 19:34.

9   Mike Bickle, "Eve: Relating to God in intimacy without shame," The Bride of Christ: Growing in Intimacy with God Series (Lecture Notes, International House of Prayer University, Grandview, MO, May 11, 2018).

10 Revelation 19:6-9.

11 Genesis 2:23.

This is what God wanted in Genesis 1:26 when He declared His desire for a creature in His image. In the beginning, we were made in Jesus' image, but sin corrupted us. Through the cross, our spirit man was washed and renewed so that we could relate to Jesus spirit to spirit once again. We came from Jesus, and we have the ability to be friends with Him because we are bone of His bones and flesh of His flesh.[12]

JESUS' LONGING FOR A BRIDE

In the Hebrew language, when Adam said, "Bone of my bones and flesh of my flesh," it was a loud and excited affirmation.[13] Adam was shouting, "At last, here is one of my kind. This is the one that I can relate to. This is the one that I can fully love and be loved by. This is the one that I've been longing for!" Remember when he was naming the animals and his longing for a companion was being awakened? We don't know how long it took to name all the animals, but we do know his longing was growing. In this moment, all his stirrings burst out in one satisfied and celebratory shout.

Jesus wanted Adam's longings to go deeper and deeper in that process so that when he finally received his bride, he would fully appreciate her value. Through the process of making and presenting Eve to Adam, I believe Jesus said, "This is how I feel about you, Adam. This is what I say to you, you are bone of My bone and flesh of My flesh. You are My companion forever. You are the one I have longed for. I am going to join Myself to you in a human body forever! Do you feel the longings inside of you for a bride? This is the same desire I

---

12 Ephesians 5:30.

13 Matthews, *Genesis 1-11:26.* 220.

have for you. Are you aware of how beautiful she is to you and how amazing it feels to be with her? This is how I feel on the inside of My heart for you. The emotions and the affections you're feeling for her now are what I feel for you! These are but a glimpse and a whisper of what I feel for you right now!" I believe Jesus was saying this to Adam. And I believe it is what Jesus is saying over you right now.

LONGING AT CREATION AND THE CROSS

God longs for a relationship with us with an intensity and capacity that only He could contain. Many of us instantly discount that thought because it sounds exaggerated. We think, "Yeah, for the other guy maybe, but I'm not that good or that special. How do I know that God is so passionate about me? Isn't that a little bit exaggerated?" It's not an exaggeration, and we have proof of that in the cross. The same passion and longing that drove Jesus to the cross for us is the same passion and longing that was in His heart while He created in Genesis one and two.

This next statement will confront any unworthy feelings you may be experiencing in your life. Jesus was naked on a cross and crushed by the Father as the greatest display of selfless love the world has ever seen.[14] He was humiliated in an undignified death and held nothing back, saying, "Here I am, this is My heart. This is who I am, and this is how far I will go in My love for you. I'll lay bloody on a cross if I can have the bride that I fashioned for Myself."

That was His display of passion on the cross, that was His passion in the beginning of creation, and that is His passion for us now. I don't think we even

---

14 Isaiah 53:3-10; Romans 5:5-8; John 15:13; Galatians 1:4; 1 John 4:10; Revelation 1:5.

know the beginning of Jesus' desire for us as His bride. He came into a human frame, lived for 30 years, died a violent death on the cross, was crushed by the Father bearing the weight of the sins of the world, and went through demonic warfare and suffering, all because He was longing for friendship with us. Let the reality of the longing of the cross confront the lies that say He isn't passionate for us or that we are unworthy of His love.

GOD FEELS AND WEEPS

As we look at the cross, coupled with the creation story, we must say, "Jesus, You are longing on the inside." God is emotional. He is not detached, stoic, and unmoved. To view the creation story correctly, and to understand the intensity of God's longing heart, we have to open our hearts to the truth of His emotions.

One example of this is when Jesus approached the city of Jerusalem before His last Passover. The Bible says that He stopped outside the city to weep over its coming destruction.[15] His desire for repentance caused Him to weep. Weeping isn't casual—it's usually intense and only takes place when deep pain is in the human heart. I believe a deep longing was stirred up as Jesus approached the city and knew that He was going to be rejected. He longed for them to be with Him, but He knew that they were going to reject Him. In this story, the lack of human response to God's love cut Him to the core of His being.

In the story of Lazarus' death, Jesus again expressed raw emotion. As Mary approached Him weeping, Jesus saw her heart and wept and groaned with her.[16]

---

15 Luke 19:41.

16 John 11:33-36.

What did it look like for the Son of God to groan in the spirit and weep, and what does this display say about the intensity of Jesus' emotions?

God weeps and feels. He longs with such an intensity that we will need all of eternity to comprehend it. God feels more emotion and desire than we ever feel because He is perfect and eternal. We think we're emotional at times, but God's emotions are infinite. Do you believe God could be so deeply pained with longing for friendship with you that He could weep in heaven?

JESUS' LONGING FOR ADAM DURING CREATION

Jesus was uniquely stirred with longing during the creation story. He created the galaxies, plants, and animals for the first five days, but He knew that on the sixth day the burning desire of His heart was going to be fulfilled. Jesus' longing and anticipation grew day by day for His bride.

I'm sure Jesus didn't have to sleep at night for each of those five days but imagine how hard it was for you to sleep in the days leading up to exciting events in your own life. The week before my wedding was filled with emotions and anticipation. I did not sleep well. I found myself lying in bed, dreaming about the wedding day that I'd been waiting for my entire life. For six months, we had planned and prepared for one day, our wedding day, and our emotions were only building with greater intensity in that last week.

If we could feel that much longing as humans, how much more could the Creator feel who is filled with perfect love? Oh, the longing He must have felt the evening before Adam was formed! Remember, He's not passive, and He's not unmoved. He's the God of desire and all-consuming fire. We must keep this perspective in mind while pondering the story of the wedding between God and humanity.

In the first five days, Jesus designed a cosmic sanctuary within which He cultivated friendship with the image-bearer. Jesus slowly formed Adam's body and then breathed His breath into Adam to bring him to life. There's a priceless picture to envision at this point, one that informs our entire theology about what God is like, how He feels about us, and how He relates to us today.[17] The question is what was Jesus feeling and doing as Adam began to open his eyes for the first time, and what was Jesus' face like when Adam first saw Him?

Was Jesus silent and somewhat still? Was He emotionally disconnected? Was His expression serious? Did Jesus look unimpressed or a little discouraged with Adam? Was He thinking He could have done a little bit better job making Adam or that Adam was a mistake? I believe many people, if they were more self-aware and honest, would say that Jesus had a negative expression on His face when Adam opened his eyes.

Then I (Jesus) was beside Him (Father) as a master craftsman, and I was daily His delight, rejoicing always before Him, rejoicing in His inhabited world, and my delight was with the sons of men.—Proverbs 8:30-31

When the morning stars sang together, and all the sons of God shouted for joy.—Job 38:7

What was Jesus thinking, feeling, and doing during those first moments of Adam's life? Proverbs 8 and the book of Job describe the mood of heaven during the creation events as joyful and celebratory. Heaven was singing and so was God.

17 Allen Hood, "The Playfulness of God" (Audio Lectures: International House of Prayer University, Grandview, MO).

Jesus was beside His Father as the master craftsman, and They were rejoicing over the things that They created. I believe Jesus, the most joyful being in the universe, had the biggest smile and was singing and dancing as Adam opened his eyes for the first time.

> *And it happened, as the ark of the LORD came to the City of David, that Michal, Saul's daughter, looked through a window and saw King David whirling and playing music.*—1 Chronicles 15:29

The Hebrew word for "rejoicing" in Proverbs 8 is the same word used for King David dancing and whirling as the ark of the covenant was ushered into Jerusalem. The word that describes Jesus rejoicing over creation in Proverbs, and David dancing before the ark means to laugh or dance out of joy and pleasure.[18] I believe Jesus was singing love songs, shouting for joy, and whirling around in an emotional display of celebration because of His bride's arrival. He is the God who rejoices over us with singing, "*The LORD your God in your midst, the Mighty One, will save; He will rejoice over you with gladness, He will quiet you with His love, He will rejoice over you with singing.*"[19]

I imagine Adam taking his first breath, opening his eyes for the first time, and seeing Jesus rejoicing before him. Adam might have thought the same things we typically think, "Why do you like me so much? I'm just dust, and everything that I am is from You anyway. I'm not that special or that amazing for You to rejoice in me. I haven't done that much for You, and I'm not devoted enough to be worthy of Your rejoicing." I imagine Jesus saying something like this, "Adam, I'm the

---

18 Strong's Hebrew #07832 - https://www.studylight.org/lexicons/eng/hebrew/07832.html
19 Zephaniah 3:17.

joyful God who is filled with love, life, and pleasures forevermore. I can't help but overflow onto you! And I've made you unique among all the created order. It's not based on how much or how little you think you've done to impress Me, but it's based on what I'm like in My heart and what I've designed you to be. I love you; I'm moved by your love for Me, and I enjoy you, Adam!"

Jesus is saying these same things over you all the time. You are not an accident. You are not a mistake. He is not disappointed in you or shut down towards you. Your birth and storyline were not missed as if you're just one person out of billions of others on the earth. Jesus longed for your birth with weeping and groaning, and He celebrated your birth with shouting and dancing. Even now, His heart is burning with longing for your friendship. He is dancing and singing songs of love over you with unbridled emotion. He's laughing with joy over your life because of how happy He is and how beautiful He's made you to be.

NAKED AND UNASHAMED

The unearned love and enjoyment that Adam experienced with God in those first moments are exactly what we can experience in our relationships with God through the blood of Jesus. Adam hadn't done anything good to earn Jesus' rejoicing or anything wrong to disappoint Him in those first moments. In the same way, we come to God as righteous, accepted in His presence, and enjoyed, not because of our good works or devotion, but because of what He is like in His heart and what He has accomplished for us.

Adam and Eve were naked, vulnerable, and intimate with each other without the factor of shame. They were fully confident to be themselves around each other. In the same way, Jesus wants to make us confident in His grace and His desire for us so that we go deeper in our relationship with Him. He wants us to openly share the deepest parts of our hearts, affections, and desires with Him as well as our fears, hurts, disappointments, and weaknesses. He wants vulnerability and transparency with a spirit of confidence rooted in the revelation of His heart towards us.

Shame is one of the major hindrances to receiving God's love and experiencing Him more. Shame is feeling anything less than 100% confident in God's smile towards you, and shame results in a guarded heart. Many Christians feel some level of ungodly shame before God due to past sins, current struggles with sin, feeling un-devoted, or just not feeling worthy. Shame causes us to "turn our face" from the Lord during times of prayer and worship because we're unsure of how He really feels about us. We might not know we turn our face a little bit while interacting with God, but the message of God's longing is so intense that it will bring such levels of shame to light.

PRAYERFUL RESPONSE

In closing, here's a prayer that impacts me whenever I meditate on this story. Take several minutes to close your eyes and picture Jesus standing in front of you. Picture yourself by Him as if you were Adam in his first moments of opening his eyes. Slowly ask Him these questions, "Jesus, do you long for me in my weakness? How much do you feel for me right now?" Wait for a couple of minutes to see if He whispers back to or brings a picture to mind. Write down what He says and then talk to Him about it.

If you feel like His words are revealing lies you have been believing, speak them out loud to Him in prayer and break your agreement with them. "God, I have believed the lie that_____ , and I break my agreement with that lie right now." End by agreeing out loud with the truths you learned about Him in Genesis 2 and with what He spoke to you just now. Then ask Him for a greater experience of His longing heart and meditate on this story as many days you need in order to sense God's heart for you.

▌WEEKLY ASSIGNMENT

This week, your assignment is to meditate on Genesis 2:7 at least one day as a way of soaking in the truth that Jesus longs for you. As a focus, meditate on what God was feeling while forming Adam, and what He was doing as Adam first opened his eyes. Take extra time to pray through the prayerful response section above. Write down what touches your heart and continue to talk to God about these things in your meditation times.

Meditating on this verse and praying through hindrances to receiving God's intense longing is the pathway to experiencing His love for you moving forward. These assignments are designed to help you pinpoint the walls in your heart that are blocking the experience of God's love for you. Take your time with them so that God can address foundational issues.

DISCIPLESHIP MEETING GUIDE
MODULE 2: FRIENDSHIP WITH GOD – CHAPTERS 5 & 6

MEETING FOCUS:

The purpose of this week's meeting is to discuss the intensity of God's longing for you and pray through hindrances to that truth.

DISCUSSION QUESTIONS (IN ORDER OF IMPORTANCE):

1. ***Chapter Questions:***
   a. Chapter 5 – Discuss your journaling and Genesis 1:26 meditation assignment from this chapter. What do you think it means to be made in God's image?
   b. Chapter 6 – Discuss your journaling and Genesis 2:7 meditation assignment from this chapter. What do you think Jesus was feeling and doing while He was forming Adam and when Adam's eyes opened the first time? What do you picture Jesus' face to have looked like and why? What might that reveal about your perception of God?
   c. Is the idea that God burns with longing for you easy or hard for you to receive? Why do you feel that way? Did the prayerful response from the end of the chapter make you aware of any feelings of shame or feeling unworthy of God's longing?
   d. Together, pray through any lies that come up in the chapter six discussions by confessing specific lies you're aware of, agreeing with the truth out loud, and asking God to touch you with the truth.
2. ***Spiritual Pursuits:*** *Do a brief follow-up to give more time to the above chapter questions or skip if needed.*
   a. Practically, how is your prayer schedule going? Do you need to make small changes to your schedule or Spiritual Pursuits? How are your Bible reading, meditation, and prayer list times going? And how is God touching you in each of them?
3. ***Heart Issue:*** *Do a brief follow-up to give more time to the above chapter questions or skip if needed.*
   a. If you have time, briefly discuss your heart issue (from *Spiritual Pursuit Document*).
4. Briefly review the assignments for the next two weeks together.

MEETING NOTES:

7

THE HAPPY GOD

HAPPINESS IS HIS FOUNDATION

The revelation of God's longing heart and happiness flow together in the love of God. His depths of passion and mercy, as revealed in the creation and gospel storylines, are only possible because of His infinite happiness. This means that happiness is the foundation of His longing and pursuit of us in the midst of our weakness. In these next two chapters, the focus will be on God's joyful heart, His enjoyment of our lives, and His desire to fill us with His pleasures.

What we believe about God's happiness shapes our perception of Him. Without the Holy Spirit's revelation of God's happy heart, our foundational perspective of Him will be dramatically tainted and limited. This may seem like an exaggeration, but when this truth starts to get inside you, you realize how intensely your heart wars against the idea of God's happiness, and you see how it's foundational to His personality. Rejection, self-hatred, feeling unworthy, feeling unenjoyable, and feeling shame in God's presence will all be demolished in the revelation of His joy. The foundation of these broken thoughts and emotions is built on the lie that God is everything but infinitely happy.

God's happiness is the doorway to trust and intimacy. Our hearts will naturally open up to the other aspects of God's personality if we can rightly see and experience His happy heart. This is because it creates a safe context to draw near to Him in intimacy. In relationships, we don't open up to people who are unhappy, angry, or disappointed in us because they aren't safe. However, we readily open up to those who are happy and enjoy us. God's happiness pulls down our guards so we can truly "go there" in intimacy and transparency with Him.

DREAM OF JESUS' JOY

While I was writing this chapter, my daughter had a profound dream that encouraged me. In her dream, Jesus appeared by her bedside at night with a purple robe that radiated the colors of the rainbow. As she looked at Him, He had a huge smile and began to laugh loudly with deep joy. Then He spoke to her while still laughing and said, "Moravia, I don't want night-night (what we call bedtime) to be that long!" After saying this, He continued laughing and walked out of her room. She knew from the dream that Jesus enjoyed spending time with her and that He was overwhelmingly excited for her to wake up. This dream paints a picture of what God is like in His joy and how He relates to us in the overflow of His delight.

MY JOURNEY

My journey into God's joyful heart started during my senior year in Bible school. The Holy Spirit began to highlight passages in the Bible that revealed God's joy in a way that I hadn't noticed before. At the same time, I started reading

John Piper's well-known book, *The Pleasures of God*. For about a month, this book and key verses in the Bible seemed to penetrate the deepest places of my heart, bringing me into another level of freedom in my relationship with God.

As the light of His joy increased in my heart, two deep-seated lies became very clear to me. First, I felt unworthy of God's joy and passionate love. And second, I felt a measure of rejection in His presence because I didn't feel fully enjoyed. I knew that God loved me, but deep down, I thought He was unhappy, moody, and even angry at me. At some level, I felt like I was a child who was adopted by a grumpy father. One who took me in out of pity but was annoyed with my needs and treated me differently than his biological children. I didn't feel entirely accepted and enjoyed by Him. And I felt like He didn't fully embrace me as my father.

During my high school years, I played a lot of sports and had to travel quite often. At times, I had to ride with other families because my parents couldn't go. That was hard for me. The families welcomed me in their cars, hotel rooms, and wherever they went during the trips, but I always felt like I was a burden. I was never confident that they wanted to bring me into their family for the weekend.

I didn't feel comfortable with them like their kids did, and I had to make sure I took care of myself even though I was under their guidance. I had to pay them for gas, food, and my part of the hotel room, but all of that was naturally taken care of for their kids. Sometimes I would have to switch hotel rooms or switch families for different parts of the trip. I remember the awkwardness of parents figuring out who I would be with and feeling like even more of a burden.

When God began to reveal the depths of His happiness to me, I realized that I had been feeling like a burden to Him. It was as if I was the only orphan in His family. I felt like He had let me into His spiritual family because I needed help, but I didn't occupy the same place of love and privilege as His actual children.

I had been experiencing amazing truths about His heart during my time at Bible school, but the crazy thing is that there were still deep layers of these lies within me I wasn't even aware of. The extreme depths of His happiness are what brought these lies to the surface because they forced me to reconcile His happiness and enjoyment of my life with my perceived worth.

During that season, there were times when a paragraph from John Piper's book or a phrase from the Bible would hit me so hard that I would be instantly filled with joy, causing me to alternate between laughing and weeping for periods of time. During those encounters, I felt like God was penetrating deep-seated beliefs concerning what He was really like and how much He felt for me. At times, the joy was from God, and other times it was the fruit of feeling relieved that God wasn't angry or sad. My heart felt free to laugh because I found deep rest in believing God was infinitely happy and deeply enjoyed my interactions with Him.

GOD'S HAPPY HEART

In Your presence is fullness of joy and the pleasures forevermore.—Psalm 16:11

The only way we can understand God's joy and original intention for us is to ponder what God was like in His joy and pleasure before He created anything. As we meditate on the truth of His happiness, we'll understand how He could be so joyful. This understanding will help us grasp His motivation for creating us. God's enjoyment of us is not based on anything but the unchanging joy He experiences within Himself outside of any creature or circumstance. We can only come into the revelation of being enjoyed as we enter into the revelation of His joyful personality.

There are three foundational ideas to understand when pursuing revelation about God's happiness. First, He is filled with life within Himself, and nothing can add or take away from it. Second, He has the fullness of life within Himself. Third, joy and happiness are more than an experience for Him—they are part of His personality.

GOD IS FILLED WITH LIFE WITHIN HIMSELF

God is eternal, uncreated, and infinitely filled with life within Himself. This means He has been His own source of everything for all of eternity. We must understand that He is filled with life apart from us or any other creatures and that His life will never decrease. Otherwise, we will wonder if He has enough supply for Himself and if His internal life is dependent on us. God is an unending river that can fill every heart in the world every day and still never decrease in His life source. This is what makes Him so stable in the face of the darkness and neediness of the nations.

God is the only being in the universe who does not depend on another source for the life that moves inside of Him. He doesn't rely on anything outside Himself to experience perfect joy. God is His own fountain of life and happiness, *"For in You is the fountain of life; in Your light we see light."*[1] Because of His emotional life source, His heart is strong, never moody or needy, and never lacking anything that needs to be given as the Father of all things. He adopts masses of broken, needy, attention-seeking children into His family every day—yet His heart is full and never wavering as He cares for them.

---

1   Psalm 36:9.

GOD EXPERIENCES THE FULLNESS OF LIFE

The second foundational idea is that the life that God experiences moment by moment is the fullness and the perfection of life—and that never changes. The Father, Son, and Spirit have experienced and will continue to experience the fullness of life, joy, and pleasure every moment of every day. They have never in any way lacked in these areas for all of eternity. This is saying a lot because God's joy container is massive. He has an uncreated heart and an infinite capacity to experience pleasure.

In Psalm 16, David says that in God's presence there is fullness of joy and pleasures for all of eternity. Because God Himself is the source of the fullness, those in His presence get to enjoy what He enjoys. God cannot be denied the fullness of joy and pleasure at any moment. We only have human words and human perspectives that are informed by the Bible to define and measure God's joy. However, we can ask the Holy Spirit this question: "What does it mean for an uncreated, eternal, and infinite Being to experience fullness according to His definition of fullness?"

We get a better perspective on His capacity for the life that surges inside of Him by looking at the natural created order. Out of God's internal life source, He was able to speak a word and create a billion galaxies. Not only did He create the stars and galaxies with a word—He still sustains them with His words.[2] Jesus upholds the visible and invisible universe with the power that flows from His lips. This creative and sustaining power is but a whisper of what the fullness of life and joy within God looks like when visibly displayed.

---

2   Hebrews 1:2-3.

GOD'S PERSONALITY IS HAPPY

According to the glorious gospel of the blessed God, which was committed to my trust.—1 Timothy 1:11

The third foundational idea is that joy, happiness, and pleasure are part of God's personality. They are who He is—not just what He experiences. A beautiful aspect of God's glory that makes Him holy and completely other-than-us is His divine happiness. In his book, John Piper quotes 1 Timothy 1:11 and says that it could be translated to say, "*The gospel of the glory of the happy God,*" which means that God is happy and that the glory of His happiness is revealed through the storyline of the gospel.[3] The good news of the gospel is that God is infinitely happy—it's in His DNA. The extravagant love and generosity offered to us through the gospel are but expressions of what is in His heart.

God's glory is another way of saying God's heart or personality. His outward glory is the physical expression of His internal life. When that glory is released outwardly, we experience a part of God. Every aspect of God's personality is physically seen around Him by the angels and saints in heaven. An example of this is in Exodus 34, where Moses cried out to see God's glory. God answered Moses' cry by declaring aspects of His personality. God's glory is the same thing as His personality.

God's happiness is part of His glory and holiness, and those in heaven worship God because of it. Night and day, the four living creatures are singing about His holiness, which refers to God's complete distinction from creation. They sing "Holy, Holy, Holy" because they don't have the fullness of words to describe something so infinite and beautiful.

---

3 John Piper, *The Pleasures of God (Sisters, OR: Multnomah Publishers, 2000)*, 25-26.

Part of what they are discovering and singing about is God's infinite and uncreated happiness. They see and feel it in His presence, and it is beautiful to them. It is easy to imagine God's throne room as being filled with power, majesty, and angels trembling in the fear of God. However, it is equally true that God's throne room is filled with an atmosphere of joy and gladness and that those around God experience the heights of happiness and pleasure, "*Honor and majesty are before Him; strength and gladness are in His place.*"[4]

God has expressed His happy personality throughout the Bible. One display is through the Father's pleasure over His Son. In Isaiah 42, written nearly centuries before Jesus' birth, the Father declared His overwhelming pleasure over His Son. Then in Jesus' lifetime on the earth, the Father again declared His deep pleasure over His Son during His baptism and transfiguration, "*This is My beloved Son in whom I am well pleased.*"[5] I think the Father was doing more than just affirming His Son to others and connecting prophecies from Isaiah to the Gospels. I think He was bursting with joy and wanted to communicate His affection to His Son. Jesus received His Father's joyful celebration and was deeply moved by His words.

Psalm 45 reveals Jesus' glad personality and the Father's happiness. First, it says that Jesus has been anointed with the oil of gladness more than anyone else. He's the glad King. Second, Hebrews 1:8 tells us that Psalm 45 is about the Father singing a love song over Jesus, so as we read the Psalm, we do so from the perspective of the Father, "*My heart is overflowing with a good theme; I recite my composition concerning the King; my tongue is the pen of a ready writer. You are fairer than the sons of men.*" Through the Psalmist, the Father communicated that His

---

4   1 Chronicles 16:28.

5   Isaiah 42:1; Matthew 3:17, 17:5.

heart was overflowing for Jesus and that He saw the supreme beauty of His Son as compared to all of humanity.

In Luke 15, Jesus lays out three different parables that reveal and highlight God's joy and happiness in the context of His celebration over the lost coming back into His family. The story of the prodigal son is the third parable in the sequence, and it ends with the father gathering his household to feast and dance in celebration. God and the angels dance and rejoice in heaven when just one sinner repents because God is joyful and happy within Himself.

JOYFUL CREATOR

God's eternal joy was His motivation in creating the universe. Before Genesis 1:1, The Father, Son, and Spirit lived with divine pleasures surging through Their hearts. As three distinct Persons, They each experienced the fullness of joy within Themselves. In relationship, They lavished Their perfect love and joy on each other and fully received each other's love and enjoyment without any hindrances of shame, unworthiness, mistrust, rejection, accusation, or other broken filters. For billions of years, They lived in this perfect friendship of love and joy. Out of this infinite overflow, the Trinity created the universe.

Unlike what I had believed, God was not begrudgingly or hesitantly creating. With each creative word, there was a raging river of life and joy breaking out of His heart like water exploding out of a mighty dam. No selfish or needy motivation was in God's heart as He stood ready to speak out the words of life that would form the galaxies. There was simply an overflowing heart that was so extravagant and so filled with joy and pleasure that it had to create more things on which to lavish His love.

Then I was beside Him as a master craftsman; and I was daily His delight rejoicing always before Him, rejoicing in His inhabited world, and my delight was with the sons of men.—Proverbs 8:30-31

The theme of the Trinity's love and joy for one another continued throughout the six days of creation and expanded to enjoying its fruit. Proverbs 8:30-31 gives us a glimpse into the heart of Jesus and the Father during those days.[6] Jesus, as the master craftsman, architect, and skilled artisan, was beside the Father.[7] As the Son, He knew the dreams and plans of His Father and spoke them into existence each day. In this way, He built the universe with unimaginable precision and wisdom.

During the building process, the Father couldn't help but be distracted by delighting in Jesus. Each day that Jesus built something new, His Father overflowed with love and pleasure over His Son in the same way He had for billions of years. In this passage, Jesus is the one saying His Father delighted in Him daily, meaning He knew and celebrated His Father's display of affection. It's as if Jesus were saying, "Friends, I was daily His delight! Day after day My Father was lavishing Me with praises and singing and joyful affirmations!"

In the overflow of being enjoyed, Jesus rejoiced every day in front of His Father. Each day of creation involved Jesus rejoicing with supernatural joy next to the Father. This means Jesus was laughing, singing, and dancing out of excitement. He celebrated everything He made with the Father and rejoiced in its eternal purpose. The Spirit isn't mentioned here, but the picture is clear; the Trinity was

6 Wisdom is personified in Proverbs 8, and much of the chapter is referring to the events of creation (8:22-31).

7 Instead of "master craftsman", some versions say, "one brought up", which means someone trained in a skill.

infinitely excited and visibly rejoicing, because They were always filled with joy and They anticipated enjoying creation.

Jesus rejoiced in His Father's inhabited world, and His unique delight and pleasure were in the sons of men—His eternal bride. The God of infinite happiness and pleasure delighted in the creation of His bride and fellowship with her in the garden paradise. His infinite emotional capacity and happy personality lead me to believe that He exploded with longing and rejoicing as Adam's eyes first opened to see His face. I'm confident Adam was lavished on in the same way that Jesus was lavished on by His Father's joy and affection.

▌WEEKLY ASSIGNMENT

In response to this chapter, continue to meditate on Genesis 2:7 with the perspective of God's happiness from Proverbs 8:30-31. All of us have wrong or limited perspectives regarding God's happiness and motives for creation, so let God wash your heart during your meditation times. Because we're broken and our parents and leaders have been broken and limited, though sincere, we have hurts and demonic (skeptical) perspectives concerning what God is really like as a father and husband. I believe God will speak and begin a healing journey for your heart to be able to see His heart and intentions more clearly.

8

ENJOYED BY GOD

ENJOYED AND PURSUED

We were created by God to be enjoyed. I believe it's a core spiritual need to know God enjoys us and that His joy for us isn't dependent on our accomplishments. Our primary calling is to be enjoyed by Him and to enjoy Him every day. We partner with Him to increase His kingdom, but our first calling is to be loved and enjoyed in an intimate relationship. In light of this revelation, I've started praying daily, "Lord, enjoy me and search me out today as I enjoy and search You out."

PSALM 149 - GOD TAKES PLEASURE IN US

Let Israel rejoice in their Maker; let the children of Zion be joyful in their King. Let them praise His name with the dance; let them sing praises to Him with the timbrel and harp. For the Lord takes pleasure in His people. He will beautify the humble with salvation.—Psalm 149:2-4

In Psalm 149, the writer calls us to enjoy God and express it without any emotional or physical reservations. We are filled with joy and rejoice in song and dance because He takes pleasure in us. The experiential revelation that God is happy and enjoys our lives awakens love and rejoicing in us. This revelation of His happiness is one of the sources that fuels our worship.

Though God experiences the fullness of joy within Himself already, He feels specific pleasures because of our relationship with Him. There are emotions within God's extravagant heart that are attentive and responsive to our every movement. If He were an unemotional God who was disconnected from us, He wouldn't have pleasure in us. But He's a Father and Husband who is defined as Love (God is love), and His heart delights in our interactions with Him.

It is easy for many to believe that they are a bother to God or are annoying and too needy, but God chooses to engage with us because He wants to. Nobody is forcing Him to like or interact with us. It was His choice to create us, rescue us from sin, and marry us. The way He relates to us in joy is all based on His pleasure-filled personality.

JESUS SEARCHES AND PURSUES

Psalm 139 declares that God searches us out and surrounds us on every side. Have you ever wondered what exactly God is searching for in you at different moments of the day? He's God; shouldn't He have known everything about you before you were even born? There is a mysterious dimension to God's omniscience by which He can know all things and yet still be able to know us progressively and relationally.

Intimacy in God's kingdom comes through real, moment-by-moment interactions with God and Jesus delights in the search of love as He studies us and interacts with us at the heart level throughout each day. He engages with us in tangible experience and fellowship in the way a husband searches and pursues his wife.

When we said yes to salvation through Jesus Christ, we agreed to an eternal marriage covenant that permitted Him to inhabit the innermost places of our beings. We've laid down our rights to be our own and hold anything back from Him. In marriage, you give your spouse permission to go deep in you and become one. Jesus has the same license to live in us and enjoy us, and He considers His access holy.

Friend, Jesus is searching out your heart today, and He's not just looking for hidden sins. Those eyes are looking into your emotions and drinking your love. His heart is hearing and sensing every movement of love and desire in you and then responding to it.

Psalm 139 begs the question, "Why would God want to search me out, and why is He consumed with thoughts about me like the sands of the sea?" Of course, there is a mystery to search out within this answer, but the simple truth is that this is just what He's like, and this is just how precious we are to Him. He defines our worth because He sculpted us into His image with His hands, and He gets to decide how much we move His heart with pleasure!

ENJOYING GOD'S PLEASURES

Does God want us to enjoy Him and experience pleasure in Him? The short answer is yes! There is a longing within God's heart for us to drink deeply of His pleasures and to be fully satisfied in Him. His will is for us to experience divine pleasure in our interactions with Him and for His pleasure to overflow into our lives.

John Piper says it this way, "God is most glorified when we are most satisfied in Him."[1] We glorify God by experiencing spiritual pleasures in Him and radiating joy and gratitude in His pleasure-filled personality. It's godlier to experience joy in God than not to. The heart that is satisfied in God and filled with pleasure is the heart that testifies of God's happy and extravagant personality.

DRINK OF HIS PLEASURES

And let him who thirsts come. Whoever desires, let him take the water of life freely.
—Revelation 22:17

They are abundantly satisfied with the fullness of Your house, and You give them drink from the river of Your pleasures.—Psalm 36:8

Revelation 22 and Psalm 36 are both referring to the river of life that flows from God's throne and inviting believers to drink from it by communing with God. The river has its source in God's Being, therefore, it carries His life and His presence. Psalm 36 adds that it's "the river of Your pleasures," meaning that it carries the infinite and eternal pleasures of God within it. Those who drink of God's presence in prayer experience the supernatural pleasures of knowing Him.

God wholeheartedly invites you to drink of His presence and His pleasures. Like an extravagant Father, He wants you to be abundantly satisfied and overflowing in your relationship with Him. God isn't stingy or withholding anything of His presence; instead, He calls you to come as often as you'd like and drink as much

---

1 John Piper, *Desiring God (Colorado Springs, CO: Multnomah Books, 2011)*, 10.

as you'd like without any reservation or cost. The only requirement is that you're thirsty and have enough desire to go to the river. God has taken the initiative to call you to the life source, but are you thirsty enough to respond? Are you thirsty enough to change your lifestyle to spend more time drinking of God's presence and pleasures in prayer?

ABIDE IN GOD'S LOVE AND JOY

I am the vine, you are the branches. He who abides in Me, and I in him, bears much fruit; for without Me you can do nothing.—John 15:5

In John 15, Jesus affirmed His desire for us to connect to the supernatural life that flows out of God. He encouraged His disciples to receive all that they could from God, otherwise, they could bear no fruit.

As the Father loved Me, I also have loved you; abide in My love.—John 15:9

After calling them to abide in the vine, Jesus explained that abiding is specifically about remaining in the supernatural experience of His love. Abiding in God's love is a supernatural lifestyle of discovering and experiencing God's unlimited affection for us. I say unlimited because Jesus loves us to the same infinite degree that the Father loves Him.

As in Revelation 22, God makes the invitation to live in His love and doesn't withhold anything. It's like He's saying, "Come in, come in! Drink of My love as often as you'd like, because you were designed to receive and give love with all of your being. I want to love on you and have your entire being overflowing with confidence in your worth and beauty to Me. I want you to live in the fellowship of the God who is love. If you knew the love and joy I experience with My Father, you would live the way that I live and bear the fruit that I bear!"

If God were stingy and not wanting us to live in His pleasures of intimacy, He would have said, "I love you, but I'm only going to show My love for you sometimes, because showing you too often would make you self-centered, wouldn't be practical, and would distract you from the real work of the kingdom. Push through your life challenges by faith and perseverance alone and focus on impacting other people."

These things I have spoken to you, that My joy may remain in you, and that your joy may be full.—John 15:11

Then Jesus gave His companions even more clarity concerning His heart and motivations for calling them into abiding in His love. With His whole heart, He wanted them to live in His joy. And not just a little joy here and there, but the fullness of joy, and that it would remain in them through the Holy Spirit. God wants us to live in the experience of His love and the fullness of His joy, and for us to bear fruit in the overflow, all of which glorifies Him.[2]

PRAYER FOR SPIRITUAL PLEASURES

That Christ may dwell in your hearts through faith; that you, being rooted and grounded in love, may be able to comprehend with all the saints what is the width and length and depth and height – to know the love of Christ which passes knowledge; that you may be filled with all the fullness of God.—Ephesians 3:17-19

---

2   John 15:8.

Paul experienced the truths of John 15 and prayed them over his churches. In Ephesians 3, he prayed that they would experience the vast expanse of Jesus' love for them. He knew that if the churches were grounded in God's love as an abiding experience it would transform their thoughts, emotions, desires, and choices. Paul lived in the love of God and knew that it was his only life source; therefore, he desired that the churches experience the same. As in John 15, we only bear fruit and glorify God if we live in the experience of His love, and we only achieve the fullness of our destinies if we experience His love.

ENJOYED IN THE PROCESS

It is essential to understand that God enjoys us during our growth process and that we're meant to experience His pleasure as we pursue victory over sins and lies. Because we are always in a process of growing, the wrong mindset that God can't enjoy us until we're victorious will hinder our experience of His love. If we feel enjoyed by God right now, it will give us the confidence to turn to Him for help instead of turning away from Him to clean ourselves up.

Experiencing His joy and free affection is what satisfies our longings so that we don't fall into sinful patterns. Because we're image-bearers, God designed in such a way that we only work right if our eternal longings are satisfied and fascinated in Him, and this only happens if we can freely receive from Him while getting victory over sin and brokenness. If we can't receive it right now, we are cutting off the very life source God has ordained to bring us into victory. His enjoyment opens the door for our hearts to receive God's pleasures and affections, and it breaks off ungodly striving, pride, and the orphan mentality that pursues freedom outside of the Father's power.

PROBING QUESTIONS

I ask people how much they genuinely believe (being honest with themselves) God enjoys them in this season of their life on a scale of 1-10, with 10 being the fullness of enjoyment. The follow-up question is, why do they believe God enjoys them at that level? Depending on their answer, another question is, when will God fully enjoy them?

Usually, people say that God enjoys them somewhere between 1-5. Their reason is that they have specific struggles with sins or lies and aren't as spiritually disciplined as they think they should be. Then I ask them when they believe God will enjoy them at level 10. After thinking, people give me one of three replies. The first response is that God will fully enjoy them once they have overcome all their sin issues and have the spiritual disciplines down. The second group replies by saying God won't fully enjoy them until they're perfected in the resurrection. The third is that God won't fully enjoy them because they're human, and He isn't that joyful.

These reflective questions probe what we honestly think about God and how He relates to us right now. If you were totally honest and not just giving good Bible answers to what you should believe, how would you answer these questions? It's imperative to be aware of how you would answer these questions because any false belief systems hinder you from receiving the experience of His delight over you. If you can be honest, you can identify and break agreement with lies and sow truth in your meditations.

REASONS GOD ENJOYS US

God can enjoy us in the growth process for at least four reasons. The first reason is that His heart is completely different from ours and overflows with happiness and love. Because of His infinite happiness, enjoying us in every season is an easy thing for Him. His heart is so complete and filled with delight that He even gets pleasure from forgiving and extending mercy!³

The second reason is that God has transformed us by the blood of Jesus. Through the blood, we have been given full access to God's presence, and He relates to us as though we had never sinned, *"Therefore, having been justified by faith, we have peace with God through our Lord Jesus Christ."*⁴ Jesus' blood completely removed the relational barrier of sin in our lives.

The third reason God can enjoy us is because we're fearfully and wonderfully made in His image. God made us beautiful and enjoyable from the beginning, and Jesus' blood has fully restored that image and position with God for those that love Him. We have to trust the design and value God has given us as restored human beings and not discount what He has made. If we aren't agreeing with our created value and beauty before God, we're pridefully saying we disagree with God about the most important thing He has ever made, which is the image-bearer. To refuse or cautiously receive His enjoyment and extravagant affection is to say that how God made us was wrong and that the value He puts on our lives is wrong.

The last reason God can enjoy us is because of His perspective. He sees us through the cleansing blood of Jesus, and He sees the fullness of our love and obedience, not just the sins we struggle with. Our perspective is skewed and limited, but His is perfect. He can see every movement of love and sin in us, and He knows how to hold them in perfect proportion to one another.

We are mostly aware of our lusts and sins, but God sees and counts our sincere desires to obey Him, and He relates to us according to our pursuits. He calls the

---

3 Micah 7:18.

4 Romans 5:1.

small but growing godly desires real even before they begin to blossom. Then, like seeds in the ground, He prophesies them over us by affirming, celebrating, and calling them forth.[5] We see our stumbling in areas, but He sees a sincere reach to love Him, and He affirms us in those areas until we get the victory.

One gaze from our heart and one movement to love and obey Him is seen and greatly valued by Him. But, unfortunately, we're hardly aware of our small movements of love for Him. We rightly focus on how our sins bring relational pain to God's heart, but we must also cultivate an awareness of our love and obedience to God and celebrate it in the same way that He does. It is hard for us to celebrate the love and godliness that we do see in our lives, but we have to because God does.

I believe a big part of why we aren't as aware of the level of genuine love for God in our hearts as we are of our sin issues is because of our lack of understanding of God's joy and gentleness. We don't see the entirety of our hearts because of a lack of revelation. A wrong perception of God's heart causes us to overestimate our sin and lack of devotion compared to our love and obedience.

HOW DOES SIN IMPACT GOD'S ENJOYMENT?

When we sin, how is God affected, and how does it impact how He feels about us? Our decisions to sin do affect God because He's a person and the relational dynamics are real. But He is not like a human with swaying emotions, and His enjoyment doesn't diminish toward us once we have sinned. God can enjoy us in the overall sense while still being pained at the moment by a sinful choice in the same way that a parent can be pained over a child's disobedience but still enjoy them.

---

5 Romans 4:17.

In our brokenness, we waiver in loving and enjoying others when there is sin, but God is consistent in His love and can maintain that heart flow even while addressing our sin. When we sin, God is relationally grieved because He enjoys deep friendship and agreement with us. When we break that fellowship in a sinful moment, our present-tense connection with Him is hindered and He is grieved. Confessing our sin to God heals the momentary disruption of fellowship.[6]

REPENTANT VS. PERSISTENT

There is still an enormous difference between a believer who stumbles into sin and hates it and a believer who willfully persists in sin. The one who struggles in a sinful pattern calls it sin, repents of it, and sets their heart to obey God in that area. God thoroughly enjoys that person because they sincerely love Him.

The believer who willfully sins is not repenting. They want to live in sin, and they are choosing to let it disrupt their fellowship with God. This approach pains the Lord's heart. He is so patient and so gracious, but at some point, that person is not enjoyed by God anymore. God still loves that person, but the severe disagreement doesn't make friendship possible. Instead, God pursues them and calls them to turn from their sin so that their fellowship can be restored.

As many as I love, I rebuke and chasten. Therefore be zealous and repent. Behold, I stand at the door and knock. If anyone hears My voice and opens the door, I will come in to him and dine with him and he with Me.—Revelation 3:19-20

---

6   1 John 1:9.

Jesus came to the church of Laodicea, whose love for God was waning, with one message, to turn back to loving God with all your heart. The jealous heart of the Lover comes out in this rebuke. His pursuit and rebuke were motivated out of love and longing to have deep fellowship with them. Jesus knocked on the door of their compromising heart and invited it to open up to Him in obedience and friendship.

If you are not in agreement with God in any area of your life, decide right now to turn from it, receive forgiveness, and come into an enjoyable relationship with God. He's been knocking on your heart, asking you to turn from your sin and toward Him wholeheartedly.

If you sincerely love God and want to obey Him but feel guilt or shame from things that you have already repented of, bring them to God again and ask Him to wash you with the experience of forgiveness. Declare the truth that you are forgiven. Then, pray about confessing those areas to a trusted friend and have them speak forgiveness over you. King David freely received the happiness of being freely forgiven, *"Blessed are those whose lawless deeds are forgiven."*[7] Set your heart to receive the happiness of forgiveness by meditating on the truth that you're freely forgiven and enjoyed by God until it begins to heal your thinking.

FIVE ACCUSATIONS

I've observed five accusations that hinder people from experiencing God's pleasure over their lives. These accusations act as closed doors that block the river of the Holy Spirit from going deeper into us as an experience. As we address each wrong mindset, our minds and hearts open their doors and allow an experience

---

7   Romans 4:7-8.

with God to happen. As you read each accusation, take a few minutes to respond to God in the ones that you know you have believed. As an initial response, repent out loud for agreeing with the accusations and slowly confess the truth. If you realize an accusation is a significant hindrance, consider meditating on the truth in your prayer times and bringing it up to your Discipleship Mentor.

#1 ACCUSATION

God isn't joyful and filled with pleasure, so why would I even pursue experiencing Him in that way?

Biblical response: God is eternally and infinitely happy and filled with pleasure. He is the most joy-filled Being in the universe, and all things receive their life from the life that surges in Him.

#2 ACCUSATION

God doesn't want me to be filled with joy and pleasure.

Biblical Response: God is the perfect Father and Bridegroom who wants to lavish you with happiness. His heart is to fully satisfy the longings He's given you. He's overflowing with happiness, and He's longing and inviting you to just come to Him and drink. *"Ho! Everyone who thirsts, come to the waters; and you who have no money, come, buy and eat. Yes, come, buy wine and milk without money and without price. Why do you spend money for what is not bread, and your wages for what does not satisfy? Listen carefully to me, and eat what is good, and let your soul delight itself in abundance."*[8]

---

8   Isaiah 55:1-2.

God wants to delight you with the abundance of pleasure, and He wants to challenge us to choose to "let our souls delight in abundance" instead of resisting pleasures!

#3 ACCUSATION

I don't feel fully forgiven of all my sins, so God isn't completely happy with me. It would be unjust for me to receive freely from Him right now.

Biblical Response: You were fully forgiven of your sins the day you made a covenant with Jesus and were washed by His blood. Any recent sins are fully forgiven and are not hindrances once you have confessed them and repented to God. He delights in mercy, and He delights in forgiveness. He loves to lavish you with extravagant joy in your weakness and in the maturing process. God thoroughly enjoys you right now if you have a sincere heart to grow in righteousness in the areas He shows you. Receive the happiness of forgiveness and magnify His mercy.

#4 ACCUSATION

Even if God is joyful and filled with pleasure, I'm a weak and broken human being, and I couldn't possibly deserve God's extravagant enjoyment. Isn't it prideful to say that God could enjoy me wholeheartedly?

Biblical Response: It is false humility and pride to resist His pleasure over you because you feel unworthy. By resisting His pleasure, you're telling Him that His blood wasn't good enough to reconcile you to Himself fully. It is humility to receive something you haven't earned freely. God is glorified when you are humbled and receive His mercy, grace, and extravagant pleasure. But, by resisting His full pleasure over your life, you are also telling Him that He can't enjoy the image-bearer that He dreamed up and formed.

#5 ACCUSATION:

Even if God does want me to experience joy and pleasure, I can't have too much joy because I feel the need to mourn my brokenness and the brokenness of the world around me. Overflowing with His joy doesn't seem fair because the rest of the world isn't experiencing that joy.

Biblical Response: There is a place for mourning sin and having compassion on the world, and it's holy to be broken in intercession. God is aware of our brokenness and the world's needs, and He feels it, but at the same time He experiences pleasure and joy. Therefore, we can give way to the Holy Spirit's leading in times of mourning and weeping in intercession and give way to God's happiness at all other times.

In John 15, Jesus said that He wanted joyful intercessors and joyful evangelists who showed the world another life source. The broken world needs to see God's happiness in the church to know there is an answer to their problems. You will be more fruitful if you let His pleasure move in your heart. Isaiah 55 says, *"Let your soul delight itself in abundance."* Choose to open your heart to fully delighting itself in God, knowing that it's God's desire.

▌WEEKLY ASSIGNMENT

This week, meditate on Psalm 149:4 at least one time this week. Also, pray about the three probing questions and discuss your answers with your Discipleship Mentor. Honestly answer what you believe deep down instead of answering with what you should believe.

1. *On a scale of 1-10, 10 being the fullness of His enjoyment, how much do you honestly believe and feel God enjoys you today?*

2. *Why do you believe He enjoys you to that level?*

3. *When will God be able to fully enjoy you?*

As you answer each of these, confess lies you believe about you and God, and agree with the truth out loud. Write down any questions you still have regarding if you can be fully enjoyed by God. Take your time with this because it is as foundational to intimacy with God as freely receiving His longing for you.

DISCIPLESHIP MEETING GUIDE
MODULE 2: FRIENDSHIP WITH GOD – CHAPTERS 7 & 8

MEETING FOCUS:

The purpose of this week's meeting is to discuss God's happiness and pleasure over your life and pray through hindrances to these truths.

DISCUSSION QUESTIONS (IN ORDER OF IMPORTANCE):

1. *Chapter Questions:*
   a. Chapter 7 – Discuss highlights from the chapter and discuss your Genesis 2:7/ Proverbs 8:30-31 meditation assignment. Did the meditation time impact your heart in any specific ways? Do you have a view of God as being infinitely happy?
   b. Chapter 8 – Discuss highlights from the chapter, your Psalm 149:4 meditation assignment, and the three probing questions assignment.
   c. Based on the three probing questions assignment, pray through any lies that come up regarding shame or feeling unworthy of God's full enjoyment by confessing the specific lies you're aware of, agreeing with the truth out loud, and asking God to touch you with truth in your meeting.

2. *Spiritual Pursuits:*
   a. Practically, how is your prayer schedule going? Do you need to make small changes to your schedule or Spiritual Pursuits? How are your Bible reading, meditation, and prayer list times going? How is God touching you in each of them?

3. *Heart Issue:*
   a. Share how your heart issue has been going this past week. With heart issue discussions, process, confess, encourage, and pray together for God to release transformation.

4. Briefly review the assignments for the next two weeks together. This is not necessary if you are having a group gathering to introduce the next module topic.

MEETING NOTES:

_____

_____

_____

_____

_____

_____

_____

_____

_____

_____

MODULE 3

MEDITATION

MODULE INTRODUCTION

Hopefully, after spending more time with God the past few weeks and reading about His longing to encounter your heart, you feel a greater desire to know Him. If so, these next chapters on Bible meditation will be really good for you because slow and deep conversation with God is the primary way we all grow in friendship with God. Meditation is the practical response to the vision of intimacy you read about in the last module.

Meditation is core to experiencing God and necessary for every believer to enter into, and it's not limited to any personality type. Meditation will set your heart in a posture of deep connection with God. That connection will help you flow more naturally in the other prayer expressions laid out in this book. It is fair to say that all the other prayer expressions build upon how your heart learns to interact with God in meditation. This is the longest module of the program because of this foundational truth.

The purpose of the first chapter is to give you vision and faith to go deep in meditation until you encounter God more deeply. The following chapters are focused on providing detailed practical instruction on how to engage God at the heart level in meditation. As you step into this topic, I encourage you to open your heart to the idea of meeting God in meditation and trying each practical suggestion for a while without giving up.

The meditation assignments include weekly meditation times and processing reflection questions related to hearing God's voice in meditation. These assignments are set up to help you process the topic of meditation, get a rhythm in meditating weekly on your specific Bible verse, and study God's interactions with you in meditation. If you take the time to meditate and reflect on your times with Him, you will become more sensitive to God's movements in meditation and grow in your journey by learning how He interacts with you.

ASSIGNMENT OVERVIEW
MODULE 3 - MEDITATION

Schedule a 2-4 hour group meditation day at the end of week twelve in place of the monthly group gathering. Gather in a prayer room together, meditate on your individual verses, and debrief together at the end of the meditation time.

Week Nine Assignments:

❑ Read Chapter 9 – "***Biblical Meditation.***" Journal thoughts and questions about the three specific sections in the chapter: *Meditation Defined, Learn God's Interactions, and Heart Posture - Proverbs 2.*

❑ This week, decide on a single Bible verse or short Gospel story to meditate on for the entire module (suggested 2-3 times per week).

❑ Fill out a new *Spiritual Pursuits Document* for this module. The pursuits can stay the same or change but filling out the form monthly helps you refocus and develop a rhythm of intentionality.

❑ Continue following your daily prayer schedule and your Spiritual Pursuits.

Week Ten Assignments:

❑ Read Chapter 10 – "***Five Ways to Interact with God.***" Journal your thoughts and questions, including which of the five is the most natural for you and which is the most difficult.

❑ Continue to meditate on the Bible verse or short Gospel story you selected for this module (suggested 2-3 times per week).

❑ Incorporate each of the five meditation expressions in your meditation times throughout the module.

❑ Continue following your daily prayer schedule and your Spiritual Pursuits.

❑ **Meet with your Discipleship Mentor.**

Week Eleven Assignments:

❑ Read Chapter 11 – "*Ten Practical Tips in Meditation Part One.*" Journal thoughts and questions about the practical tips.

❑ Continue to meditate on the Bible verse or short Gospel story you selected for this entire module (suggested 2-3 times per week).

❑ Continue following your daily prayer schedule and your Spiritual Pursuits.

Week Twelve Assignments:

❑ Read Chapter 12 – "*Ten Practical Tips in Meditation Part Two.*" Journal thoughts and questions about the practical tips.

❑ Continue to meditate on the Bible verse or short Gospel story you selected for this entire module (suggested 2-3 times per week).

❑ Continue following your daily prayer schedule and your Spiritual Pursuits.

❑ Participate in the 2–4-hour group meditation day.

❑ **Meet with your Discipleship Mentor.**

Week Thirteen Assignments:

❑ Read Chapter 13 – "***Seven Heart Progressions.***" Journal thoughts and questions, including answers to which stages have you experienced since the beginning of this module, which stage do you have the most questions on, and which stage are you looking forward to?

❑ Continue to meditate on the Bible verse or short Gospel story you selected for this entire module (suggested 2-3 times per week).

❑ After one of your meditation times this week, fill out a *Meditation Observation Document.*

❑ Continue following your daily prayer schedule and your Spiritual Pursuits.

Week Fourteen Assignments:

❑ No chapter reading.

❑ Continue to meditate on the Bible verse or short Gospel story you selected for this entire module (suggested 2-3 times per week).

❑ After one of your meditation times, fill out a *Meditation Observation Document.*

❑ Continue following your daily prayer schedule and your Spiritual Pursuits.

❑ **Meet with your Discipleship Mentor.**

Week Fifteen Assignments:

❑ Read Chapter 14 – "***Quieting the Mind.***" Journal your thoughts and questions including answers to: do you struggle with quieting your mind in prayer and why, and are there lifestyle changes to make to have a quieter mind?

❑ Continue to meditate on the Bible verse or short Gospel story you selected for this entire module (suggested 2-3 times per week).

❑ After one of your meditation times, fill out a *Meditation Observation Document.*

❑ Continue following your daily prayer schedule and your Spiritual Pursuits.

Week Sixteen Assignments:

❑ No chapter reading.

❑ Continue to meditate on the Bible verse or short Gospel story you selected for this entire module (suggested 2-3 times per week).

❑ After one of your meditation times, fill out a *Meditation Observation Document.*

❑ Continue following your daily prayer schedule and your Spiritual Pursuits.

❑ **Meet with your Discipleship Mentor.**

SPIRITUAL PURSUITS

DATE: _____

1. **Bible reading direction and plan**
    (Write down what you will read and when you will read it):

2. **Meditation verse** (Choose a verse that speaks truth into your heart issue):

3. **Sin/character issue from which to get freedom:**

4. **Lie from which to pursue deliverance:**

5. **Gifting to pursue** (Include simple ways you can pursue it):

6. **Weekly Prayer Schedule**—Write down your plan for the *specific times* you are committed to spending with God each day, and *what specifically you plan to do during those times*. Include what your study or meditation focus will be. Refer to the example schedule in Chapter Two. (e.g., Monday 6-6:30 am—Tongues, 6:30-7:30 am—Meditation on Song of Solomon 1:2)

Monday

Tuesday

Wednesday

Thursday

Friday

Saturday

Sunday

9
BIBLICAL MEDITATION

THE BLESSING OF MEDITATION

In Psalm 1, David laid out a glorious promise for those who engage God in deep heart meditation. Through personal experience, he affirmed that every person that delights in and meditates on God's Word will have a heart flowing with life. They will be like a tree planted by a river that brings life to it in every season.

We find our deep connection to God through meditation. As a result, we experience His life in our hearts like the tree's roots going deep to draw water from the soil by the river. Meditation is where we feast on the Lord and receive nourishment for our souls. In comparison to eating natural things, spiritual food is put on the table as we read the Bible, engage in worship, listen to Bible teachings, or have edifying conversations. But we eat, chew, digest, and absorb the life of those spiritual foods through meditation.

These spiritual things can stir and inspire us, but the God-given way to partake of the deeper life is to slowly speak and sing His Words back to Him in deep heart communion. Unfortunately, many believers are frustrated at their lack of experiencing God and transformation. This lack is probably due to their neglect of intimate meditation on the Word. They might know how to be inspired in spiritual things, but they haven't taken the time to eat His Word and digest it unto an authentic heart experience and transformation.

Like David, God promised Joshua that he would act wisely and prosper in leading Israel into their land if he meditated day and night.[1] I believe God encouraged Joshua to continue in the meditation lifestyle he had seen and cultivated under Moses' leadership.[2] King David and Joshua were both national leaders with lots of responsibilities; however, God rooted both of them in meditation so they would flow in supernatural life and blessing and prioritize friendship with Him.

The last Biblical promise is intimacy with God in meditation. Psalm 119 embodies the promise and displays where God can take the human heart in receiving love and spiritual pleasures. There are three themes in Psalm 119. The first is rejoicing in and loving God's Word.[3] The Psalmist rejoiced in God's Word as in riches, had a value for revelation in God's Word, and experienced joy in encountering God in His Word.

The second theme is experiencing the delight and pleasure of God in His Word. The Psalmist oriented his life around the highest joy of experiencing God through His Word, the chief pleasure available to the human heart.

---

1 Joshua 1:8.

2 Exodus 33:11.

3 Psalm 119:14, 47-48, 54, 72, 97, 103, 111, 119, 127, 129, 140, 159, 161-163, 165, 167.

The third theme is the cry for God's revelation through His Word. The Psalmist repeatedly asked for understanding, eyes to be opened, and the Word to teach him about God.[4] The primary entry point into the revelation of God is the Word ignited by the Holy Spirit. Therefore, we need Him to give us understanding.

MEDITATION DEFINED

In my past, meditation only meant focusing my mind on Bible verses while being in solitude, silence, and stillness. While I still believe in silence and stillness, I've broadened my understanding of how to meditate and become more specific in its purpose. *My working definition of meditation is that it's a focused and persistent searching of an area of God's Personality through deep conversation over His Word.*

In meditation, we search out one area of God's heart at a time by praying through single words until the Spirit brings us into an experience in the truth. It is focused and persistent in the sense that we focus on one idea about God, one word in a verse, and we dialogue with Him long-term until we experience Him. For example, we take a Bible verse, and we lock into it for weeks or months, and say, "God, I want to explore this area of Your personality. I want to discover it. I want to be on a treasure hunt with this one thing specifically, and I'm not going to stop until I meet You in powerful ways."

Meditation is about exploring, experiencing, and enjoying God in His Word. It is way more than just a spiritual discipline; it's about going on a fascinating exploration of His heart. We meditate to explore an aspect of God in a precise and focused way. His personality is a vast ocean of beauty and love that we will search

---

4 Psalm 119:12, 18-20, 26-29, 33-34, 64, 66, 68, 71, 73, 124-125, 130, 133, 135, 144, 169, 171, 175.

out for billions of years. Through meditation, we enter into a slow exploration of that endless beauty.

Our purpose for existing is to discover God's Personality so that we can know Him. We step into that eternal calling now by giving ourselves to exploring Him in meditation. This process leads us to experience Him as a real Person when the truth becomes a discernible experience. Experiencing Him is enjoyable because it satisfies the God-given longing to know Him as a Person.

If our eternal purpose is to explore, experience, and enjoy God, why not begin that journey right now? Why wait until eternity to go deep into God's heart? If meditation is the primary way to enter into that eternal calling, why not go deep in it now?

God has designed us in such a way that we only work right if we first meet Him intimately and then overflow from that place to impact others. He is to be known and enjoyed before He is to be partnered with in ministry. God is a jealous Husband who wants all of our hearts in a deep and enjoyable relationship with Him. He wants to impact others with us, but not at the expense of our relationship with Him, and not if our relationship with Him is mostly based on doing ministry with Him.

 ## DOOR INTO GOD'S HEART

When talking about meditation, we must be clear that the source of our meditation is God's Word. In His Word, God has communicated the depths of His heart to us. It is a supernatural door into His eternal heart.

Why is His Word so significant? Words have the unique ability to communicate the invisible interior life of a person. Our deepest thoughts, emotions, desires, and plans are mostly expressed through our words to others. In the same way, God's Word has communicated the fullest expression of His heart to us so that we can understand the invisible workings of His heart.

The Bible isn't just a boring storyline. In it, we see how God has interacted with people, and we can understand what He's like and How He relates to us. In the testimonies of the Bible, we hear literal conversations God had with people, and we hear His plans and desires for us. The Bible is filled with revelation about His heart!

LEARN GOD'S INTERACTIONS

Meditation is a lifelong journey in understanding how God interacts with you in the Word. It's more than learning practical techniques to get insight into Bible verses—it's learning how to posture yourself before God to understand how He interacts in real space and time. He's an actual Person with a personality and unique ways of relating and interacting, and we have to set our hearts for a lifelong journey of learning Him in meditation.

Interacting with God in meditation is a spiritual skill that needs to be cultivated with great care. A long-term perspective is necessary because it causes us to pay closer attention to how God interacts with us, which causes our spiritual senses to be more sensitive. Cultivating the spiritual skill also increases our awareness that we're talking to a legitimate person who is really thinking, feeling, and communicating with us right then.

This active learning process makes me ask God questions to understand and sense Him more. I'm asking Him, "How do I relate to You in meditation? What

are You doing right now in my heart? What am I sensing? How are You speaking to me? How do I respond to You right now? Teach me how You move and how You ebb and flow in my conversations with You."

TWO LEVELS OF REVELATION

It is helpful to understand that there are two levels of revelation in meditation. Revelation begins in the thought realm and grows into revelation in the emotional realm. Distinguishing them can help identify where you are in the progression of revelation and develop a Biblical expectation of what you can receive from God in meditation.

Revelation in the thought realm is the first phase of an encounter. It comes in the form of divine ideas, thoughts, questions, and clarity concerning phrases in a Bible verse. These thoughts are probably from God and captivate our attention for a few minutes and create a hunger for more.

If given time, revelation in the thought realm will develop into revelation in the emotional realm. In these moments, God is experienced intimately by many of our spiritual senses. In these moments, He takes an idea and makes it an experiential reality that becomes real inside us and allows us to feel Him as a person.

God wants to encounter us in our emotions. We will step into emotional encounters more often if we're patient and have a higher vision than thought realm revelation. I consistently see people stop meditating once they experience inspired thoughts, but they are frustrated that their experience and transformation aren't deeper. Most likely, their vision for revelation is too low; therefore, their pursuit of more of God at the moment gets cut short.

HEART POSTURE - PROVERBS 2

PROVERBS 2:5 - THE KNOWLEDGE OF GOD

Proverbs 2:1-5 summarizes what the heart posture and pursuit of the knowledge of God look like in meditation. Verse five is the goal of the pursuit that is listed out in verses one through four. In verse five, we are promised an encounter with God if we walk out the heart posture and pursuit listed in these verses. Be encouraged; God has given us a roadmap to follow.

My son, if you receive my words, and treasure my commands within you, so that you incline your ear to wisdom, and apply your heart to understanding; Yes, if you cry out for discernment and lift up your voice for understanding, if you seek her as silver, and search for her as for hidden treasures; then you will understand the fear of the LORD, and find the knowledge of God.
—Proverbs 2:1-5

PROVERBS 2:4 - HIDDEN TREASURE

In verse four, the heart requirement is laid out—the person seeking depth must value encountering God as a precious treasure. As a result, they must have a hunger in their heart that causes them to change their lifestyle to seek God. Without understanding that God is a precious treasure within reach, we won't have the hunger necessary to pursue Him in meditation. Hunger ushers us into encounters with God, and it's fueled by a vision for more satisfaction in Him.

How much time, effort, and emotion would you give to finding a treasure chest in your backyard if you knew there were a million dollars in it? If you had any sense in you, you would drop everything right now and go home to begin your search. You would pay and do anything necessary to find that treasure chest because you would know that when you find it, life would be different. The vision for the treasure motivates you to push through the obstacles and delays until you find it. Likewise, God is a hidden treasure waiting to be discovered through the process of meditation. He hides Himself to be found by us, but there is a discovering process that we must press through.

Some people meditate for a few minutes here and there and don't experience God, but they lack the revelation that they are to search out God as if He were a precious treasure in their backyard. Their mentality says, "It didn't work for me, so I'm moving on." No! There are a million dollars in your backyard. Just stay with it, and you'll find the treasure.

PROVERBS 2:2 – SPIRITUAL HEARING

Verse two calls us to incline our hearts, which is a posture of listening to God in meditation. The inclining heart says, "Holy Spirit, I want to hear Your voice as I read these words. I want to hear Your voice speaking to me as I meditate on this phrase." So, it's a spiritual ear that we're inclining, and we're saying, "God, the Word is right there, but I want the Holy Spirit to open my ears to hear Your voice in this passage."

For everyone who partakes only of milk is unskilled in the word of righteousness, for he is a babe. But solid food belongs to those who are of full age, that is, those who by reason of use have their senses exercised to discern both good and evil.—Hebrews 5:13-14

In the process, God is training us to hear Him and respond to Him. In the stillness and invisible dialogue, He's tuning our ears to His frequency. As you incline your spiritual ears intentionally during your meditation times, you end up inclining your ears more naturally throughout the day. This inclining posture strengthens your spiritual discernment. Hebrews talks about having your spiritual senses exercised through interacting with God, and it's specifically talking about hearing and sensing Him in the Bible.

If anyone has ears to hear let him hear.—Mark 4:23

And with many such parables He spoke the word to them as they were able to hear it.—Mark 4:33

*"He who has an ear, let him hear what the Spirit says to the churches."
—Revelation 2:7*

In Mark 4, Jesus highlighted the fact that hearing Him in His Word is supernatural, and then He called us to cultivate spiritual ears that hear the Spirit of God.[5] Later in the chapter, it says that He could discern when the people could not hear Him. This means that Jesus knew when their spiritual hearing was done and that His words would be wasted. At the heart of Jesus' message to hear the Spirit, He's saying, "Pay close attention to what I'm saying. Give time and energy to searching out My word while asking the Spirit for revelation. As you search out My words in meditation, expect layers of meaning and encounter to unfold."

---

5   Mark 4:23.

The author of Hebrews also referenced spiritual hearing in that he could not teach in-depth on specific topics because he knew the listeners were spiritually "dull of hearing."[6] Meditation is a focused pursuit of truth until it becomes alive on the inside of us. Therefore, meditation is the practical response to Jesus' exhortation to break out of dull hearing.

PROVERBS 2:3 – HUNGRY PRAYERS

Verse three tells us that meditation includes hungry prayers for understanding and experience with God. Once you meditate on something long enough, a deeper cry for the experience of that verse gets awakened. Often, I will be meditating on something on a specific day, and then I'll get a little stirred to encounter that truth, so I'll spend a while pacing and saying, "God, I want to feel this. I want to experience it. Let my heart burn with this." So there's an intercessory thing that can happen. An element of meditation that we need to understand is that we will see the truth, and we might be inspired by it a little bit, but there will be a journey to enter into a powerful experience with that truth. We meditate, set our minds, and sing, but there's also a place for asking God, "I want to feel this verse. Holy Spirit, write it on the inside of me!"

---

6   Hebrews 5:11.

WEEKLY ASSIGNMENT

For your assignment this week, choose which Bible verse or short Gospel story you would like to meditate on for this entire module. You could continue meditating on your verse from the previous modules or choose a new one that speaks into your heart issue. During each meditation time, include writing your thoughts, questions, and prayers to God so that you can discuss your meditation experiences in-depth during your Discipleship meetings. Also, journal your thoughts and questions on three sections of this chapter: *Meditation Defined*, *Learn God's Interactions*, and *Heart Posture - Proverbs 2*.

10

FIVE WAYS TO INTERACT
WITH GOD

INTRODUCTION

Most of the main meditation expressions included in this chapter are based on a well-known meditation model taught by Kirk Bennett, a leader at the International House of Prayer in Kansas City. His training manual, *Revelation by Meditation*, launched me into meditation. The meditation expressions Kirk teaches are reading, writing, praying, singing, and speaking. I have modified it a little bit for this chapter: picture, read, write, pray, sing. Each of these engages something unique in us that helps maintain conversation with God and open our deep places to God. Incorporating these expressions helps take the truth deeper because we were made to meditate and learn by engaging multiple faculties of our minds, hearts, and bodies.

I usually start my meditation time by going in the order listed in the next section, but then I flow between them without a specific order until I move on to a new phrase in a Bible verse. Below, I've written out what I do in my meditation times and why I do it this way to clearly communicate learned values and give practical examples. But don't feel restricted to a specific order. Instead, use the example order as a template for your initial journey into deep meditation, and then see how your heart flows in the expressions after a few months of going deeper. In saying this, approach this chapter as a student by trying all the meditation expressions for months before minimizing or ruling any of them out.

PICTURE GOD

In all my prayer and worship expressions, I always close my eyes and picture the descriptions of Revelation 4:2-3, God on His throne in all His colors. This is a helpful way to engage with Him as a person and stay focused, especially in meditation times. Colossians 3:1-3 says to set our minds (imagination) on things above where Jesus is seated and where we are seated spiritually.[1] Doing this isn't just using our imaginations for fun or to help us concentrate. Setting our minds on the images God has given us brings us into the spiritual reality of where we live with Jesus in the throne room. It's a real place in heaven, and we have literal access there by the blood of Jesus.[2]

Picturing God is so critical to prayer that it is one of the modules in this program, so I encourage you to look at Revelation 4:2-3 and begin to picture God in your times with Him. When you speak or sing to Him, it will make the conversation more intimate and real. Imagining takes a little more focus and energy, but it will become natural over time, and it's worth it!

---

1 Ephesians 2:6-7.

2 Hebrews 10:19.

READ

Start by reading your meditation verse. Read through it slowly several times so that you get an initial feel for what it may be saying. During this time, the Holy Spirit will cause one word to stick out to you by drawing your attention to it on the page or by stirring your interest in the word. You don't have to over-analyze if God is highlighting it to you to meditate on it, but often there is some impression-level leading from the Spirit. If you're unsure if He's highlighting a word, just start meditating on the first word in the verse and meditate through the verse sequentially.

WRITE

Slowly write down the entire verse on a notepad as many times as is helpful to engage your heart. Next, write down the first phrase you want to meditate on, and write it as many times as you want. As you do this, questions and thoughts might come to mind, so take your time and write those down. Then I have a conversation with God by praying and singing my thoughts to Him. I write down new thoughts that come during that conversation, or I re-write my thoughts repeatedly. At different times in my meditation time, I go back over things I've written, and I engage with the words by circling and underlining things that seem inspired, and then I write more notes in the margins.

ENGAGING THE MIND

Writing is a powerful and practical way of engaging God. In my experience, writing is the most necessary meditation expression in getting clarity and staying engaged at the heart level. Practically speaking, writing helps keep you focused and process what you are thinking. Thoughts float around in our minds and tend to be unclear until we have to articulate them on paper or speak them aloud. I often think I have clarity on something until I'm forced to write it down. At which point, I realize I don't have clarity and respond by meditating more and processing my thoughts.

Clear thoughts lead to deeper encounters, so they're worth fighting for. When we wrestle to get clarity on a truth and come away with detailed sentences, something clicks in the mind and heart. After writing clear statements, there is usually a flow of thought that follows and an increase of God's presence.

Writing forces our minds to engage in a deeper level of learning and exploration. It engages new sections of our minds, connecting them together neurologically in the process. Also, writing involves more functions of our hands and body, all of which increase the focus and engagement of our minds and hearts. This has been proven to impact memory and other brain functions related to learning, which I believe has the potential to practically help with renewing the mind in truth.

There is something transformative about slowly forming letters on a page to articulate an idea that makes it seem tangible and real. When I write, I feel the truth solidify in my thoughts and emotions. It's like my eyes and my heart see the words being written down letter by letter, and at the same time, my heart begins to accept the idea as truth. At this point, I feel the letters begin to be written on my heart.

STEWARDING REVELATION

Another benefit is that writing helps capture and steward key questions or revelations that you may forget. In my meditation notepad, I go back to circled and underlined sections and pray them back to the Lord several times. Years later, I still have meditation times when I go back to pray ideas that seemed inspired and anointed when I first meditated on them.

PRAY

Slowly speak thoughts, questions, and truths back to God with repetition. Start by speaking the actual Bible verse to the Lord repeatedly in a way that connects you to Him. Picture Him in your imagination and speak to Him as a real person. As you pray out loud, you may find that clarity and more language come to your heart about the verse. Write those thoughts down and pray them again. At times, review your journal and pray out phrases and questions you've written down that move your heart or seem significant.

Speaking to God out loud will help connect your heart to Him, even if it's just a whisper. It's not enough to just think thoughts to God; the greater power is in speaking them. God has designed our tongues to be the steering wheel of our entire being, so whatever we speak out loud gives leadership to the rest of our being.[3] Praying out loud brings focus and causes our attention to be given to what we're saying to God. Praying out the truth is a form of spiritual agreement with God, and therefore changes the spiritual atmosphere around us and transforms our thinking and feeling.[4]

WAYS TO PRAY IN MEDITATION

1. Speak the verse's exact words to Him and any thoughts about the verse. Based on what you have written down, speak anointed truths to Him. Thank Him and praise Him for the truths.

2. Make the truth personal and speak it to Him, "Father, I am the one that You love. You love me in the same way that You love Jesus. I am loved by

---

3   James 3:1-12.

4   Romans 10:8-10.

You." Then take the truth and speak it over yourself from God's perspective. "Jeff, I love you with the same intensity that I love My Son, Jesus. You are loved, Jeff. You are enjoyed by Me. I'm thinking of you throughout the day, Jeff."

3. Pray out your questions about the truth of the verse for a while. I take 10-15 minutes just asking God one question while walking and communing with God by praying in tongues.

4. Ask for experiential knowledge of the verse. I often pray, "God, I see the truth of the verse, but I don't feel it, and my heart isn't moving yet. Help me to experience it on the inside. Give me experiential knowledge of this truth." I do this intermittently in my meditation times, but I also spend extended amounts of focused time doing this.

5. Pray and sing in tongues at different times and engage your mind in conversation with God about the verse. Engage your mind with a question or truth while you commune spirit to Spirit with God.[5] Engaging your spirit will make you more sensitive to His voice and more receptive to the truth.

6. Once you feel a level of clarity and internal focus, silently commune with God with the verse's truth. Communing prayer is simply being with God while focusing on the verse in your heart. Picture God in your imagination and bring one phrase or truth to mind as you gaze on Him.

7. Respond to anything you sense God speaking to you in the verse. If He's bringing conviction of sin, take time to confess your sin and repent and receive His forgiveness. If you feel negative emotions or unbelief in your heart because of the verse, be honest and talk to the Lord about them so that He can speak the truth into them. Or maybe you need to speak the

---

5   1 Corinthians 14:14-15.

truth into a situation in your life and resolve in your heart to choose the truth daily in that specific situation.

SING

The singing expression of meditation is simple and very enjoyable. Singing is naturally engaging, intimate, and worshipful. Because of these, it can easily flow from our hearts. This creates new opportunities within meditation because it's so easy and enjoyable to sing something out repeatedly.

Our prayer room always has worship playing, so it's a very natural environment to sing prayers back to God. But if I'm at home, I turn on worship instrumental music with no words, turn on regular worship songs, or just play my guitar so I have something to sing with during meditation. If you play an instrument even a little bit, play a couple of simple chords and sing your meditations. If you're more experienced in music, put your meditations together into a simple song and let it become one of the songs you sing over your heart.

I believe singing allows the deep places of our hearts to be expressed and unguarded and therefore opens up our deep places to have His words dwell in us and transform us.[6] I say this from experience and because music and singing are such a significant theme in the Bible, which I believe shows us that they are a core part of our human makeup and God's divine makeup. Music moves us because God made us musical; therefore, something in us comes alive when we sing to Him. It's the language of our hearts.

Heaven is filled with worship and singing, and we're exhorted to worship and sing on the earth.[7] I've also read several testimonies of people who have seen

---

6 Colossians 3:16.

7 Revelation 4:7-11, 5:8-13; Psalm 96:1-13, 119:54; Isaiah 54:1.

heaven and said that music and singing are a part of the fabric of heaven. This worship reality in heaven reflects God's value for singing. Even God sings and makes melodies.[8]

Singing is intimate, enjoyable, and vulnerable, so some people have a hard time singing to God in worship or meditation. I've noticed that speaking the truth to God can be easier than singing the truth. There have been times in my past where I could agree with a truth in the Bible by speaking it out, but then when I would try to sing it out, I wouldn't be able to do it because I couldn't believe it. In those moments of trying to sing, my conviction of what I believed to be true was revealed because singing opens our hearts.

When I feel restricted in singing the truth, I dialogue with God about why I'm not grabbing the truth more freely. When I have clear thoughts of what is in my heart, I repent for believing specific lies or holding onto anger and offense, and then I speak the truth out loud again and begin to sing. I may not be able to grab onto the truth with all my heart in the initial times of singing, but my heart always gets more tender to the truth and grabs on in due time.

One specific example of this was when I was meditating on Song of Songs 1:15. For months, I had felt oppressed with feelings of self-hatred, loneliness, comparing myself to others, and the fear of never getting married. I meditated on this verse every day for a month but couldn't do the singing part of meditation until one week in because my heart was so bound up in lies. I couldn't bring myself to sing it out loud. I identified the main lies and areas of offense towards God in those moments and spoke them out to Him, at times, with tears of desperation.

As I meditated on the truth, it slowly began to fill my heart with faith to grab onto it. When I started to sing it out loud with more confidence, my deliverance began to manifest. I sang short statements like, "Behold, Jeff, you are beautiful

---

8   Zephaniah 3:17; Revelation 4:5; Psalm 42:8, 32:7.

198

to Me. Look at how I've made you. You are the one that I love with all My heart. God, I'm beautifully and wonderfully made in every way. I am the one You love. I say no to self-hatred and loneliness because they're lies."

I felt the deep places of my heart breaking agreement with the lies as I sang, and I felt the deep places receiving the truths I was singing. There were many tears in those moments and noticeable shifts in my emotions of feeling peace, joy, and hope because I truly felt beautiful and enjoyed by God. I not only received discernible deliverance from the demonic oppression in that month; something significant was established in my heart to the point that it launched me into a new spiritual season of confidence before God and people.

Singing truths to God seems to be the one expression that people most often dismiss or minimize. I've seen many of those people give singing a chance at some point and be convinced of its place in meditation. I've also seen many others never try singing meditations, probably because they feel the intimacy and vulnerability of singing to God and pull back in fear. Whether you think you sound good or not or are used to singing in meditation or not, I encourage you to jump right in to singing the scriptures to God and watch Him move on your heart. If you feel the uncomfortable openness and vulnerability of singing, stay with the meditation and bring your struggle to the Lord. He has met me there, and I am confident He will meet you there. Singing is for you, and it will be intimate and fruitful over time, so don't give up on it.

WAYS TO SING IN MEDITATION

1. Sing the same things to God that you would normally speak to Him. Go back and forth between singing and speaking out your thoughts, questions, and declarations in the same way that you would flow between speaking and singing in tongues.

2. Create choruses or short songs from the truth and sing them out over and over again.

3. The truths might begin to touch your heart and awaken spontaneous choruses, so sing those out for a while.[9] Singing spontaneously around the verse will bring you into more clarity, and it will bring you into a deeper experience in the moment. I've found great emotional healing and deliverance manifest in my times of singing meditations, and it seems like the singing moments bring me into worshipful climaxes that open my heart to express and receive more deeply.

MEDITATING ON GOSPEL STORIES

We have a unique treasure to meditate on in the Gospel stories; God fully manifested in a human body for all to behold! Nothing in the Bible compares to meditating on Jesus in the Gospels. In His stories, we get to see how the invisible God talks to His people, what tone of voice He uses, what attitude He has, what body language He displays, and how He interacts with real people in real situations. Jesus' disciples and eyewitnesses have truly given us a gift in writing down His interactions for us to dive into in meditation to encounter God as a real person.

The gospels are also powerful because, in them, we get to meditate on stories. We were made to read stories and then to enter into stories with our imagination. We connect to the characters and the scenery in a story, and they become somewhat real to us. Each gospel story has characters and scenery that we can relate to, and then we get to see how Jesus interacts with them, which creates a context for Him

---

9 Colossians 3:16; Ephesians 5:18-19.

to show us how He interacts with us. In one moment, we can be meditating on how He interacted with a person, and in the next moment, the Holy Spirit puts us in the story, and we experience Jesus' interactions with us.

Meditating on Jesus in stories makes Him more real as a Person because the earthly scenery, as opposed to heaven, is so familiar to us and allows us to relate to Him differently. We relate to the stories, and we relate to the scenery, smells, interactions, and when we do, God becomes a real Person to us by revelation. The truth of God becoming flesh living among us finally hits home in these moments. I often find myself saying the same thing in these moments of revelation, "God, You are a real Person who interacts with me in a personal way."

I encourage you to regularly mix in gospel story meditations between your other meditation topics and give them time to unfold over the course of weeks. Fall in love with the Person of Jesus who fully embodies and displays God's heart towards you. Engage all your senses and enter into the story by picturing the people, the landscape, the sounds, and Jesus' interactions. The Holy Spirit will take your holy imagination and create a living context for Jesus to interact with you.

 ## PRACTICAL TIPS FOR GOSPEL MEDITATION

READ THE STORY

Pick a Gospel story and read the entire story a few times so that you have an overall idea of what is happening in the story. You will pick up new details just by reading it a few times.

PICTURE THE SCENE

Then read it slowly one last time and get a growing picture in your imagination of what was happening in the story. Partner with the Holy Spirit and develop all the different aspects of the scenery of the story: the colors, smells, sounds, people, moods, and landscapes. You want this story to be as real as possible in your heart, because the more real the story, the more real the interactions with Jesus will be to your own life. God wants to reveal Himself to you in the details of the story. Journal the landscape of the story, your thoughts and questions, impressions about Jesus, and anything else that you want to capture in writing.

ASK QUESTIONS

You've probably noticed a few details in the story that interest you more than the others, so start there in your meditation and ask Jesus questions. Go phrase by phrase and ask Him questions about the story like, "What did You think when they did that? What did You feel at that moment? How did You feel about that person? What did You say to them? Why did You say that?"

IMAGINE INTERACTIONS

Go phrase by phrase, and picture each interaction that Jesus had with people. Go with the bunny trails in the story that aren't technically in the Bible story. For example, focus on one of the people in the story and imagine their background, their life, and what happened to them after the story. Imagine parts of the conversation that took place that are not detailed in the Bible.

TELL JESUS WHAT YOU SEE

Tell Jesus the things you notice about Him in the story. Speaking observations back to Him is prayer. Pause often and reflect on what you've read and seen about Jesus in the story. When you see displays of His heart, thank Him for that attribute of Himself and ask Him to touch you with that same aspect of His heart. "Jesus, I see Your compassion for that woman! You are so aware of our hearts in every circumstance, and Your heart is filled with compassion for us, thank You. Open my eyes to experience Your compassion."

ENTER THE STORY

In your holy imagination, picture yourself being the person Jesus is talking to in the story. Fully enter into their situation and have a real dialogue with Jesus from their perspective. Imagine yourself as one of the people Jesus healed, as one of those that lavished Him with perfume, or as one of those that were at the foot of His cross. When I do this, I receive tremendous insight into what was happening in the story, but also a real face-to-face moment of interaction with Jesus and experience of His words personalized to me.

WEEKLY ASSIGNMENT

In your meditation times this week and onward, practice each of the five meditation expressions. As you do this, you will notice that some of them will be easy and enjoyable while others might be harder. Even if they're hard, or you don't sense a connection to God in them, take a student's posture and don't decide against them for several months or more. As a part of this week's assignment, write down your experience with each expression in your meditation times, and process them with your Discipleship Mentor at your next meeting. Included in this, write down which expression is most natural for you, and which one is the hardest.

DISCIPLESHIP MEETING GUIDE
MODULE 3: MEDITATION – CHAPTERS 9 & 10

MEETING FOCUS:

The purpose of this week's meeting is to discuss the importance of meditation, review practical tips for meditation, and talk in-depth about your meditation verse.

DISCUSSION QUESTIONS (IN ORDER OF IMPORTANCE):

1. *Spiritual Pursuits:*
   a. Talk through your meditation journal from the last two weeks in-depth. How are your meditation times going? What is God doing in your heart during these times? How is it impacting your heart issue?
   b. Practically, how is your prayer schedule going? How many days this week have you walked out your prayer schedule? Do you need to make small changes to your schedule? How are your Bible reading and prayer list times going?
   c. Briefly review your new *Spiritual Pursuits Document.*
2. *Chapter Questions:*
   a. Chapter 9 – Discuss your journal response assignment (*Meditation Defined, Learn God's Interactions,* and *Heart Posture - Proverbs 2*). How would you define meditation? Would you say you understand the significance of meditation to your life in God?
   b. Chapter 10 – Discuss your journaling from the chapter, including which of the five meditation expressions is the most natural, the most difficult, and how implementing them has been going for you. Have you tried singing your meditations yet?
3. *Heart Issue:*
   a. Share how your heart issue has been going this past week. With heart issue discussions, process, confess, encourage, and pray together for God to release transformation.
4. Briefly review the assignments for the next two weeks together.

MEETING NOTES:

_____

_____

_____

_____

_____

_____

_____

_____

_____

_____

11

TEN PRACTICALS
PART ONE

INTRODUCTION

The purpose of these next two chapters is to flesh out practical ways of meditating on God. Many of these have been taught to me by leaders that have gone deep in meditation in their own lives, and their teachings have helped me and instructed me on my journey. Then other practicals I have learned by giving much time to meditation over the past fifteen years. In that time frame, I have observed how God has interacted with me consistently in meditation, and I've observed how my heart responds to His movements. Use these practical tips as a launching pad for learning how God interacts with you in meditation.

FIVE PRACTICAL TIPS

#1 - SCHEDULE STRATEGICALLY

Think through your weekly schedule and find the best times for you to meditate. Two major hindrances in meditation are falling asleep and being distracted by other life issues, so schedule times when you know you'll be more awake physically and attentive to the Lord mentally and emotionally. Schedule the best times for you to meditate, the best days that will give you the most time and pick the location that facilitates it the best. Don't fit meditation into your lifestyle; make needed changes in your lifestyle and schedule to prioritize meditation times.

For me, scheduling strategically means meditating in the morning on days that I have the most time. I do this because my mind is the clearest in the morning and I know I need certain amounts of time. For the location, I prefer to meditate most times at my church because I stay more focused, have less propensity to fall asleep, and because I can be louder and play worship.

On top of your regular weekly devotional times with God, try and carve out longer sacred times (one hour or multiple hours) for meditation occasionally. The longer time frames allow God to increase our heart size over time so that we have the capacity to experience more of Him more often. For some, this may be possible once a week, and for others, it may be once a month. Extended times in prayer allow your mind and emotions to dial down even more than they do in the shorter meditation times. The more you dial down and focus on God, the more sensitive you'll be to hearing God's voice and sensing His movements in meditation. You may be surprised by how God meets you, and you may be surprised by how enjoyable it is.

#2 – STAY WITH ONE VERSE

The first part of going on a journey in meditation is picking a Bible verse. As a part of the values of this discipleship program, I suggest choosing a verse based on what you're desiring and needing truth in. If you need freedom from fear, anxiety, rejection, shame, or feeling unworthy of God's love, find verses that speak truths into these lies to dismantle their spiritual strongholds. In general, I choose verses that clearly reveal God's heart or verses that reveal my worth and value to Him. That's not all that I meditate on, but that's the majority of my focus.

The next part of the journey is sticking with the verse until you begin to experience God in its truth. I encourage you to schedule 1-2 focused meditation times throughout your weekly prayer schedule and then stay with your verse for at least a month. I've been on my most recent verse on God's pleasure for several months now, and it keeps going deeper and deeper. If you give it a month or longer, the Spirit has more time to walk you through the process of revelation and transformation. If an encounter with God and heart transformation are the goals of meditation, then stay with a verse until you observe those happening.

In the process of meditation, it's Biblical to expect tears to flow, to have hope and joy filling your heart, and to feel like God is moving on your emotions to some degree. I tell people to stay committed to their verse until they're crying or weeping because it answers the "how many weeks do I meditate on this verse" question. These experiences are signposts along the way indicating that the truth is dismantling lies and renewing your soul. I say weeping because that's a strong emotional experience, and I think that's our portion consistently. Our hearts can become tender as we stay with a Bible verse long enough.

#3 – DEVELOP A PHRASE

Developing a phrase means taking your time to let one word or one idea from your verse expand and open to you in meditation. As you pray and sing through it, the word will begin to have more and more meaning and may even lead you in multiple directions of thought, which are new things to explore with God. If you picture meditation as being in a huge mansion for the first time, meditating on one word is like going into a mansion. Each new idea or question that stems from that one word is like exploring a new room in the mansion. After exploring a new room, the one word you began with should only get more exciting over time.

Therefore, move forward slowly. There is no rush to move forward to a new phrase or a new verse. Success in meditation isn't just "completing" a word or "getting through" the passage but encountering God's heart in your emotions and mind. What's motivating you to get to the next thing? Slowness is a part of God's process. He could just download us with all the information we need so we could share it or be transformed, but He wants a slow dialogue. He's not interested in just giving information outside of intimate experiences with Him.

Here's an example of words unfolding from one of my meditations on Psalm 45:1, "*My heart is overflowing with a good theme.*" My meditation started with "my heart is overflowing." Within that phrase I spent days going in different directions: God awakens my heart, my emotions can overflow and should be felt, God can inspire my emotions with discernable love for Jesus, my tongue is the pen of the ready writer because my heart is overflowing, and I was made to overflow. The next phrase was "good theme," which developed into the following ideas: Jesus is a good theme, He's the theme or current that runs through my heart, the first thing on my mind and encompassing, I see Your beauty and goodness in everything, the theme of my interior life, and Jesus is an all-consuming theme.

#4 - REPETITION IN ALL THINGS

Be repetitive in all things with meditation. Repetition slowly brings your mind and emotions into a truth with God. It's not to be confused with the vain disconnected repetition Jesus warned about or filling the air with words thinking it's prayer and more spiritual. It's about engaging with God over a truth through slow repetition of words with a meaningful heart engagement.[1] Some people automatically think repetition is religious, but it is foundational to meditation if you engage your heart in it. My encouragement to you is to be repetitious with the five different meditation expressions (picture, read, write, pray, sing) and to embrace the simplicity of it.

#5 - ASK GOD QUESTIONS

Asking God questions is also very foundational in the meditation process. The questions that come to my heart while meditating become the central piece of my conversation with God. Questions determine the direction of the conversation and create hunger in me to pursue Him unto deeper answers. They open up new areas of thought to explore, make truths more personal and applicable, and they give God specific things to answer. Asking questions and dialoguing over answers is a very fruitful discipleship model in the church, how much more so when we're asking the Great Discipleship Mentor questions.

Deep questions and deep answers fascinate me on the inside. Questions unlock the answers that reveal the heart in a friend, and the same principle is true in conversation with God. We explore God's heart by asking Him questions and pursuing answers, which produces fascination. Years ago, I was meditating

---

1 Matthew 6:7.

on Genesis 1:1 and learned something about asking questions. For a few days during my meditation, I was specifically asking God the question, "What were You doing in eternity before You created the angels or anything else?" The question itself was stirring me and bringing me into a stronger sense of eternity. One day, the Holy Spirit whispered to me and said, "That's a good question, Jeff! Keep asking about that." The impression I got from Him was that He would give me a deeper sense of the answer and open my eyes to understand it more in the Bible as time went on.

Asking God questions is a pattern throughout the Bible. King David connected asking questions about God with meditation and gazing on God's beauty.[2] Job received a tremendous revelation about God as Creator after asking questions about God.[3] Daniel received multiple open visions from God because He was asking God questions.[4] As a pattern, Jesus always gave more understanding to those who asked Him questions after His teachings.

Even brain research affirms the power of exploring God through asking Him questions. This is a quote from an educational leader, "When our curiosity is piqued, our Limbic Reward System lights up and brain pleasure centers are stimulated through the release of dopamine. And not only does dopamine make us feel happy, but it also enhances connections between cells that are involved in learning. Our brains are wired to learn! Learners of all ages who retain and can activate their own curiosity are empowered to learn more effectively. Our brain's hippocampus, which is associated with the creation of memories, sees increased activity in curious minds. So the questions we ask and the answers we seek out on

---

2   Psalm 27:4.

3   Job 38:1-41:34.

4   Daniel 7-12.

our own not only make us feel good but are also more likely to be committed to our memories."[5]

The author's point is that curiosity and interest, which in meditation we call hunger and exploration, stimulate more parts of the brain to pursue a truth. The process of asking questions actually releases pleasure to the person because they're pursuing a truth through questions. This is evidence that God has designed the brain to engage more fully when it's in a question-asking mode and answer-seeking mode. It also proves that God has designed the brain to release pleasure to the person to encourage that approach.

Studies also show that our brains naturally focus more when they are interested in something and ask questions or are asked a question. "Questions trigger a mental reflex known as 'instinctive elaboration.' When a question is posed, it takes over the brain's thought process. And when your brain is thinking about the answer to a question, it can't contemplate anything else."[6] God has designed us to ask questions and to be consumed with desire and focus while pursuing a truth.

There are three significant takeaways from brain research that excite me. Number one, God made our brains to explore things. Number two, what we explore is more deeply connected to the rest of our thoughts and emotions because of the deeper process of exploring. Number three, our brains are naturally consumed and focused when we have a question to explore.

---

5 Denise Alquist, "Achieve Better Learning: Utilize Curiosity to Stimulate Brain Function," August 11, 2017.
https://www.gettingsmart.com/2017/08/achieve-better-learning-utilize-curiosity-to-stimulate-brain-function/

6 David Hoffeld, "What your Brain Does When It Hears a Question," February 21, 2017.
https://www.fastcompany.com/3068341/want-to-know-what-your-brain-does-when-it-hears-a-question#:~:text=Questions%20On%20The%20Mind,can't%20contemplate%20anything%20else.

As you start meditating on a sentence, pay attention to the initial questions that arise in your heart to the Lord. Write down your questions and then pick one to focus on and ask God about it until He begins to speak into it. I may take a few minutes on one question, a few hours on another, or days for others that have stirred me with hunger. In the mansion analogy, each new thought in meditation is like a new room to explore in God. If that is the case, one question is like the door that we knock on until it opens up with revelation into the new room of thought. I ask God a question with persistence with the expectation that He will fulfill Matthew 7:7 and open the door of revelation.

Ask Him general questions about Him and the truth in the verse, but then also make it personal and specific by asking detailed questions of how this truth applies to you. For example, If I were meditating on God's joyful heart, I would ask, "Do You feel joy towards me today? Why do You feel joyful towards me? Does Your joy change because of my sin or weakness? What did You feel for me when I chose righteousness today? Why don't I feel Your joy very often? Is there anything hindering me from receiving joy?"

WEEKLY ASSIGNMENT

In your meditation times this week, focus on developing one word in your verse and asking God questions. There's no pressure to develop the word on your own or figure out all the questions to ask. As you go through the process of writing, praying, and singing your meditations, they will both begin to flow naturally.

12

TEN PRACTICALS
PART TWO

█ INTRODUCTION

You are weeks into deeper meditation, and I'm sure you're growing in it already! Continue to stay consistent in your times and with the same Bible verse even when it's hard because it will transform you and become an inner lifestyle. Any challenges you're facing will be overcome as you continue on. Remember, you're growing in your weekly prayer lifestyle, so any new lifestyle and prayer rhythms are going to be challenging at first.

Hopefully, you are observing and sensing God moving on your heart in new ways and having the Bible phrases become alive inside. If so, be encouraged that you're experiencing God and being tenderized. Also, know that your Bible verse is releasing light into the specific areas of your heart in which you're pursuing freedom and transformation. As you read the practical suggestions in this chapter,

I think you'll see how God is leading you into deeper truths and experiences within your verse, and that more is right around the corner.

#6 – RESPOND TO THE EBBS AND FLOW OF THE HOLY SPIRIT

At different points in your meditation times, you will sense God's presence touching your heart and body. When you feel His presence come upon you, respond by giving Him your attention. I've found that God's presence will come upon me little by little like waves slowly coming back and forth onto a beach. In these moments, the verse's truth feels alive, and I feel God's presence like a little breath coming into me or the sensation of heat resting on me.

He will come for a moment and then pull back. If I give Him my attention in the moment, the waves often intensify and progress into an emotional experience with Him. I believe those waves of His presence are invitations to engage with Him longer in order to enter into even deeper encounters with Him.

The principle here is that God touches us and then pulls back to see how we will respond. He initiates the experience but then draws back and allows us to respond based on the measure of hunger and desire that we have for Him. He gives more of Himself based on our level of desire for Him.[1]

In the parable of the Sower, Jesus spoke to the crowd with a parable until He knew they couldn't receive any more from Him. He was able to perceive when they were at their physical and spiritual limit of listening. Then He would stop talking until someone responded to His words with a hunger for more understanding.[2]

---

1   Mark 4:23-25.

2   Mark 4:33-34; Matthew 13:36.

Jesus did something similar when He encountered two disciples on the road to Emmaus. He walked with them and taught them about Himself in the scriptures to the point that their hearts were burning with revelation. But when they arrived in Emmaus, Jesus made it look like He would keep walking and end His revelation session with them. At the moment, they had to choose to respond to the experience of revelation with a desire for more or to be content with Jesus leaving them for the night.[3] They made the wise choice in the moment to constrain Him and ask Him for deeper fellowship, and because of this, Jesus came into the house with them and completely opened their spiritual eyes to see Him. They were being encountered to a degree on the road, but their eyes were not fully opened to know that it was Jesus until they constrained Him and asked for more.

Jesus moves in the same way during our meditation times. He'll reveal Himself to a measure and release His presence upon us, but then He will wait and give us the opportunity to respond in the moment. There will be times when you feel your heart moving with a measure of revelation but stay engaged and ask Him for more because you may have eye-opening experiences like the disciples in Emmaus.

I usually experience waves of His presence that get my attention, leading to a progressive experience in the same prayer time. Within this time frame, the waves may pause for lengths of time, and my meditation posture may shift from silence to being more active in prayer. Also, it may all unfold over one or two hours of waiting on Him, not necessarily within five to ten minutes of initially feeling His presence.

In a recent meditation time, I felt God's presence at a distinct moment, so I began softly praying and staying focused on the truth that was resting on my heart. About thirty minutes later, I felt God pulling on my heart even more. I knew a deeper experience was probably around the corner, so I put everything down,

---

3   Luke 24:16-32.

focused my heart on Him, and let Him whisper phrases to me. Tears began to flow down my cheeks as I felt God's words going deeper into my heart. Within minutes, there was a deeper groan as my heart unlocked, and God's presence rushed in. I gave way to the experience and wept on and off for a while. In between weeping times, I continued to stay engaged in a quiet dialogue with the Lord asking questions and staying focused on His presence and what He was stirring in me.

#7 – STAYING FOCUSED MATTERS

Though very common, momentary distractions are giant enemies to fruitful meditation. Staying focused on God matters because encounters come as we set our minds on God for longer periods. The longer you can stay relatively concentrated on God and your meditation, the more you'll be impacted. So when you feel your thoughts wandering, bring them back to meditation by utilizing the five prayer expressions (picture, read, write, pray, sing).

I value longer times of meditation in the morning because my mind is naturally calmer, focused, and not stirred up by the interactions and responsibilities of the day. I don't look at my phone, emails, or checklist for the day, and I try not to have conversations with people during my scheduled meditation times. These little things stir my mind up in different directions and hinder me from entering into deeper communion with God. In the same way, think about small things that distract you and make some changes to remove them or steward them differently.

#8 – BE HONEST WITH GOD

The purpose of meditation is to agree with the truths of the Word, but a part of that is recognizing when you don't agree with it. When you identify a lie, be honest with God in conversation as a way of grabbing onto the truth and getting healing. As you meditate on a verse, you may realize that you resist that specific truth for some reason deep in your heart. I believe the Holy Spirit is making you aware of those parts of your heart so that you can confess it and dialogue with God.

This may include telling Him you haven't felt loved by Him in certain situations and that you've withdrawn or become angry at Him. Possibly, you haven't believed He answers prayer because certain times it didn't seem like it, and you've stopped praying for things out of unbelief. Or maybe you feel convicted by the truth and need to confess your sin and commit to righteousness.

It is helpful and healing to be honest with the Lord about the lies you believe. It's not as helpful to only confess the truth repeatedly without making it personal. The overall value is that you believe the Word to be true, but the honest conversation with God allows you to address your pains and unbelief and create new room for His Words to become alive in you.

#9 – ENGAGE ALL YOUR SENSES

Meditation is about engaging all our senses in conversation with God, even using the natural senses to serve the spiritual senses. We do this in part by picturing, reading, writing, praying, and singing, but other ways include arts, dancing, acting out the verse, or songwriting. Artistic expressions would be painting or drawing the truth you're meditating on or asking the Lord for a picture of what He's speaking to you in meditation. Dance expressions would be taking time to dance in a way that expresses the truth of the verse or in a way that expresses your response to God.

#10 – WALLS OF QUIETNESS AND BOREDOM

Resist giving up or being distracted in meditation when there are walls of quietness and boredom in your heart. Quietness and boredom are part of the meditation process, and they are actually fruitful. God is doing something in your heart in these portions of time, but there's also a deeper experience right around the corner if you can push through. I believe the quietness and boredom are the Lord teaching our souls how to wait and respond to Him in hunger, or they're moments where He is breaking our distracted patterns and increasing our spiritual attention span.

The experience of boredom signifies that our heart has come to the end of itself and needs fresh fascination. We experience moments of boredom throughout the day and constantly satisfy it by busyness, eating, entertainment, and small distractions with our phones. But in meditation times, we don't have these options. This sacred time and space allows God to become our fascination and the thing our hearts turn to in the moments of boredom through the day.

God wants to train our hearts to drink from Him for fascination instead of the small fountains of distraction we have trained our souls to depend on. Today's culture and technology have allowed us never to face quietness and boredom. There's a constant supply of entertainment through media and phones so that we can engage in activity for any minute or even seconds when something is not engaging us. Because of this, meditation is counter-cultural and very necessary for training our souls to engage in God instead of media or activity.

Quietness and boredom are also signs of our spiritual barrenness in the revelation of God. Meditation should bring everyone to a place where they feel like they don't know God well because He is infinite and eternal. The awareness that you don't know that much about God experientially in a specific attribute is a revelation from the Holy Spirit. But many people don't have much depth in their friendship with God yet, so the feeling of quietness and unfamiliarity with God can be more intense and uncomfortable.

I've found that people avoid deeper meditation times because the quietness and depth of conversation reveal spiritual barrenness and a lack of understanding of who God really is. Our activity in prayer and Bible reading and our activities in life can cover these areas up. But in the stillness, and with the singular focus on a Biblical phrase, the reality of our hearts comes forth. This is actually a good thing that can bring us closer to Him, depending on how we respond. The wrong response is to push away from the barrenness and cover it up with the things. The right response is to face it and let God produce a hunger that will pull us into His heart for satisfaction.

I once had a friend I was introducing to meditation who tried a couple of short meditation times and told me that he didn't like it and didn't feel comfortable with it. I believe what he was really experiencing was that all the white noise and distractions in his life were removed in meditation and he didn't feel comfortable being alone with God because he didn't yet have a friendship with Him. God wants to strip away all the things that deceive us into thinking we have more intimacy with Him than we really do so that we can experience real friendship with Him.

I remember feeling this same way when I began having more contemplative prayer times focused on talking to the indwelling Holy Spirit. I would talk to Him and speak phrases of the Bible about the Holy Spirit to Him, but I felt weird talking to Him because He felt like a stranger. I confessed that to Him, and He met me there, but that's a reality we must overcome. Meditation forces us to have an intimate conversation with a stranger in a quiet room with nobody else around. In this case, the stranger is God. But soon, the awkward unfamiliarity with Him will change into a safe and familiar friendship.

WEEKLY ASSIGNMENT

During this week's meditations, focus on the ebbs and flows of God's presence. In the moment, be purposeful to observe when He's touching your heart, and practice responding to Him.

Schedule a 2–4-hour group meditation day for the end of this week in place of your monthly group gathering. During that time, gather in a prayer room with worship or worship instrumentals playing loud enough for everyone to feel like they can pray without disturbing others. If helpful, talk together before meditating and after, and maybe even at the halfway point to pray with each other and share what God is doing in your hearts.

The purpose of a longer meditation day is to stretch yourself by positioning your heart in meditation longer than usual. The benefit of this is that your soul will quiet down more, and you'll receive more from the Lord. The other purpose is to give you a taste of what a longer prayer day could feel like and look like for your personal life moving forward. The benefit of doing it in a group is that you will encourage and strengthen each other in the room.

DISCIPLESHIP MEETING GUIDE
MODULE 3: MEDITATION – CHAPTERS 11 & 12

MEETING FOCUS:

The purpose of this week's meeting is to review the 10 practical tips for meditation and talk in-depth about your meditation times.

DISCUSSION QUESTIONS (IN ORDER OF IMPORTANCE):

1. *Spiritual Pursuits*:
   a. Talk through your meditation journal from the last two weeks in-depth. What is God doing in your heart during these times? How is it impacting your heart issue?
   b. Practically, how is your prayer schedule going? How many days have you walked out your prayer schedule? Do you need to make small changes to your schedule? How are your Bible reading and prayer list times going, and how is God impacting you through them?

2. *Chapter Questions*:
   a. Are you trying each of the five meditation expressions (read, write, pray, sing, picture)? How is each one going for you?
   b. Chapter 11 – Discuss your journaled thoughts and questions. Talk through practical tips #3 (developing a phrase) and #5 (asking God questions).
   c. Chapter 12 – Discuss your journaled thoughts and questions. Talk through tip #6 (stewarding the ebbs and flows of God's presence).
   d. Group Meditation Day - Discuss anything necessary in preparation for the meditation day.

3. *Heart Issue*:
   a. Share how your heart issue has been going this past week. With heart issue discussions, process, confess, encourage, and pray together for God to release transformation.

4. Briefly review the assignments for the next two weeks together.

MEETING NOTES:

_____

_____

_____

_____

_____

_____

_____

_____

_____

_____

13

SEVEN HEART PROGRESSIONS

INTRODUCTION

Throughout my meditation journey, I've observed seven different stages that I call the progression of the heart. These are not hard and fast stages, but I believe there are some observable progressions God takes us through as we give ourselves to a verse for weeks or months. This progression is my attempt to put language to the invisible things that I've noticed happening during meditation in my heart and the hearts of those I've been around.

It seems beneficial to be aware of any progression God takes our heart through so that we don't get discouraged in the journey. Instead, we can be encouraged that God is doing something purposeful in us in each stage and have faith that another level of revelation may be right around the corner. In my experience, many people stop meditating after one or two stages of the heart progression and conclude that they've experienced the fullness. But knowing there are multiple stages and depths of experience increases expectations and perseverance to walk through the entire process.

#1 – INTRODUCTION TO THE THEME

There is an introduction to the verse's themes in stage one, and initial questions are brought to the surface. There may be an initial hunger or excitement to understand the verse. Depending on how long my meditation times are, it might take a few prayer times to get past this introductory stage.

#2 – QUIETNESS, BOREDOM, AND UNBELIEF

There is often a quietness at this stage. I will still have questions and thoughts about the verse's main ideas that I'm thinking about, but not much is happening on the inside. This is usually where I have to face boredom, distraction, and possibly hit "walls" of unbelief towards the truth. The walls are probably a combination of human brokenness and demonic accusation.

At this point, I tend to get bored or distracted and can check out. Here's what I'm thinking when I'm bored, "I'm not feeling it. What can I look at on my phone to distract me? This is boring. Is this what it's supposed to feel like? Is there something wrong with me? Should I be on a different verse? Maybe I'll go do something else for a while and then try again."

Quietness is a healthy part of the process because it prepares our hearts to receive from God in the next stages. Many times, it's the calm before the storm of revelation comes. I see God smiling during this stage, saying, "I have a purpose in letting you feel the quietness and boredom. I want your hunger stirred up by the pain of boredom. Keep responding to me, and I'll meet you in this verse."

#3 - HUNGER IS STIRRED

In the third stage, my heart is stirred with hunger to experience the verse' truth in a more profound way. The boredom and quietness of the previous stage pushes against my apathy, allows me to wrestle with discontentment, and then produces a holy hunger. This desire breaks me out of the boredom and lights a fire in my heart to keep pursuing God in my meditation. There's hunger at all seven stages, but I would say this is where the foundational hunger is birthed and fueled.

Throughout this stage, there's greater clarity about the truths in the thought realm, but it's not yet an experience of truth in the emotional realm. There's some satisfaction because of some revelation, stirred desires, and clear conversation with God, but it's mostly an appetizer that gets me hungry for the deeper things. My heart feels awakened with a vision for more, and because of that, the intensity of my pursuit of truth increases.

#4 - INITIAL HEART ENCOUNTER

In the fourth stage, God takes the hunger and clarity of the previous stage and turns it into emotional encounters that are very intimate and satisfying. In this stage, I begin to feel connected to the verse's truth and God's heart in a real way. The verse begins to have a sweetness to it, and my heart begins to move when I whisper key Bible phrases to God. What may have started as a discipline of meditation in earlier stages now turns into enjoyable prayer in this stage. Because there is an increased measure of heart revelation, the heart is stirred with a desire to spend more time with the Lord in meditation.

#5 – DEEPER ENCOUNTER AND DEEPER HUNGER

In the fifth stage, God consistently encounters me in a deeper way, and I experience tears, joy, and feel waves of His presence washing over my emotions. This is incredibly satisfying because it's a sustained experience over several meditation times and through the days as I whisper the truth to Him. Oddly enough, these deeper experiences produce a disruptive hunger and desire to know and experience God more in the verse's truth at any cost. I'm crying out in these moments, "God, Your love is so amazing; it's so unending. Oh, there's so much more! I have to taste that again!"

Only God can fully satisfy our hearts and, at the same time, produce a greater longing in us for more of Him. The depth of encounter opens my eyes to see that there is even more truth to experience, which produces that desperate hunger. This is the hunger that births lovesick cries for understanding spoken of Proverbs 2, "*Cry out and lift your voice.*"

This disruptive hunger and desire bring us into the next stages of revelation in two ways. First, this hunger and desire increases our hearts' size so that we can experience more of God when He touches us again. The larger our hearts, the greater the experience of pleasure and intimacy when He moves on our hearts.

Second, this level of hunger causes you to desire more experience with God desperately, at any cost. This hunger motivates you to move things around in life to get more time with God and be more willing to say no to small things that don't help your spiritual life. He pulls us into His presence by giving us the gift of desire, which changes everything and acts as an inner current pulling us towards Him. Desire and thirst cause you to forsake everything and run to His river for life. Desire takes you farther than discipline ever will. This is when you want to stay up later or get up earlier to be with Him, or when you see every short break as an opportunity to be with Him. This is when you discern the negative impact of idle time and words, small moments of entertainment, and ungodly relationships.

#6 – DELIVERANCE

The sixth stage is really fun! In it, the verse's truths penetrate my heart and shine a light on the root system of lies contrary to the verse. This is a positive thing, and it's a sign that revelation is increasing. A divine exchange of truth happens in this stage where I break agreement with lies and grab onto the truth more deeply.

Hebrews 4:12 says that God's words are living and powerful as they move inside of our hearts. They are actively probing, bringing light, exposing darkness with truth, and then cutting off the darkness. When His words get into our hearts, they discern every one of our thoughts and intentions, and act like a brilliant searchlight revealing the root systems of lies which have lain hidden inside of us.

Realizing your brokenness isn't a sign that you're more broken than before or that God is angry with you. It means that His Word is making you aware of the brokenness you were unaware of so that you can break the agreement and be set free at a deeper level. If you give meditation time, His words will penetrate like a sword into your deepest thoughts, emotions, and the twisted paradigms of what you know about God and yourself.

By this stage, the Holy Spirit has already addressed some layers of lies, but there is a deeper work to be done to release a significant deliverance from strongholds. Strongholds are negative belief systems in our thoughts and emotions that function as open doors for demons to energize those lies supernaturally. Demons live within those belief systems, and then they seek to build on those belief systems and make them more pervasive. But the Holy Spirit shines His light on them through meditation so that we can rise up in faith in agreement with truth and break agreement with the lies that are strangling our hearts.

This stage brings deliverance because His Word has had time to go deep within our hearts and become a double-edged sword that aggressively cuts off lies and disobedience. His Word pierces us and penetrates us, which I believe is a real experience we can have in the Spirit. A sword piercing someone is a violent act in the same way God pierces us with His sword. What I'm describing is more than just a conviction of a lie or a sin. It's a supernatural experience where the sword of truth goes in you, and you say "Yes, and amen" to it at an incredibly deep level. You come out of an experience like this, and you feel a bit different.

These are intense experiences with the truth where there is a lot of emotion and weeping. In these moments, real demonic strongholds are being torn down. This is not a casual experience, though I believe in different levels of the sword experience and honor those as authentic and powerful. This is a more intense experience where we're seriously gripped with the conviction of the truth, and we feel the divine confrontation on the inside.

There was a month that I was meditating on all of Genesis 1, and verse 1:26 stuck out to me like never before. I stayed with the verse for weeks and meditated on the truth that God created me because He was joyful and was burning with desire for me. The truth began to go deeper and deeper in me.

In the last stages of my meditation, the emotional experiences were so intense that I would either be laughing with joy and relief or weeping out of gratitude for what God was like. He was confronting stuff in me that was so deep that I began to respond with pure joy saying, "God made me 100% because He wanted to. I wasn't a mistake, and I wasn't an accident! I'm not just a little minion that God made who annoys Him and asks for money and help all the time."

It was the same idea hitting me at a deeper level, but I stayed with it. Because I stayed with it long enough, there began to be intense exchanges happening in me where I was wrestling with God, "Are You really like this? Are You really joyful by Yourself? Did You really overflow with joy while creating, and did You really make us because You desired us? If You have desire, how much could You have if You're an all-consuming fire?" Those words penetrated the deepest places in me and causing me to laugh with joy for long periods. It was God touching my heart, confronting thoughts of rejection, thoughts of being annoying, and thoughts of not being fully enjoyed by God. Stay with your meditation and wrestle with God over His truth. His words will impart strength and faith to break agreement with the lies, where in the past, you may not have had the strength to say no to the enemy.

 # #7 – BREAKTHROUGH IN REVELATION

After some deliverance has taken place, there is a profound sense of ownership of the verse's truth, resulting in much singing, weeping, rejoicing, and freedom. We choose to sing during the entire meditation process, but there's another place in encountering God to where the song is in you because the truth is in you. In this place, the truth awakens praise and a deep song to the Lord.

This is a deeper place of encounter with God, and it's more sustained than before. It can even become a well of encounter that you can go back to months or years later. The truth becomes fresh breath and satisfying water to our souls, and it seems much easier to receive the truth without wading through internal arguments and demonic accusations. When I get breakthroughs in a verse to a deep level, I can just sit with my Bible open and speak the truths back to God with gentle weeping. Just whispering the truth back to Him in this condition is enough to live by, and it makes me feel very content.

I don't think we ever exhaust the revelation available to us in a verse. In this stage, we enjoy the benefits of an open heart and agreement with His truth. It's as if you've spent much time and energy digging for a well and removing all the hindrances, and now you've got a healthy flow of water coming more naturally. When the well is established, you enjoy the fruit of the labor, and now you drink as much as you want. In the same way, you get to stay at this newly dug fountain and drink of all the revelation that God has for you.

VISION FOR FULLNESS

Hopefully, after reading the heart's progression in meditation, you feel faith to keep going with your Bible verse. Encountering God and experiencing deliverance is your portion if you continue meditating with a high vision for all that God has for you. Many people stop meditating on a verse after walking through one or two stages and assume that there is nothing more to experience, but more is available.

But these are the ones sown on good ground, those who hear the word, accept it, and bear fruit: some thirtyfold, some sixty, and some a hundred.—Mark 4:20

In the parable of the sower of the seed, Jesus revealed that there are several heart conditions people have compared to different soil qualities. This parable is both sobering and exciting, and it applies to the idea of having a high vision for God's Word touching us in meditation. Jesus referenced four different soils; three soils were unreceptive, and only one was fit for the Word to penetrate. Good soil is the heart that takes time to hear God in meditation and doesn't give up until an encounter happens.

Within the good soil, there is a substantial range of fruitfulness. Some hearts will receive thirty, sixty, or a hundredfold fruit from the same seeds of God's Word. This fruitfulness isn't based on God's choice; it's based on the individual's choice to give God's Word time to penetrate and awaken. I encourage you to set it in your heart to not only have the good soil that Jesus described but to have the richest soil that produces the hundredfold fruit of revelation.

 ## WEEKLY ASSIGNMENT

As a part of your assignment this week, reflect on the heart progression stages. Identify which ones you may have experienced in your past meditations, which ones you may have walked through with your current meditation, and which stage you are looking forward to. As you process, be encouraged that the Lord is doing something intimate and specific with you. He has a tailor-made journey for your heart in the verse you've chosen to go deep in. Also, be persistent in meditation with a fresh perspective that God will progress your heart to the final stages to bring encounter and deliverance.

Once a week for the next four weeks, fill out a *Meditation Observation Document* right after a prayer time. This assignment is designed to help you identify and process God's movements. The reflective questions on the document will help you observe how God is interacting with you and help you recognize which Biblical phrases He's unfolding to you right now.

MEDITATION OBSERVATIONS

Meditation Passage:_____ **Date:**_____

1. What was the main thing God was communicating to you during today's meditation time?

2. In what ways did you sense God interacting with you (images, inspired thoughts, inspired emotions, physical presence, whispers). At what moment were you feeling Him the most?

3. How did you respond in the moments of feeling God's presence the most?

4. In today's meditation journaling, which sentences seemed the most significant to you (felt God's presence, had clear language for truth, exposes a lie, clear question)?

5. Did you learn anything about how to interact with God during meditation?

MEDITATION OBSERVATIONS

Meditation Passage:_____   **Date:**_____

1. What was the main thing God was communicating to you during today's meditation time?

2. In what ways did you sense God interacting with you (images, inspired thoughts, inspired emotions, physical presence, whispers). At what moment were you feeling Him the most?

3. How did you respond in the moments of feeling God's presence the most?

4. In today's meditation journaling, which sentences seemed the most significant to you (felt God's presence, had clear language for truth, exposes a lie, clear question)?

5. Did you learn anything about how to interact with God during meditation?

DISCIPLESHIP MEETING GUIDE
MODULE 3: MEDITATION - CHAPTER 13

MEETING FOCUS:

The purpose of this week's meeting is to discuss the progression of the heart in meditation, talk in-depth about your meditation times, and give extra time to discussing your heart issue.

DISCUSSION QUESTIONS (IN ORDER OF IMPORTANCE):

1. *Spiritual Pursuits:*
   a. Talk through your meditation journal from the last two weeks in-depth. What is God doing in your heart during these times? How is it impacting your heart issue?
   b. Practically, how is your prayer schedule going? How many days have you walked out your prayer schedule? Do you need to make small changes to your schedule? How are your Bible reading and prayer list times going, and how is God impacting you through them?
2. *Chapter Questions:*
   a. Are you trying each of the five meditation expressions (read, write, pray, sing, picture)? How is each one going for you?
   b. Chapter 13 – Discuss your journaled thoughts and questions. Discuss which stages have you experienced since the beginning of this meditation module? Which stage do you have the most questions on? Which stage are you looking forward to?
   c. Discuss your *Meditation Observation Assignment* pages from the last two weeks with the emphasis on learning how God is interacting with you.
3. *Heart Issue:*
   a. Discuss your heart issue in more depth (from Spiritual Pursuit Doc). With heart issue discussions, process, confess, encourage, and pray together for God to release transformation.
4. Briefly review the assignments for the next two weeks together.

MEETING NOTES:

_____

_____

_____

_____

_____

_____

_____

_____

_____

_____

_____

14

QUIETING THE MIND

COMMON CHALLENGE

One of the most challenging things to overcome in prayer is a distracted and busy mind. In surveying people before writing this book, this was the most common struggle people identified in their prayer lives. When they sit down and close their eyes to pray, most people said that their minds go a little crazy thinking about their to-do lists for the day, replaying recent conversations, worrying, thinking about the next meal, or having random wandering thoughts.

Being distracted in prayer is the fruit of a heart culture and personal lifestyle. Trying to quiet the mind in prayer isn't simply addressing one small problem: it's addressing an entire way of being. As a picture, the mind is like a huge pot of water that is stirred up each day by a distracted way of being. When looking at the water, we see the current moving in one direction around the pot, representing our thoughts flowing in a current of busyness. Then, when we go to be still in prayer, we become extremely aware that the water is still moving around in a strong current and have to fight against it. This imagery reflects both the lingering effect that busyness has on us and the truth that it's only recognized in prayer times.

If this has been your experience, take courage; it's normal, and you can conquer it. In prayer, I used to find myself thinking about random things, replaying movies I had watched, or being somewhat filled with anxious and fearful thoughts about life circumstances and responsibilities. Before I knew it, fifteen minutes would go by, and there wouldn't have been any real conversation with God. As I grew in my prayer life and removed distractions, my mind began to quiet down quicker in prayer. Some days it takes me ten minutes to get focused. Infrequently, I'll be really distracted or weighed down by something for an hour or two. But for most of the time, I can enter into focused conversation with God within minutes. This quietness then continues through my day.

OVERCOMING DISTRACTION IS CRITICAL

Acknowledging your distracted mind and overcoming it can be very difficult at first. Still, it's critical because our thoughts are the starting place for engaging God in conversation and the doorway to encounter and transformation. When our conversation with God is disrupted, it affects our connection to Him and limits our experience of Him. A distracted mind hinders our ability to dialogue with God, ask real questions, and hear His voice. These aspects of relating to God are necessary to experience Him and receive His deliverance power.

Our experience of God will increase when we can pray in a focused way for longer periods, and that will only happen if our minds can be quiet longer. This same principle is true when spending time with our friends. If you are distracted by your thoughts, phone, and other people while sitting down at a restaurant with a friend, you end up not hearing them or connecting with them. Likewise, if we are distracted in our conversations with the Lord, we won't hear all that He is saying to us, and we won't be as impacted.

WEANING THE MIND – PSALM 131

Surely I have calmed and quieted my soul, like a weaned child with his mother; like a weaned child is my soul within me.—Psalm 131:2

Like King David, we have to go through the process of quieting and calming our minds. David compared quieting his soul to weaning a child, which is a messy process. In this process, we have to wean ourselves from the things that have created a distracted soul in us and have given us a false sense of life.

Weaning is a process that takes time and energy. It refers to the process of transitioning a child from one source of life and comfort to an entirely different one. Children are fussy and uncomfortable in the process because they are so used to the pattern of drinking from their mom and receiving the emotional comfort that it brings. But after they finish the long and challenging process, they are at rest with their new food source and no longer crave their mom's milk. In Psalm 131, the fully weaned child could sit with its mother without craving and fussing for her milk. When a child can do this, you know they are fully weaned!

We all have to face our distracted and fussy souls as we pursue weaning and calming it long-term. Like a baby, we all have things and distractions we drink from that have become part of our daily rhythm. To transition to more spiritual food, we have to be aware of and accept the weaning process. The transition will be messy as you retrain your mind to focus on God as your source of life and comfort, but you will have a calm mind, and you will learn to feast on God's satisfying presence.

HOW TO CULTIVATE A QUIET MIND

Cultivating a quiet mind is done by changing your lifestyle and what you do in prayer. If you change in both areas and give your mind a season to grow quiet, you will experience dramatic results. Lifestyle changes include identifying and removing the things in your daily life that stir your thoughts up and the things in your daily rhythm that cause you to have a short attention span.

MEDIA USAGE

For me, I've identified a few things that lead to my mind being distracted consistently. Media is one of them. If I watch shows or videos, my mind replays them repeatedly throughout the day and during my prayer times. If I'm consistently checking my phone for texts, emails, news updates, or checking other things, I find that I end up wanting to check those during my prayer times. When I have a pattern of checking my phone out of boredom, it trains my mind to have a short attention span.

Phones give us 24-7 access to every form of entertainment and communication available. The danger with this is that our minds are being trained to be stimulated all the time. This has massive negative implications for our attention spans in the place of prayer. Even if what you are entertained by doesn't initially seem evil to you, it can still fuel distraction and increase your appetite for entertainment and fantasy. If you know you struggle with distraction during prayer, consider completely removing media entertainment (social media, movies, YouTube, phone games, video games, etc.) for a few months to see how peaceful your mind becomes.

Consider changing your cell phone lifestyle by limiting usage to specific times and needs. Set clear boundaries on how much you use your device and what you use it for. For example, my wife and I try not to use our phones before or during our morning prayer times, and then we put them away in the evenings during family times. Also, I don't use my phone as a Bible study resource or note-taking resource during my prayer times. I prefer not to rely on my phone for everything in life. I don't want to be stirred by notifications, and I don't want to have the most distracting thing in my life in my hands when I'm the most tempted to be distracted.

Phones can take you out of deep thought in the moment, and then they will stir up your mind around the topic you just read about for a few minutes or even longer. Focusing on God and deeply connecting to Him is like getting an airplane off the ground and soaring in the air. In prayer times, it takes a while to get going on the runway and into the air. Then it takes some time to ascend, level out, and soar in that place of connecting to God. Distractions have the potential to make you start the flight process over again to get back into that smooth flying place to where your mind is fixed on God.

FEAR AND ANXIETY

Do you have a pattern of being fearful or anxious about things in your life, and do those things come to your mind when you want to pray? God could be highlighting a heart issue. Ask the Lord where you are anxious and what you need to do to have peace in that area again. Identify what specifically stirs up those anxieties and have a prayer time where you give those areas of anxiety to the Lord.

Bring this issue to your Discipleship Mentor to process and pray through, and watch the Lord change it over time.

Practically, God could be addressing a part of your lifestyle and schedule that is giving you anxiety unknowingly. You can address some levels of anxiety by creating and following a weekly schedule with committed planning times. Some people are anxious about things that need to be thought through or done simply because they don't have an appropriate time and place to think through them. Schedule a time to deal with the things that weigh on you through the day and train yourself to not think about it after those scheduled planning times.

FANTASY

Although fantasy can be expressed in many ways, the common fruits are a distracted imagination and a frequent pull to escape into a mental pretend world. Fantasy is a relevant challenge to identify and address because its negative fruit will manifest itself in prayer times as you try to wean yourself from these distractions.

Different forms of fantasy include sexually focused fantasy, playing out situations, replaying memories or conversations, daydreaming about the future in specific ways as a way of comfort and distraction, reading books as an escape, shopping online, and engaging in forms of social media.

Though all the forms of fantasy have a spiritual impact and need to be addressed, I want to focus on pornography and sexually focused fantasy. If you struggle with these issues regularly, you're probably having to fight against imaginations in prayer times. These are distracting and can lead to feeling shame in God's presence.

If you're not already doing this, it is worth asking friends and leaders for help and accountability if you struggle with looking at sexual images. Accountability will greatly reduce your options of what you are distracted by. The next step for removing distractions is to war against your pattern of indulging in fantasy to escape.

God has strategically given us Revelation 4 to help focus our imaginations on the imagery of God's throne room. Focusing on His throne room replaces immoral and superficial images, helps you not to wander, and has a supernatural benefit to it. Jesus said that our eyes are the lamp of our bodies and that if they are good, they will impact our entire being.[1] Setting your mind on His throne room enables the light of God's glory to enter our spiritual eyes, which then fills our entire being with God's light and begins to wash away immoral images and desires.

If you know you struggle with escaping something through fantasy in other ways, now is the time to call it what it is and war against it. Bring it to the Lord and your Discipleship Mentor for repentance and healing. As you do this, you will walk in the contentment and quietness that God desires for you. If you're not sure if what you think about is fantasy, take time to think through what you're actually doing and what fruit it's bearing. Also, bring it before the Lord in prayer and ask Him what He's saying about it.

PRAYER LIFE

Think through what time of day you pray and how long you're scheduling prayer because these can impact your effectiveness. If you are distracted but don't know what time is best, try praying at different times. The best time for me to pray is early in the day so that I don't have to "unwind" or process my day in my prayer times.

---

1   Matthew 6:22-23.

Is the length of your prayer times long enough to be able to quiet down? If they're too short, your mind won't have enough time to dial down in the moment, and it also won't have a chance to break distracted cycles. Consider scheduling longer prayer times than what you're used to currently. It takes time for our minds to quiet down for every prayer time. By increasing the length of your prayer time, you will get more focused time, which is when you will receive the most from the Lord. Experiencing that quiet mind for longer periods each day in prayer will carry through to the rest of your day and help you cultivate a quiet mind as a lifestyle.

CHOOSING WHITE NOISE

You might struggle with distraction because you want to be distracted. You might be creating "white noise" in your daily life so that you don't have to face the reality of the condition of your heart, how life looks for you, or what your relationship with God is really like. White noise is a sound that people play while sleeping to block out random noises, whether it be a sound machine or something else. In context to choosing distraction, white noise is the things you fill your life with that don't allow for silence and deep thinking. It's a noise that occupies your mind so that your true thoughts and emotions don't come to the surface.

Reflect on your life and see if you regularly distract yourself with things to do, a filled schedule, always watching or listening to things, or always thinking of something so that you don't have silence and stillness in your life. If this applies to you, talk to God and ask Him to replace the distraction and false satisfaction with His peace and satisfaction. Turn away from all the distractions and tell your Discipleship Mentor your struggle so they can help you get freedom. Completely shutting off the noise might sound impossible and horrible to you, but life is better on the other side. You will face reality and find peace, contentment, and progress, and you'll experience the supernatural fruit of the Spirit.

PRACTICAL CHANGES

DON'T PLAN BEFORE PRAYER

It can be a huge temptation to be in planning mode before prayer times. This may be planning for the day, the week, or planning different things in life. This can take a lot of mental investment, so it's not easy to stop thinking about those topics once you start. Save planning times for other times in the day and train yourself to stop thinking about your planning topics outside of your planning times.

RESIST DISTRACTED THINKING

Bringing every thought into captivity to the obedience of Christ.
—2 Corinthians 10:5

When a distracting thought comes to you, exercise the muscle of your mind by resisting it and focusing back on God. At times, this only takes one moment of resisting, but other times, it takes several moments of refocusing on God. As this exercise becomes a lifestyle, the pattern of distraction will be transformed into a pattern of quietness. If you can't stop thinking about something, take a minute to write it down so you feel like you can deal with it later. If that doesn't help, dialogue with God about the things on your mind until you feel like it's resolved. In group prayer settings, you also have the option of asking a friend to pray for you.

Sometimes people wonder if their distracting thoughts are God directing them to do something else in the moment. This is definitely a possibility. At times, God will bring something or someone to mind prompting us to reach out to them, send them encouragement, or pray for them. My first response is that distractions do not mean "walking in the Spirit." My second response is that God won't redirect us most of the time when we're meditating on a truth. In my opinion, if this is happening most days, it's probably not God. What He will do is take the meditation truth and make it personal by bringing up memories or situations so we can process its application.

PRAY AND SING OUT LOUD

Speak and sing your prayers out loud instead of just thinking your prayers. Speaking out loud has a real spiritual impact, but the mind also naturally focuses better if you talk out loud. God has designed our mouth to be the steering wheel of our entire being.[2] Our thoughts, emotions, desires, and bodies are directed by the things that we speak out, so be intentional to speak out most of the time, even if it's just a whisper. I am more focused and have way more clarity when I speak and sing out loud versus just thinking my prayers. From my experience, praying out loud and writing down prayers are the two most powerful ways to stay focused during prayer.

WRITE PRAYERS

Get a journal or a notepad and write some or all your thoughts, questions, and conversations with the Lord in your prayer times. Writing will engage more parts of your mind in prayer, which will help you stay focused. Writing also helps you get more clarity in what you're talking about with God. You have to have clarity

---

2   James 3:2-6.

to write something down, and once it is written down, you never lose it. If you're just thinking prayers and only speaking them out loud occasionally, you will lose track of what you were talking about with the Lord, and you'll miss some of what He is whispering to you.

WORSHIP

I usually have worship playing during my prayer times because it helps focus my thoughts and emotions on God. Worship music changes the atmosphere and helps direct the heart towards God. For me, worship music includes live worship at the local prayer room I'm a part of, a worship recording in the background, or I play my guitar and worship while I talk to the Lord.

MOVE

Slow movements during prayer really help people stay focused in your thoughts and emotions. Moving around is significant enough for me that for most of my prayer times, I slowly walk back and forth or gently rock in my chair. Rocking has been a common motion among praying Jews for centuries, and research shows it aids in concentration in people of all ages.

PICTURE GOD

I talk about picturing God often throughout this discipleship program because it is so helpful, but people often don't try it. Use your imagination to picture God in His throne room instead of focusing your mind on nothing. This will help your mind stay focused, and it will make you feel like you're actually talking to a real person. A simple way to begin doing this is to read Revelation 4:2-3 during every prayer time and picture one description of God and His throne in your imagination. Focus on that image of Him as you talk and sing to Him.

WEEKLY ASSIGNMENT

As part of this week's assignment, reflect on this chapter and identify if you struggle with a distracted mind in prayer. If so, ask the Lord what internal or external things are causing distraction, and write down what you want to change in your life as a response. If you set your heart to make life changes, you can expect to have a quiet mind in prayer in the next few months. When you close your eyes, you will focus on God, hear His whispers, and have little to no thoughts coming to your mind outside of prayer. Through the day, you'll be as clear and peaceful and able to connect with God while you're doing other things.

MEDITATION OBSERVATIONS

Meditation Passage:_____ **Date:**_____

1. What was the main thing God was communicating to you during today's meditation time?

2. In what ways did you sense God interacting with you (images, inspired thoughts, inspired emotions, physical presence, whispers). At what moment were you feeling Him the most?

3. How did you respond in the moments of feeling God's presence the most?

4. In today's meditation journaling, which sentences seemed the most significant to you (felt God's presence, had clear language for truth, exposes a lie, clear question)?

5. Did you learn anything about how to interact with God during meditation?

MEDITATION OBSERVATIONS

Meditation Passage:_____ **Date:**_____

1. What was the main thing God was communicating to you during today's meditation time?

2. In what ways did you sense God interacting with you (images, inspired thoughts, inspired emotions, physical presence, whispers). At what moment were you feeling Him the most?

3. How did you respond in the moments of feeling God's presence the most?

4. In today's meditation journaling, which sentences seemed the most significant to you (felt God's presence, had clear language for truth, exposes a lie, clear question)?

5. Did you learn anything about how to interact with God during meditation?

DISCIPLESHIP MEETING GUIDE
MODULE 3: MEDITATION – CHAPTER 14

MAIN FOCUS:

The purpose of this week's meeting is to discuss hindrances to having a quiet mind, talk in-depth about your meditation times, and give extra time to talk and pray about your heart issues.

DISCUSSION QUESTIONS (IN ORDER OF IMPORTANCE):

1. *Spiritual Pursuits:*
   a. Talk through your meditation journal from the last two weeks in-depth. What is God doing in your heart during these times? How is it impacting your heart issue?
   b. Practically, how is your prayer schedule going? How many days have you walked out your prayer schedule? Do you need to make small changes to your schedule? How are your Bible reading and prayer list times going, and how is God impacting you through them?

2. *Chapter Questions:*
   a. Are you trying each of the five meditation expressions (read, write, pray, sing, picture)? How is each one going for you?
   b. Chapter 14 – Discuss your journaled thoughts and questions. Do you struggle with having a quiet mind? If so, why, and what can you change in your lifestyle? Take time to pray together about any hindrances to having a quiet mind.
   c. Discuss your *Meditation Observation Assignment* pages from the last two weeks with the emphasis on learning how God is interacting with you.

3. *Heart Issue:*
   a. Discuss your heart issue in more depth (from Spiritual Pursuit Doc). With heart issue discussions, process, confess, encourage, and pray together for God to release transformation.

4. Briefly review the assignments for the next two weeks together. This is not necessary if you are having a group gathering to introduce the next module topic.

MEETING NOTES:

MODULE 4

PRAYING IN THE SPIRIT

MODULE INTRODUCTION

The topic of praying in the Spirit is an exciting topic for many. But for some of you, it might bring up fears, anger, spiritual insecurities (feel less spiritual than others or less loved by God), offenses, confusion, questions, or hurts from past experiences. Whatever your experience has been with the Holy Spirit or the topic of praying in the Spirit, know that this module is a safe context to process with others, dig into the scriptures, and take a step forward.

There are a variety of Biblical perspectives on this topic that are worth searching out. Having said that, here are specific perspectives that this module is centered around: *(1) speaking in tongues is for today, (2) tongues is available to every believer, (3) personal tongues is distinct from the corporate gift of tongues, (4) the apostle Paul emphasized tongues as a lifestyle, (5) there is always more of the Spirit available to every believer, (6) there are multiple infillings of the Spirit available after salvation, (7) infillings of the Spirit are usually discernible experiences, (8) tongues is usually the initial manifestation of the Spirit but sometimes takes time and coaching to vocalize it, (9) it's Biblical to pray in tongues as a group without needing interpretation.*

The assignments are geared towards those who have received tongues in the past or will receive it within the first weeks. They are focused on establishing your daily rhythm of praying in tongues long-term. For those who haven't spoken in tongues yet, take the assigned prayer times to study the verses and ask the Spirit to fill you until it happens. For those who aren't at a place to pursue tongues, take the assigned prayer times to study the verses and process questions and challenges with your Discipleship Mentor.

ASSIGNMENT OVERVIEW
MODULE 4 – PRAYING IN THE SPIRIT

Continue to follow your prayer schedule and Spiritual Pursuits each week. Schedule a time to pray in tongues as a group during Week 20.

Week Seventeen Assignments:

❑ Read Chapter 15 – "***Receiving The Holy Spirit.***" Journal your thoughts and questions on the chapter.

❑ If you have received tongues, pray in tongues for 15 minutes at least three days a week. If that's not a challenge, consider praying 30-60 minutes every day of the week. Write a paragraph on how each prayer time goes for you, was it difficult or easy, did you sense God's presence or any spiritual benefits?

❑ If you haven't received tongues at this point, study the Bible verses from the chapter and pray about the topic of tongues for 15 minutes three days this week.

❑ Fill out a new *Spiritual Pursuits Document* for this module. The pursuits can stay the same or change but filling out the form monthly helps you refocus and develop a rhythm of intentionality.

Week Eighteen Assignments:

❑ Read Chapter 16 – "***Praying From Our Spirit-Man.***" Journal your thoughts and questions on the chapter.

❑ If you have received tongues, pray in tongues for 15 minutes at least three days a week. If that's not a challenge, consider praying 30-60 minutes every day of the week. Write a paragraph on how each prayer time goes for you.

❑ If you haven't received tongues at this point, study the Bible verses from the chapter and pray about the topic of tongues for 15 minutes three days this week.

❑ Do a simple study on the words "*mystery*" and "*mysteries.*"

❑ **Meet with your Discipleship Mentor.**

Week Nineteen Assignments:

❑ Read Chapter 17 – "***Communing with God in Tongues.***" Journal your thoughts and questions on the chapter.

❑ If you have received tongues, pray in tongues for 15 minutes at least three days a week. If that's not a challenge, consider praying 30-60 minutes every day of the week. Write a paragraph on how each prayer time goes for you.

❑ If you haven't received tongues at this point, study the Bible verses from the chapter and pray about the topic of tongues for 15 minutes three days this week.

❑ In addition to one of your daily tongues times, pray in tongues for 30 minutes once. If you've been praying longer than 15 minutes each day, try doubling your time for one day. After the longer tongues time, write down if and when you felt a breakthrough moment during the prayer time.

Week Twenty Assignments:

❑ Read Chapter 18 – "***Praying with Groups.***" Journal your thoughts and questions on the chapter.

❑ If you have received tongues, pray in tongues for 15 minutes at least three days a week. If that's not a challenge, consider praying 30-60 minutes every day of the week. Write a paragraph on how each prayer time goes for you.

❑ If you haven't received tongues or aren't ready to pursue it, study the verses from the chapter and pray into the topic during the assigned prayer times.

❑ In addition to your other tongues times, plan and participate in one 30-minute group tongues time.

❑ **Meet with your Discipleship Mentor.**

Week Twenty-one Assignments:

❑ Read Chapter 19 – "***Different Uses of Tongues.***" Journal your thoughts and questions on the chapter.

❑ If you have received tongues, pray in tongues for 15 minutes at least three days a week. If that's not a challenge, consider praying 30-60 minutes every day of the week. Write a paragraph on how each prayer time goes for you.

❑ If you haven't received tongues or aren't ready to pursue it, study the verses from the chapter and pray into the topic during the assigned prayer times.

❑ In addition to your other tongues times this week, pray in tongues for 30 minutes one time. This could be an individual prayer time, a group tongues time, or a prayer time with your Discipleship Mentor.

SPIRITUAL PURSUITS   *DATE:* _____

1. **Bible reading direction and plan**
   (Write down what you will read and when you will read it):

2. **Meditation verse** (Choose a verse that speaks truth into your heart issue):

3. **Sin/character issue from which to get freedom:**

4. **Lie from which to pursue deliverance:**

5. **Gifting to pursue** (Include simple ways you can pursue it):

6. **Weekly Prayer Schedule**—Write down your plan for the *specific times* you are committed to spending with God each day, and *what specifically you plan to do during those times*. Include what your study or meditation focus will be. Refer to the example schedule in Chapter Two. (e.g., Monday 6-6:30 am—Tongues, 6:30-7:30 am—Meditation on Song of Solomon 1:2)

Monday

Tuesday

Wednesday

Thursday

Friday

Saturday

Sunday

15
RECEIVING THE HOLY SPIRIT

INTRODUCTION

The purpose of this chapter is to give an overview of the topic of the infilling of the Spirit and receiving tongues. As you enter into this new module, it is important to understand what God has made available to you by the Holy Spirit. If you are unfamiliar with the Spirit and tongues, the following sections will inspire you to embrace all that God has for you. If you are active in praying in the spirit, you will be inspired to pursue fresh infillings of the Spirit and learn to impart the Spirit to others!

The following sections will break down the topic of the infilling of the Spirit by defining what it is, exploring its prominence and impact in the early Church, and connecting it to praying in tongues. The last portion of the chapter will focus on Jesus' promise for all believers to pray in tongues and give practical advice on how to receive tongues for the first time. My summary perspective is that all believers can pray in tongues, there are multiple infillings of the Spirit available and necessary for spiritual growth, and that tongues are a significant gift from God that is worth pursuing.

THE INFILLING OF THE SPIRIT

DEFINITION

"For John truly baptized with water, but you shall be baptized with the Holy Spirit not many days from now."—Acts 1:5

"But you shall receive power when the Holy Spirit has come upon you."
—Acts 1:8

The infilling of the Spirit is synonymous with the baptism of the Spirit and refers to specific moments when the Spirit releases an increase of His presence and power in and on a believer. The Holy Spirit comes into our spirit-man and resurrects it at salvation, so in one sense we have the Spirit after that moment. But the infilling of the Holy Spirit is when He fills, not just our spirit-man, but our souls and bodies, and then He rests upon us to minister in greater power. Another way to say it is that the Spirit came to live in us at salvation, but we become immersed (baptized) in Him, and have greater empowerment to walk in Him at the infilling experience.

THE PROMISE OF THE FATHER

"Behold, I send the Promise of My Father upon you; but tarry in the city of Jerusalem until you are endued with power from on high."—Luke 24:49

The infilling of the Spirit is the "Promise of the Father" that Jesus emphasized during His earthly ministry and right before His ascension. Jesus said that it was better for Him to go to heaven so He could send the Spirit and fill His people![1] The Holy Spirit's union with the Church through the infilling experience is the catalyst of the New Testament Church.

The central theme of the book of Acts is the Spirit's power upon the church to witness to the nations. This theme is summarized in Acts 1:8 and then highlighted throughout the book as believers were filled with the Spirit and operated in power. Acts 2 is the climax of the book in which the "Promise of the Father" was released to God's people who were waiting in prayer. The first church was birthed at the infilling of the Spirit, and everything in the church and the book of Acts flowed from that place.

The theme of the Holy Spirit in Acts reveals God's passion for the Spirit and how central He should be in the Church. The Spirit, the infilling, and tongues have been said to be divisive or optional topics, but Acts shows us that they are vital topics. Experiencing more of God's presence and power isn't limited to the infilling and tongues. Bible study, meditation, purity, and others are necessary as well, but these Holy Spirit topics (infilling and tongues) are unique and central to God's long-term plans of bringing us into fullness.

---

1   John 16:7.

MY INFILLING EXPERIENCE

The infilling of the Spirit and praying in tongues has been a catalyst in my life since college. I've had several defining moments with God, but one of the most significant ones was being filled with the Spirit. As I look back on that day, I know that it changed my life and set me on a new spiritual trajectory.

My journey to receiving tongues started when I went to a Holy Spirit conference as a newer believer. The preacher taught on the infilling of the Spirit and the power of tongues and said, "Pray in tongues for thirty minutes a day and it will change your life." I was interested in tongues after that conference, but it wasn't until the end of that year that I seriously pursued it. At the end of that year, for about a month, I asked for tongues every night. I knelt on my bed, put my face in my pillow, and asked God to fill me with His Spirit. As I prayed each night, I tried to speak something out, but I never sensed God's presence or any kind of flow in tongues.

At the end of that month of praying, I began a fast for my college campus. As I prayed into my pillow that first night of the fast, I felt God's presence on me and I began having syllables come to my mind. When I stepped out in faith and spoke out the syllables, I felt God's presence on my body like heat. I began to be overwhelmed with God's heart and wept for my campus. For the first time, I started receiving prophetic images in my mind; they were of students participating in sin or being depressed and broken. With each new image, a fresh weeping would come over me. Though speaking in tongues felt weird to me in the experience, I continued speaking out the few syllables that were flowing to my mind.

I didn't have a theology for everything that happened in that prayer time, but I knew that something had shifted in me, and I noticed immediate fruit in my life. I began experiencing God's felt presence more often and in stronger ways. My desire to live more focused on Jesus and be in the Word increased. Conviction of sin and sincere longing for righteousness increased, and I began a journey of walking in the gifts of the Spirit.

BIBLICAL ACCOUNTS – INFILLING AND TONGUES

There are five stories in the book of Acts that recount infillings of the Spirit. These accounts show us that the infilling of the Spirit (1) can be distinguished from the salvation experience, (2) is a discernible experience, (3) and is connected to receiving tongues. These accounts also show us the high value the apostles placed on the infilling experience in that they promoted it and made sure others were aware of it wherever they ministered. These five testimonies continue the Acts 1:8 theme of the Spirit filling and empowering believers to be witnesses to the nations.

The first story is in Acts 2:1-4. The 120 disciples were already saved and some of them had already received the Holy Spirit.[2] However, in this encounter, they were filled with more of the Spirit. This encounter was discernible in many ways and the result was them speaking in tongues.

The second story is in Acts 8:5-17. Because of Phillip's preaching and miracles, multitudes in the city of Samaria gave their lives to Jesus and were baptized in water. Days or weeks later, John and Peter made the 35-mile trip to help minister to the new believers. The story infers that when they arrived, they perceived or understood by questioning the people that they hadn't yet received the infilling of the Spirit. It says that they had only been baptized in Jesus' name. This means that John and Peter cared enough about the infilling experience to ask about it, didn't

---

2 John 20:22.

266

assume it happened at their water baptism, and weren't worried about offending or confusing the new believers by offering more of the Spirit. The apostles laid hands on them, and they were filled in a discernible experience; visible enough for Simon to see it and want the same impartation power. Tongues are not mentioned in this story, but it's fair to believe it happened because of the pattern outlined in Acts.

The third account is in Acts 9:3-18 where Paul gave his life to Jesus in a supernatural encounter and was blinded for three days while he fasted and prayed. Jesus sent Ananias to prophesy, release healing, and specifically pray for Paul to be filled with the Spirit even though he was probably already saved. This experience isn't detailed, but I assume Paul's infilling experience was as discernible as his healing. Also, tongues are not mentioned in this account, but it's safe to assume it happened at the same time because of the pattern outlined in Acts and because he referred to praying in tongues in his writings. In continuation of the Acts 1:8 theme, Paul immediately went out transformed and in power as a witness to the Jews in Damascus.

The fourth account is in Acts 10:44-48. While Peter was preaching the gospel to Cornelius and his household, the Holy Spirit fell in a recognizable way, and they all spoke with tongues. In this experience, their salvation experience was coupled with the infilling of the Spirit. Notice that Peter and his friends specifically highlighted the gift of the Spirit and the infilling of the Spirit in the moment, not their salvation. This story is significant because these were the first known Gentiles to receive the gospel and the gift of the Spirit with tongues.

The fifth story is in Acts 19:1-6 in which Paul met some disciples in Ephesus. Paul assumed they were believers in Jesus, and the first question He asked is whether they had been filled with the Spirit yet. He didn't assume they received the Spirit at their salvation, and he wasn't worried about offending or confusing them. Paul cared about the infilling of the Spirit because this was the promise of the Father to the New Testament Church!

After questioning them, he realized they hadn't heard the full gospel yet, so he led them to Jesus, baptized them, and then prayed for them in a distinct way for the infilling of the Spirit. The Spirit came upon them in a discernible way and then all twelve of them spoke in tongues and prophesied. This story is significant because as you read the rest of it, Paul and these Spirit-empowered disciples brought Ephesus into a mighty revival that turned the entire region upside down. I believe Luke wove the disciples' infilling experience into the Ephesus revival account to highlight the Acts 1:8 theme of the Spirit filling and empowering believers to be witnesses.

MULTIPLE INFILLINGS

EPHESIANS 5 – KEEP BEING FILLED

Besides the initial infilling of the Spirit, there is an ongoing invitation to be filled with fresh or greater measures of the Spirit. Paul said, *"And do not be drunk with wine in which is dissipation, but be filled with the Spirit."*[3] In Greek, the verb "be filled" emphasizes an ongoing activity as opposed to a one-time action. In his Ephesians commentary, John Stott explains it this way:

"In the Greek there are two kinds of imperative, an aorist describing a single action, and a present when the action is continuous. Thus, when Jesus said

---

3 Ephesians 5:18.

268

during the wedding reception in Cana, 'Fill the jars with water' (Jn 2:7), the imperative is aorist, since the jars were to be filled only once. But when Paul says to us, 'Be filled with the Spirit', he uses a present imperative implying that we are to go on being filled. For the fullness of the Spirit is not a once-for-all experience which we can never lose, but a privilege to be renewed continuously by continuous believing and obedient appropriation."[4]

As you grow in friendship with the Holy Spirit, you can receive consistent refreshings of His presence and power that renew godly desires, break off lust, apathy, and confusion, and empower you to move in the gifts of the Spirit. These fresh fillings may be small moments where you sense God's power touching you, or they may be more intense experiences, but every experience is empowering.

ACTS – SECONDARY INFILLINGS

There are a few examples of these smaller infilling experiences in the book of Acts. In each of the following stories, the word "filled" in the original language is a verb, meaning an action is taking place at the moment.[5] In other places in Acts, leaders are described as being "full" of the Spirit, in which case the original language is using an adjective to communicate they had received the Holy Spirit.[6] So there is a differentiation between the words "filled" and "full" as you read the stories.

---

4 John Stott, *The Message of Ephesians*. The Bible Speaks Today Commentary Series (Downers Grove, IL: InterVarsity Press, 1979), 209.

5 Strong's Greek #4130 - https://www.studylight.org/lexicons/eng/greek/4130.html
Strong's Greek #4137 - https://www.studylight.org/lexicons/eng/greek/4137.html

6 Acts 6:3, 11:24; Strong's #4134 - https://www.studylight.org/lexicons/eng/greek/4134.html

In Acts 4, Peter was touched by the Spirit and filled in a fresh way to empower him to speak boldly and prophetically to the religious leaders.[7] In Acts 13, the Spirit filled Paul to speak prophetically and release blindness on Elymas the Sorcerer.[8] Later in the chapter, the Spirit filled Paul and Barnabas again resulting in joy amid persecution, *"And the disciples were filled with joy and with the Holy Spirit."*[9]

ACTS 4 – ANOTHER CORPORATE INFILLING

The apostles had multiple experiences with the Holy Spirit, and each one released a greater experience of the Spirit's presence and power in their lives. They had the Holy Spirit, but at the same time, they asked for more of Him and never saw it as a contradiction or a lack of faith in what they had already received. The apostles first received the Holy Spirit when Jesus breathed upon them after His resurrection.[10] Then at Pentecost, they were filled even more with the Spirit. In Acts 4, which was one or two years later, they experienced another corporate infilling.[11] The Spirit shook their house, freshly filled them, and launched them into a season of greater presence and power. The supernatural fruit of their infilling is revealed in Acts 4:31-5:16: power evangelism, boldness, unity, radical giving and sacrifice, fear of the Lord, salvations, signs and wonders, and crowds being healed and delivered.

What we learn from the Biblical accounts is that God always has more of His Spirit or fresh touches available to every believer. For some, the first step

---

7 Acts 4:8.

8 Acts 13:8-12.

9 Acts 13:52.

10 John 20:22.

11 Acts 4:31.

to receiving more of God's Spirit is the initial infilling of the Spirit with God activating tongues and the other power gifts of the Spirit. For those that have already had an initial infilling experience, God wants you to believe and ask for fresh infillings of the Spirit that impart a fresh or greater presence and power.

ALL BELIEVERS CAN PRAY IN TONGUES

It is important to have clarity on whether all believers can pray in tongues. I've seen people give up on pursuing tongues when it didn't happen right away because they assumed they were not one of the people God had chosen to have it. But if they had more understanding from the Bible, they might have continued the pursuit with the expectation that they would receive it. Below are the five reasons why I believe all believers can receive tongues from the Holy Spirit.

OUR SPIRITUAL DNA

We are first spirit beings, and tongues activate our spirit-man to communicate directly with God. God is Spirit, we are spirit, and tongues allow our spirit-man to lead our thoughts and emotions in prayer. I believe God wants all of us to be able to commune with Him spirit to Spirit and for all of us to have our spirit-man leading our minds and emotions in prayer. Within this perspective, praying in tongues is simply an expression of our identity and DNA as spirit beings.

This foundational perspective changes the conversation about tongues. No longer is the first question if God wants to give tongues, but rather, does God want to relate to every believer spirit to Spirit? I think the answer is yes, God wants the benefits of praying in tongues to be experienced by all.

JESUS PROMISED NEW TONGUES

The second reason I believe all believers can receive tongues is that Jesus said that all His followers would speak in new tongues, along with healing the sick and casting out demons.[12] Jesus connected tongues with things that every believer is anointed to operate in through the power of the Spirit. As an outworking of Jesus' promise, all the Acts accounts that include tongues indicate that everyone received it: the 120 in the upper room, Paul in Damascus, everyone in Cornelius' household, and the 12 disciples in Ephesus received tongues.

PERSONAL VS. CORPORATE

The third reason is that praying in tongues is different from the corporate gift of tongues and interpretation. Some people automatically assume they are the same, but Paul distinguishes them in 1 Corinthians 14. Personal tongues are for all believers at any time, are for personal edification, are spoken to God, and don't need interpretation.[13] Corporate tongues are for all believers to some level but are only released in the timing of the Spirit,[14] are for corporate edification, are spoken to people, and need interpretation to edify others as a prophetic word. Most of 1 Corinthians 14 is focused on bringing right order and humility in the context of the corporate gift of tongues in the context of a corporate gathering.

---

12 Mark 16:17-18.

13 1 Corinthians 14:2, 4, 5, 18, 28.

14 1 Corinthians 12:11.

PERSONAL EXPERIENCES

My experiences and the experiences of others are not equal to the Bible, but they are worth considering in this topic. In over 15 years, I have seen thousands of believers operating in personal tongues in prayer, and I've seen several hundred receive the infilling of the Spirit with tongues. Out of all the experiences, I have only seen a small number of people not immediately receive tongues after a discernible experience with the Spirit. Most of those people received tongues later after some practical coaching and prayer that unlocked their hearts.

HOW TO RECEIVE TONGUES

ASK GOD UNTIL

Ask God for tongues with persistence until you receive it. In Jesus' teaching on asking for the Spirit, He said to come with persistence and to ask, seek, and knock until the door was opened.[15] You might receive the Spirit and tongues within seconds of asking, or you might have to ask several times; just stay with it because He wants to give it to you!

Asking for it is proactive, which is what God desires. Some people believe that God will fill them with the Spirit when He wants to without them pursuing it at all. God can do that, but it's more Biblical to say that we have to desire it, ask for it, and pursue it. Three times in 1 Corinthians 14 alone, Paul said that our part is to desire and pursue the gifts of the Spirit zealously.[16]

---

15 Luke 11:8-13.

16 1 Corinthians 14:1, 12, 39.

STUDY THE BIBLE

Study the Bible on the topic of the infilling of the Spirit and tongues to get clarity, stir your hunger, and remove any unbelief. If you've grown up with teachings against it or have had any personal reservations on the topic, personal study and responding to the truths you see will open your heart to receiving it when He does fill you.

RECEIVE PRAYER

I recommend having others who've received the Holy Spirit lay their hands on you and pray for an infilling. The pattern in Acts was for people to lay hands on others to receive the Holy Spirit and tongues. Laying on of hands was also Jesus' method of releasing God's power.[17]

Have them ask God to fill you with the Holy Spirit and then have them pray in tongues out loud. In the prayer time, focus your attention on God, and be aware of how His presence touches you. You don't have to experience a lot, but most times there's a clear presence that comes (gentle presence, heat, tears, joy, or peace). When receiving prayer, do not feel pressure to make anything up or copy their syllables; just wait for God to touch you.

SPEAK OUT

When others pray over you or when you're by yourself, open your mouth and speak if you feel God moving in you and sense syllables come to mind. If you

---

17 Laying on of hands - Luke 4:40; Mark 16:18; Acts 6:6, 8:17-18, 9:17, 13:3, 19:6, 28:8; 1 Timothy 4:14, 5:22; 2 Timothy 1:6; Hebrews 6:2.

don't feel anything stirring in you, don't feel like you need to speak anything out. In my experience, I felt a small urge to speak out, and then I had a few syllables to speak. There will be some level of flowing in tongues, but you will have to step out in faith to some degree when it first comes. As in the Acts accounts, there will be a deeper sense of worship and thanksgiving coming out of you when you speak in tongues.

With others praying over you, there is the freedom to quietly speak out the syllables that are coming to you without feeling the pressure of knowing if tongues are flowing or not. I remember it feeling good to my heart, but feeling weird and foreign to my mind, so I suggest speaking out the few syllables that flow to you. If there is no flow of tongues whatsoever and no discernable presence of God, keep waiting on God in the prayer time and then try again later if needed.

In my opinion, you can receive tongues in an experience but struggle to verbalize it. If you and the others felt God touching you with His presence, there's a good chance you did receive the Holy Spirit and tongues. Some people need extra time and coaching to step out in praying the tongues that they received in the prayer time. If this is you, take time every day to wait on God and then speak out any syllables that come to your mind and see if you feel more of a flow in tongues than before.

GROW IN IT

After you receive it, set aside time to pray and sing in tongues every day. Once you have tongues, you don't have to wait for another experience to pray in tongues. You can do it whenever you choose because your spirit-man has been activated in it. Praying every day will help you cultivate a new flow in prayer and build your faith in the truth of tongues.

HINDRANCES TO RECEIVING TONGUES

The first thing I've seen hinder hungry believers from receiving tongues is past unbiblical theology that believed tongues were demonic or not for today. Past beliefs can create fear and unbelief. When someone isn't receiving tongues and they share their past beliefs, I lead them in repenting and agreeing with the truth of tongues for today. If they are unsure of their beliefs, I ask them to study the verses on the infilling and the verses from 1 Corinthians 14 until they're ready to repent and pray again.

The second hindrance is a wrong expectation of what will happen when tongues are received. Some people expect God to take over their body and mouth to speak in tongues. Even with my intense infilling experience and others I've witnessed, there is usually conscious participation to speak out what is bubbling inside. When this assumption is there, it creates passivity and doesn't allow for their personal participation. Sometimes this perspective is there because people sincerely don't want it to be fake. In this situation, it is helpful to coach people through participating with their mouths in faith when there is some level of bubbling up inside.

The third hindrance is an intellectual struggle of unbelief that requires repentance and surrendering to God's ways. Some people want more of God in tongues, but the "foolishness" of the simplicity of "babbling" in tongues is a stumbling block to them. God's ways are foolishness to the minds of men and praying the same unknown syllables repeatedly is probably the clearest expression of this! For those struggling with this, I have them repent and ask God to help them enter into faith in this prayer language.

DON'T GIVE UP

If you have not received tongues, I encourage you to pursue them with all your heart. I've seen it frustrate many people when they haven't received an infilling experience or tongues soon after asking for it. Over time, it seemed like God gave it to everyone but them. To pray for it, or be prayed over several times, became too painful because it never happened, and it affirmed the accusation that God treats them differently. It becomes easier to retreat to the belief system that tongues are not for everyone because it removes the pain of asking God again. I encourage you to challenge this temptation.

The hindrances listed in the above section may be the only things holding you back. But the short delay may also be God's pathway to addressing deeper lies you believe about His Father's heart that loves to give to His children. Maybe He's using the issue of tongues to make you aware that you don't believe in His goodness toward you. If you continue your pursuit of the Spirit with an open heart, God will use the process to further heal you of these lies.

WEEKLY ASSIGNMENT

The initial assignment for this module depends on your current experience with tongues.

1. For those who haven't received an initial infilling of the Spirit and spoken in tongues, journal your thoughts and questions on the topic and study the verses from this chapter. If you feel clear about pursuing the Spirit and tongues after studying, take time this week to ask for it in prayer or receive prayer from others. If it doesn't happen this week, keep pursuing it throughout the module.

2. If you have received tongues, your assignment is to pray in tongues for 15 minutes a day for at least three days this week. After each prayer time, write down a paragraph of how these prayer times go for you such as if it was easy or difficult, if you sensed God's presence, if you learned how God interacts with you, and if you sensed any benefits from doing it. If 15 minutes is not a challenge to you, consider praying 30-60 minutes every day of the week throughout the module instead.

16

PRAYING FROM OUR SPIRIT-MAN

INTRODUCTION

There are three essential truths to focus on from this chapter. The first is that praying in tongues is the prayer of our spirit-man. The second truth is that our spirit-man speaks supernatural revelations about God called mysteries or hidden truths. Last, our souls and bodies will come under the influence of the Holy Spirit and our spirit-man as we sow time and effort into tongues. As you focus on the topic of tongues for the next few weeks, give it time to bear fruit in your heart. I trust that as you pray in tongues every day, you will begin to discern moments of alignment and spiritual breakthrough that will encourage you in your prayer journey.

MY JOURNEY - CONTINUED

I had my initial infilling of the Spirit experience during my junior year in college. After that, I began praying and singing in tongues regularly, in prayer times, and walking around campus. My spiritual life was noticeably stronger and different in that initial season. Looking back, I can trace the beginnings of many of my giftings and spiritual hunger to that time.

Soon after college, I started Bible school at IHOP in Kansas City. During my first semester, Corey Russell taught a class on intercession in which we prayed in tongues for the first thirty minutes of every class. I had a value for praying in tongues for a few years before this class but praying in tongues that long gave me a higher vision for encountering God in tongues. Many times, God met us in those thirty minutes with deeper cries of intercession, joy, worship, repentance, freedom from lies, praying for one another, and increased revelation during the teaching times. Like the preacher said in college, praying in tongues thirty minutes a day in that class did impact my life.

Before my junior year of Bible school, I read the *Walk of the Spirit* by Dave Roberson. In his story, Dave prayed in tongues several hours a day when he began pastoring full-time. After a few months, God began to release words of knowledge and miracles in his life. I was intrigued by Dave's story and the apostle Paul's references to always praying in the Spirit and speaking in tongues more than anyone, and I decided to try and pray in tongues for a few hours a day for that summer.[1]

It was hard in some ways, but God met me in those times and convinced me of the significance of tongues. It became normal for me to cry and long for God's presence consistently while reading the Bible. I learned what small daily spiritual breakthroughs felt like in the Spirit (shifting from operating in my soul to walking in the Spirit).[2] Also, I started learning how to wait on God in prayer and respond

---

1 Ephesians 6:18; 1 Corinthians 14:18.

2 Galatians 5:16, 18, 25.

to ebbs and flows of His presence as each hour passed. During those long hours of praying in tongues, I would listen to worship, meditate on a Bible verse, pray through my prayer list, or wait on God in tongues.

For the next few years, I was blessed to be around many leaders and friends who had a history of praying in tongues, which gave me a lot of opportunities to grow by praying in group settings. To this day, praying in tongues for extended times and praying in group settings are still dynamic parts of my prayer life. They are so integral to my communion with God that I cannot imagine my prayer life without them. By experience, testing, and trial and error, I can say that praying in tongues is fruitful and worthy of the pursuit of every believer. Let this next section on the realities of praying from your spirit-man stir your faith to press into tongues even more.

WHAT IS PRAYING FROM OUR SPIRIT-MAN?

OUR SPIRIT-MAN PRAYS

For if I pray in a tongue, my spirit prays, but my understanding is unfruitful.
—*1 Corinthians 14:14*

I will pray with the spirit, and I will also pray with the understanding.
—*1 Corinthians 14:15*

Praying in tongues is the prayer of our spirit-man under the inspiration of the Holy Spirit. This is significant because our spirit is the one part of our being (spirit, soul, body) that has experienced the resurrection and is already living in fullness. It has been fully joined to the Holy Spirit, given access to God's heart and throne room, and is able to interact with God spirit to Spirit.[3] This means our spirit-man can see, hear, sense, and feel God in the same way as those around His throne room right now. So when our spirit-man prays, it speaks from the place of spiritual clarity and revelation.

When we pray in tongues, our spirit-man is allowed to lead our souls and bodies into the experience of God's life that dwells within it. After sin entered into creation, humans have been wrongly led by the broken and lustful appetites of their souls and bodies. Praying in tongues reverses this broken pattern by allowing our spirit-man to take the initiative in connecting to God and aligning the rest of our being under the inspiration of the Spirit. Our thoughts, emotions, longings, and physical appetites can walk in the Spirit when this happens.

Also, because the make-up of our being is first spiritual, the prayers of our spirit-man are real expressions from the deepest places of our beings. Tongues are not just anointed words that God prays through us as if disconnected from a relationship. They are Holy Spirit-inspired expressions in partnership with what our spirit-man is thinking and feeling in response to what it sees, hears, and senses in the Spiritual realm. These deep expressions are personal thanksgiving, praise, loving adoration, prophecy, and intercession.

OUR SPIRIT-MAN SPEAKS TO GOD

For he who speaks in a tongue does not speak to men but to God, for no one understands him; however, in the spirit he speaks mysteries.—1 Corinthians 14:2

---

3   1 Corinthians 2:9-12, 6:17; Ephesians 2:6-7, 18; Hebrews 10:19-20.

But if there is no interpreter, let him keep silent in church, and let him speak to himself and to God.—1 Corinthians 14:28

The corporate gift of tongues and interpretation is directed and spoken to people for their edification but praying in personal tongues is directed and spoken to God to bless Him and interact with Him. It's not a superstitious prayer that is disconnected from an authentic conversation with God, and it's not just spoken into the air or the spiritual realm. When we pray with our spirit-man, we talk to God as a person. Our spirit communicates real things to His heart, and God speaks real things to us. When I pray with my spirit-man, I picture God and remind myself that I'm entering into genuine dialogue and heart exchange with God as a person. Rather than "enduring" praying in tongues as a spiritual discipline, we can enter into a deep, enjoyable, and present-tense communion with God.

I led a small group of students one year, and one of the guys seemed to be struggling with our times of praying in tongues as a group. I noticed he just looked at the wall while praying in tongues, so I asked him why. He said he constantly distracted himself while praying in tongues because he thought there was no connection with God. I brought up this idea of picturing and praying to God spirit to Spirit, and it shifted his paradigm and helped him experience intimacy with God in tongues.

OUR SPIRIT-MAN SPEAKS MYSTERIES IN THE HOLY SPIRIT

However, in the spirit he speaks mysteries.—1 Corinthians 14:2

Speaking mysteries in the Spirit is a significant statement that needs to be unpacked and understood. First, Paul says that we pray "in the Spirit." Praying in tongues is mentioned three times in the New Testament, and each time it is referred to as "praying in the Spirit."[4] This phrase means that the Holy Spirit anoints our spirit-man to see and supernaturally perceive God. I love what Corey Russell says about this, "When we pray in tongues, we pray into the realm of the Spirit - the place of revelation where divine mysteries are unlocked and communicated to our spirits. It is true that, as believers, we have the Holy Spirit, but we need to get into the realm of the Spirit."[5]

In the New Testament, the phrase "in the Spirit" means either a momentary prophetic encounter with the Holy Spirit or a general living in the power of the Spirit. Both meanings have significant implications in the context of praying in tongues. The Apostle John had open visions and heavenly visions in the book of Revelation and described himself as being "in the Spirit."[6] Jesus said that King David had an open vision of Jesus in Psalm 110 and called Him Lord "in the Spirit."[7] Paul had prophetic encounters with the Holy Spirit about his ministry in each city and referenced being "in the Spirit."[8] When we pray in the Spirit, we draw on the Holy Spirit as the Revealer, and He awakens our spiritual senses to the spiritual realm. I believe the things we speak out are prophetic insights that our spirit-man is allowed to perceive in the realm of the Spirit.

Second, Paul says that we "speak mysteries." Speaking mysteries is not mystical and ethereal; it refers to speaking deep truths of God's thoughts, emotions, and plans back to Him. In the New Testament, mysteries are purposefully hidden

---

4 Jude 1:20; Ephesians 6:19; 1 Corinthians 14:2.

5 Corey Russell, *The Glory Within* (Shippensburg: Destiny Image, 2012), 80.

6 Revelation 1:10, 4:2, 17:3, 21:10.

7 Matthew 22:43-44.

8 Acts 20:22-23.

truths about God's Heart and His plans that He wants to unfold to those who are spiritually hungry. The Greek word for "mysteries" is used twenty-seven times in the New Testament. It refers to something hidden from the spiritually passive or ungodly, or something profound and worth searching out in partnership with the Holy Spirit.[9] It never means something that is unsearchable or out of reach.

Paul used the word "mysteries" or "mystery" to describe the revelation of God and His plans through Jesus and the message of the gospel. Paul was a steward of the mysteries of God. He had insight into the mystery of the gospel by revelation, and he preached the mysteries of the gospel to the lost. Paul used the word in context to the glorious realities of Jesus and the gospel that need to be searched out for all eternity: Jesus' marriage to the Church, Jesus' human and divine nature, resurrected bodies, the unification of heaven and earth at Jesus' second coming, Israel's blindness, and the Jews and Gentiles becoming one new man in Christ.

If indeed, you have heard of the dispensation of the grace of God which was given to me for you, how that by revelation He made known to me the mystery.…. which in other ages was not made known to the sons of men, as it has now been revealed by the Spirit to His holy apostles and prophets.—Ephesians 3:3-5

Let a man so consider us as servants of Christ and stewards of the mysteries of God.—1 Corinthians 4:1

Paul and Jesus also used the word "mysteries" when revealing things to the hungry and hiding them from the passive or ungodly. Jesus spoke in parables so that

---

9   Mysteries - Matthew 13:11; Mark 4:11; Luke 8:10; Romans 11:25, 16:25; 1 Corinthians 2:7, 4:1, 13:2, 14:2, 15:51; Ephesians 1:9, 3:3-4, 3:9, 5:32, 6:19; Colossians 1:26-27, 2:2, 4:3, 2 Thessalonians 2:7; 1 Timothy 3:9, 3:16; Revelation 1:20, 10:7, 17:5, 17:7.

people had to choose if they were going to pursue greater clarity in conversation with Him or if they were going to walk away from Jesus. God gives the hungry and godly believers insight into the mysteries of His kingdom, but He hides them from the passive and ungodly. To use the language of 1 Corinthians 2, when we pray in tongues, God opens the hidden mysteries and makes them known to us because they are taught by the Spirit and spiritually discerned by us if we are spiritual people.[10]

And He said to them, "To you it has been given to know the mysteries of the kingdom of God; but to those who are outside, all things come in parables.
—Mark 4:11

But we speak the wisdom of God in a mystery, the hidden wisdom which God ordained before the ages for our glory, which none of the rulers of this age knew; for had they known, they would not have crucified the Lord of glory.
—1 Corinthians 2:7-8

In context to praying in tongues, the word "mysteries" means that our spirit is praying out hidden truths about God's heart, the glories of the gospel, and God's eternal plans through Jesus. For example, that means that we can explore the profound, eternal mystery (hidden truth) of our marriage to Jesus by meditating the Bible and praying in tongues. As we do this in each meditation time, we progressively become more aware of the revelation of the mystery by Biblical clarity, thoughts, and emotional experiences with His presence and truth. Praying in tongues with meditation helps us receive from the Holy Spirit because

---

10 1 Corinthians 2:13-14, 3:1.

we're postured to hear and understand Him with our spirit-man instead of our natural man.

WE EDIFY OURSELVES

> *He who speaks in a tongue edifies himself, but he who prophesies edifies the church.*—*1 Corinthians 14:4*

To be edified means to be built up by the Spirit or to experience the life of the Holy Spirit in a greater measure. Edification is revelation, peace, joy, hope, faith, strength, and righteousness. God releases life and power in us as we engage our spirit in prayer. Paul's encouragement in 1 Corinthians 14 was for the church to excel in prophecy because it released God's power to individual hearts. Yet, personal tongues release supernatural power to our souls and bodies in the same way that prophecy does as we speak to others.

Edifying ourselves is a good thing, not a selfish thing because it's all unto strengthening our friendship with Jesus and abiding in the vine. Resist believing the lie that praying for yourself or focusing on personal spiritual growth is ever wrong. Those edified and flowing in the Holy Spirit (intimacy with God) are the most impactful to other people.

Paul wasn't devaluing tongues in 1 Corinthians 14, and he emphasized that when he said, *"I thank my God I pray in tongues more than you all."* He was correcting issues that this specific church had with their corporate use of tongues. He also encouraged them to be zealous for personal edification through tongues and corporate edification through prophecy and the gifts of tongues and interpretation.

BLESS WITH THE SPIRIT-MAN

Otherwise, if you bless with the spirit, how will he who occupies the place of the uninformed say "Amen" at your giving of thanks, since he does not understand what you say? For you indeed give thanks well but the other is not edified.
—1 Corinthians 14:16-17

This phrase highlights the reality that our spirit is expressing something personal to God instead of the idea that the Holy Spirit is just singing through our spirit in an impersonal way. As our spirits experience God's beauty by the Holy Spirit, we respond with praises back to God. There's a unique place of worship that our spirits automatically live in that our souls must enter into through prayer progressively. Our spirits are joined to Jesus in His throne room, so they see what the Living Creatures see and have the same praises to declare.

In Acts 2:11, the Apostles were blessing God with their spirits, "*We hear them speaking in our own tongues the wonderful works of God.*" In Acts 10:46, Peter heard Cornelius and his household praising God with their spirits after receiving the infilling of the Holy Spirit, "*For they heard them speak with tongues and magnify God.*" Paul also said we could give thanks well, which means we can pour out our worship of thanksgiving by singing in tongues.

PRAY WITH OUR SPIRIT AND UNDERSTANDING

For if I pray in a tongue, my spirit prays, but my understanding is unfruitful. What is the conclusion then? I will pray with the spirit, and I will also pray with the understanding. I will sing with the spirit, and I will also sing with the understanding.—1 Corinthians 14:14-15

In this passage, understanding refers to our thoughts and emotions, while unfruitful refers to their lack of engaging and experiencing spiritual benefits from tongues. This can happen because our minds don't automatically engage with God when we pray and sing from our spirit-man. However, we can choose to engage them, and they can be fruitful. Paul encouraged believers to flow between prayer and worship from their spirit-man and their understanding to bring the most fruitfulness. Combining the two is powerful because our thoughts and emotions were meant to flow in prayer and worship under the leadership of our spirit-man.

PRAY FOR INTERPRETATION

Therefore let him who speaks in a tongue pray that he may interpret.
—1 Corinthians 14:13

Paul's encouragement to interpret tongues mostly concerns the corporate gift of tongues that are prophetic words to a group. However, asking for interpretation and speaking it out is not necessary regarding personal tongues because it's directed to God and for personal edification. I think it's okay to ask for understanding of what we're praying with our spirit, but not necessary. I believe the interpretation comes naturally to our thoughts and emotions in our prayer times and then progressively throughout the day in these ways and more: receiving revelation in the Word, praying inspired prayers, having spontaneous ideas come to mind throughout the day, clarity and wisdom, and receiving prophetic impressions for others.

I don't believe Paul was worried about interpreting what we say word for word. In 1 Corinthians 14, the Greek word for "interpret" emphasizes communicating a general message instead of a literal word for word translation.[11] Unless someone is speaking out an earthly language with clear sentence structures, interpretations of personal tongues are probably only communicating the main ideas God is speaking through the person.

WEEKLY ASSIGNMENT

For this week's assignment, pray in tongues for three days or more for at least 15 minutes each time. After each prayer time, journal a few sentences on how it went for you. If you have time and desire or already pray in tongues as a lifestyle, try scheduling 30-60 minutes every day of the week. Wherever you are in your rhythm, stretch yourself for more time and watch how God meets you. If you've not received tongues yet, take the assigned prayer times to pray about and study the topic of tongues from the chapter

The purpose of these prayer and journal assignments is to build your rhythm and usher you into spiritual breakthrough moments where you feel the life of the

---

11 Prior, David. *The Message of 1 Corinthians.* The Bible Speaks Today Series (Leicester, England: Inter-Varsity Press, 1985), 240.

Spirit touching you. Once you experience these moments, you'll be encouraged and more excited to keep praying. By reflecting afterward, you will become more aware of how God moves during your prayer times, and you'll be more sensitive to the fruit. Writing down questions and challenges will also help you search them out during this module.

Also, based on 1 Corinthians 14:2, do a simple study on the words "mystery" and "mysteries." On a Bible search website (like www.biblegateway.org) type in one word at a time and review all the verses that have that word. Write down what you learn about the words based on the others verses.

DISCIPLESHIP MEETING GUIDE
MODULE 4: PRAYING IN THE SPIRIT – CHAPTERS 15 & 16

MEETING FOCUS:

The purpose of this week's meeting is to discuss **your most relevant** questions about praying in tongues and process how your daily tongues times are going.

DISCUSSION QUESTIONS (IN ORDER OF IMPORTANCE):

1. ***Spiritual Pursuits:***
   a. Practically, how is your prayer schedule going? How many days have you walked out your prayer schedule? Do you need to make small changes to your schedule? How is your Bible reading, meditation, and prayer list times going, and how is God impacting you through them?
   b. Briefly review your new *Spiritual Pursuits Document*.
2. ***Chapter Questions:***
   a. Chapter 15 – Discuss your most relevant questions (Bible and practicals) about receiving the Holy Spirit and tongues based on the chapter. Focus on the most helpful questions instead of smaller questions that can be discussed another time.
   b. If you have been praying in tongues, how have those times been going for you based on your journaling? If you haven't received tongues, discuss your studies and the times you've prayed into the topic so far.
   c. Chapter 16 – Discuss your most relevant questions on the chapter, focusing on the idea of praying mysteries with your spirit-man. Discuss your study on the words "mystery" and "mysteries."
3. ***Heart Issue:***
   a. Share how your heart issue has been going this past week. With heart issue discussions, process, confess, encourage, and pray together for God to release transformation. ***Pray in tongues together and ask God to release power to the heart issue.***
4. Briefly review the assignments for the next two weeks together.

MEETING NOTES:

17

COMMUNING WITH GOD IN TONGUES

BENEFITS OF PRAYING IN TONGUES

In this chapter, you will read about some of the benefits of tongues and how to commune with God for extended times. The benefits section is first because understanding some of these will help you navigate your prayer times. They will also give you language for what you might experience in your prayer assignments.

HOLY SPIRIT INSPIRATION

We can experience spiritual breakthroughs daily by praying in tongues. A spiritual breakthrough is when you experience a shift from operating out of your soul and body to operating in the Holy Spirit. In these breakthroughs, our thoughts, emotions, wills, and bodies come under the leadership and inspiration of the Holy Spirit in a discernible way. Galatians 5 calls it walking in the Spirit.

These breakthroughs usually happen after I pray for fifteen to thirty minutes, but sometimes they happen sooner or later. Many pastors and authors describe similar experiences around that same time frame. In these breakthrough moments, I sense a sudden increase of the Spirit's presence in and around me, and I sense things in my being come into alignment and under His inspiration. I feel various levels of peace, joy, hope, clarity on life, courage, desire for God, longing for righteousness, faith to intercede, Bible verses come to mind, and I begin operating in the various gifts of the Spirit such as prophecy and healing.

Before these breakthroughs, I either feel okay or weighed down by negative thoughts, emotions, and accusations. Most of the time, all that negative stuff goes away as I pray and come under the influence of the Holy Spirit. If I feel levels of fear, anxiety, accusation, or confusion, I know that praying in tongues will break it all off. These kinds of experiences are what convinced me of the power of praying in tongues in my twenties and still give me vision to experience God's inspiration daily.

Outside of these breakthrough moments, there is a general fruit of inspiration in my life from tongues that impacts prayer, worship, Bible study, and ministry to others. Here are some examples. God brings prayers to mind and inspires my emotions in prayer. He inspires spontaneous songs and choruses during worship times. He also gives prophetic impressions for me and others. God releases wisdom and practical strategies for things I'm leading, whether that be ministry or how to disciple my kids in each season. Also, He inspires my emotions with love, joy, peace, and the other fruits of the Spirit.

FAITH, STRENGTH, AND RESOLVE

When I pray in tongues, I feel a progressive increase of faith, strength, and resolve in my heart. Sometimes I feel disconnected from God and experience negative emotions such as anger, fear, and confusion, but things shift in those prayer times. Faith rises within me, and I feel God imparting strength to me. I feel resolve and strength increase to the degree that I feel determined to say no to lies or sin patterns that I didn't have the strength or the resolve to say no to.

In these experiences, I feel my spirit rising in faith to lead and speak to my soul like the Psalmist, "*Why are you downcast, O my soul? And why are you disquieted within me? Hope in God, for I shall yet praise Him for the help of His countenance.*"[1] I speak to my soul from a place of faith and strength and break my agreement with darkness.

He who speaks in a tongue edifies himself.—1 Corinthians 14:4

But you, beloved, building yourselves up on your most holy faith praying in the Holy Spirit.—Jude 1:20

To edify oneself has the same meaning as in Jude when he says to build oneself up in the Spirit. The picture of the word is of a building being established on the inside. God strengthens us on the inside and builds up our most holy faith. God's power increases in our thoughts and emotions, and He fills our inner man with supernatural might and fortitude.[2]

I feel faith regarding who God is, who I am to God, and what He says He's going to do. For example, once when I was driving to my hometown, I prayed in tongues most of the six-hour drive. Driving into town, I felt surges of faith for what God wanted to do in Sioux Falls. The clear feeling of faith and clarity remained for a few days because of that prayer time.

---

1   Psalm 42:5.

2   Ephesians 3:16.

I've had to conquer doubts, fears, and challenges in different seasons when God has directed me into new parts of my calling. In those seasons, I've prayed into the new direction and prayed in tongues for days or weeks at a time. The result has always been a more vibrant faith for what God would do and an inner resolve and emotional strength to walk it out.

SPIRIT OF REVELATION

Praying in tongues releases a greater flow of revelation from the Holy Spirit to my thoughts and emotions. This is the fruit of speaking mysteries with my spirit-man. I experience revelation in understanding the Word and experiencing God as a person.

Often, I pray in tongues when reading the Bible or meditating, and I ask the Holy Spirit to teach me all things. When I do this, phrases stick out to me and expand in meaning. Ideas flow to me as I read and pray, God's Word becomes clearer, and I experience a deeper hunger to know Him in the Word.

God ministers experiential knowledge to my heart in Bible study, meditation, worship, or when praying in the spirit. This is what Paul called the spirit of revelation in the knowledge of God. In these times with the Lord, my thoughts become focused on Him, my emotions feel His emotions, and there's a tangible sense of intimacy and oneness with Him. The spirit of revelation is a regular experience when praying in the spirit is a lifestyle.

DEEPER EXPRESSION OF PRAYER AND WORSHIP

Praying with my spirit allows me to express the deepest places of my being to God in ways that natural words can't always do. Also, singing in tongues allows me to express the deeper places of gratefulness and praise to God. In praying and singing, I feel like I'm expressing who I am to God, but it also overflows into my thoughts and emotions and inspires them to express themselves in deep ways. My emotions open up to God, and I feel more love and thankfulness for Him.

SPIRITUAL GIFTS

Praying in the Spirit ushers in all the gifts of the Spirit. Praying in tongues engages our spirit-man and allows the Holy Spirit to flow through us in power. When I pray in tongues, I am more sensitive to God's voice, His leading, the spiritual realm around me, and I'm more conscious of His power moving through me. I have heard this principle said in one form or another in many books and testimonials throughout my life, and I have experienced it myself. When I refocus on praying in tongues, I see more healings, prophecy, words of knowledge, divine appointments, and power in delivering others from demonic strongholds. Because of this, I try to make it a point to pray in the Spirit for extended times before leading worship, preaching, or praying over others.

 ## COMMUNING IN TONGUES

Communing conveys the idea of an intimate sharing of thoughts and emotions with God. In it, God communicates the deep things of His heart, and we share ours in a way that flows back and forth. At the same time, there is a tangible experience of each other's person or presence that goes beyond the verbalizing of ideas. It's a present tense being with God as a person that is more intimate than communicating. Communing is expressing deep things by sharing your presence while communicating can just be verbalizing ideas to another person without intimacy.

The best picture for communing with God is John the Beloved leaning on Jesus' chest at the Last Supper. John talked to Jesus at the table and heard His words, but he also heard Jesus' heartbeat and felt His physical nearness. Jesus also heard John's words and was able to feel his physical nearness. Between the two of them, there was a communing or sharing of hearts outside of the words they spoke.

In my opinion, Biblical meditation and praying in tongues uniquely postures us to commune with God. As we commune with God in tongues, we get to experience a supernatural flowing from our spirit to His Spirit. The main points in this section give practical ways of connecting and communing with God and giving language to what you might experience in your prayer times. As in meditation, you are learning how God interacts with you in prayer, so be a student of His presence as you read this and apply it to your prayer life.

PRACTICALS IN COMMUNING

You can apply the practical instructions below to any praying and singing in tongues times. But the primary context I'm speaking into is longer, focused times in tongues that are directed towards receiving from the Holy Spirit. As you grow in praying for longer periods, you will experience different levels of communion with God. Some of the practical instructions below will make more sense to you during these longer prayer times. Also, there are two stages I refer to in this section (**stage #1 – connecting and stage #2 – revelation**) that give language to the spiritual progression you may experience in your prayer times.

PICTURE GOD

When you pray in tongues, it is really helpful to picture God in your imagination. Our sanctified imaginations are spiritual eyes God has given us to engage with the Spiritual realm.[3] Setting your mind on Him will help your understanding be fruitful and will significantly increase the feeling that you're interacting with a real person. Picturing God takes the majority of the effort in prayer, but it's worth it because it's where prayer becomes real.

Personally, I don't feel connected to God as a person or experience the power of tongues until I focus my mind on Him. Once I get focused, there is a small but instant shift inside of me. I liken this effect to putting a car in gear so it can drive forward. You can pray in tongues without picturing and engaging God as a person, but it's like pushing the gas pedal and revving the engine when the car is in park. When you connect to Him in your mind and emotions, it's like connecting the engine with the transmission to make the car go.

I set my mind on a picture of God in three different ways: on His throne from Revelation 4, Jesus standing by me from Revelation 1, or the Holy Spirit in my spirit as a glorious light. Throughout your prayer time, refocus your mind on the image of God. Don't feel bad for putting a lot of energy into this. As you do this, the spiritual muscle of picturing Him will become more and more natural.

TALK TO GOD

Remember, when you pray or sing in tongues, you're communicating something real from your spirit to God's heart. So, engage your mind and emotions like it's a real conversation. When you do this, you will experience more intimacy with Him, and you'll feel a greater expression and opening of your own heart.

---

3 2 Corinthians 3:18; Colossians 3:1-2.

PRAY AND SING LOUD

I always encourage people to pray and sing loud enough to hear themselves (talking volume or louder). Most new people tend to be quieter, either because they are not confident in tongues or are unsure of how loud they are allowed to speak. I believe there is a spiritual dynamic to praying louder than usual, which helps our faith and heart engage. When I do this, I feel more faith in tongues, and I feel like I'm giving my spirit permission to lead my being in prayer. I suggest praying louder at the beginning of your prayer time and then following the Holy Spirit's current about whether you continue to pray louder or softer.

STAGE #1 – CONNECTING

Usually, for the first 15-30 minutes of praying in tongues, there's what I call the "connecting stage." This is where you focus on gradually connecting to God and getting into the Spirit. During this time, you may feel distracted, uninspired, or feel like you're plowing hard ground spiritually. Don't be discouraged in this stage, and don't stop praying because it's hard. It will shift, and you'll feel God's life flowing through you at any moment.

I suggest alternating between praying in tongues and praying out in your language until you sense God's presence during this stage. I've found that this helps people engage all of themselves in prayer. I suggest focusing your prayers on asking God for revelation and power in your heart, praises, and declarations of truth, or thanking Him for the Holy Spirit in you with language from key New Testament verses.[4]

---

4 John 14:26, 15:26, 16:13-15; 1 Corinthians 2:10.

PRESS PAST DULLNESS

Keep praying in tongues even if you feel nothing and are distracted. You might not feel anything initially, and you might be distracted, but staying steady in tongues will change your heart within an individual prayer time. Sometimes praying in tongues feels laborious and feels like I'm plowing up hard ground, but it doesn't faze me anymore because it almost always shifts in the prayer time.

PRAY UNTIL THE BREAKTHROUGH

Pray in tongues and commune with God until you feel the tangible shift or spiritual breakthrough in your heart and body. If you are used to praying in tongues for one or two minutes here and there, you won't fully experience the breakthrough moments God has for you through tongues. Again, this breakthrough might happen within a few minutes of prayer, or it might take longer, but it's worth praying into each time.

STAGE #2 – REVELATION

After taking time to connect to God in your heart, you will begin to sense God inspiring your thoughts and emotions progressively with faith, clarity, His manifest presence, and a sweet flowing of tongues. This is the breakthrough moment I described earlier. My interpretation of what's happening in this stage is that our spirit-man is rising inside of us and the rest of our being is starting to come under the leadership of God's Spirit in our spirit. When this happens, it releases supernatural inspiration. Inspiration will usually increase during the prayer time.

Once you step into this stage, you will feel more grace to pray, and it will be more enjoyable. In the connection stage, it can seem like you're going against the wind, but it feels like the wind is pushing you in the revelation stage. At this point, your focus is to commune with God's presence and follow the leading of the Spirit.

SPEAK OUT

Once you feel God inspiring you with His presence and power, pay attention to your thoughts, pictures in your imagination, emotional stirrings, and ways God manifests on you. These may be gentle or strong impressions and stirrings, and God will lead you in what to pray by inspiring you in these areas. Sensing and then speaking out the inspired thoughts and emotions will make you more aware of God's voice, and it will help bring your soul into an agreement with what God is doing in your spirit-man. These inspired areas are probably interpretations of what your spirit-man is praying out. Pray out the thoughts and emotions in your native language as long as you want and flow between tongues and your language.

RESPOND

As you continue to flow between praying out the things God is putting on your heart and praying in tongues, respond to God in anything He reveals to you. As you get into a flow, God will bring revelation of Biblical truths to you, encounter your emotions, convict you of sin, bring you into His prayers, or reveal things for you to do. In whatever He brings up, respond to Him accordingly. As you respond, His presence will often increase and take you deeper into the same things or bring other things to your heart. Also, by responding to Him, you'll become more sensitive to His leadership.

FOLLOW HIS WAVES

The Spirit's presence and power will come and go throughout your prayer time like waves coming and going on a beach. These waves may last a few minutes or longer. They are identified by some of these: an increase of His felt presence, an increase of faith or thanksgiving, or a burden of prayer. As you feel a wave of His presence, respond to it in the way that seems right until you feel the wave withdraw.

Here are some examples of what I experience and how I respond. If I feel His presence and my faith increase like a small surge of power, I naturally pray louder, and my tongues sound a little different. I pray louder and pray ideas out in faith until I feel His wave withdraw. Sometimes, I feel a wave of love, joy, and peace touch me, and I breathe His life in and receive from Him by praying softer and communing with Him. When a wave of intercession comes, I alternate between praying in tongues with the prayer topic in mind and praying in my language.

When you feel the wave of the Spirit withdraw, continue to pray in tongues and engage with Him until you feel another wave. Praying between the waves is like positioning yourself in the water to ride the next good wave. Don't assume that your prayer time is done after one wave because His waves will keep coming if you give Him more prayer time. During the summer that I began praying in tongues for hours, waves of different sizes would come upon me for as long as I was willing to wait on the Lord in prayer. Because of that, I encourage you to stay in prayer as long as you want to wait on the Lord's presence.

WEEKLY ASSIGNMENT

This week's assignment is to continue praying in tongues for at least three days (at least 15 minutes) and journal thoughts, questions, and observations from your time. In addition, schedule one day when you can pray in tongues for at least thirty minutes continuously. Observe how God moves on you in your longer prayer time and try to discern if you experience a breakthrough moment (as listed in the *Holy Spirit Inspiration* section). If you do, write down what it felt like and what fruit you experienced afterward.

If you have not received tongues, take the assigned prayer times to continue your study of praying in tongues and pray for the infilling of the Spirit and tongues. Journal your thoughts, questions, and challenges from your prayer and study times to process with your Discipleship Mentor.

18
PRAYING WITH GROUPS

INTRODUCTION TO GROUP TONGUES

Praying and singing in tongues with a group of people for extended periods is a powerful but uncommon experience for many that I meet. Even in churches or prayer ministries where tongues is accepted or promoted, it seems less common for there to be a corporate culture of group tongues. Church cultures and rhythms of praying in tongues as groups will increase as individuals grow daily in praying in the Spirit, and as people take initiative to create groups that pray in tongues together so people can experience the power of it. By doing both, faith and testimonies around individual and group tongues will increase, as well as experience and wisdom in moving in the Spirit together.

GROUP BENEFITS

The benefits of praying in a group are the same as individual prayer except multiplied and accelerated. This corporate grace applies to anything else in the kingdom because God loves unity and family in the same way that the Trinity is family. Compare the benefits of group tongues with the benefits of a worship team. One person can play guitar and worship in their room and it's impactful, but when that person plays guitar on a full worship team, the dynamics and benefits multiply. With a team, there are multiple sounds that flow together, varieties of spiritual giftings that bring strength, fuller perspectives to discern God's direction in the moment, musicians playing off one another's sounds and creativity, and going somewhere together in God's heart together, which creates a shared spiritual experience.

STRENGTH AND FAITH

On top of the individual benefits of praying in tongues (faith, strength, resolve, spiritual sensitivity, interpretation of mysteries, and so on), the group dynamic adds strength, group discernment of the Spirit's leading, and a shared experience in God. When we pray together, there is a practical and spiritual strength and faith released to the group to stay focused while believing for more of God's presence. Practically, this happens by seeing each person lean into prayer in the moment. When you're distracted, discouraged, or oppressed, it's strengthening to look at a friend next to you praying in tongues. Spiritually, when more people pray together the Spirit's activity multiplies

DISCERNMENT

Discernment increases in groups because each person is connecting to God with their spirit-man and becoming spiritually sensitive. When everyone is sensitized to God's presence, each person can speak into what they feel the Spirit highlighting or affirm what others are saying and praying out. This breeds more clarity and confidence around the Spirit's leadership. When there is group agreement, each person is more empowered to enter into the moment.

SHARED EXPERIENCE

The last group benefit is the shared experience in God, which means we all sense, hear, and feel led to respond to God in similar ways in the prayer time. This group encounter leads to spiritual unity and agreement that is deeper and quicker than if someone has to be convinced of a vision or value through teaching. Whether it's direction for the future, the conviction of a sin issue, or a prayer focus, the group has heart agreement because of the Spirit's power. Many times, I've seen groups experience God's heart or perspective over something which resulted in a shared clarity, conviction, resolve, and even practical action steps. Acts 13:1-3 describes this sort of group encounter and the resulting fruit of unity and commissioning.

The process of praying unto a shared experience has two benefits. First, believing for and pressing into the breakthrough moments builds group spiritual resolve long-term. Second, group discernment of the Spirit's leading teaches those same people how to discern the Spirit's voice and leadership for anything else. My leadership teams know how to discern God's voice for church direction and decisions because they've learned how to follow Him together in group tongues times. I believe this process increases the bond of the Spirit, which is indispensable for a leadership team.[1]

---

1   Ephesians 4:3.

BIBLICAL PERSPECTIVE

CONTEXT OF 1 CORINTHIANS 14

Some believers have reservations about group tongues because of Paul's statements in 1 Corinthians 14, but I think those can be resolved. To begin the discussion, it is important to understand that Paul was writing to people that may have been coming from pagan backgrounds that involved demonic trances and speaking or prophesying in demonic tongues. Some of Paul's guidance or corrections were probably addressing spiritual mixture (pagan expressions mixed with spiritual gifts) and their expectations of how the Spirit would manifest on them and through them.

CORPORATE TONGUES VS. PERSONAL TONGUES

The next clarification is that Paul was correcting the corporate use of the gift of tongues and interpretation that are spoken to people during speaking times in corporate gatherings, not prohibiting personal tongues that are spoken to God in prayer and worship times. The four values Paul wanted to see in their corporate gatherings were clarity, edification, submission to church leadership, and honoring one another in the gifts. When he limited tongues to one person at a time and asked for an interpretation, he was addressing people who were climbing over one another to give corporate prophecies in tongues. They had wrong motivations to be seen and heard because of their gifting, and they may not have understood the Spirit's order. Such practices led to confusion in the services, a lack of edification, and possible competition that was dishonoring to others.

COMMUNICATE

Praying in tongues with a group can be celebrated within Paul's values when leaders communicate the values and Biblical perspectives of group tongues. When leaders teach on the difference between the gift and personal tongues and establish that everyone is directing their prayers to God, it removes the possible confusion and distractions of Paul's scenario. If the group agrees that they're all speaking to God, there is no confusion as to needing interpretation or only allowing one person to speak at a time. Group tongues honor Paul's values and lead to edification, clarity, submission to leadership, and honoring one another.[2]

LEADING GROUP PRAYER

These practical suggestions are for people leading focused group times (15 minutes or longer) of praying and singing in the Spirit and can be used for times of waiting on the Spirit, singing, or group intercession. These suggestions are almost identical to the ones from the previous chapter with some nuances that are unique to groups and leadership. Like the previous chapter, I reference the connecting and revelation stages because the goal in leading group prayer times is to envision and guide people into the breakthrough moments.

GIVE DIRECTION

As the prayer time leader, tell the group what the purpose of the prayer time is, how long the prayer time is going to be, how they can engage together throughout the time, and what the breakthrough moments might feel like. During the prayer

---

2   Acts 2:11, 10:46.

time, speak out any directions or encouragements that would be helpful for the group. As the leader, you will probably sense when people are distracted or disconnected at different points. The best thing to do is to speak out or pray out short encouragements about the power of tongues and invite them to refocus on God in prayer. People that are newer to praying in groups will probably need consistent guidance and encouragement in prayer times.

PICTURE GOD

Encourage everyone to picture God the entire prayer time (Father on the throne, Revelation 1 Jesus, or the indwelling Holy Spirit). Focusing our hearts on Him in this way creates a much more intimate connection. Whenever you sense people disconnecting in prayer, encourage them to refocus their hearts on that image.

PRAY LOUD

Encourage people to pray loud enough to hear themselves and to feel the freedom to pray louder when they need to or feel an increase of God's power. Praying louder causes us to rise in faith and confidence, which produces a more wholehearted prayer engagement in prayer times. Sometimes, it is helpful to ask people to start out louder to get hearts engaged and overcome any awkwardness of praying in a group setting. There are times when God's presence will move in a prayer time and bring people to silence and quiet tongues, but when that presence is not moving, quiet tongues can indicate that people are disconnecting and lacking faith in what they are doing. In these moments, you can refocus the group by reminding them to picture God, ask them to stand up, and invite them to pray louder as a way of engaging their spirit-man.

STAGE #1 – CONNECTING

I call the first section (15-30 minutes) of prayer time the "connecting stage" because people need to connect to God individually but also as a group. Unity in the Spirit matters in a group context, so everyone needs to engage in prayer and learn how to flow in tongues as a family of believers. The level to which individuals engage in prayer does affect what the others experience in the prayer time. God's presence and power will begin to move and inspire the group as each person intentionally connects to Him.

During this initial stage, ask people to pray in tongues out loud and for people to take turns speaking out prayers in their own language. Both of these help engage hearts and facilitate the process of everyone connecting to God. When people speak out their own prayers, it helps everyone focus and it brings unity to the room. When someone prays out loud and everyone agrees with it in prayer, there is unity in the group's pursuit. This unity of purpose is part of what I mean by connecting to God as a group. The purpose of praying in a group is that you enter into God's heart unified and together in the Spirit.

Instead of praying into your prayer points right away, consider focusing on asking for the spirit of revelation and the Spirit's presence to manifest in the group. I suggest holding off on your prayer list for that time until there is some inspiration from the Spirit in the room. People could also focus prayers on speaking out verses about praying in tongues or thanking God for specific promises and spiritual realities in the Bible. For example, I pray out verses about the Holy Spirit's ministry and presence in me, and then I ask for those to manifest in me in the prayer time. I also pray out the truths of what I'm doing by praying in tongues, "God, we speak mysteries to You in the realm of the Spirit. We speak the deep things of Your heart back to You from our spirit-man."

STAGE #2 – REVELATION

After individuals and the group connect to God, there will be an increased sense of God's presence, faith, and inspired thoughts and prayers. A group context is different from an individual prayer time in that there is teamwork in the realm of the Spirit. Like a worship team, everyone in a group prayer time has a role to play, and everyone needs to flow together in prayer to walk in the Spirit and experience spiritual breakthroughs. When the Spirit begins moving in the group, He will use each person to release spiritual impartation, lay hands and pray, and release confirmation to others concerning what God is doing in the group.

Direct people to speak out the prayers (their native language) that are stirring in their hearts because many of these will be inspired by the Holy Spirit to guide the prayer time. I believe that these inspired thoughts and prayers are interpretations of the mysteries that people were praying out with their spirit-man just minutes before. If others are being stirred with the same thing, they can pray out loud in the same vein one person at a time. If you want the group to stay on a prayer topic longer, or respond in a certain way, speak out about what you're feeling and guide the group.

As in individual prayer times, these breakthrough moments may lead to praying, declaring truth in place of lies, the conviction of sins, or encountering God emotionally. As various ones sense God's life moving in them, encourage them to fully express it to God. This allows the group to support them in prayer and maybe even step into the experience with them.

FOLLOW HIS WAVES

The Holy Spirit's presence and power will come in waves, and the group will respond to Him by praying louder and responding with clarity. If needed, encourage people to fully express themselves in volume, words, or physical posture. When a wave of the Spirit pulls back, people will naturally respond by praying quieter. If needed, encourage people to continue responding to what God just did in that wave of His presence if they feel the desire to; otherwise, encourage them to continue in tongues while waiting for another wave. After the first wave, the group will naturally flow in tongues and enjoy it, so these secondary waiting times are enjoyable and serve to stoke the flame the Holy Spirit just awakened. The Spirit may even continue to touch people during these calmer moments.

GROUP SINGING IN TONGUES

I will sing with the spirit, and I will also sing with the understanding.
—1 Corinthians 14:15

And do not be drunk with wine, in which is dissipation, but be filled with the Spirit, speaking to one another in psalms and hymns and spiritual songs, singing and making melody in your heart to the Lord.—Ephesians 5:18-19

Singing in a group has all the same dynamics as praying in a group, but two unique dynamics are singing simple melodies together and singing choruses together. As the leader, guide people by singing in tongues to a very simple melody or by asking a singer in the group to do this. Guide people to listen to the melody and then to sing in tongues in a way that flows well with the lead singer.

Once there is a flow in worship, invite people to sing out the praises in their hearts from their understanding. They can sing out loud to themselves, or they can sing loud enough for everyone to hear. Spontaneous singing will naturally lead to people making short choruses for everyone to sing together. Follow these choruses as one way that God will lead the group.

INTERCESSION IN TONGUES

Praying always with all prayer and supplication in the Spirit, being watchful to this end with all perseverance and supplication for all the saints.
—*Ephesians 6:18*

In this well-known passage on prayer and spiritual warfare, Paul encouraged believers to always pray in the Spirit in intercession and supplication. We can assume Paul did this as a lifestyle and knew its power. Interceding in tongues is easier than only praying from our understanding, it is unifying for a group, and it connects us to faith and the will of God in our prayers. In context to the topic of spiritual warfare in Ephesians 6, interceding in the Spirit helps us persevere in prayer and connects us to the prophetic spirit for our prayer topics, which is what being watchful refers to.

INDIVIDUAL INTERCESSION

Most of your intercession can be done by praying in tongues. If you're praying through your prayer list by yourself, bring one prayer point to mind and then pray in tongues. Intermittently, pray out the prayer point in your own language. Faith, clarity, and emotions will grow as you continue to pray out. If tongues are easily flowing out of you and you're feeling an increased burden from God in prayer, feel free to speak out your own prayers as much as you want.

Give full expression to what you feel inside during intercession, and don't hold anything back. When you intercede in tongues, you're allowing the deepest place of who you are to express itself to God. Your emotions will often be opened in this process, and you'll feel the desire to pray louder or cry under the prayer burden that God is giving you.[3]

GROUP INTERCESSION

Depending on how much time you have for your prayer time, take time to connect to God in tongues before praying through your prayer list. Then, as the leader, let people know when you're transitioning to interceding as a group. Have people take turns praying out their prayers and encourage everyone else to continue praying out loud in tongues while staying focused on the current person's prayers. Also, encourage people to intermittently speak out phrases from the current person's prayers. Keeping the one praying in mind and speaking out their phrases increases unity in the group.

---

3 Romans 8:26.

WEEKLY ASSIGNMENT

This week's assignment is to pray in tongues with a group for at least 30 minutes. After the prayer time, reflect with the group and write down your observations of how it went, what you experienced, and any practical questions you have. You may or may not love group tongues right away, but like everything else, give it a few months before you evaluate it. Also, if you've had reservations about praying in tongues out loud or reservations about group tongues because of statements in 1 Corinthians 14, bring them for discussion with your Discipleship Mentor and study the verses together.

For those who are studying tongues or asking for it, it is still beneficial to join the group tongues times. Being around people engaging in tongues is a great way to learn about it or ask for it, and you can still join in the prayers. If you don't feel comfortable doing that, talk with your Discipleship Mentor about your desires and then you could take that time to continue studying and praying about the topic.

DISCIPLESHIP MEETING GUIDE
MODULE 4: PRAYING IN THE SPIRIT – CHAPTERS 17 & 18

MEETING FOCUS:

The purpose of this week's meeting is to process your praying in tongues time and to pray about your heart issue.

DISCUSSION QUESTIONS (IN ORDER OF IMPORTANCE):

1. ***Spiritual Pursuits:***
   a. Practically, how is your prayer schedule going? How many days have you walked out your prayer schedule? Do you need to make small changes to your schedule? How are your Bible reading, meditation, and prayer list times going, and how is God impacting you through them?
2. ***Chapter Questions:***
   a. Chapter 17 – Discuss your journaled thoughts and questions from the chapter. Share how your 30-minute tongues time went and discuss the idea of experiencing breakthrough moments. Do you understand the idea, and have you experienced a breakthrough moment before?
   b. If you have been praying in tongues, how have those times been going for you based on your journaling? If you haven't received tongues, discuss your studies and the times you've prayed into the topic so far.
   c. Chapter 18 – Discuss your journaled thoughts and questions from the chapter. What was the most helpful Biblical perspective or practical suggestion for group prayer times? Do you have reservations about praying in tongues in groups?
3. ***Heart Issue:***
   a. Share how your heart issue has been going this past week. With heart issue discussions, process, confess, encourage, and pray together for God to release transformation. ***Pray in tongues together and ask God to release power to the heart issue.***
4. Briefly review the assignments for the next two weeks together. This is not necessary if you are having a group gathering to introduce the next module topic.

MEETING NOTES:

_____

_____

_____

_____

_____

_____

_____

_____

_____

19
DIFFERENT USES FOR TONGUES

INTRODUCTION

This chapter focuses on how praying in tongues can be used in various individual and group contexts. Praying from our spirit-man can be integral to every aspect of our relationship with God and can bear fruit in every situation. As you read this chapter, write down some of the ways you could integrate tongues into your life. The last section highlights some testimonies of well-known historical leaders to encourage you in your daily lifestyle.

SEEKING DIRECTION

Praying in tongues is one of the main ways I seek God's direction for small or large decisions in my life (practical needs, family, job, ministry, and life-calling-related decisions). Praying mysteries to God with our spirit-man includes praying out prophecies about our future, which is God's will or God's plan for our lives.

As we pray out God's plans for our lives in tongues, our minds and emotions become aware of those plans, agree with them, and live them out. Paul prayed for believers to be filled with the awareness of God's plans through wisdom and spiritual understanding.[1] I believe the spiritual understanding Paul prayed about refers to prophetic insight that comes by engaging the Holy Spirit in prayer.

When necessary, I start by scheduling special times to do nothing else but pray in tongues to ask God for direction. I prefer having an hour or more scheduled each time so that I have time to get deeply connected to God and quiet my mind. I pray in tongues while holding my request firmly in my mind before God. I ask God for direction, sometimes silently, sometimes aloud, while also journaling any thoughts or pictures that come to mind. During one of these intentional prayer times, clear thoughts come to mind about what I'm supposed to do, and if they do not, I pray until they do.

Out loud, I pray the thoughts or images that come to mind back to God in English and ask Him if this is what He's speaking to me. I do this intermittently as I continue to pray in tongues. If peace and agreement in my heart increase and God's presence increases on me while speaking the impressions back to Him, I feel more confident that what I'm sensing is from God. If these don't increase while speaking the impressions back to Him, I write them down and go back to just praying in tongues until more clarity comes to mind. At some point, I sense clarity and God bearing witness to what I'm feeling to the degree that I can move forward.

SEEKING STRATEGY

I regularly seek God's plans and strategies for my life, my marriage, parenting, finances, and ministry. Similar to praying for direction, I pray in tongues with my

---

1   Colossians 1:9.

topic in mind before the Lord for one prayer time, or more if needed. With the topic of parenting as my example, I pray in tongues while, in my mind, I ask God how to parent and disciple my daughter in this season of her life. I speak out my questions and prayers and ask for His ideas and strategies.

As I do this, more prayer points or questions come to mind to talk to Him about. I take as much time as I want to pray into the prayer points for my daughter or to wrestle with God over questions I have about her heart and life. Usually, some ideas, timelines, goals, and approaches start coming to mind while praying. Sometimes they all come at once like a download of clarity, other times they come slowly throughout the prayer time. Either way, I take time to write them down. Not only do the ideas come, but I feel God impart strength, faith, and excitement to my heart to carry out the ideas.

SEEKING REVELATION

I pray in tongues for revelation about Bible verses that I'm meditating on or studying, and I seek revelation to interpret dreams and prophetic words. If I'm talking to God about a verse, I pray in tongues out loud and ask Him for insight and experience of the truth until ideas start to flow to my mind and emotions. Sometimes I pace and pray out the verses and pray in tongues for a few minutes and then go back to my Bible, and things become clearer. Other times, I pray in tongues and study something for weeks until understanding comes. I ask, seek, and knock on the door of revelation until the Bible verses begin to open to my understanding. Lack of clarity in the Bible does not usually mean we're supposed to move on; it means we're supposed to lean into the Holy Spirit to give Him time to teach us.

DIFFERENT USES FOR TONGUES

Also, God gives me more understanding in interpreting dreams and testing prophetic words when I pray in tongues. When I'm interpreting a dream, I read the whole dream and pray in tongues until I sense clear thoughts come regarding the dream's overall theme or meaning. Then, I slowly read the dream and pray in tongues to interpret specific sentences where I feel God's presence.

I test prophetic words through prayer, Bible study, and community.[2] For the prayer portion of the testing, I read the prophecy and pray in tongues with the words in mind. If I feel God's presence increase on me and feel clarity concerning the prophetic words, I take that as God encouraging me that it's from Him or at least an encouragement to continue the testing process. I put the prophetic words to the side if I don't feel either of these things from God. If I feel like it's from God, I continue to pray in tongues until I feel ways to respond to God in my heart and prayer.

BREAKING DEMONIC SWIRLS

Praying and singing in tongues is my first response to break off demonic swirls of accusation and oppression. A demonic swirl is when you feel an overwhelming amount of accusation in your mind and physical darkness over your body. The swirl might catch you up in specific fears, confusion, insecurities, rejection, hopelessness, anger, or sinful temptations. These might be intense experiences where you feel like you can't resist, or just powerful enough to hinder you from feeling and thinking normally for the day. Praying and singing in tongues is powerful in combating this

---

2 Testing prophetic words and dreams also takes Bible study and community. See if the prophecy is Biblical and carries God's heart as a Father or if any Bible verses help interpret. Use your Church community to pray and sense with you if it is God, and what it might mean. This includes prayer, study, and discussion.

because demonic swirls try to weigh you down and get you to live from your soul, not your spirit-man. Tongues cause your spirit-man to rise up, and they fill your heart with faith and might.

I have to choose to engage in prayer and worship; otherwise, the swirl will only intensify. I pray and sing in tongues and declare truth back to God in direct opposition to the swirl that I'm feeling in the moment until I feel completely free from the demonic swirl. In between praying in tongues and declaring truths, I rise up in faith and rebuke every demon that's attacking me. I know I've broken through the demonic swirl when I feel a dark presence lift off me, feel God's presence rest on me, and feel my thoughts and emotions calm down and feel control over them. I encourage you not to settle for just feeling better in these moments, but to pray and worship until you feel like you're thriving on the inside by the Spirit's power.

COMMUNING WITH THE HOLY SPIRIT

I enjoy scheduling prayer times to take one or two Holy Spirit Bible verses and lightly pray in tongues in a receiving mode. I take the fruit of the Spirit verses in Galatians 5 or a Bible verse about the Holy Spirit's ministry, and I speak the phrases of the verses and position my heart to receive His ministry in those ways.[3] I pray in tongues while doing this to commune with Him and maintain the spirit-to-Spirit connection. For example, I'll picture the Holy Spirit in me as the river of life, and I'll thank Him for the fruit of peace that dwells in my spirit-man because of His union with me until I feel His peace filling me. "Holy Spirit, thank you for dwelling within me. Thank you for the peace of God that dwells in

---

3 Galatians 5:22; 1 Corinthians 2:10.

my spirit-man because of you. I receive that peace into my thoughts and emotions right now." I'll slowly and repetitively pray something like this for as long as I want, and the experience of God's peace will usually increase.

HISTORICAL TESTIMONIES

These are three encouraging testimonies of the power of tongues as a lifestyle and ministry value. These individuals, among many more, were shaped and fueled in their well-known ministries because of their aggressive lifestyle of praying in tongues. These testimonies, along with the apostle Paul's emphasis and fruit from tongues, have stirred my faith and helped me press into it as an intentional lifestyle. Let these bolster your faith as you continue to learn about the Biblical value of tongues and grow in it during your daily life.

JOHN G. LAKE

John G. Lake was marked by the infilling of the Spirit and praying in tongues. He lived in the early 1900s, and his ministry's fruit still inspires believers today to reach for more of the power of God. Throughout his life, he planted many churches, multiplied leaders in Africa, was a powerful preacher, and saw hundreds of thousands of people healed and delivered from demons. John said this about his famous ministry, "I want to talk with the utmost frankness and say to you that tongues have been to me the making of my ministry. It is that peculiar communication with God when God reveals to my soul the truth I utter to you day by day in my ministry."[4] John credited his intimacy with God and his

---

4   Roberts Liardon, *John G. Lake: The Complete Collection of His Life Teachings* (New Kensington: Whitaker House, 1999), 373.

healing power to the communion he experienced with God while praying in tongues.

John went on to describe the fruit that he saw in his own life. "I went into fasting and prayer and waiting on God for nine months. And one day, the glory of God in a new manifestation and a new incoming came to my life. And when the phenomena had passed, and the glory of it remained in my soul, I found that my life began to manifest in the varied range of the gifts of the Spirit, and I spoke in tongues by the power of God, and God flowed through me with a new force. Healings were of a more powerful order. Oh, God lived in me, God manifested in me, God spoke through me. My spirit was deified, and I had a new comprehension of God's will, new discernment of spirit, new revelation of God in me."[5]

SMITH WIGGLESWORTH

Smith Wigglesworth, one of the most influential healing revivalists from the early 1900s, was also changed when he received the Holy Spirit. After speaking in tongues, his preaching became anointed, healings increased, and preaching on the Holy Spirit became one of his primary life messages.[6] "It is a wonderful thing to pray in the Spirit and to sing in the Spirit, praying in tongues and singing in tongues as the Spirit of God gives you utterance. I never get out of bed in the morning without having communion with God in the Spirit. It is the most wonderful thing on earth. It is most lovely to be in the Spirit when you are dressing, and you come out to the world and the world has no effect on you. You begin the day like that, and you will be conscious of the guidance of the Spirit right through the day."[7]

---

5 Liardon, *John G. Lake: The Complete Collection of His Life Teachings*, 372.

6 Smith Wigglesworth, *Greater Works* (New Kensington: Whitaker House, 1999), 186.

7 Smith Wigglesworth's Sermon on the Gift of Tongues.
   http://www.smithwigglesworth.com/sermons/eif18.htm

JACKIE PULLINGER

Jackie Pullinger, a well-known evangelist to heroin addicts in Hong Kong since the 1960s, said that praying in tongues changed her life and became the foundation of her ministry. She saw very little fruit in her ministry when she began her work in Hong Kong, but after receiving tongues and praying in the Spirit for fifteen minutes a day for weeks, she started leading people to Jesus. "After about six weeks, I noticed something remarkable. Those I talked to about Christ believed. Now I found that person after person wanted to receive Jesus. At my conversion, I had accepted that Jesus had died for me; now I began to see what miracles He was doing in the world today."[8]

Jackie worked with heroin addicts and soon discovered that the horrible withdrawal symptoms could be entirely cured by praying in tongues. At the time of writing her book, she had discipleship houses where young boys could receive Jesus, be filled with the Spirit, and be delivered from heroin addictions. Without fail, if the boys would trust her and pray in tongues, the withdrawal symptoms would never come, and they would be free of the addiction within several days. If they did not pray in tongues, the withdrawal symptoms would increase until they laid down their pride and prayed in tongues.

Soon, some of the boys who were set free stayed in discipleship houses to coach other boys. "In another sense, the work became easier and easier because the boys who had come off drugs themselves were very good at helping the 'new boys.' They happily cooked meals and did housework, and they had endless patience. They sat with the new arrivals, encouraging them to pray and praying with them. Having recently been through withdrawal, their faith was high. The other boys

---

8 Jackie Pullinger, *Chasing the Dragon* (Ventura: Regal Books, 2001), 65-66.

listened to them with some respect when they said, 'It works - once you begin to pray, the pain goes. Just ask Jesus and pray in the Spirit.'"[9]

Here is Ah Tong's testimony from Jackie's ministry. "We gave him no medication, not even aspirin. We did not even give him cigarettes to help him in his withdrawal from heroin. Every time he began to feel a slight pang, he went back to praying and using his new prayer language. His withdrawal period was pain-free. No vomiting, no cramps, no diarrhea, no shivers. With this miracle, Ah Tong began a new life."[10]

YOUR PORTION

Your portion in praying in tongues is a spiritual breakthrough and an overflowing heart. If praying in tongues daily is a newer idea to you, resist unbelief about God's purpose for tongues and fill your heart with Bible verses about the power of praying with your spirit-man. In the early days of growing in tongues, Satan will always try to lie to you about this topic and say that it's not fruitful or that the historical testimonies won't apply to your life. But you can say yes to the Biblical promises and to the testimonies of this chapter until you begin to experience it for yourself.

---

9 Pullinger, *Chasing the Dragon*, 100.

10 Pullinger, *Chasing the Dragon*, 22-23.

WEEKLY ASSIGNMENT

On top of your daily tongues times this week, schedule a 30-minute tongues time. You can pray individually, in a group, or with your Discipleship Mentor. Reflect on your prayer time and write down your observations. If you are still seeking tongues or studying the topic, continue "asking, seeking, and knocking," because God is a good Father who will give you all things and show you all things!

MODULE 5

DELIVERANCE

MODULE INTRODUCTION

The purpose of this deliverance module is to equip you in understanding how to walk out freedom from sin and lie patterns as a long-term lifestyle. In this module, you will learn about demonic strongholds, how to identify and pray through them, and how to walk in spiritual freedom. For the next few weeks, your focus will be on praying through the patterns you've been talking about with your Discipleship Mentor. With a focused and well-rounded Biblical approach to freedom, levels of breakthrough can happen in every season. As a reminder, here are the four ways in which this discipleship program is set up to train you in a lifestyle of freedom:

1. **Encounter God** – Experiencing intimacy with God is the starting place for walking in freedom, and it's the way to maintain freedom long-term. Learning the prayer expressions positions you to encounter God.

2. **Intentional pursuit of freedom** – Sin and lie patterns are transformed the quickest when they are identified and addressed in a focused way. Orient your Bible pursuits (meditation, Bible study) around the truths you need to receive freedom.

3. **Accountability** – We have you meeting with a Discipleship Mentor to encourage you in your life in God and grow you in a lifestyle of accountability. Accountability relationships are a part of walking out freedom because they bring you out of hiddenness, shame, levels of

passivity in pursuing God, and help to bring you into a greater sense of being fully known and celebrated by God and others.

4. **Deliverance prayer** – Receiving deliverance prayer is a major part of experiencing freedom from negative patterns, which is why it's the focus for an entire module. It is healthy to receive deliverance prayer in every season, and the more you do it, the more you'll be equipped to pray with others. Deliverance prayer supernaturally addresses demons and broken parts of the heart that are energizing darkness and hindering transformation.

ASSIGNMENT OVERVIEW
MODULE 5 – DELIVERANCE

For Weeks 23-25, schedule a 1 ½ - 2-hour deliverance prayer time in place of your weekly Discipleship Mentor meetings. These deliverance prayer times can be done with a local Sozo ministry (bethelsozo.com/sozo-network/) or with your Discipleship Mentor. Continue to follow your prayer schedule and Spiritual Pursuits each week.

Week Twenty-two Assignments:

❑ Read Chapter 20 – "***Demonic Strongholds.***" Journal your thoughts and questions about the chapter.

❑ Take one prayer time to identify strongholds God is highlighting in this season.

❑ Fill out a new *Spiritual Pursuits Document* for this module. The pursuits can stay the same or change but filling out the form monthly helps you refocus and develop a rhythm of intentionality. Be intentional to add praying in tongues to your prayer schedule while maintaining your Bible reading, meditation, prayer list, and corporate prayer times.

❑ **Meet with your Discipleship Mentor.**

Week Twenty-three Assignments:

❑ Read Chapter 21 – *"**Deliverance Guide.**"* Journal your thoughts and questions about the chapter.

❑ **Meet with your Discipleship Mentor for a Deliverance Prayer Time.**

Week Twenty-four Assignments:

❑ Read Chapter 22 – "***Walking Out Freedom: Prayer.***" Journal your thoughts and questions about the chapter.

❑ Complete the forgiveness prayer time in one of your prayer times this week.

❑ **Meet with your Discipleship Mentor for a Deliverance Prayer Time.**

Week Twenty-five Assignments:

❑ Read Chapter 23 – "***Walking out Freedom: Church Family.***" Journal your thoughts and questions about the chapter.

❑ Answer the Church Family related questions.

❑ **Meet with your Discipleship Mentor for a Deliverance Prayer Time.**

SPIRITUAL PURSUITS   DATE: _____

1. **Bible reading direction and plan**
   (Write down what you will read and when you will read it):

2. **Meditation verse** (Choose a verse that speaks truth into your heart issue):

3. **Sin/character issue from which to get freedom:**

4. **Lie from which to pursue deliverance:**

5. **Gifting to pursue** (Include simple ways you can pursue it):

6. **Weekly Prayer Schedule**—Write down your plan for the *specific times* you are committed to spending with God each day, and *what specifically you plan to do during those times*. Include what your study or meditation focus will be. Refer to the example schedule in Chapter Two. (e.g., Monday 6-6:30 am—Tongues, 6:30-7:30 am—Meditation on Song of Solomon 1:2)

Monday

Tuesday

Wednesday

Thursday

Friday

Saturday

Sunday

20

DEMONIC STRONGHOLDS

JESUS WILL DELIVER YOU

The Spirit of the Lord God is upon Me, because the Lord has anointed Me to preach good tidings to the poor; He has sent Me to heal the brokenhearted, to proclaim liberty to the captives, and the opening of the prison to those who are bound.—Isaiah 61:1

Jesus is anointed to deliver those who are bound in sin and struggles. The Father sent Him to the earth to liberate us from the effects of sin and darkness, and He anointed Jesus with the full power of the Spirit to accomplish such a work. In fact, this is part of the gospel message. Jesus quoted Isaiah 61 the first time He identified Himself as the Messiah, which means that deliverance and freedom are core to Jesus' identity and the gospel message.[1]

---

1   Luke 4:14-21.

Jesus' preaching of the kingdom was always accompanied by the works of the kingdom in healing and deliverance. He commissioned His followers to do the same, and they turned cities upside down as they cast out demons.[2] Casting out demons was synonymous with the preaching of the kingdom for Jesus and the early church because the gospel promises freedom from the kingdom of darkness. As the church, we have the same commissioning and power to break demonic bondages and cast out demons. You can be confident that God will use others to help deliver you, and you will help deliver others by God's power.

Then His fame went throughout all Syria; and they brought to Him all sick people who were afflicted with various diseases and torments, and those who were demon-possessed, epileptics, and paralytics, and He healed them. —Matthew 4:24

Then the seventy returned with joy, saying, "Lord, even the demons are subject to us in Your name."—Luke 10:17

And these signs will follow those who believe: In My name they will cast out demons; they will speak with new tongues.—Mark 16:17

Heal the sick, cleanse the lepers, raise the dead, cast out demons. Freely you have received, freely give.—Matthew 10:8

---

2 Acts 5:16, 8:7, 16:18, 19:11.

Jesus is the great liberator who destroys the work of the Devil![3] No demonic stronghold is too strong for Him, and no pattern is too deep or too long-term for Him. Whatever brokenness you or others have, it is not too broken for Him. Jesus can set you free from the power of the Devil and sin.

JESUS IS ZEALOUS FOR YOUR FREEDOM

Jesus is zealous to set you free, and your freedom matters more to Him than it does to you. His eyes are on you, and His heart is filled with compassion towards your condition. Real desires are moving in His emotions for your freedom right now! God is not just waiting in heaven for you to figure things out by yourself; He's your leader, Husband, and Father. Jesus is in the trenches with you, and He's fully involved in your issues at the deepest level. Resist the lie that He's passive and disconnected from your problems, and trust that He's taking the initiative to bring you into freedom in each season.

Jesus is a jealous Bridegroom who wants every part of your heart freed up so that you can receive His affections and give Him all of yours. He's been tenderizing you and weakening the walls of lies in your heart as you've been growing in friendship with Him these past few months. Now Jesus wants to tear down the walls through deliverance. If you have felt unbelief around your deliverance or frustration over failed attempts to get free, break your agreement with unbelief out loud today and renew your hope in Jesus' desire and power to deliver you.

---

3   1 John 3:8.

INTRODUCTION TO SPIRITUAL STRONGHOLDS

For the weapons of our warfare are not carnal but mighty in God for pulling down strongholds, casting down arguments and every high thing that exalts itself against the knowledge of God, bringing every thought into captivity to the obedience of Christ.—2 Corinthians 10:4-5

What exactly are spiritual strongholds? In the natural, strongholds are fortresses or castles protected by thick and tall walls to keep out enemies. In the spiritual, strongholds are places in the soul and body where walls are built up to protect something. These strongholds are godly if they are walls of truth and righteousness, or these strongholds are demonically influenced if they are walls of sin and lies. In both cases, strongholds are built up through agreement with truth or lies.

GODLY STRONGHOLDS

Godly strongholds are built up brick by brick by meditating on the Bible and making righteous decisions day after day. As we grow in agreement with God's values and truths, godly strongholds are made stronger and become harder for the enemy to penetrate with lies or temptations. These strongholds create places in our minds and hearts for God to manifest and dwell in a greater experiential way.[4] God came to live in our spirit-man the day we gave our lives to Him, but He inhabits places in our minds and hearts when we grow in agreement with truth and righteousness over time.

---

4   John 14:21, 23; Ephesians 3:17.

DEMONIC STRONGHOLDS

"Be angry, and do not sin": Do not let the sun go down on your wrath, nor give place to the devil.—Ephesians 4:26-27

When an unclean spirit goes out of a man, he goes through dry places, seeking rest and finds none.—Matthew 12:43

Demonic strongholds are built up by agreeing with sin and lies day after day. In reality, a stronghold can begin with agreeing with a lie or participating in a sin a few times. From there, it can build on itself into something larger. If we grow in agreement with a sin or a lie, we allow that stronghold to get taller and stronger. Agreement with darkness gives legal access to demons to dwell in those places of the heart and mind and demonically energize sins and lies. Demonic strongholds create supernatural barriers that block the truth from truly entering the heart, and they darken thoughts and emotions. Demons are looking for places to live, and they want to destroy people, so they do everything in their power to create strongholds or homes for themselves in humans.[5] In Ephesians 4, Paul warned believers not to "give place" to the devil, which is the same word in Matthew 12:43 when demons are seeking rest in dry "places."

If God perhaps will grant them repentance, so that they may know the truth, and that they may come to their senses and escape the snare of the devil, having been taken captive by him to do his will.—2 Timothy 2:25-26

---

5   Matthew 12:43-45.

Demonic strongholds are torn down brick by brick by agreeing with God through confession, repentance, forgiveness, and Biblical meditation. These spiritual means are a huge part of "renewing the spirit of our minds."[6] Deliverance prayer times help tear down bricks because they are focused on agreeing with God and breaking agreement with lies and sins through confession and repentance.

ADDRESSING DEMONS IS NECESSARY

As they went out, behold, they brought to Him a man, mute and demon-possessed. And when the demon was cast out, the mute spoke.—Matthew 9:32-33

Then they came to Jesus, and saw the one who had been demon-possessed and had the legion, sitting and clothed and in his right mind. And they were afraid.—Mark 5:15

To get victory over demonic strongholds, you must deal with the stronghold and the demon behind any lie or sin pattern through repentance, forgiveness, and agreement with truth. Though not all the time, demons can block or be the source of physical, emotional, or mental illnesses.[7] Therefore, spiritual hindrances must be addressed in spiritual ways. Because of this principle, self-help methods and counseling methods that don't include the spiritual methods aren't very effective.

I don't believe the world's solutions to human problems can offer deep freedom through non-spiritual means. God has established the spiritual realm in such a way that there must be a spiritual transaction (repentance, forgiveness, casting

---

6 Ephesians 4:23.

7 Luke 13:10-16; Mark 9:17; Matthew 9:33, 12:22.

out demons, agreement with truth) with Him to deal with a pattern that is rooted in spiritual things. Demons don't leave until the stronghold is torn down, and ungodly patterns don't stop until the demon is cast out, so why pursue methods that don't first address the root cause? The world mostly offers coping methods to deal with brokenness, but Jesus has a supernatural solution.

SPIRIT, SOUL, AND BODY

May your whole spirit, soul, and body be preserved blameless at the coming of our Lord Jesus Christ.—1 Thessalonians 5:23

For the flesh lusts against the Spirit, and the Spirit against the flesh; and these are contrary to one another, so that you do not do the things that you wish. —Galatians 5:17

Christians can have demonic strongholds in their souls (thoughts, emotions, will) and physical bodies (physical appetites and physical health) but not in their spirit-man.[8] Some people don't believe that Christians can have a demonic presence in them because they believe that the Holy Spirit completely possesses them after salvation. After salvation, the Holy Spirit resurrects our spirit-man and then lives in him. But our souls and bodies are not changed at salvation; the Holy Spirit progressively renews them as we participate with God in growing in revelation and character, which is called sanctification.

Our bodies have supernatural access to the Holy Spirit's life for divine healing and conquering physical lusts and urges. However, the fullness of salvation will

---

8   Romans 7:23; James 1:14-15.

not come to our bodies until we receive our glorified bodies at Jesus' return.[9] A common way of communicating this principle is that our spirits are saved, our souls are being saved, and our bodies will be saved.

> *But if you have bitter envy and self-seeking in your hearts, do not boast and lie against the truth. This wisdom does not descend from above, but is earthly, sensual, demonic. For where envy and self-seeking exist, confusion and every evil thing are there.*—James 3:14-16

Our souls and bodies are open to demonic influence and strongholds because of our salvation's progressive and future nature. This means that you can still engage with lies or sins and open doors to demonic influence even after being a Christian. Therefore, you need Jesus to heal and deliver you from past lies and sins and any demonic strongholds that have been created because of demonic influence.

LEVELS OF DEMONIC INFLUENCE

There are varying levels of demonic influence within the category of demonic strongholds. These levels are important to understand and identify so that you can deal with strongholds properly. Understanding the idea that there are levels of demonic influence also removes the idea that someone with a demon is automatically fully possessed by a demon.

LEVEL #1 – ATTACK/ACCUSATION

Every believer has to resist momentary accusations or temptations from the demonic realm at times. This shouldn't be a constant reality throughout the day.

---

9   Romans 8:23.

The amount that it happens and the amount that it moves us depends on our spiritual maturity in Christ. Satan accuses the church night and day to get us to agree with his lies so that demons can build strongholds.[10] The enemy can also attack by causing circumstances to flare up, stirring up relational conflict (usually through accusation), releasing physical heaviness, tempting us to lust, and stirring up our emotions in a heightened way. As believers, we're called to resist and quench these "fiery darts of the wicked one."[11]

LEVEL #2 – OPPRESSION

In my opinion, there are many levels of oppression, and most deliverance needs would fall into this category. I believe most Christians have some level of oppression they could address. Oppression is a heightened measure of demonic influence that is consistently experienced in specific areas (thoughts, emotions, behavior, physical symptoms) due to spiritual strongholds. We still choose to think, feel, and do negative things out of our free will, but the enemy adds supernatural energy to those areas in the moment and helps to keep us in ungodly cycles.

Oppression is different from attack because there is some level of agreement at the heart level with the lies or accusations, and it manifests in the way a person behaves or thinks. An oppressed person experiences the same temptations with heightened urges and accusations (or overwhelming negative emotions) that seem hard to break out of on a near-daily basis. In these moments, they almost always give way to them. Example temptations, accusations, and overwhelming

---

10 Revelation 12:10.

11 Ephesians 6:16; 2 Corinthians 12:7.

emotions could be fear, rejection, shame, loneliness, confusion, anxiety, bitterness, levels of panic attack, anger, addictions, and lustful or perverted sexual desires.

LEVEL #3 – HINDERED

This level of demonic influence is a severe level of demonic influence and is stronger and more consistent than the oppression levels. People in this category feel tormented by dark thoughts, heavy emotions, or perverted desires. They also struggle to spend time with God due to experiencing intense accusation in their hearts and feel powerless in battling a sin or lie and have little to no hope to overcome it. People in this category find it hard to sustain normal living because they are severely "hindered" in one ore more ways.

LEVEL #4 – DOMINATION (POSSESSION)

Christians cannot be dominated by or possessed by a demon because it requires a very deep level of agreement. Domination means that the demon has an extremely high level of control over a person. Some people use the term "domination" instead of possession because it communicates the feeling of being overwhelmed by a demon while still having a free will. It is common for Christians who are newer to the deliverance topic to assume everyone with a demonic stronghold is possessed, but this isn't the case, and it leads to many misunderstandings and unnecessary fears.[12]

---

12 Matthew 17:14-18; Luke 4:33-35, 8:27-33.

DISCERNING STRONGHOLDS

#1 - OBSERVE PATTERNS

There are several ways to determine if you have some level of a stronghold in your life. The first way is to take an honest look at your life and write down any lies, negative emotions, or sins that you struggle with on a daily or weekly basis. What lies do you struggle with consistently? What triggers you into an emotional swirl, and when does it usually happen? What sin do you act out consistently?

Let the following physical description help you to identify strongholds that you may not be aware of. My dad uses the language of "emotional bruises" when talking about identifying personal strongholds. Physical bruises are very sensitive to the touch, and they hurt a lot if someone bumps into them. The level of pain associated with being bumped by someone doesn't make sense in the moment, but it makes sense if you understand that there is trauma deep in your tissue. Emotional bruises are similar in that they're caused by something in your past and create a deep wound that needs healing. That past wound can be "bumped" by people or circumstances around you and cause an illogical amount of emotional pain. The emotional pain or swirl of accusation isn't necessarily the fault of the person or the circumstance in front of you; it's the result of the past wound that wasn't healed.

You can also ask close family and friends what they see in your life. You may not identify some patterns because they have become normal to you, but others have an outside and possibly clearer perspective than you do, which can be helpful. They can see your sins towards others or themselves, see unhealthy patterns of living, and they can hear you speak out lies that you believe. Going back to the bruise analogy, you naturally protect your emotional bruises from being "hit by others or circumstances" by arranging or orienting your life in certain ways. Those around you might be able to see your bruises and how you're protecting them.

#2 – ASK GOD

The second way to discern strongholds is to take a prayer time to ask the Holy Spirit if you have a stronghold. He will bring a word to mind, an image, or an overall awareness of an issue with memories of when you fall into the pattern. Ask the Holy Spirit questions about what He brings to mind to get further clarity on the heart issue.

#3 – EXAMPLE STRONGHOLDS

The third way to discern a possible stronghold is to review a list like the one below to see if you identify with any of them. If you know you struggle with something on this list, take time to ask God for clarity about how and when it affects you. Here is an example stronghold list:

1. Fear
2. Anxiety (stress, worry, panic attacks)
3. Passivity/laziness
4. Unbelief
5. Unforgiveness/bitterness
6. Legalistic
7. Control/manipulation
8. Pride/arrogance
9. Self-hatred (personality, gifting, body)

10. Anger

11. Rejection

12. Abandonment/orphan spirit

13. Sexual perversion (past or current pattern)

14. Occult practices/witchcraft/drug use

15. Traumas

16. Heaviness/depression

17. Fear of death

18. Jealousy

19. Lying

20. Spirit of infirmity (sickness)

EVIDENCE OF BROKEN STRONGHOLDS

When a stronghold is addressed, and any level of demonic influence is removed, some immediate fruits are clarity of mind, increased godly desires (worship, righteousness), a sense of intimacy with God, and the ability to identify and resist old patterns. Strongholds and demons are supernatural and have a real impact on the human heart, so when they're broken, there should be a supernatural relief from the darkness and an increase of God's felt presence. I say this to help you realize that you're in a spiritual battle, to give you hope to address the strongholds, and encourage you that deliverance prayer times can be intimate and joyful times with God.

I see these fruits in those I lead through deliverance prayer, but I've also experienced them myself when I've received prayer. In my first deliverance prayer time, I received freedom from a spirit of anger. As I asked God to highlight an issue to address, He brought the word "anger" to mind three times, so my friends and I asked Him to reveal the root sins or memories connected to anger. Each time He brought up a memory of me acting out in anger, I repented and felt something loosening from my heart. As I repented of the last memory and rebuked the demon, I felt something lift off me and felt an increased peace and God's presence come upon me. After that day, I was better able to recognize the past anger patterns and resist them. I was more patient, and I felt more empowered to resist or healthily process anger when it arose instead of it overtaking me.

In another scenario, I prayed for a person who was addicted to drugs, alcohol, and cigarettes who experienced these same fruits after prayer. In our prayer time, God highlighted trauma and unforgiveness as sources of his addictions. As he forgave each person by name and repented of believing specific lies, we all felt darkness leave and God's presence come. The person felt such a release that he sat for several minutes breathing in peace and then laughing in joy. At the end, he began to weep and praise Jesus out of gratitude. As a fruit of addressing strongholds and demonic influence, this person never struggled with his addictions again in the four years that I knew him. He even went on to go through Bible school and thrive in the midst of hard life circumstances.

These supernatural moments are your portion, too. God is near you, and He has the supernatural power to deliver you from any issue you've struggled with. He's overseeing your deliverance, and He wants all your heart freed up to receive His love and give Him your love.

WEEKLY ASSIGNMENT

As an assignment response to this chapter, take at least 30 minutes in a prayer time this week to ask God for clarity in identifying which strongholds He's wanting you to address right now. Using the three suggested ways to identifying strongholds in the chapter, write down your own observations of broken patterns in your life. Write down the thoughts, images, memories, and emotions God brings to mind. Included in this, ask God about the heart issue you've been praying about and discussing since the beginning of the program. What you sense from the Lord in this prayer time will be the prayer agenda for your deliverance prayer sessions throughout this module.

DISCIPLESHIP MEETING GUIDE
MODULE 5: DELIVERANCE – CHAPTER 20

MEETING FOCUS:

The purpose of this meeting is to discuss the topic of spiritual strongholds and prepare for the deliverance prayer sessions of this module.

DISCUSSION QUESTIONS (IN ORDER OF IMPORTANCE):

1. *Chapter Questions:*
   a. Chapter 20 – Discuss any journaled thoughts and questions from the chapter.
   b. Identifying Strongholds assignment - In-depth, share how your prayer time went and what you sensed God revealing to you about your strongholds. We will focus praying through these strongholds in the deliverance prayer times this month.

2. *Spiritual Pursuits:*
   a. Practically, how is your prayer schedule going? How many days have you walked out your prayer schedule? Do you need to make small changes to your schedule? How are your Bible study, meditation, prayer list, and tongues times going, and how is God impacting you through them?
   b. Briefly review your new *Spiritual Pursuits Document.*

3. Briefly review next week's homework together. Decide when your first deliverance session will be and what needs to be done before in preparation for it.

MEETING NOTES:

_____

_____

_____

_____

_____

_____

_____

_____

_____

_____

21

DELIVERANCE GUIDE

(WRITTEN BY BETHANY MOOTZ)

▍INTRODUCTION

This chapter is a practical guide to praying through strongholds with a Biblical approach (confession, repentance, and forgiveness). The practical steps and values are very similar to most inner-healing and deliverance models. After reading it, you should understand the basic flow of what a prayer time can look like, how God will speak, and how you can respond to His leading. More training and experience will always be helpful, but the simple truths of this guide are substantial enough to equip you to begin receiving and facilitating basic prayer times. These tools are designed to be used with one or two people praying over another person, but they will also help you pray through strongholds in your own prayer times moving forward.

As you read through what a deliverance prayer time can look like and consider your own deliverance sessions in this module, understand that they are intimate and presence-filled times with Jesus. You will encounter the Psalm 139 God who, in delight and desire, searches and knows your every detail and reveals His thoughts towards you in the smallest of moments of your past. Jesus never brings fear, shame, or condemnation in these prayer times. He only brings clarity, love, comfort, and forgiveness.

SPIRITUAL OPEN DOORS

Let us lay aside every weight, and the sin which so easily ensnares us, and let us run with endurance the race that is set before us, looking unto Jesus, the author and finisher of our faith, who for the joy that was set before Him endured the cross.—Hebrews 12: 1-2

Through the grace of the cross, Jesus has forgiven and empowered you to run your spiritual race. Running your grace-empowered race includes choosing to lay aside everything that hinders you. Hebrews 12 says to throw off "weights" and "snares." Sins ensnare and are open doors to darkness. Weights are lifestyle choices, emotional wounds, or anything that weighs you down while running your race. What areas of your life do you need to lay aside or throw off so that you can run with endurance and joy?

Open doors give the demonic kingdom legal permission to influence us and occur when we agree with darkness or have in the past. Once opened, the enemy works to grow them into strongholds. Open doors remain open to the enemy's influence until we actively shut them through spiritual means.

Identifying open doors isn't a "witch hunt" or a systematic figuring out the names of demons you might have. Instead, it can be a lifestyle where it's a delight to ask God what hindrances He wants to highlight and free us from. It's an intimate conversation with Jesus our Bridegroom to bring forth greater freedom and love.

THREE OPEN DOORS TO DARKNESS

When you seek the Holy Spirit for clarity in your prayer times, there are three common areas that He will highlight to you as open doors to darkness.[1] Even though the open doors overlap, separating them helps deal with each open door in Biblical ways.

1. **Sins** you commit – unforgiveness/anger, involvement in sexual sins, occult (innocent or purposeful), viewing or listening to sinful entertainment, lying, covetousness, jealousy, anger, drunkenness, drug use, etc.

2. **Injustices** against you – physical, sexual, and emotional abuse, differing levels of emotional trauma, rejection, betrayal, etc. Injustices could also include things that were not done for you.

3. **Lies** you have agreed with – things people have told you, things you have believed on your own because of your circumstances or the worldly culture (rejection, abandonment, fears, self-hatred, etc.)

BIBLICAL RESPONSES TO OPEN DOORS

1. **Sins** you commit – respond by ***confessing the sin*** out loud and acknowledging it as a sin. ***Repent of the sin*** by praying out loud that you choose to turn away from the sin and war against it in God's grace. ***Ask for forgiveness*** from God.

---

1 Shelley Hundley, "Simplified Ministry Training—Praying for Deliverance and Healings," (Lecture Notes, International House of Prayer University, November 22, 2009).

2. **Injustices** against you – respond by ***forgiving others, God, and yourself.***

3. **Lies** you believe – respond by ***breaking agreement with each lie.*** Pray out loud that you reject the lies. Then break agreement with each lie specifically.

GOD'S CLEANSING TOUCH

As you respond to what God highlights, He responds to you! After you have confessed and received forgiveness in the prayer time, it's important to seek healing and cleansing from God for each open door. He wants to remove the darkness from your heart and replace it with truth, light, and His love. Expect to feel God's presence on your body and emotions as He washes the effects of sin and pain away. After prayer, your thoughts and emotions should feel freer and more peaceful because spiritual defilement will have been washed away. Defilement is a spiritual residue of darkness from sin and lies that rests on us and affects our thoughts and emotions until God washes it away.[2]

1. **Sins** you commit – He comes to cleanse you of defilement and forgive you. After confession, there is usually a feeling of being cleansed, forgiven, and embraced by God. ***Receive His forgiveness for your sins.***

2. **Injustices** against you – He comes to cleanse, bring comfort, remove pain, release inner healing, and restore what was stolen. After forgiving, there is usually a sense of hope and peace and a sense that God is with you. There can also be a sense of emotional relief as pain is released to God. ***Picture Him washing you and removing your pain.***

3. **Lies** you believe – He comes to cleanse you and build a stronghold of truth. While praying to hear His truth, you will hear God whisper

---

2   Matthew 15:11-20; 1 Corinthians 3:17; 8:17; Hebrews 12:15; James 3:6; Revelation 3:4.

His perspective over you and feel His heart towards you. ***Give God time to speak His truth over you, and write down whatever He speaks.***

SIMPLE DELIVERANCE MODEL

Before you begin your prayer time, pray and command every demon to submit to the Lordship of Jesus, "In the name of Jesus, we command every demon to submit to Jesus. We say that you will not manifest in this room or in our hearts in any way." Before you begin a deliverance time with others, remind everyone that demons should not talk or manifest in any way. If there is a demonic manifestation (fear, anxiety, shaking, nausea, sleepiness, confusion) during the time, stop and command every demon to submit to Jesus.

STEP #1 - ASK

Identify the symptom that you or someone you are praying with is dealing with. This can be done before or during the prayer session using the steps from the previous chapter. It's like going to the doctor; what are your symptoms, and what do you need freedom from (fear, anxiety, addictions, pornography, anger, etc.)? Take a few minutes to ask the Lord what issue He's highlighting. God will bring a thought or picture to mind communicating what you need to pray about. Other times He may communicate through an inner knowing, which is like a "gut feeling." Or you can begin with the clearest negative symptom you are aware of in your life.

STEP #2 – REVEAL

Alone or together, ask God to highlight any of the three open doors (sins, injustices, or lies) that are connected to the symptom you've identified. In detail, write down what you sense God highlighting. Take your time during the entire process. God could highlight a memory of a clear injustice, lie, or sin, or it could be a thought that seems random. I've learned that the first few thoughts are most likely God talking, even if it doesn't make sense initially.

In this highlighting time, ask the Lord to reveal the root memory or the first time you agreed with your specific issue, not necessarily all the times you've acted out in the particular issue. For example, if you deal with anger, you don't necessarily have to address it every time you've been angry. In a deliverance time, God will highlight the memories where the pattern of anger began (example: acting out in anger or injustice that caused anger) and where the spirit of anger was first given legal access.

STEP #3 – REPENT

Respond to each open door God highlights by slowly praying through them one at a time. We must break agreement (repent) and resist the enemy and then respond to what God highlights **by speaking these out loud:**

1. **Sins** you commit – respond by *confessing the sin* out loud and acknowledging it as a sin. *Repent of the sin* by praying out loud that you choose to turn away from it and war against it in God's grace. *Ask for forgiveness* from God.
2. **Injustices** against you – respond by *forgiving others, God, and yourself.*
3. **Lies** you believe – respond by *breaking agreement with each lie.* Pray out loud that you reject the lies and then break agreement with each lie specifically.

STEP #4 – PROPHESY TRUTH

This step always includes a cleansing from defilement and pain. The open door might be closed, but now it's time to receive His forgiveness and comfort. Now's the time to let Him come into your emotional pain, bring inner healing, and let Him speak His truth over you. He does this because He wants to begin building strongholds of truth in place of the torn down demonic strongholds.

The way to receive the truth is to ask God for His perspective about the memory you just prayed through. In these memories and hurts, ask God where He was, how He felt, and what He was doing and saying to you. Allow Him space to prophesy truth over you. Usually, it's best for the person receiving prayer to hear God and share it before the prayer leader shares what God speaks to him or her.

For example, after praying through a time in my life where I felt rejected, in my imagination I took time to watch Jesus come into the negative memory and show me where He was. It was like I was a little girl again, and I saw Him looking at me with love and holding me at that moment. He was completely and thoughtfully engaged and singing over me! The real memory's emotions were the exact opposite of this, but after I broke agreement with the lies and shut the open doors, I felt His love being deposited into that memory. I felt accepted, and I felt restored in my emotions.

If there isn't a tangible emotional feeling of love, peace, or joy from God, or if you don't feel Him speaking quite yet, go back to Step 2 and Step 3. Tangible experiences almost always happen when God has done a full work, so there could be more memories that need to be highlighted and prayed through. If the scheduled session doesn't give time for this, have the prayer session recipient go back through steps 2 and 3 by themselves and then schedule another deliverance session. It is normal to need multiple prayer sessions.

STEP #5 - REBUKE

After praying through each door (repenting and prophesying truth), take time to command every demon connected to the sin and lie patterns to leave the individual. Empower them to speak a prayer like this out loud, "In Jesus name, I command every demon connected to these lies and sins to leave my life. I close all spiritual doors, and I say no to these lies and sin patterns." I encourage you to speak this out at a normal volume and not to hype up the moment. Your authority to cast out demons comes from Jesus' Kingship, not the loudness of your voice. Rebuking in a calm way magnifies Jesus' authority, diminishes the perception of demonic control, and teaches all those involved in the prayer time how to be supernaturally natural.

Rebuke after all doors are closed – Rebuking demons should only be done after you have responded to all the things God highlights pertaining to the one issue you're praying about. When it seems like God has stopped highlighting things, and the person receiving prayer has been feeling freedom in the prayer time, rebuke the demon. It's possible that demons leave when things are repented of, but it's still good to rebuke them out loud at the end. Demons must leave when all the legal doors have been closed and are commanded to leave the property. If there are still legal doors to close, the demons have a legal right to stay, so casting them out too early will be less effective.

What it feels like – When a demon is cast out, there should not be any demonic manifestations (shaking, vomiting, coughing, nausea, choking, fear). This is a helpful expectation to communicate to the person receiving prayer so that they are not worried about or waiting for a demonic manifestation as a sign of deliverance. If there is a demonic manifestation at any point in the deliverance process, stop and command every demon to submit to Jesus. When demons leave, there will usually be an obvious experience of God's presence, a feeling of heaviness or cloudiness lifting off the person, and a feeling of emotional and mental peace and stillness. It is even common for people to cry or praise Jesus out of relief and gratitude.

FORGIVENESS

Forgiveness is a very important part of pursuing freedom because so many dark things are wrapped up in unforgiveness or are the fruit of unforgiveness (bitterness, anger, control). When forgiveness is released, the foundations of demonic strongholds crumble and emotions become free. It is so simple but so powerful in deliverance prayer times.

First of all, forgiveness is a command from Jesus, not an option.[3] His eternal nature is to forgive, and the foundation of the gospel message is forgiveness. He delights in showing mercy and forgiving thousands of times, and He wants us to be like Him and experience the freedom of being merciful.[4] Everything that you have done to others or others have done to you can be forgiven.

Forgiveness is an acknowledgment of wrong things that have been to you.[5] When God highlights an issue to forgive in your prayer times, you should not minimize or dismiss it. Pray something like this, "Father, I acknowledge that this person wronged me (say what they did) and that it affected me." Forgiveness is also entrusting God to release justice to the person that wronged you and to the

---

3   Mark 11:25-26.

4   Matthew 18:21-22; Micah 7:18.

5   R.T. Kendall, *Total Forgiveness—Revised and Updated*, (Lake Mary, FL: Charisma House, 2007), 23-24.

broken situation in His timing.[6] This releases your right to bring vengeance or collect the practical or emotional "debt" that is owed you.

Forgiveness allows for pain, anger, and other things to be released to God so He can fill your heart with His life. Pray something like this, "Father, I entrust You to judge this person and this situation in Your timing and in Your way. I release all rights to bring vengeance upon this person and this situation, and I release all the pain and anger to You. I completely forgive them for their debt to me."

For more severe situations, forgiveness does not mean that you have to be friends with someone who's hurt you.[7] Once you have forgiven, you will be able to set godly boundaries with those who have hurt you and still aren't safe. In certain situations, this takes time to figure out with the counsel of others outside the situation. In God's healing power, you will grow in compassion for them and pray for them without having to relate with them.

CONFESSION

Confess your trespasses to one another, and pray for one another, that you may be healed.—James 5:16

If we confess our sins, He is faithful and just to forgive us our sins and to cleanse us from all unrighteousness.—1 John 1:9

---

6 Romans 12:19.

7 Ibid., 5.

Similar to forgiveness, confession and repentance are important parts of pursuing freedom. Confession and repentance are God's ordained way of restoring fellowship with Him, closing spiritual doors to darkness, and removing spiritual defilement. It's important to understand what these are and how to pray them during your deliverance sessions. This is also helpful in your daily walk with God.

Confession is acknowledging and taking responsibility for personal sin before God in order to restore fellowship with Him. Our sins don't cut us off from our relationship with God, and our confession doesn't earn right relationship with God. However, they do restore intimate fellowship with God. Like any human relationship where there's been sin, confession brings healing by acknowledging the relational hurt and dealing with it. When you sin, you're in disagreement with God. When you confess sin, you come back into agreement with God and can relate to Him with an open heart.

An overall legal forgiveness was applied to your life by the blood of Jesus at your salvation experience, but small relational forgiveness throughout your life between you and God is applied when you confess to Him. When confession happens, God washes away the spiritual defilement that rested on your thoughts and emotions as a result of your sin and renews a sense of intimacy with Him. I believe this is the tangible "cleansing from unrighteousness" that is described in 1 John 1:9.

When confessing sin to God or others, don't minimize or explain it away. Also, don't try to make it bigger than it is to prove you're sorry. Simply say what you did without explanation and own it before God. Pray something like this, "Father, I confess (say in detail) what I did as a sin against You. I ask You to forgive me of my sin and wash away all spiritual defilement from the sin."

REPENTANCE

Repentance is the turning of your heart towards God and away from darkness (sins or lies). At the heart level, repentance is a choice to love and agree with God with all your being. You can set your heart and shift your affections towards God, His truth, and His righteousness through repentance. Repentance is powerful because it breaks spiritual agreement with darkness and aligns your inner man with God's kingdom. I picture repentance as choosing to get out of a fleshly river with its strong current and getting into the Spirit's river with its strong current. Repentance positions you to walk in the current (the power) of the Spirit a little more each time you make the choice.

Repentance follows confession because you commit to pursuing loving obedience in the area that you confess to God as a sin or lie. Pray something like this, "Father, I turn away from my sin (speak out your sin), and I turn my heart towards You. I set my heart to walk in obedience in this area with Your help. I set my heart to war against this sin with Your help."

For thus says the High and Lofty One… I dwell in the high and holy place, with him who has a contrite and humble spirit, to revive the spirit of the humble, and to revive the heart of the contrite ones.—Isaiah 57:15

Jesus is tender, and a gentleman, and will never force you to "give up" or repent of anything that you want to hold onto. But if you are done holding on to sin or pain or darkness, He is willing and able to free you. Notice here I didn't say that you have to be 100% brave and 100% free from fear going into a prayer time to get freedom; you just have to have a willing heart and say yes to Him in your weakness.

This is a bold statement, but it's been true, I have never seen someone who is hungry and humble not experience deliverance and inner healing. The few who haven't received deliverance in a prayer time weren't interested in repenting of the sins God highlighted; therefore, God couldn't set them free. Choosing to repent of sin is necessary, and when someone isn't willing to repent, the deliverance session should stop because there's no way forward until they are willing.[8]

 ## PERSONAL TESTIMONIES

When I (Bethany) was in Bible school, I heard about deliverance and experienced my first prayer session. I went into my deliverance time prepared with a list of what God highlighted to me. The patterns were that I felt shut down in front of most people and had uneasy emotions when I was with people because I was fearful of their opinions about me. I spoke and thought negatively about my personality and body.

During my deliverance session, the prayer team and I brought these symptoms to God one by one, asking Him to highlight the time each of them began. As we did this, I suddenly remembered a few things that had been said or done to me in my past. At least three memories came up during our prayer time.

The first memory was when I was 18 months old. Because of respiratory sickness, I was placed in a plastic tent for about twenty-four hours without being held or comforted. I didn't remember that experience affecting me emotionally,

---

8   Pablo Bottari, *Free in Christ—Your Complete Handbook on the Ministry of Deliverance*. (Lake Mary, FL: Charisma House, 1999), 109.

but it seemed like God wanted to bring comfort to my heart and show me where He was when I didn't know what was going on. When the leaders led me through a prayer of asking God where He was in that hospital room, God showed me a picture of Him coming close to me in the tent. He watched me and held me when no one else was allowed to. What He communicated to me with that picture took that negative memory and filled it with comfort and peace.

The second memory was the day my little brother was born, and I was sad, confused, and scared about seeing my mom on the hospital bed. In the memory, God comforted my adult heart with the truth that He had seen and ministered to me at that young age and that He (and my parents!) were there when I felt scared and alone. I broke agreement with fear and rejection and every scheme of the enemy that began at the time of those memories. During that prayer time, the fears of rejection, of my mom dying, and the fear of being replaced by my brother were all healed.

The third memory was when I was five years old, and someone said a few negative words about my body. It was a comment I and others joked about for many years. After I told everyone in the prayer time the memory, I started crying! Then I was embarrassed because it seemed too small to make me cry, so it all caught me off guard. I had to acknowledge that it was a painful comment that did affect me. I broke agreement with the negative comments, forgave the person that said it, and asked God for the truth of what He thought about me and my body. God truly ministered to my heart in the process. Afterwards, my thoughts and emotions felt freer as God told me He saw me, cared about me, and loved me for all that I was. I no longer felt uneasy in my emotions in front of people, and negative thoughts about my personality and body no longer plagued me.

WEEKLY ASSIGNMENT

For the next three weeks, you will receive deliverance prayer. You can receive prayer from your Discipleship Mentor or a local ministry that is experienced in deliverance prayer similar to what is described in this chapter. If necessary, one international ministry I recommend utilizing is Bethel Church's Sozo ministry that has a long track record of praying through deliverance and training people. They have a global network of trained leaders that might be in your region. If you haven't already, schedule a 2-hour deliverance prayer session for each of the next three weeks.

LEADERS DELIVERANCE GUIDE

The following steps seek to bring freedom to people in a compassionate way. We desire to reflect the love of Jesus in how we pray, minimizing pain, discomfort, and shame while also addressing the roots of the bondage, which enables the individual to remain free. The prayer time reinforces the authority that the individual has in Christ—we simply agree and partner with them as they arise in the authority Jesus has given.

When you are in the actual prayer time, keep a piece of paper out to take notes. When God highlights a memory to the person, write it down. Next, write down the sins, lies, or injustices that are highlighted within the memory. Give space in between each memory so that you can thoroughly pray through steps three and four until there are measures of breakthrough.

STEP #1 – ASK – DISCUSS THE PERSON'S PRAYER NEEDS.

A. Locate the symptom(s) that the person is dealing with and wants to be free of. Allow the person to set the tone for what God is doing in them. They can get clarity on this prior to the prayer time. Ask, "What are your symptoms? What do you need freedom from?"

B. **Prayer** – Before you begin to pray through the symptom, calmly command every spirit to submit to the Lordship of Jesus. *"In the name of Jesus, we command every demon to submit to Jesus. We say that you will not manifest in this room or in our hearts in any way."* Pray for God to increase in the room and have the person receiving prayer pray out their desires for the session.

STEP #2 - REVEAL - ALLOW GOD TO REVEAL AREAS OF OPPRESSION.

A. In prayer together, ask the Spirit to highlight to them: any of the 3 open doors connected to the symptoms.
1. **Sins** they have committed or responses to the abuse, etc.
2. **Injustices** that they need healing from in order to get free.
3. **Lies** they have believed and agreement they have had with the enemy.

B. Pray until they have thoughts, or a memory connected to their symptoms. Ask them if the Lord said anything or if thoughts are coming to their mind. Take notes and write down what they say and if you sense God highlighting anything. Closer to the end of this step, you can humbly and loosely submit anything you received to them, but let the person confirm or deny what you suggest, and mostly rely on them hearing God.

C. If a few memories were highlighted, begin with the one that either had the most emotion on it, the one they want to begin with, or simply the earliest memory in their life.

STEP #3 - REPENT - BREAK AGREEMENT WITH DARKNESS.

A. **Confess/Repent of any sins** they committed that were highlighted – Have them pray or lead them in prayer and repent and ask God's forgiveness for sins they have done.

B. **Break agreement with lies** – Allow Him to guide them in turning away from lies. If it's not apparent, ask the Holy Spirit what are the lies they have been believing? And wait until they hear from Him. After lies are located, they can pray to break agreement with the lie themselves, but some might need help doing this.

C. **Forgive from the heart** – Forgive the people involved, themselves, and God. Help them if they are struggling and keep it simple. Don't rush into forgiveness if you sense they are first needing to be comforted by God in the memory. Sometimes it is helpful to ask God where He was before forgiving, so they can feel God's ministry and comfort and safety.

D. **Break agreement with demons** – Have them verbally renounce their agreement with the demonic oppression associated with their symptoms by having them speak something like this: *"In the name of Jesus, I break my agreement with all demons connected to these lies and sins in my life. I close all spiritual doors, and I say no to these lies and sin patterns."*

STEP #4 – PROPHESY TRUTH – ALLOW GOD TO SPEAK HIS TRUTH INTO THEIR MEMORIES.

A. **Pray for Healing** – Pray for the person to receive healing from the effects of sins committed against them and forgiveness and healing for the effects of the sins they have committed—inviting God to come into every area.

B. **God's Response** – Ask God to come with forgiveness and comfort, let Him remove and come into emotional pain, bring inner healing, and speak His truth. ***Note**: Inner healing will occur over time so don't feel pressure to get His full perspective over them. You cannot cast out pain, so help them direct their loss, grief, and pain to Jesus.*

1. Ask God to let the person see how He felt/feels for them. Allow space for Him to speak/prophesy over the person and do what He needs to. Pray for Him to speak, then wait so that person can hear.

2. Usually, if the person cannot hear from God there might be more doors to shut. If there feels like a block or a wall where the person cannot hear God's perspective, stop and ask God together what is hindering the person from receiving truth.

3. If there isn't a tangible emotional feeling of love, peace, or joy from Him, or if they don't feel Him speaking quite yet, go back to Step 2 and Step 3. If nothing is tangible, there could be more open doors that need to be highlighted and opposed. If this session doesn't give time for this, have the individual do this in their personal prayer life and/or schedule another deliverance session.

4. If there is time, pray through other highlighted open doors and do Step 3 and 4 again.

STEP #5 – REBUKE – COMMAND THE DEMONS TO LEAVE.

A. **Rebuke after all doors are closed** – Rebuking and casting out a demon should only be done after they have responded to all the things God highlights. When it seems like God has stopped highlighting things, and the person receiving prayer has been feeling freedom in the prayer time, rebuke the demon. Demons have to leave when all the legal doors have been closed and they are commanded to leave the property. If there are still legal doors to close, the demons have a legal right to stay, so casting them out too early will be less effective.

B. **What it feels like** – When a demon is cast out, there should not be any demonic manifestations (shaking, vomiting, coughing, nausea, choking, fear). If there is, command every spirit to be bound again. When demons leave, there is usually an experience of God's presence, a feeling of heaviness lifting off, and an emotional peace. The person may cry or feel the desire to worship Jesus out of relief and gratitude.

C. **End prayer session** – Once you feel like things are finished within the highlighted open doors, you can have all leaders pray, prophesy over, and bless the person. End the session by thanking God for what was done. Take appropriate notes in order to pick back up where you left off for their potential next deliverance session.

D. **Spiritual Plan** – Help them make a plan to get rid of anything connected to their sins–items used in occult worship, drugs, pornography, and other sin patterns. They should also commit to continuing their prayer schedule, meditating on appropriate Bible passages to counteract the lies they are struggling with, and staying in a community of believers.

22

WALKING OUT FREEDOM: PRAYER

(WRITTEN BY BETHANY MOOTZ)

AFTER PRAYER MINISTRY

After receiving deliverance prayer, there are several things to be aware of to maintain your new freedoms and build up godly strongholds. This includes understanding demonic strategies, continuing the lifestyle of praying through heart issues, and making life changes as a response to the things you've been freed from. Maintaining freedom also consists of building up godly strongholds through prayer and growing in community and accountability in your local church.

RESIST DISCOURAGEMENT

Being confident of this very thing, that He who has begun a good work in you will complete it until the day of Jesus Christ.—Philippians 1:6

After a deliverance session, it will be common for you to be more aware of the heart issues that God's been highlighting. You might feel like the issue is still there, is partly gone, or completely removed. Either way, don't be discouraged! Thank God for what He has done and stay with the process for more freedom. God can break down thick walls in a two-hour prayer time, but pursuing freedom includes setting up multiple prayer sessions, living out a lifestyle of prayer and meditation in an intentional godly community.

For a righteous man may fall seven times and rise again, But the wicked shall fall by calamity.—Proverbs 24:16

Building up a godly stronghold to replace any stronghold of lies takes time. God delights in the process and so can you! Give yourself the grace to be weak; not being passive in addressing your heart issues but understanding you might stumble in the process. There's grace to stumble, and there's grace to get up again and again unto victory. Within the journey, let God lavish His love on you. He wants to be close, and you shouldn't push Him away because you think you aren't clean enough. In the humility of receiving God's joy in the maturing process, you can enjoy His nearness and surrender to His radical love.

INTERNAL STRONGHOLD VS. EXTERNAL ATTACK

There is a difference between an outside demonic attack versus an internal stronghold of lies. In general, external attacks are less powerful, less frequent, and easier to discern as demonic than internal strongholds. God's way to deal with external attacks is to acknowledge, confess, and rebuke the lies you are feeling to God and the people in your life. Repent of anything needed. As you break off the lies, position yourself to receive God's supernatural life into your heart to help you.

If you are having to rebuke the same lie or resist the same level of sin day after day, this could be a clue that you are still dealing with an internal stronghold of lies, which means that somewhere you have agreed with this lie and the demon has authority to lie to you. These consistent lies need to be addressed and prayed through to complete the deliverance.

DELIVERANCE LIFESTYLE

Receiving deliverance prayer from a group is really helpful because of the family dynamic in the Spirit, but we want you to be empowered to pray through things in your alone times as a lifestyle. A simple way to begin this is to have a certain day each week or month where you ask God, "Where and what do I need alignment in?" In these times, God will highlight sins that need to be repented of, new or old lies that you've been believing again, and places where you've been hurt and need to release forgiveness.

Your heart will increase in health if you keep talking to Jesus about your hurts and issues. If praying about this weekly sounds too overwhelming, start with once every one to two months. Set a reminder on your phone, and take one hour to align your heart, repent, confess, forgive, and recommit to what God desires you to be like. These "alignment days" are my favorite because Jesus always ministers to my heart in a refreshing and healing way.

As an example, in one of these alignment times, God highlighted multiple people to forgive. I slowly forgave each person in each circumstance until I felt pain, anger, and unforgiveness lift from my emotions. As my heart experienced freedom, I connected to God's love and compassion for them and started praying blessings over them and our friendships.

In my life, God has tenderly and intimately highlighted things that need to be addressed through confession and repentance. It's a good feeling when He asks me to consider where I am wrong or who I need to forgive in certain situations. I have learned that His correction is His Fatherly love, and that it makes me grow. Moving forward, God wants you to have the perspective that He cares for you and will keep you in alignment with His heart as a tender Father.

BUILDING UP GODLY STRONGHOLDS

You can maintain your freedom and grow in freedom by building godly strongholds. After tearing down demonic strongholds, Jesus wants to build up a strong fortress of truth inside of you. Building these godly strongholds takes time, but you can partner with Jesus to accelerate the process. If you focus on the Word as your spiritual weapon and utilize what you've learned about prayer in the past modules, the fruit of your deliverance prayer sessions will be multiplied.

PRACTICAL CHANGES

Therefore do not let sin reign in your mortal body, that you should obey it in its lusts. And do not present your members as unrighteousness to sin. —Romans 6:12-13

If your right eye causes you to sin, pluck it out and cast it from you; for it is more profitable for you that one of your members perish, than for your whole body to be cast into hell. And if your right hand causes you to sin, cut it off and cast it from you; for it is more profitable for you that one of your members perish, than for your whole body to be cast into hell.—Matthew 5:29-30

If you have a weakness in your life, it will benefit you to get rid of the things that trip you up in that area. In conversation with Jesus, consider each broken pattern you prayed through in your deliverance sessions and ask God what stumbling blocks you can get rid of. God admires and encourages you to use godly violence or aggressiveness in removing the hindrances in your life.

Jesus' advice to pluck out eyes and cut off hands applies to perversion and adultery but also to every area of temptation, whether lies or sins. Yes, if you tend to look at things on your phone that you shouldn't, get rid of it at all costs. But if you waste hours viewing "innocent" things, consider ending your subscriptions and setting up godly boundaries in your life. If you tend to say or think ungodly things around certain people, consider changing friends. Some changes can seem severe or too hard, but Jesus' exhortation implies costliness and challenge. However, in the costliness of change, know that the pleasures and freedoms you will experience in the Lord will far surpass what you lay down.

> *Do not be deceived, God is not mocked; for whatever a man sows, that he will also reap. For he who sows to his flesh will of the flesh reap corruption, but he who sows to the Spirit will of the Spirit reap everlasting life. And let us not grow weary while doing good, for in due season we shall reap if we do not lose heart.—Galatians 6:7-9*

In Galatians 6, Paul describes the principle of sowing and reaping that gives insight into your spiritual life. Whatever a man sows in his daily life, he will reap in the next season. This means your current spiritual and emotional life are the fruit of what you sowed during your previous season. The confronting reality of Galatians is that nothing is neutral. We're either sowing seeds towards spiritual fruit or fleshly fruit through each day with our lifestyle choices and thoughts. This is probably why Paul said to take "every" thought captive because every thought is a seed and has future impact if allowed to grow.[1]

Within this sowing and reaping principle, seemingly small or "innocent" non-sinful things can be subtle seeds towards the growth of your flesh. Likewise, small lifestyle choices towards God will multiply a harvest of freedom and godliness. As you make life changes to sow into your spiritual freedom, heed the exhortation of Galatians 6:9, "*let us not grow weary while doing good, for in due season we shall reap if we do not lose heart.*"

Are you reaping negative fleshly things you've sown? Are you depressed? Bored? Dissatisfied? Anxious? Angry? Discontent? Or are you "reaping" God's peace and life on a day-to-day basis by "sowing" prayer, fasting, meditation, and time in the Word, cultivating friendships with other believers, and denying your flesh? It is worth intentionally changing your lifestyle to walk and sow in the Spirit, and it will greatly benefit you because these are the things that build up godly strongholds.

SATISFACTION IN PRAYER

As with any relationship, consistent time with God keeps you grounded and connected to His heart. Disconnection with God is the enemy of continued freedom. If you need power from an electrical outlet, you have to stay engaged or connected to the electric outlet to get the power consistently. Likewise, your daily prayer times with Jesus are how you plug into the power outlet of God. Now, more than ever, it is important to keep your prayer schedule, to engage at a heart level with Jesus (not just a checklist mentality) and hear Him speak His love into you.

---

1 2 Corinthians 10:5.

A major part of getting and maintaining freedom is experiencing satisfaction and fascination in God's presence. Many sins and broken patterns are healed just by finding satisfaction in God because many areas of brokenness are wrongly trying to satisfy God-given longings. Remember, your most basic need is the spirit of revelation, the experiential knowledge of God's heart. I'm telling you, strongholds crumble when your heart is moving and crying daily in God's presence. I greatly value counseling and programs as a means to freedom and wholeness, but what if you started by giving God more time every day and truly getting a flowing heart?

In this discipleship program, you're being equipped to pray one to two hours a day because this amount of time seems like a minimum amount of time needed to begin experiencing God in transforming ways. Wherever you're at in your level of desire for God and amount of time with God, I encourage you to re-evaluate how much prayer time you can get each day. If you're closer to one hour a day, consider increasing it by fifteen to thirty minutes every day for now, and then consider moving towards two hours a day in the next few months.

Pursuing this amount of time isn't religious or legalistic; it's a basic relationship principle in the kingdom of God. In my personal life, with kids, work, and life's demands, I know that I need at least two hours a day with God to get my heart flowing and growing. In my marriage, we both understand that we need long amounts of time with God, so every day, we alternate who gets a few hours of prayer and who is responsible for the kids when they wake up. Because of this reality, the weekends aren't sleep-in days; they are opportunities to get more time in prayer to encounter the beautiful God!

BIBLE MEDITATION

Because meditation is the primary way to engage with and encounter God, continuing your specific verse meditations is critical. After deliverance, meditation will position you to be satisfied in God, strengthen you to resist old patterns, and build godly strongholds. Small agreements with God's truth in meditation times will be putting one brick on top of another to build strong walls of truth. If your deliverance times have served to dismantle demonic walls and blinders, now is the time to go deep in the heart of God through meditation without the barriers that once hindered your heart from experiencing truth.

PERSONAL PRAYER LIST

Having a personal prayer list and scheduling weekly times to pray through it is another tool in fighting lies. I suggest putting your main heart issues on your prayer list and seriously praying for them every week. This is so simple but so powerful! Take a few minutes and pray in tongues while asking God for truth or strength in your heart issue. Ask Him to deliver you from temptation and to give you strength. Rebuke demonic attacks from even happening in these areas. Review your prayer list and Bible meditation verse every couple of months and change them depending on what truths you're pursuing.

A few years ago, I (Bethany) felt the Lord highlighting the fear of man as an issue in my life. In response to what He was highlighting, I meditated on key verses to fill me with truth in context to fear of man, and I put "freedom from fear of man" on my daily prayer list.[2] For a few months, I prayed in tongues over my heart crying out for a breakthrough. In those prayer times, I received God's burden for full freedom for myself and felt His zeal and emotions for me.

One day, I was with a person who normally intimidated me and caused me to fear their opinions of me. In discussion, they said something small that I didn't

---

2 Zephaniah 3:16-17; Galatians 1:10.

agree with. I normally would have crumpled inside and smiled and nodded on the outside because I was afraid of their rejection and their reaction in every way.

However, I felt God saying, "Bethany, stop smiling and disagree with them out loud." I resisted, but God continued, "No, it's ok, disagree with them." I shared my perspective and disagreed with them without being angry or fearful, and this person agreed with me. I almost fell over! I felt like a part of the stronghold of the fear of man was knocked down that day. I pursued more freedom in that season but praying for myself and stepping out that day was a huge starting point, and it made me confident in the fruitfulness of the intentional pursuit of freedom.

WEEKLY ASSIGNMENT

For this week's assignment, take 30-60 minutes in one of your prayer times to ask God who you need to forgive (refer to the personal deliverance section). Close your eyes and ask God to bring people to mind that you need to forgive. When a person comes to mind, you will probably know what you need to forgive them for. Out loud to God, forgive them for the specific things they did or said until peace replaces the emotions of pain and anger. If you don't feel anything change in your emotions, continue to talk to God about the situation, speak forgiveness again, and pray blessings over them. If God brings more people to mind than you have time for, schedule another forgiveness prayer time.

23

WALKING OUT FREEDOM: CHURCH FAMILY

(WRITTEN BY BETHANY MOOTZ)

COMMUNITY AND ACCOUNTABILITY

From whom the whole body, joined and knit together by what every joint supplies, according to the effective working by which every part does its share, causes growth of the body for the edifying of itself in love.—Ephesians 4:16

In this hour of history, God is restoring the definition and glory of the local church as His primary means of transforming believers and society. God has strategically placed a significant piece of your freedom in the people that make up your local church. Churches are meant to be places of deep friendships that pursue God together and edify (build up) each other in love. If you haven't already, now is the time to focus on building deep spiritual friendships within your church and posturing your heart to receive all the discipleship you can receive from your leaders.

"WITH THOSE"

Flee also youthful lusts; but pursue righteousness, faith, love, peace with those who call on the Lord out of a pure heart.—2 Timothy 2:22

God has ordained Biblical community and relational accountability to be a weapon against the darkness, and a tool for believers to walk in personal freedom. In my opinion, you will grow twice as fast if you deeply engage in a hungry community of believers. To a degree, we pursue righteousness alone, but in 2 Timothy 2:22, there's another place for pursuing righteousness in your church community "with those who call on the Lord out of a pure heart." We are exhorted to flee sinful desires and pursue righteousness with like-minded people who have hungry and pure hearts because they will provoke us, convict us, talk us into more righteousness, and encourage us along the way.

CONFESSING TO OTHERS

Some people think that if they're open to God, they don't have to be open or confess to other people, but that isn't how God set it up. When you are open with others, your heart is more open with God. He has designed the church community to operate like this; community with each other is community with God. The capacity of your heart to love Jesus and to fulfill your destiny increases according to your openness to your church community. I tell young people that are not in a true community that they're only going to reach fifty percent of their spiritual destiny alone. Our spiritual growth and deliverance are deeply connected to our level of friendship with other wholehearted believers.

And if he has committed sins, he will be forgiven. Confess your trespasses to one another, and pray for one another, that you may be healed.—James 5:15-16

God already knows you have sinned and will forgive you if you ask Him to, but the Biblical value is that it has to be exposed on the human level before you can receive full healing and breakthrough from God. It is through vulnerability with others that healing flows. Jesus paid for the cleansing of your sins already but will apply more cleansing as you confess and repent to others in your community.

When things remain in darkness, our perspectives and wrong thinking are allowed to stay. But when we confess and expose hidden things, we allow truth to flood our souls. I'm not talking about shouting your sins from the rooftops. I'm talking about being transparent with a trust-filled, safe environment where you know and do life with the people you are confessing to; those who will hold you accountable to getting out of sin and love you in the midst of your weakness.

You are vulnerable to demonic swirls of accusation when you are isolated because God never meant for us to be alone. These same accusations can only be broken off through God's gift to us, which is community. We know ourselves more fully as we interact with one another because we see unique aspects of ourselves and how God created us as we connect with others. Godly relationships are where people are calling each other to greater places of loving God and each other and breaking through life circumstances together.

As iron sharpens iron, so a man sharpens the countenance of his friend.
—*Proverbs 27:17*

We desperately need God to point out our blind spots and bring inner healing where we've been hurt by people. There are many hindrances to having community and friendships: past hurt relationships and not wanting to be hurt again, wrong perspectives (I have to wait and be pursued instead of initiating a relationship), fear of being known in weakness or sin, I don't have time for it, I don't know how to be a friend or be friendly to people, etc. Ask God for the humility to see where you need an alignment or a deeper healing work so that you can begin to see from His perspective the gift of grafting into your church community.

God wants us to form friendships around prayer, fasting, the Word, and the spirit of revelation. If friendships are not formed around pursuing God together, they will not be life-giving or Biblical. If you go deep in God with other people, your discussions will center around who God is and what He is doing in each of you. I believe these kinds of friendships are within the definition of what church is supposed to be—a group of committed friends intentionally pursuing God together in deep relationship.

In a church community, you will have conflict. The lack of perfection in any community is guaranteed. No community does relationships perfectly. You will want to keep the deep places of your heart hidden for fear of rejection and shame. You will not want to forgive and respond in humility towards a sincere but weak brother who hurt you. But if you desire wholeheartedness and to continue receiving breakthroughs from the Lord, you need one another and you need committed loving relationships.

All of us have an excuse as to why we hide little things, but if you are not going to be open, you are closing your heart off from receiving from the very community you are a part of. You're also hindering the community from true unity. If you do not open up, who will? The hard parts of community life shouldn't hinder us from wanting and desiring to be a part of the culture of a community where vulnerability and accountability are celebrated, and weakness is handled Biblically.

PRAYER ACCOUNTABILITY

Prayer accountability is having a regular checkpoint with a few people of mutual commitment to confess sins, encourage each other in spiritual pursuits, and pray for each other. Prayer accountability can best happen with companions in the faith, people you see regularly and can run alongside you and pick you up when you fall, and vice versa. Right now, you have this with your Discipleship Mentor, but God wants this for you for every season, however it looks. If you've never had this type of relationship before, pray about what people might be a good fit for you when you transition out of this program. The best place to look for someone who could be a prayer accountability partner is in your current local church.

A simple model for prayer accountability is to discuss each person's spiritual pursuits: prayer life (prayer/fasting schedule, meditation verse, Bible study direction), heart issues, and gifting. The *Spiritual Pursuits Document* in this program is set up to be used for future accountability friendships. Set up a regular meeting time, and then decide what they want to share and be accountable for. Ask each person to share what God has been doing in their heart through prayer and the Word, how they've been doing with walking out their prayer schedule, how they've been doing with their heart issue, and how they are growing in their giftings. Encourage the group to listen, ask good questions, encourage, challenge, prophesy, and release God's forgiveness when sins and weaknesses are confessed.

Through relational accountability, you can more easily overcome sin patterns and heart issues, feel the heart of God as you are loved and accepted in your weaknesses, extend the merciful forgiving heart of God to others, and learn to be vulnerable and open with no shame or hiding. There is profound grace to grow with accountability as you confess openly to those who know all your weaknesses, and time after time, they still love you and cheer you on. Confession can be more than sharing sins. It can include confessing doubts, fears, struggles, pain, but also truths and victories!

 # WEEKLY ASSIGNMENT

Besides continuing to pray through your heart issues this week, take some time to consider your understanding of God's plans for the local church. Answer the following questions. *How involved and connected are you with your church family? Based on Ephesians 4:12 and 16, what does it mean to be edified and to edify others in your church? What does is look like to have deep spiritual friendships in your church? What could a prayer accountability friendship look like for you?*

MODULE 6

BIBLE STUDY

MODULE INTRODUCTION

Before getting into this module, I want to encourage you that your passion for God and your yes to daily prayer moves God's heart, even if your yes feels small most days. God is looking for friends on the earth who give Him the time and love He deserves, and He's finding that in you. In addition, the way you're pursuing prayer is the wisest thing you can do in this hour of history. What you are cultivating in God will be your strength and life source in every season and will be the very thing you lead others into.

The purpose of this Bible study module is to give you the vision, confidence, and tools you need to go deep in the study of the Word of God. You will learn the practicals of how to pursue the Biblical truths God highlights to you in each season, which is one of this program's primary goals. You will also learn about three different study approaches (general reading, topical studies, and book studies), how to do word studies, and how to utilize study resources (Bible study websites, commentaries, Bible dictionaries, Greek/Hebrew resources).

The module assignments include a topical study, a study on a book of the Bible, and a word study. These assignments will train you to do in-depth study on topics that are relevant to you moving forward, but personalize the assignments by using them to study the truths you are pursuing right now. In preparation, review your *Spiritual Pursuits Document* and determine if anything needs to be changed, and pick your study and meditation direction. I suggest studying and meditating within the same truth, and possibly even within the same verses so that you can focus and go deep through both means.

ASSIGNMENT OVERVIEW
MODULE 6 – BIBLE STUDY

Continue to follow your prayer schedule and Spiritual Pursuits each week. As a follow-up to the deliverance module, continue to pray through heart issues during part of each Discipleship Mentor meeting. Also, schedule an Extended Group Prayer Day (2-4 hours) for week 28 or 29.

Week Twenty-six Assignments:

❑ Read Chapter 24 – "***Bible Study Approaches.***" Journal your thoughts and questions about the chapter.

❑ Begin the Topical Study assignment. This is a two-week assignment.

❑ Fill out a new *Spiritual Pursuits Document* for this module. The pursuits can stay the same or change but filling out the form monthly helps you refocus and develop a rhythm of intentionality.

Week Twenty-seven Assignments:

❑ No chapter reading this week.

❑ Complete your Topical Study assignment.

❑ Schedule an Extended Group Prayer Day for week 28 or 29.

❑ **Meet with your Discipleship Mentor.**

Week Twenty-eight Assignments:

❑ Read Chapter 25 – "***Book Study Part 1.***" Journal your thoughts and questions about the chapter.

❑ Begin your Book Study assignment (research the book's background, read the book through several times, and create a general outline). This is a three-week assignment.

Week Twenty-nine Assignments:

❑ Read Chapter 26 – "**Book Study Part 2.**" Journal your thoughts and questions about the chapter.

❑ Continue your Book Study assignment by going more in-depth (2-3 more layers) on your existing outline. Finish this detailed outline this week.

❑ **Meet with your Discipleship Mentor.**

Week Thirty Assignments:

❑ No chapter reading this week.

❑ Finish your Book Study assignment by writing your own commentary on each verse within one section of verses (5-10 verses).

Week Thirty-one Assignments:

❑ Read Chapter 27 – "**Word Studies and Interpretation.**" Journal your thoughts and questions about the chapter.

❑ Complete your Word Study assignment.

❑ Write down a 1–2-month Bible study plan to put in the next module's *Spiritual Pursuits Document.*

❑ **Meet with your Discipleship Mentor.**

SPIRITUAL PURSUITS   *DATE:* _____

1. **Bible reading direction and plan**
   (Write down what you will read and when you will read it):

2. **Meditation verse** (Choose a verse that speaks truth into your heart issue):

3. **Sin/character issue from which to get freedom:**

4. **Lie from which to pursue deliverance:**

5. **Gifting to pursue** (Include simple ways you can pursue it):

6. **Weekly Prayer Schedule**—Write down your plan for the *specific times* you are committed to spending with God each day, and *what specifically you plan to do during those times*. Include what your study or meditation focus will be. Refer to the example schedule in Chapter Two. (e.g., Monday 6-6:30 am—Tongues, 6:30-7:30 am—Meditation on Song of Solomon 1:2)

Monday

Tuesday

Wednesday

Thursday

Friday

Saturday

Sunday

24
BIBLE STUDY APPROACHES

MEDITATION AND STUDY

God wants to bring Bible study and meditation together in your life. It is normal for them to be pitted against each other, or for personality types to gravitate towards one or the other, but they are meant to flow together and fuel one another. Bible study will help you understand the fuller context and meaning of a Bible topic, while meditation will position you to encounter God in the truth in a deeper way. Bible study gives you information and understanding to meditate on, and meditation brings up questions to study. Both aspects are forms of searching out God's heart, and both are needed to experience transformation.

If you maintain the meditative heart posture you've been cultivating in this program, you will be able to healthily grow in intimacy with God in Bible study. You will be challenged by the focus and thought the study assignments will require, but you'll be blessed by your labors. I encourage you to enter into the initial tension of Bible study and meditation and to find your way in it without abandoning one or the other.

WHY STUDY THE BIBLE

GOD'S HEART REVEALED

The Bible is the revelation of the heart of God written down for us to engage with, and when we talk to God about it, light fills our understanding and transforms us. As a Person with real thoughts, emotions, and desires, God has revealed Himself in the Bible and wants to be known by us. He wants to take the written Word and make it the Living Word by releasing encounters with Jesus. When we talk about Bible study, it means to study and peer into God's personality, values, and His ways so that we can know Him and become more like Him as His bride.

Sometimes Christians automatically slip into a non-relational academic mindset when they think about the idea of Bible study. Deep down, they believe it's merely a mental pursuit of right Christian doctrines and principles. You can be a believer and still approach Bible study in a non-relational way, but this doesn't have to be the case for you. If you can keep the perspective that you're pursuing God's heart from the place of longing, and that you can keep a meditative posture while studying, you can see Bible study as being relational and similar to meditation. This perspective will allow your desire for God to express itself in the form of searching Him out in Bible study.

"You search the Scriptures, for in them you think you have eternal life; and these are they which testify of Me. But you are not willing to come to Me that you may have life."—John 5:39-40

Jesus rebuked the religious leaders of His day for studying the Scriptures without a relational perspective. They searched out His plans through study, but they weren't willing to talk to God about the things they were studying, and they were not willing to obey the Spirit's leading. Jesus rebuked their approach. He desired that they would find life in Him through prayerful study. This passage does not discourage Bible study; it encourages conversation and encounter with God in Bible study, and it promises intimacy and life.

JESUS AND THE APOSTLES

Going deep in the Bible includes meditation and study because the two flow together in searching out God. The apostles valued both and gave most of their ministry time to Bible study, meditation, and prayer so they could experience God and know His values.[1] We know they had Biblical depth because they were people who understood God's kingdom and the Messiah before Jesus called them to be disciples. They continued their pursuit of the scriptures after Jesus' ascension so they could form the early church around new revelations. The New Testament writings are a fruit of their Biblical understanding.

As the Son of God, Jesus valued the role of study and meditation in understanding His Father and knowing His ways. As a Jewish boy in Galilee, He would have grown up memorizing the Torah and learning through meditation and study.[2] By the age of twelve, He had cultivated enough understanding of the scriptures to dialogue with Jewish teachers in the temple and amaze those around Him.[3] Jesus equated Bible study with knowing what His Father was doing, *"Did you not know that I must be about My Father's business?"*[4]

---

1   Acts 6:2, 4.

2   Luke 2:40.

3   Luke 2:46-47.

4   Luke 2:49.

Jesus displayed the fruit of His Biblical understanding throughout His entire life. In the wilderness, He used His Biblical depth to discern and war against Satan's lies and temptations.[5] In His teaching ministry, Jesus brought new understanding and new interpretations to the Bible and amazed people with His wisdom and authority. Through study and communion with His Father, He understood His role as Messiah from Biblical prophecies, and He knew His Father's timing for the cross, the resurrection, and His second coming.

BUILT-UP BY THE WORD

"So now, brethren, I commend you to God and to the word of His grace, which is able to build you up and give you an inheritance among all those who are sanctified."—Acts 20:32

There are three phrases in Acts 20:32 that are significant regarding the power of the Word. In context, Paul spoke this to the Ephesian elders for the last time. In this meeting, he entrusted them to the power of God in His Word as their means of growth.

Paul called the Bible "the word of His grace." God's Word releases grace and transforming power to the human heart. Engaging Him in the Word is the source of receiving His empowering grace in your thoughts, emotions, and desires. Mike Bickle says this, "There is a supernatural activity that happens when the written Word of God touches the human heart under the anointing of the Spirit."[6]

---

5 Matthew 4:3-10.

6 Mike Bickle, "Bible Study Action Plan: Power of a Focused Life Series," 2003. International House of Prayer University, Grandview, Missouri, MP3, 55:18, https://archive.org/details/ThePowerOfAFocusedLife.

His Word is "able to build you up." His Word has the supernatural ability to build up your heart in the Spirit. In module four, you learned that praying in tongues builds you up, but His Word also builds up and is the primary way He encounters and edifies the believer. His Word will fill your heart with His fiery love and fascination and awaken your spiritual desires for Him. His Word will wash away lies and accusations and the lusts of the flesh and bring you into a place of truth, righteousness, and empowerment. A built-up soul finds satisfaction in God and grows in distaste for the deceitful pleasures of darkness.

His Word will "give you an inheritance among all those who are sanctified." Your inheritance in God refers to all that He has promised you in this age and in eternity. Paul says that the Bible will give you an inheritance because everything in your life hinges upon you experiencing God's life in the Word. As you fill your heart with His Word, it will renew your thoughts, invigorate your emotions, and set you on a holy course to fulfill your destiny. You will only realize your inheritance if you come to God as the life source, and the starting point is His Word.

Therefore lay aside all filthiness and overflow of wickedness, and receive with meekness the implanted word, which is able to save your souls.—James 1:21

James called the Bible the "implanted word." The Word is like a divine seed that is thrust into the soil of the human heart. In the right conditions, the small seed will take root and produce divine fruitfulness. The implanted word "is able to save your souls." If you give yourself to the Word and respond to the Word in meekness, it will progressively transform and deliver you from brokenness and darkness and renew it into the glorious image of God

You must lay hold of the Word of God with intentionality to experience the glorious promises of fruitfulness. If you're casual in making time for God in the

Word, you will end up being in the Word less often, and it will bear less fruit in your soul. But if you carve out time and have a plan, you will give God time and space to awaken your heart. An awakened heart will begin to demand more and more time to feast on the Word of God and lead to transformation and more satisfaction in God.

BIBLE STUDY APPROACHES

There are three approaches to Bible study that I use and suggest to people wanting to grow in the Word. Each one of them has its specific benefits. As you read each description, consider how you could apply them in your study life.

GENERAL READING PLAN

The simplest way to study the Bible is to pick a book or books of the Bible to read on specific days of the week. This is most people's default study approach. The benefit of doing this is that it is so simple and so easy to do that you can quickly get a rhythm in it and enjoy it. Two other benefits of general reading are that you can see the big picture and central themes of a book or Bible section and follow the author's storyline because you're reading it straight through. This simple study method helps grow a hunger for the Word, leading to a desire for more in-depth study. When I have a general reading plan, I connect to the storyline, which helps me pick up my Bible to continue reading when I have a few minutes here and there.

1. Start by deciding what you want to read based on the truths that you want to grow in. Pick one book of the Bible like Romans or Ephesians or pick a section of the Bible like the Gospels, the Psalms, or the entire New

Testament. If you're not sure what to read or are not very familiar with the Bible, I would recommend reading through the New Testament several times. You could read it through every two months if you read about five chapters a day.

2. Plan to read a certain number of chapters each day or plan to read for a certain amount of time each day. An example would be to read five chapters a day or to read for an hour a day. If you decide to read one book, depending on its size, you may even be able to read the entire thing each day.

3. Take time to turn what you're reading into conversation with the Lord. When a verse moves you, or you want to say something to the Lord about what you're reading, stop and talk to Him for a minute and then continue reading. These reading times aren't meant to be deep meditation times, but your heart will engage God more and receive more if you have a conversation with Him.

4. Have a notepad with you while you read and write down a few thoughts, questions, observations, and things you would want to study later.

TOPICAL STUDY

Topical Bible study is an approach that focuses on studying the Bible by specific topics. A topical study requires a little more work than just having a general reading plan, but it's still simple and easy for everyone to do. The benefits of this approach are that you can focus on the specific topic you want to study, and you can gather a broad number of verses and information on the subject. This approach is a perfect way to pursue one of the truths you know you need in this season.

A topical study will cultivate a longing for truth and create spiritual momentum in your heart for specific topics. When you search out topics, you naturally engage the parts of your heart that were made to search and discover God. Each day you go deeper into a topic, new layers of truth and understanding will open up. As this happens, you will encounter God in the truth and become hungrier for a fuller understanding. Like searching out a treasure, your heart will want to keep engaging as you see the truth unfolding in front of you.

1. Start by picking one Bible topic that you want to study to help free you from your current heart issue or empower you in a gift you want to grow in.

2. In a topical study, the first step is to gather information on the topic. Start by finding Bible verses on the topic and compiling them in a notepad or on your computer. You can find verses or chapters on your topic in three ways: write down verses you already know of, look up keywords on a Bible website, and look up the topic in a Bible dictionary or Topical Bible. These three extra resources reference verses by topic and give commentary on the topic. The main website I use for word searches, Bible dictionaries, and Topical Bibles is www.studylight.org. I'll guide you in using this specific website, but you can access the same resources on other Bible study websites.

3. Go to www.studylight.org and click "Bible Study Tools" and then select "Bible Concordance (Topical Bibles)," "Bible Dictionary," or "Bible Encyclopedia." I suggest using the International Standard Bible Encyclopedia because it is clear and has extensive information. Enter your topic in the search bar of whatever resource you choose, and then write down the verses they reference in your notepad or computer.

4. After gathering information on the topic, review and study all your verses while writing down your thoughts and specific questions on any verses. Continue to read the verses to find answers to your questions. If there isn't

much information or many verses, this may be a quick study. If there are a lot of verses and outside information, you could take your time over the course of weeks to study and pray through the topic.

EXAMPLE TOPICAL STUDY

If I were to pick forgiveness as my topic, I would type in variations of the word (forgiveness, forgiven, forgive) in the Bible search option on a Bible study website. Then I would copy all the relevant verses into my computer. Afterward, I would go into a Bible Dictionary and Nave's Topical Bible on the website and click on forgiveness as a topic. I would copy all their verses and ideas and copy them in my document. Lastly, I would take several days to look at all of the verses and write down truths and questions from the verses. If there was a key verse, I would consider meditating on it for a while.

Based on my questions, I might need to look up other topics to understand forgiveness better. With the topic of forgiveness, I would want to know how the blood of Jesus allows me to be forgiven. There would be some edifying bunny trails to study within this topic, leading to even more clarity.

BOOK STUDY

A book study is an in-depth study of one book of the Bible. This approach takes the most work, but it's a natural way of learning. It produces a lot of fruit because it's so comprehensive. The benefits are an immersion into the heart and thought process of the book's author and the Holy Spirit, understanding each verse in relation to the entire book, and more easily reading from the original audience's perspective. It is easy to get spiritual momentum in this type of study because you become so immersed in the book's storyline and get excited about seeing all the verses come together.

With the book study approach, you can go as in-depth as you want. The four basic things you need to do are **study the book's background** (author and audience), **discover the overview of the book** (main themes and main points), **create a personal outline** of the book, and **write your own commentary** on each verse or section. You can go as deep as you want in each of these three categories, and you can decide if you want to study the entire book or a specific section of the book.

The process of creating an outline and writing a personal commentary will help you engage the truths of the book. The process will force you to summarize and personalize what you're reading, which produces clarity and a personal response to God. After studying a book, you will be able to tell someone else what the main point of the book is in one sentence, and what each section of the book is saying in one sentence. The process will also help you grow in understanding how each verse connects to the book's main themes, which will help you interpret them better.

IMPLEMENTING BIBLE STUDY

Within your weekly prayer schedule, you have planned times to meditate, worship, pray in tongues, and study the Bible. During this module, review your prayer schedule and see where you want your Bible study times to be and what topic or section of the Bible you want to focus on in those times. If you haven't had a strong Bible reading or Bible study plan so far, this is the module to learn how to do so and put it into place in your times with the Lord.

WHAT

Decide what you want to read or study. I suggest picking part or all your Bible reading based on the truths you need in this season. Bible study and meditation can flow together, so consider doing them both on the same topic or verses. Typically, I have two different Bible study directions in my weekly prayer schedule: one for general reading in a section of the Bible that I'm interested in and another that is specific to what I want my heart to grow in.

WHEN

Decide when you want to study the Bible in your weekly prayer schedule. Do you want or need to find more time to be in the Word each week? In your schedule, write down what days and times you're going to study and what you'll be studying.

HOW

Decide how you want to approach your study. Out of the three approaches in this chapter, which one or two would you want to use for a month or more? Based on the study approaches you pick, write down a few bullet points of how you will study. For example, if you're going to do a topical study on God's love, write down each simple step of what you're going to do. Review your steps whenever you're not sure what to do in your study times.

WEEKLY ASSIGNMENT

The assignment for the next two weeks is to do a topical study and to write down a detailed Bible study plan on how to execute it. In the study plan, write down what you're going to study, what approach you're going to try, and what simple steps you're going to take in the study. Follow the steps in the chapter for your assignment. Two weeks should give you adequate time to find a rhythm in topical studies and get some depth in the topic of your choice.

This assignment is designed to be done during the Bible study days in your prayer schedule. Consider using all your Bible times for two weeks on this assignment so you can go deep. Also, the assignment is meant to be in line with the Bible topics you are already investing in, so choose a topic that you're wanting more truth in right now. Doing so will help you build godly strongholds in place of the demonic strongholds that were torn down in the last module. As you make this personal, it will impact your heart and become a testimony that strengthens you to study after this module.

DISCIPLESHIP MEETING GUIDE
MODULE 6: BIBLE STUDY – CHAPTER 24

MEETING FOCUS:

The purpose of this meeting is to discuss your Topical Study assignment and continue praying through your heart issue.

DISCUSSION QUESTIONS (IN ORDER OF IMPORTANCE):

1. *Heart Issue:*
   a. Share how your heart issue has been going since the deliverance module. Take time together to ask God for more clarity concerning the current heart issue or ask Him to highlight more things to pray through during this meeting. Use the simple deliverance prayer steps from the last module.

2. *Chapter Questions:*
   a. Chapter 24 – Discuss your journaled thoughts and questions from the chapter. Do you struggle with viewing Bible study as only academic and not relational? Do you see how meditation and study can work together?
   b. Topical Study assignment – In-depth, discuss how your assignment went for you and how God impacted your heart. In relation to the deliverance module, do you feel like this study helped build you up in truth?

3. *Spiritual Pursuits:*
   a. Practically, how is your prayer schedule going? How many days have you walked out your prayer schedule? Do you need to make small changes to your schedule? How are your daily prayer times going, and how is God impacting you through them?
   b. Briefly review your new *Spiritual Pursuits Document*.

4. Briefly review the assignments for the next two weeks together.

MEETING NOTES:

25

BOOK STUDY PART ONE

EVERYONE CAN GO DEEP

As you begin the book study chapters of this module, I want to encourage you that you are called and able to go deep in Bible study. God has depths available to you in the Word. He's given you the necessary skills to study, and there are abundant Bible resources to help you grow. In my observation, the three things that hold people back from going deep are having enough time, not knowing where to start or how to study, and feeling intimidated and unqualified. All three of these will be easy to overcome if you press in during this module.

FINDING ENOUGH TIME

The first issue is regarding having enough time for Bible study. If you don't have much time scheduled for prayer each day, you are going to feel limited in where you can go in Bible study. If you know this is the case for you, take a fresh look at your weekly schedule and see if you can find more time. That might mean saying no to entertainment or legitimate activities and being more focused in your daily schedule but finding the extra time with God is so worth it!

Consider orienting your life and schedule around getting enough time with God, and then schedule everything else after you've established those sacred times. Resist the temptation of resigning to the amount of time you have with God and take a fresh look at your schedule. Even if you can only find fifteen or thirty more minutes a day to be with Him, it will help you substantially.

Many of you reading this have pursued studies, whether in college or in job training. What if you were to apply the same intensity of study as you did for those pursuits? Jobs and schooling are worthy causes, but how much more worthy is the pursuit of the truth in God's Word?

We all experience hard seasons and have circumstances that seem to hinder us from spending more time with God, but more time with Him is the answer in the midst of hard seasons. God challenged me to spend more time with Him in a tough season when my kids were young, were going through health issues, weren't sleeping well, and our parents were going through severe health challenges. All these situations left me more tired and with less time, which resulted in me pulling back from prayer, fasting, and Bible study. Essentially, I had resigned to less quality time with God.

One day, God interrupted my thoughts and whispered to me, "You have a demon in your life." I said, "What are you talking about? What demon is in my life?" God replied and said, "You have a demon called excuses. All your challenges are real and difficult, and I know what you're going through, but this demon is exploiting them to discourage you from spending more time with Me. He's making your circumstances seem bigger than they really are, and he's convincing you that they are valid excuses for not spending enough time with Me.

I felt the Father's heart in this conversation, and it helped me say no to my legitimate excuses. He communicated that He was fully with me in my challenges, and He didn't dismiss or minimize them. But at the same time, as my Father, He was calling me higher and saying that He would help me. He wasn't just rebuking me out of anger and then leaving me to figure things out by myself.

God said something like, "I know your challenges! They are real! But I will help you spend time with Me. You can fast and pray and be in the Word more in the midst of being tired in your circumstances. I'm with you in this, and I will give you grace!" It's like He came as a father to pick me up from the ground and committed to holding me up as I walked.

KNOWING WHERE TO START

The second issue is learning how to study the Bible and knowing where to start in the process. You can learn how to study, and it doesn't have to be complicated! The most important thing is to decide what you will study for a month or two, and then write down a simple study plan. If you think it through on the front end, you will feel confident during your studies.

Part of the learning process is practicing the study methods in this module, both now and moving forward. You will gain a level of clarity and confidence from doing the assignments, but each time that you use a study approach (general reading, topical study, book study, word study) you will feel clearer and more confident. The more times you practice the different study techniques, the more natural they will be, and the more enjoyable they will be. If you give yourself to utilizing the study approaches this month while you have focus, structure, and mentors, your study growth will accelerate.

INTIMIDATION

The third issue is feeling intimidated and under-equipped to do in-depth Bible study. The idea of understanding the historical settings of the Bible, interpreting verses, and getting into Bible commentaries and other resources can seem intimidating. I relate to feeling intimidated because that's how I felt in my twenties. I never enjoyed studying anything growing up, but when I got saved, there was a desire to dig into the truth. After learning how to study from mentors, the intimidation was removed, and I felt empowered to discover the Bible. You don't have to be super smart or have a theology degree to have Biblical clarity. All you need is the Holy Spirit, a tender heart, time, and a little experience with Bible resources to have a good foundation for understanding and interpreting the Bible.

Some of the intimidation comes from not knowing the Bible or the history of Biblical times. Each year that you study, you will grow in understanding the history of Israel, Jesus' life, and the New Testament contexts. This will only come as you study over time, but it's doable and enjoyable.

OVERVIEW OF BOOK STUDY APPROACH

A book study approach studies one book of the Bible at a time to get immersed in the Holy Spirit's flow of thought. Like a story, each book of the Bible is meant to be read as one piece of truth. The Holy Spirit and human authors wrote their books knowing that each sentence was connected and built upon the ones that came before. Therefore, a book study will bring you into a greater understanding of individual sentences because you will read them in context to the book's central message. You'll also read them in context to the original audience, which is the starting place for interpreting passages and understanding the Spirit's overall message in a book.

The four essential components of a book study are to *study the book's background* (author and audience), *discover the book's overview* (main themes and main points), *create a personal outline* of the book, and *write your own commentary* on each verse or section.

Creating an outline and writing a personal commentary will help you engage the truths of the book. The process will force you to summarize and personalize what you're reading, which produces clarity and personal responses to God. After studying a book, you will be able to tell others the main point of the book in one sentence, and what each section of the book is saying in one sentence. In all of this, you will get hooked by the life of God you experience through the searching process and the growing connection to the book's storyline, and your appetite for the sweetness of the Word will expand.

STUDY THE BOOK'S BACKGROUND

A book study begins with understanding its background, which includes knowing details about the author. Who were they? When and why did they write the book? What was their relationship like with their readers? It can even be helpful to look at the author's life as a whole to understand their heart and journey. Understanding the background also includes knowing who the original audience was and what they were dealing with at the time of the book's writing.

Most of this background information can be found in Bible resources like Bible dictionaries, Bible Encyclopedias, and in the introduction section of commentaries. If you have a study Bible, it most likely has some background information before each new book of the Bible. Check multiple Bible sources to get as much understanding as possible, and then write down your information in one spot. You don't have to remember or understand all the information, but you will learn more progressively as you do this.

DISCOVER THE BOOK'S OVERVIEW

The next step is to understand the overview or big picture of the entire book. As you read, answer the questions: what are the main points and the main themes, what are the repetitive ideas, and how do all the chapters connect to each other? You can get some overview thoughts from the Bible resources, but the primary way is to read, if possible, the entire book in one sitting several times over the course of a week or two. Every time you read the book, you will see the big picture become more apparent, and you will see main themes emerge. As you read, write down all your observations. Observing and writing these things down will help you create an outline.

GENERAL BOOK OUTLINE

A book outline is a document you make that breaks the book up into different-sized sections. The general book outline is the first of three to four layers in the outlining process. In the next chapter, you will learn about the deeper layers of outlining. There are no wrong outlines, and your outline might change later. Typically, I have two different Bible study directions in my weekly prayer schedule: one for general reading in a section of the Bible that I'm interested in and another that is specific to what I want my heart to grow in. The focus is more on the benefits of the outlining process.

Creating an outline is incredibly beneficial because it guides you in a systematic way of praying and thinking through the content and flow of the book. It forces you to ask and answer the question, "What is the author saying, and how is he saying it?" Summarizing each section with a short sentence will help you personalize and own the topic of each section. By the end of the process, you will understand and be able to communicate the book's main points, summarize each section with a sentence, and walk someone through the book's flow.

1. **First outline layer** – For the first outline layer, divide the book into large sections. As a general idea, there may be two to four large sections in a book. You can identify these larger sections by big topic changes.

   In the book of Ephesians, an idea for large sections would be chapters 1-3 as the first section and 4-6 as the second section. The first section is filled with truths of who we are in Christ, and then Paul shifts to more exhortation and application in the second section. In Acts, chapters 1-12 are focused on Peter and the gospel among the Jews, and chapters 13-28 are focused on Paul and the gospel among the Gentiles.

2. **Second outline layer** – To make the second outline layer, divide the large sections into smaller ones. In shorter books, these sections might be the size of one or two chapters. In longer books, these sections might include several chapters. These smaller sections fit within the broader topic of the large sections, but they have their own focus within that. In a shorter book like Ephesians, chapters 1-3 could be broken up into three sections the size of the chapters or into two sections that are a little larger. In a longer book like Acts, chapters 1-12 could be broken into smaller sections like chapters 1-5 (Jerusalem Church established) and 6-12 (Gospel spreads).

3. **Title each section** – Write a few words or a short sentence to title each section you make. The purpose of the title is to summarize the main point of the section in your own words.

EXAMPLE BOOK STUDY - ACTS

BOOK BACKGROUND

Based on my reading from one commentary and a couple of other Bible resources, I would write down a few paragraphs of information that helped me understand the book. For a serious book study, I would have one to two pages of introductory information written down. The example below would be longer if I copied more paragraphs from a commentary, wrote more about Luke's life, and expanded on the purpose of Luke-Acts.

Luke, a minister with Paul, wrote Acts to go along with the Gospel of Luke. Luke probably wrote the book around 62 AD, when Paul was in prison for two years. The book covers about thirty years of early Church history, from Jesus' resurrection to the end of Paul's ministry. Luke relied on eyewitnesses, written documents, trustworthy oral traditions, and his own understanding of what people preached in the book. The Greek word for "acts" was used to describe famous people's heroic deeds in Greek culture. This book portrays the acts of the Spirit through the apostles.

The Gospel of Luke and Acts were explicitly addressed to Theophilus to prove the existence of Jesus and to teach about Him and His salvation story through the early Church. People believe Theophilus was either a Roman officer learning about Judaism and Jesus or a Jewish leader learning about Jesus with Luke. Luke wrote these books to prove to Theophilus and other Gentiles the validity of Jesus' life and message through an accurate and detailed account. His writings helped the world understand the gospel of the Jews and why it was being widely accepted among the Gentiles.

BOOK OVERVIEW

I start connecting to the overview or big picture of a book by reading it through in one sitting several times. Acts is a long book, so it takes me about an hour to read at a medium pace. I read slow enough to understand what I'm reading, but not slow enough to catch every detail. As I read, I write down themes, key verses, and ideas of how I would outline. This process is similar to brainstorming in that I put a lot of observations and thoughts on paper, and then I organize them later.

The book's main point seems to be the fulfillment of Jesus' promise to send the Holy Spirit and His impact on the Jews and Gentiles. Luke follows the story of the Spirit as He is poured out and then breaks out in power to bring multitudes into the kingdom. The apostles were filled with the Spirit, and then they brought the Holy Spirit to Jerusalem, Samaria, and the regions beyond. Acts 1:8 summarizes the main point of the book, "But you shall receive power when the Holy Spirit has come upon; and you shall be witnesses to Me in Jerusalem, and in all Judea and Samaria, and to the ends of the earth."

A secondary point of the book seems to be the outworking of Israel's destiny to be a light to the gentile nations. Throughout the book, the Jewish apostles are unsure how their new Messianic faith impacts their laws, religious customs, and the gentile nations around them. In the book, there is a progressive outworking of the Messianic faith. The first half of the book is focused on Peter and his ministry to the Jewish communities, as the Jews were to receive the gospel first.

The second half of the book shifts to Paul and his ministry to the Gentiles, which brings up questions about how the Gentiles should respond to the gospel.

Themes

1. *The Promise and power of the Holy Spirit.*
2. *Power demonstrations leading to the Church growing.*
3. *Jesus' resurrection from the dead.*
4. *Being Jesus' witness to the nations.*
5. *Making disciples.*
6. *Persecution and pressures - mostly from Jews.*
7. *No fear of persecution or martyrdom.*
8. *Jewish transition to Messianic Judaism.*
9. *The gospel goes to the Jews first and then to the Gentiles.*

It is helpful to understand that Acts covers around thirty years of early Church history. At one point, I studied different resources to figure out what year each chapter was happening. Luke references many religious and secular events, places, and people, so there are confident estimates on Acts' timeline. I added this time frame to my book overview, and as I read different chapters in Acts, I knew about what year it was happening.

GENERAL BOOK OUTLINE

I usually make my first outline layer into 2-4 large sections. When I read Acts, I see two large sections—one focused on Peter and another focused on Paul. I titled both sections to summarize what I understand to be happening. The first section seems focused on the outpouring of the Holy Spirit, His impact in the early

Church, and then the spreading of the gospel to the Jews specifically. The second half seems focused on Paul and his ministry to the Gentiles on his missionary journeys.

1. *The outpouring of the Spirit and the gospel to the Jews (1-12)*
2. *Paul takes the gospel to the Gentiles (13-28)*

My second outline layer breaks these larger sections into smaller ones based on themes or stories that fit together. In my reading, the first section is broken up into at least two smaller sections. The first five chapters are focused on the Holy Spirit and the Church in Jerusalem, and chapters 6-12 shift the focus to the gospel going out of Jerusalem. The second large section of Acts is centered around Paul's three missionary journeys, so I sectioned it off according to those trips.

1. *The outpouring of the Spirit and the gospel to the Jews (1-12)*
   i. *Early Church established (1-5)*
   ii. *Persecution takes the gospel to all of Israel (6-12)*
2. *Paul takes the gospel to the Gentiles (12-28)*
   i. *Paul's 1st missionary journey - sent from Antioch (13-14)*
   ii. *Paul's 2nd missionary journey - sent from Antioch (15-18:22)*
   iii. *Paul's 3rd missionary journey (18:23-21:26)*
   iv. *Paul imprisoned (21:27-28:31)*

WEEKLY ASSIGNMENT

You can do this! The Holy Spirit is with you to help you go deep in the Word and understand the things that He's written. Take it one step at a time and know that you'll grow in this depth of study as you practice it. Resist the lie that you can't understand or do an in-depth study like this and resist the temptation to be lazy in Bible study and say that this is too much work. You were made to go deep in the Word and have clarity! Every book of the Bible is available to you to understand if you give it time, and the Church needs you to encounter Jesus in your books and bring clarity to others! If you feel like you've been too casual about Bible study or have given up on the amount of time you can give it to the Word, take some time today to respond to God in any way that seems appropriate.

This week, begin your book study on a book of the Bible that is relevant to the truths you are seeking in this season. You will have three weeks to work on this book study. I suggest choosing a book that is under ten chapters long for your first time to make it easier. You will have three weeks to finish the book study assignments from this chapter and the next. Refer to the instructions in this chapter and research the book's background, read the book through several times, and create a general outline. In the following two weeks, you'll create a more detailed outline and write some personal commentary, so wherever you type out your information, format it in such a way that you can add to it each week.

26
BOOK STUDY PART TWO

PERSONAL TESTIMONY

I am always significantly impacted and grow in understanding when I study a book of the Bible, but when I first started studying, I didn't enjoy it, and it intimidated me. In my early twenties, I read the Bible as best I could, but I didn't know how to go deeper, and I didn't feel confident in using the Bible resources that were available to me. The amount of history in the Bible overwhelmed me, and I didn't know where to start. In my life, studying and reading weren't even things I enjoyed doing.

I began Bible school when I was twenty-three, and I felt the same hindrances to Bible study going into my first year. The classes and teachers were excellent, but what really helped me grow in confidence in Bible study was the simple assignments that required me to take the extra effort to dig into the background of a book and create a simple outline. As I did this, I became more familiar with Bible resources and felt confident that I could learn Biblical history little by little.

One book that I had never understood, but desired to, was the book of Isaiah. Because of feeling intimidated and unequipped, I never would have studied the book by myself. In school, I took a class on Isaiah, and our assignment was to read the entire book several times and outline the whole thing.

The outlining process took a lot of diligence and time, but my heart came alive as I began to understand God's heart and message in Isaiah concerning the promised Son of David and the future glory of Jerusalem. Once I saw how Isaiah strategically built on his central themes section by section and understood his historical timeline, all the other minor details made more sense. That study laid the foundation for me so that each time I go back to the book, I can build on the clarity and understanding that I already have. One other benefit of Isaiah's class and assignments was that I felt bolder and more empowered to tackle any book of the Bible moving forward.

Another book study that impacted me was the book of Revelation. Like Isaiah, Revelation seemed like it was off-limits because of its size and my lack of familiarity with it. I read, meditated on, and studied the book for over a year as my weekly Bible study. As a result, I saw the beauty, mercy, and zealous love of God in the book. What was once a scary mystery to me became a place of encountering the Lamb of God in clarity.

I've outlined and written brief commentaries on many books, usually for a few months at a time. For Revelation, I created a verse-by-verse outline and wrote an extensive commentary for most verses. I didn't plan on commenting on most verses, and I didn't plan on writing so much, but the book pulled me in. There was so much content, and my heart was overflowing and discovering God. One phrase would move me at times, and I would meditate on it for days with a tender heart. At other times, a Bible commentary would clarify a chapter, and I would process my understanding in my writing. My outline and personal commentary became my journal with God for that year.

DEEPER LAYERS OF BOOK STUDY

In the previous chapter, I discussed how to begin a book study by researching its background, reading it several times, and creating a personal outline. You can choose to go as deep as you want in each one of these categories. This section will discuss the subsequent layers of book study, including more outlining layers and writing a personal commentary on sections or individual verses.

BOOK OUTLINE

To review, the first layer of outlining breaks a book into large sections. As a general idea, there may be two to four large sections in a book. I break Ephesians (1-3, 4-6) and Acts (1-12, 13-28) down into two sections. The second layer breaks these larger sections into smaller ones. Depending on the size of the book you want to study, these sections may be a few Bible chapters long or the size of one Bible chapter.

The next step is to add more complex layers to your outline and title each section. The number of outline layers will depend on how long the book is and how in-depth you want to break it down. Each layer will break the smaller sections based on subpoints. Each layer is worth the extra effort.

1. **Third outline layer** – Take the sections that are one or more Bible chapters long and divide them into smaller sections. For a shorter book, these sections will be half a chapter-long or shorter. In a longer book, these sections might be one or two chapters long. In my book of Acts example,

Acts 1-5 is broken into four smaller sections around one chapter in size (1-2, 3, 4:1-33, 4:34-5:42).

2. **Fourth outline layer** – These small sections will be several verses long in a shorter book and would be a good place to stop to begin to write your commentary. In a longer book, these sections are several verses to half a chapter in size. In my book of Acts example, Acts 1-2 is broken into six sections (1:1-11, 1:12-26, 2:1-4, 2:5-13, 2:14-40, 2:41-47).

3. **Fifth outline layer** – These small sections will be around one or two verses long. In my Acts example, 1:1-11 is broken down into three sections (1:1-3, 4-8, 9-11).

4. **Title each section** – Write a few words or a short sentence to title each section you make. The purpose of the title is to summarize the main point of the section in your own words.

PERSONAL COMMENTARY

After doing all the work of reading, outlining, and titling a book or a section of a book, it's time to study individual passages and write down your study results. A personal commentary is a collection of your thoughts, meditations, observations, topical studies, and word studies from individual verses. You can do as much or as little writing as you want. So you could write a sentence in one section and pages in another.

A titled outline is an optimal and very natural place to begin studying smaller sections or individual verses. The outlining process brings you into the bigger picture of a book and the flow of thought from one section to the next, so studying smaller units and writing your ideas will be a natural next step. I type out my outlines on my laptop and then write all of my studies in the outline in paragraphs.

This format gives me the ability to have all of my content in one place so that I can reference material and build on it each day. I still reference my old outlines and commentaries when preparing for Bible teachings or Bible studies. Below is a list of things I include in my writing.

1. **Thoughts** – I write down all my initial thoughts, observations, and questions as a way of processing the Bible verses.

2. **Bible verses** – If other verses connect to the verses I'm studying, I copy and paste them into my commentary. There are no rules; at times, I have one or two pages of verses typed in just for fun.

3. **Topical studies** – When I find a topic in a verse to study in more depth, I research the topic and compile the results in my commentary. While reading Acts, I noticed there were many supernatural stories. One day, I spent an entire study time skimming through the book to find and type out every event. I copied every story into my commentary and then wrote a sentence summary about each event.

4. **Word studies** – When I find a word that I want to understand better, I do a word study and compile all of my findings in my commentary. This includes researching the word in the original language and looking at every verse that uses that word. Example words from Acts are hope, resurrection, filled with Spirit, witness, tongues, and kingdom.

5. **Commentaries** – When I'm at a stopping point in my studies on a verse or don't know what the verse is talking about, I read commentaries. Commentaries are an excellent resource in that they offer several interpretations, explain their thought process, give historical context, and reference Bible verses for further study. I write down any helpful information.

You can access multiple commentaries on most Bible study websites. If you go to studylight.org, click on "Bible Study Tools" and then select "Commentaries." Another helpful website is Biblehub.com, which allows you to see multiple commentaries side by side. All you have to do is type in your verse and click the "comment" tab at the top, and all the commentary on your verse will pull up. I encourage you to read as many commentaries on your verses as you find helpful.

If you plan to study a book in-depth for a few months, I recommend buying a hard copy commentary to track with during your study. To go deep into the big picture of a book without studying individual verses, I recommend a simpler commentary series such as *The Bible Speaks today* by Intervarsity Press. It will give you a good background, insight into the book's flow, and commentary on sections of the book. It is very understandable for beginner Bible students.

A more extensive commentary will have verse by verse commentary with Greek and Hebrew word studies and more detailed explanations of interpretations. These commentaries are constructive if you are ready to read a lot of information and if you can decide which information to focus on. For example, an extensive commentary series I purchase for verse-by-verse book studies is the *Baker Exegetical Commentary on the New Testament*.

6. **Meditations** – Bible study leads to Bible meditation. When a verse moves my heart, I meditate on it and journal in my study notes. My meditations could include writing down prayers from the truth of the verse.

EXAMPLE OUTLINES

Don't be intimidated by this outline or the personal commentary in the next section. This took some time to read through Acts and a few times of changing the outline. Also, I made it look as good as I could to be in a book. Remember, there are no rules as to how your outline should look, and you can adjust the outline as many times as you want. The process of outlining is what benefits you the most, not having it "perfect."

#1 OUTLINE LAYER

1. *The outpouring of the Spirit and the gospel to the Jews (1-12)*
2. *Paul Takes the Gospel to the Gentiles (13-28)*

#2 OUTLINE LAYER (THE NEW LAYER IS BOLDED)

1. *The outpouring of the Spirit and the gospel to the Jews (1-12)*
   a. Early Church Established (1-5)
   b. Persecution Takes the Gospel to All of Israel (6-12)

2. *Paul takes the gospel to the Gentiles (13-28)*
   a. Paul's 1ˢᵗ Missionary Journey – Sent from Antioch (13-14)
   b. Paul's 2ⁿᵈ Missionary Journey – Sent from Antioch (15-18:22)
   c. Paul's 3ʳᵈ Missionary Journey – (18:23-21:26)
   d. Paul Imprisoned (21:27-28:31)

#3 OUTLINE LAYER (THE NEW LAYER IS BOLDED)

1. *The outpouring of the Spirit and the gospel to the Jews (1-12)*
   a. *Early Church Established (1-5)*
      i. **The Outpouring of the Spirit (1-2)**
      ii. **Healing and Preaching at the Temple (3)**
      iii. **Jewish Leadership Confronted with Power – 1st Time (4:1-33)**
      iv. **Fear of God Falls on the Church – 2nd Time Jewish Leadership Confronted (4:34-5:42)**

   b. *Persecution takes the gospel to All of Israel (6-12)*
      i. **Stephen Killed – 3rd Time Jewish Leadership Confronted (6-7)**
      ii. **The Gospel Goes to Judea and Samaria – Philip the Evangelist (8)**
      iii. **Saul Converted and Commissioned to the Gentiles (9)**
      iv. **Peter Brings the Gospel to the Gentiles – Cornelius (10)**
      v. **Apostles Bless the Gentile Conversions - Antioch Highlighted (11)**
      vi. **Peter Imprisoned and Herod Killed – Paul Highlighted (12)**

#4 OUTLINE LAYER (THE NEW LAYER IS BOLDED)

1. *The Outpouring of the Spirit and the Gospel to the Jews (1-12)*
   a. *Early Church Established (1-5)*
      i. *The Outpouring of the Spirit (1-2)*
         1. **Jesus' Resurrected Ministry (1:1-11)**
         2. **Apostolic Leadership Established (1:12-26)**

     3. *Corporate Prayer and Pentecost (2:1-4)*

     4. *Tongues Amaze Jerusalem (2:5-13)*

     5. *Peter's 1ˢᵗ Prophetic Sermon (2:14-40)*

     6. *First Wave of Salvation (2:41-47)*

  ii. Healing and Preaching at the Temple (3)

     1. *Lame Man Healed (3:1-11)*

     2. *Peter's 2ⁿᵈ Prophetic Sermon (3:12-26)*

  iii. Jewish Leadership Confronted with Power – 1ˢᵗ Time (4:1-33)

     1. *Peter and John Imprisoned (4:1-22)*

     2. *2ⁿᵈ Outpouring of the Spirit – Praying Church (4:23-33)*

  iv. Fear of God Falls on the Church – 2ⁿᵈ Time Jewish Leadership Confronted (4:34-5:42)

     1. *Radical Christian Giving (4:34-37)*

     2. *Ananias and Sapphira Judged (5:1-11)*

     3. *Healing Revival on the Streets (5:12-16)*

     4. *Apostles Imprisoned (5:17-40)*

#5 OUTLINE LAYER (NEW LAYER BOLDED)

1. *The Outpouring of the Spirit and the Gospel to the Jews (1-12)*

  a. Early Church Established (1-5)

    i. The Outpouring of the Spirit (1-2)

     1. Jesus' Resurrected Ministry (1:1-11)

      a. *Jesus' 40 days of teaching (1:1-3)*

      b. *Jesus Promises the Spirit (1:4-8)*

      c. *Jesus Ascends in the Clouds (1:9-11)*

EXAMPLE PERSONAL COMMENTARY

This section includes how I organize my thoughts and studies in a book study. At the end, I included a commentary quotation and extra information from an online article to show how you can incorporate Bible resources.

1. Jesus' Resurrected Ministry (1:1-11)

   After His resurrection, Jesus was with His disciples for forty days before He ascended into heaven. During this time, He spoke to them about His kingdom and told them to wait and pray in Jerusalem until He poured out the Holy Spirit. The disciples would end up praying for ten days before the Spirit was released. There was a fifty-day gap between Jesus' resurrection and the outpouring of the Spirit, which came during the Jewish feast of Pentecost.

   This section of Acts introduces the Spirit's outpouring and the commandment to take His power to the nations. These two statements unfold through the entire book of Acts. Jesus also highlights these two things before His ascension to heaven.

   "Acts begins with a short prologue that connects the book to Luke's Gospel and introduces the key themes of Acts: (1) Jesus is alive and functioning at God's right hand; (2) the promised Spirit will come and enable the new mission in fulfillment of divine promise; (3) the message of the kingdom is to go out into all the world, starting from Jerusalem."[1]

---

1   Darrell L. Bock. *Acts.* Baker's Exegetical Commentary on the New Testament (Grand Rapids, MI: Baker Academic, 2007), 49.

Jesus' 40 days of teaching (1:1-3)

The former account to Theophilus - *Luke was writing to Theophilus, who was possibly a Roman Official who was a follower of Jesus or was interested in faith in Jesus. The former account is the book of Luke. Acts is part two of Luke's account. Acts 1 is similar to Luke 24 and then transitions into the rest of the early Church's story. In Acts 1, Luke includes proof that Jesus was seen by many for forty days and taught about His kingdom during that time.*

Jesus began to do and teach - *What Jesus began to do in the earthly ministry will be continued through His people after His ascension to the Father. He will continue to teach and do works of power through His Church. Jesus taught on the kingdom of God and demonstrated the kingdom of God with power. Jesus combined doing the works of the kingdom with teaching on the kingdom.*

Jesus presented Himself alive - *Jesus purposefully presented Himself to the Apostles and disciples to prove His resurrection and leave credible eyewitnesses. Jesus appeared sequentially to many people over forty days.[2] At one point, Jesus was seen by 500 people as proof of His resurrection. What was it like to see the resurrected Lord walking and talking and eating?*

1. *Mary Magdalene at the tomb (John 20:11-17)*
2. *The women (Matthew 28:9-10)*

---

2   Dr. Elizabeth Mitchell, "The Sequence of Christ's Post-Resurrection Appearances," *Answers in Depth,* March 21, 2012. (https://answersingenesis.org/jesus/resurrection/the-sequence-of-christs-post-resurrection-appearances/)

3. *Peter (Luke 24:34)*
4. *Two disciples (Luke 24:13-35; Mark 16:12-13)*
5. *The eleven apostles, except Thomas, and those with them (Luke 24:36)*
6. *The eleven with Thomas (John 20:26-29)*
7. *Seven disciples at the Sea of Tiberias (John 21:1-23)*
8. *Disciples and a possible large gathering of 500 in Galilee (1 Corinthians 15:6; Matthew 28:16-18)*
9. *James, Jesus' brother (1 Corinthians 15:7)*
10. *Disciples before His ascension (Luke 24:49-53)*

Jesus spoke about the kingdom of God *- Jesus continued His teaching ministry during the forty days, and one of His topics was the kingdom of God. We don't know everything He said about the kingdom, but what He said caused the disciples to ask if it was time to restore the kingdom to Israel.³ The topic of God's kingdom is related to His promises for the nation of Israel. Jesus is the king of the Jews, and He will return as the Messiah who restores all things. He will restore all things as a king in Jerusalem.*

The kingdom of God was Jesus' primary topic during His life. His kingdom is mentioned eight times in Acts (1:3, 6; 8:12; 14:22; 19:8; 20:25; 28:23; 28:31).

But when they believed Philip as he preached the things concerning the kingdom of God and the name of Jesus Christ, both men and women were baptized.—Acts 8:12

---

3 Acts 1:6.

So when they had appointed him a day, many came to him at his lodging, to whom he explained and solemnly testified of the kingdom of God, persuading them concerning Jesus from both the Law of Moses and the Prophets, from morning till evening.—Acts 28:23

Jesus, teach me about the kingdom of God. Show me what you talked about in the gospels. Show me what you talked about with the disciples before Your ascension. Show me what they knew about the kingdom in Acts and the New Testament letters. I want to know about You as King, and I want to know about Your kingdom. I want to persuade people about the kingdom as Paul did. I want to do miracles as a testimony of the kingdom like Philip did. Bring me into a greater paradigm and reality of living in Your kingdom.

OVERCOME INTIMIDATION

As you read this chapter and continue in your Bible study assignments, be encouraged that you can have an organized in-depth Bible study and love it. Some parts of the process may take more time or energy than you are used to, but it will become second nature to you if you take it step by step. The Bible study assignments will give you an opportunity to grow in these specific study approaches but continue to look at these Bible study chapters and grow in your study skills after this module.

If you feel overwhelmed or intimidated by in-depth study and struggle with thoughts that it isn't for you, now is the time to break agreement with lies and move into the things God has for you. You can understand entire books of the Bible! Break off the spirit of intimidation. You can know the Word and discover

God in any book that you desire. You have the ability to understand Genesis, Isaiah, Song of Songs, Matthew, Romans, Revelation, and any other book of the Bible. There's a line to cross in your heart as to whether you believe you can and should go deep in Bible understanding, and I encourage you to step over that line today.

WEEKLY ASSIGNMENT

The process of reading, researching, outlining, and commenting can be done to any level that you desire for any book. You could do a surface-level study of a book and get a lot out of it, or you could take more time and get even more out of it. Either way is fine. If you don't want to study an entire book and have one section you want to focus on, read the entire book and do one or two layers of outline for the book. Then do several outlining layers and write a commentary on the one chapter you want as your focus.

This week, apply the instructions from this chapter and add more outlining layers (2-3 more layers) to the outline you created last week. Next week, write your commentary on one section of verses (about 5-10 verses) that are the most relevant to you. This includes writing thoughts on the overall section and then verse by verse commentary. Remember, this isn't an assignment for a grade, this is a practical way to get you into the truths you want to impact you in this season. Resist the temptation to "just get it done." Instead, pour yourself into this study and encounter God.

DISCIPLESHIP MEETING GUIDE
MODULE 6: BIBLE STUDY – CHAPTERS 25 & 26

MEETING FOCUS:

The purpose of this meeting is to discuss your Book Study assignment and continue praying through your heart issue.

DISCUSSION QUESTIONS (IN ORDER OF IMPORTANCE):

1. *Heart Issue:*
   a. Share how your heart issue has been going since the last meeting. Take time together to ask God for more clarity concerning the current heart issue or ask Him to highlight more things to pray through during this meeting. Use the simple deliverance prayer steps from the last module.

2. *Chapter Questions:*
   a. Chapter 25 & 26 – Discuss any journaled thoughts and questions from the chapters. Do you have the vision to go deep in Bible study? Does in-depth Bible study intimidate you?
   b. Book Study Assignment – In-depth, discuss how the Book Study is going for you and what you are learning about your book of the Bible.

3. *Spiritual Pursuits:*
   a. Practically, how is your prayer schedule going? How many days have you walked out your prayer schedule? Do you need to make small changes to your schedule? How are your daily prayer times going, and how is God impacting you through them?

4. Briefly review the assignments for the next two weeks together.

MEETING NOTES:

_____

_____

_____

_____

_____

_____

_____

_____

_____

_____

27
WORD STUDIES & INTERPRETATION

THE BIBLE FUELS PRAYER

The Bible is the most powerful thing God has given to anchor and fuel our hearts. God wants His Word to be the center of our relationship with Him and for every prayer expression to flow out of it. When we make the Bible the centerpiece of our life in God, His words become like logs that sustain the bonfire of prayer in our hearts.

Reading and meditating on the Bible imparts life to us in the form of faith, conviction, and informed conversation with God. The Word renews our faith and inspires us with promises of our inheritance in God. It sensitizes and aligns our conscience to God's standards of love and purity. Lastly, the Word directs and informs our conversation with God in that what He stirs in us during our Bible times becomes the primary thing He is doing in our hearts. God directs our conversations with Him based on what He leads us to dive into in the Word, and He informs our prayer conversation with the content of His Word.

I believe that a deep pursuit of God in His Word is central to growing in a life of prayer. I find that my prayer life (worship, praying in tongues, intercession, etc.) rises or falls depending on my level of engagement with God in His Word during any given week. If I don't have regular times with Him in the Word during a week, but I'm still having focused prayer and worship times, I feel slightly disoriented in my heart and sense a lack of intimate connection with God. My faith decreases, and my conscience is weakened. If I give Him focused time in the Word and open my heart to His truth, I feel aligned in my convictions, strengthened with faith in His promises, and my conversation with Him overflows with Biblical clarity.

BIBLE-CENTERED FRIENDSHIPS

Deep and meaningful friendships are based on the place of pursuing God together. One of the ways we seek Him as friends is to go deep in the Word together. If the main thing God is doing in us revolves around what we're reading and meditating on, the most meaningful thing we could share with our friends is what God is speaking to us through the Word.

God created the human heart to function and thrive in the context of community. He designed us to be known and to know others in an intentional and meaningful way. We were created to overflow in love for people in our families and our friendships; to have intimacy without shame, to be ourselves and loved in our weakness, to be encouraged to grow at a pace faster than what we would be able to alone. To have a godly and Biblical community, there has to be a foundation that centers our relationships, and for believers, that is the Bible.

The Word is longing to find a home in our hearts, but also in our friendships. God designed us to thrive in spiritual truth and life, and we only find that kind of life in interacting with the Holy Spirit in conversation with the Bible. In the same vein, our friendships can only have unique life and truth flowing to each relationship if the Word is at the center. It is crucial to find friends that long for that same truth and life as we do.

How does this look? Discuss, digest, talk through, weep, and celebrate what each other is studying and talking to the Lord about from the Word. Share the truths that have impacted you and give language to what God is saying to you in the Bible. In these times of sharing, you and your friends will begin to receive faith, conviction, and clarity from the Holy Spirit, you'll speak truth to one another. Whenever I do this with my family and friends, my revelation increases while speaking, and they add revelation spontaneously or from an understanding they've already had. At times, God's presence rests on us and we enter into an encounter with God together. When this happens, we respond to Him in prayer, thanksgiving, or repentance.

PRACTICAL RESPONSE

There are two practical responses to this exhortation on friendships. The first response is to consider focusing a lot of your conversation time with friends around what you're reading in the Bible and what God is speaking to you through it. Help shape your friendship culture by talking to your friends and asking if they'd like to make the Word a central part of your time together. Bring your Bible to hang-outs and ask each person to share what God is doing in their heart. This is challenging to do if you or your friends aren't really reading the Bible, but if you all agree to the vision of Bible-centered friendship, you can quickly grow in Bible reading and conversation.

If you're married, make what God is doing in you and your spouse in the Word the central focus of your relationship and conversation. If you have children, bring them into this Bible culture by having them read their age-appropriate Bible with you every day and make it a part of your dinner conversations. Those of you who have siblings and parents who love Jesus, ask them if they would like to make Jesus and the Bible a regular part of the family relationship.

WORD STUDIES

A word study is the study of an individual word's meaning in a Bible verse. They are done by researching the meaning of words in their original language and comparing them in other verses. Hebrew is the original language for Old Testament words, and Greek is the original language for New Testament words. Word studies are very easy, and everyone who has access to Bible resources can do them well.

Before moving on, I want to be clear that we can interpret the Bible with clarity and depth without knowing the meaning of words in their original language. Sometimes, newer Bible students assume that knowing the true meaning of a word is always the way to understand a verse fully. But meditation, understanding the flow of thought, and knowing the original audience are the most essential interpretation elements. In some verses, word studies can bring much-needed insight, and in other verses, they only add a little flavor or meaning to the translated word.

Word studies are a natural fit and support to topical and book studies. When you study a topic, you will most likely have keywords you're searching out. These keywords can turn into word studies to add more depth of understanding.

An example word study within a topical study is the word "hope." While researching the topic of what hope is and what we're to hope in, it would make sense to understand the Hebrew or Greek meaning of the word. You might find more than one Hebrew or Greek word for the English word hope, which might impact how you understand verses on hope.

When doing a book study, you will naturally want to do word studies when writing a commentary on individual verses. When you get to a word that interests you or limits your understanding of a verse, do a word study. Based on what you discover in the study, fill your commentary with your findings.

HOW TO DO WORD STUDIES

There are two parts to doing a word study. The first part is to research the meaning of the word in the original language. The second part is to compare every verse that uses the word to understand the different contexts in which it's used. To research the Hebrew and Greek meanings, go to a Bible study website with a Bible search engine and Bible resources like commentaries and dictionaries. The resource that is needed for word studies is called an Interlinear Study Bible. This resource will show you the Bible in your language next to the Bible in the Greek or Hebrew language so you can easily see what words you're researching.

1. Go to www.studylight.org and click on the "Language Tools" tab on the top. Then select the "Hebrew" tab if you need an Old Testament verse or select the "Greek" tab for New Testament verses. Next, click on the book and chapter of the Bible you need and find your specific verse.

2. At this point, you should see every Bible verse of the chapter you selected in your language with Greek or Hebrew words above most of your words. The Greek or Hebrew words correspond to the word in your translation.

The numbers above the words are assigned to each Greek and Hebrew word based on a Bible resource called *The Strong's Concordance.*

3. Click the word that you want to study, and all its information will show up. The information will include summarized meanings of the word, what other words it comes from or is similar to, and a list of every verse that contains the word. The list of verses is necessary for the second part of a word study, which is to read all the verses containing the word. When you read every verse, you can see the different contexts in which your word is being used.

4. Click on each listed book of the Bible, and you will see every verse that uses your word. Click on every book and read every verse. Write down your observations about how the word was used or the context in which it was used. Also, write down anything you learn from the verses or themes you see. In doing this, your word study could blossom into an interesting topical study that will make the word come alive!

EXAMPLE WORD STUDY

My word study is on the New Testament Greek word for "hope." The verses that I'm starting my research in are Romans 8:24-25, *"For we were saved in this hope, but hope that is seen is not hope; for why does one still hope for what he sees? But if we hope for what we do not see, we eagerly wait for it with perseverance."* The first step is to look at Romans 8:24-25 in the Interlinear Bible to get information on the Greek word. The second step is to compare all the verses in which it is used. The third step is to summarize the findings and write down my thoughts on the meaning and use of the word.

The Greek word for hope is "elpís." The Strong's Concordance number is #1680.[1] It comes from the Greek word "elpo," which means to anticipate something with pleasure. Thayer's definition says it's a, "Joyful and confident expectation of eternal salvation." This word is used fourteen times in Romans, more than any other book in the New Testament. It is used fifty-four times in the New Testament. In almost every verse, it is translated as "hope."

Elpís is a noun and not a verb. When Paul or others used this word, they talked about hope as an object or referred to our faith in the future as an object or a thing. We have hope, or we hope in something. Most of the time, the book of Romans uses this noun form.

"Men and Brethren, I am a Pharisee, the son of a Pharisee: concerning the hope and resurrection of the dead I am being judged."—Acts 23:6

Who contrary to hope, in hope believed, so that he became the father of many nations.—Romans 4:18

But I do not want you to be ignorant brethren, concerning those who have fallen asleep, lest you sorrow as others who have no hope.—1 Thessalonians 4:13

Elpizō (Strong's #1679) is the verb form of elpís.[2] The verb is used thirty-six times in the New Testament. Out of the three times the verb is used in Romans, Romans 8:25 is one of them. In these verses, hope is an action in the heart

---

1 Strong's Greek #1680 - https://www.studylight.org/lexicons/eng/greek/1680.html

2 Strong's Greek #1679 - https://www.studylight.org/lexicons/eng/greek/1679.html

of the believer. This word is also translated as "trust" and "expect" in some versions. Some versions say to "set" or "fix" our hope on God.

For to this end we both labor and suffer reproach, because we trust in the living God, who is the Savior of all men, especially of those who believe. —1 Timothy 4:10

Command those who are rich in this present age not to be haughty, nor to trust in uncertain riches but in the living God, who gives us richly all things to enjoy.—1 Timothy 6:17

Bears all things, believes all things, hopes all things, endures all things. —1 Corinthians 13:7

Therefore gird up the loins of your mind, be sober, and rest your hope fully upon the grace that is to be brought to you at the revelation of Jesus Christ. —1 Peter 1:13

My summary understanding is that our hope is set on an object or an event, and it is something we engage within our thoughts, emotions, and will. Hope is a joyful emotion related to something in the future that can increase as an experience. The anticipation and expectation of the future bring pleasure now. Hope is confidence, expectation, and trust in something or someone. We can move our hearts to trust in or hope in God. We have to determine what we put our internal trust and hope in because it is something we set or fix our hearts on.

In Roman 8:24-25, the hope is in our future resurrected body and restored earth. Hoping in these things will produce joyful anticipation in our thoughts and emotions and cause us to "eagerly wait for it with perseverance." The clearer the future or the object of hope, the more joy and excitement we will have in the waiting.

After looking at the context of the verses that talk about hope, I would do some further studies on the broader topic of hope. First, I would want to research all the godly and ungodly things in the Old and New Testament verses that people have hoped in. After that study, I would want to investigate the present-tense effect of hope in the lives of God's people in the Bible.

INTERPRETATION PRINCIPLES

ORIGINAL MEANING

The main goal in interpreting Bible verses is to discover what God and the author were trying to communicate to the original hearers in their day and life context. Interpretation is understanding what the original message was, and application is understanding how that interpretation applies to your life context. Once you have a sense of the verse's interpretation, you can apply the timeless truth or principle to your life.

PLAIN-SENSE MEANING

The Bible is meant to be read and understood in a literal way unless there are clear stories with one main point, analogies, or symbols that need to be further understood. When a verse seems literal, take the literal or the plain sense meaning of the verse as your interpretation. If you realize you're reading an analogy, a parable, or something with symbols, understand that your interpretation may not be literal. In saying that, many of these verses do have a plain sense or a straightforward meaning that most people can understand.

You don't have to "read between the lines" or find a hidden spiritual meaning to a verse to find the true meaning or for it to qualify as a revelation from God. Read things in a literal way to develop your interpretation of verses. As you do this, God will give you deeper meanings, and He'll help you understand His heart behind His words, but it will still fit within the meaning of the verses. My suggestion is if your "deeper meaning" interpretation doesn't line up with other Bible verses, and if your friends and leaders don't see your interpretation, it probably isn't accurate, or it needs further development.

HISTORICAL-CULTURAL CONTEXT

What does historical-cultural context mean in Bible interpretation? It refers to understanding some of the histories of the people, places, and events surrounding the time frame of a book of the Bible. It also refers to understanding the cultural values and practices of the author and original readers. The history and the culture set the scene or the background for your reading. If the goal of interpretation is to understand the original message to the original hearers, then we must know what their worlds looked like.

For example, it is beneficial to understand some possible cultural practices of Corinth when reading 1 Corinthians 11 and the topic of head coverings. In the city of Corinth, head coverings and hair length for men and women were significant. They communicated cultural status and values in a completely different way than they do in American culture. To interpret this chapter without cultural understanding leads to wrong conclusions.

The Bible resources I've mentioned in this module and online articles are great resources that give insight into the history and culture of the books of the Bible. Typically, if you're tracking with a commentary in your studies, it will provide you with a good amount of background information. A little information will help you significantly, but you can study as much as you want about the history and culture behind books of the Bible, and you would reap even more understanding.

BOOK CONTEXT

Book context refers to understanding individual verses in light of the big picture message of the surrounding verses, the chapter around it, and even the entire book. Individual verses or words make the most sense when understood within the larger message that is being presented. When verses are not interpreted in context to the book and surrounding verses, they can be misunderstood and misinterpreted. Find the main context by looking at the few verses surrounding your main verse, then work your way out from there and find the larger context of the chapter and then the book. Each layer will add context to the verse you're trying to interpret.

Book context also refers to understanding the style or genre of the book or verses being read. The main genres in the Bible are narrative, law, prophetic, poetic, wisdom, Gospels, and letters. Each genre has its own way of communicating and developing main points, and this affects how we are supposed to read and interpret. Having a simple understanding of the genre will further equip you to develop an interpretation. You can pursue more information on a book's style and genre by researching its background and using commentaries.

COMPARE TO THE BIBLE

Compare your understanding and interpretation of an individual verse to the rest of the Bible to get a fuller truth and find contradictions in your interpretation. The verse you're studying may have a part of the truth on a topic, but other verses may have other parts of the truth that are needed to bring together a fuller picture of the topic. Your interpretation should never contradict other Bible verses. If it seems to contradict other verses, you probably don't have a true understanding of the verse, or you need to wrestle with a few Bible verses and see how they work together.

For example, within the topic of women in church leadership, there are several verses that seem to contradict each other. Some verses indicate restrictions on women ministering to people, while other verses describe women ministering without limitation. When one of these verses is not compared to other verses, the interpretation is limited and can be filled with error. When these verses are viewed together, a fuller message comes to the surface, changes how we interpret each individual verse, and explains the seeming contradictions.

WEEKLY ASSIGNMENT

Your first assignment this week is to think and pray about how you can apply your Bible study tools in your weekly times with God moving forward. Each module is meant to equip you in your times with God, so how can you apply Bible study in your prayer schedule? Write down what you want to read or study in the Bible for the next 1-2 months, what your approach is going to be (general reading, topical study, book study), a simple action plan, and when you'll study in your prayer schedule.

Your second assignment this week is to do a word study from a verse you did a personal commentary on during the last two weeks of the book study assignment. I encourage you to pick a word that would help you understand a verse or a word that seems significant to you. Follow the directions from this chapter and write your findings in your commentary.

DISCIPLESHIP MEETING GUIDE
MODULE 6: BIBLE STUDY - CHAPTER 27

MEETING FOCUS:

The purpose of this meeting is to discuss your Book Study and Word Study assignments and continue praying through your heart issue.

DISCUSSION QUESTIONS (IN ORDER OF IMPORTANCE):

1. *Heart Issue:*
   a. Share how your heart issue has been going since the last meeting. Take time together to ask God for more clarity concerning the current heart issue or ask Him to highlight more things to pray through during this meeting. Use the simple deliverance prayer steps from the last module.

2. *Chapter Questions:*
   a. Chapter 27 - Discuss your journaled thoughts and questions from the chapter. What are your thoughts on the Bible-centered friendships section?
   b. Study assignments - In-depth, discuss what you wrote in your personal commentary in the Book Study. Also, share about your Word Study assignment. Share how both assignments impacted you.

3. *Spiritual pursuits:*
   a. Together, create a schedule and plan for including the new Bible study tools into your prayer schedule. Decide what you will read or study next, what approach you'll take, and if you need to make changes to your prayer schedule.

4. Briefly review the assignments for the next two weeks together. This is not necessary if you are having a group gathering to introduce the next module topic.

MEETING NOTES:

MODULE 7

THRONE ROOM

MODULE INTRODUCTION

The purpose of this module is to equip you to access your position in God's throne room and behold God's beauty with your spiritual eyes (imagination). The first chapter will focus on your access and position as a priest in God's throne room, while the following three chapters will walk you through the throne room descriptions from Revelation 4. Through the process of meditating on His throne room, God will train your mind to see Him every time you talk or sing to Him. Your conversations with Him will become more tangible, and your faith in the power of prayer will increase.

Throughout this module, I'll frequently reference the idea of beholding or gazing at God's beauty. Beholding God or gazing on God means meditating on the Biblical descriptions of God's physical presence in His throne room and looking at Him with your spiritual eyes. Gazing on God means we enter into the beautiful throne room scene with our spiritual eyes and then stay there with a gazing posture like the living creatures with all eyes all over their bodies. I like the words beholding and gazing because they have the sense of looking and focusing on God's beauty in an attitude of wonder and holy fascination.

For your assignments, you will meditate on specific descriptions of God and His throne room from Revelation 4. Take the time to picture the descriptions in your prayer times and know that the Holy Spirit will help you paint the picture over time. As you meditate on the verses in the next chapters, go deep in what each description reveals about God, but give the most attention to entering into the actual images. Wait for the Spirit to bring you into an encounter with God. Revelation will come through Biblical ideas, but it will also come through multi-sensory (hearing, feeling, seeing, smelling) experiences through your spiritual senses, and then ideas and truths will flow from that place.

ASSIGNMENT OVERVIEW
MODULE 7 – THRONE ROOM

Continue to follow your prayer schedule and Spiritual Pursuits each week. During week 34 or 35, schedule one 30-minute group tongue time. In the prayer time, pick one throne room description and meditate on it together by praying in tongues, picturing the description, and taking turns praying out the truths of the description.

Week Thirty-two Assignments:

❑ Read Chapter 28 – "**Seated in God's Temple.**" Journal your thoughts and questions about the chapter.

❑ Read the throne room Bible chapters and briefly pray phrases of Revelation 4 during a prayer time this week.

❑ Fill out a new *Spiritual Pursuits Document*. The pursuits can stay the same or change but filling out the form helps you refocus and develop a rhythm of intentionality. Include your new Bible study plan while maintaining the other prayer expressions in your schedule.

Week Thirty-three Assignments:

❑ Read Chapter 29 – "**God's Throne and Glorious Colors.**" Journal your thoughts and questions about the chapter.

❑ In one prayer time, picture the descriptions from the chapter and journal your experience.

❑ **Meet with Discipleship Mentor.**

Week Thirty-four Assignments:

❑ Read Chapter 30 – "***God's Glory Storm.***" Journal your thoughts and questions about the chapter.

❑ In one prayer time, picture the descriptions from the chapter and journal your experience.

Week Thirty-five Assignments:

❑ Read Chapter 31 – "***Around God's Throne.***" Journal your thoughts and questions.

❑ In one prayer time, picture the descriptions from the chapter and journal your experience.

❑ Participate in one 30-minute group tongues time. Together, focus on one throne room description while praying in tongues and in your understanding.

❑ **Meet with Discipleship Mentor.**

SPIRITUAL PURSUITS   *DATE:* _____

1. **Bible reading direction and plan**
   (Write down what you will read and when you will read it)**:**

2. **Meditation verse** (Choose a verse that speaks truth into your heart issue)**:**

3. **Sin/character issue from which to get freedom:**

4. **Lie from which to pursue deliverance:**

5. **Gifting to pursue** (Include simple ways you can pursue it)**:**

6. **Weekly Prayer Schedule**—Write down your plan for the *specific times* you are committed to spending with God each day, and *what specifically you plan to do during those times*. Include what your study or meditation focus will be. Refer to the example schedule in Chapter Two. (e.g., Monday 6-6:30 am—Tongues, 6:30-7:30 am—Meditation on Song of Solomon 1:2)

Monday

Tuesday

Wednesday

Thursday

Friday

Saturday

Sunday

28

SEATED IN GOD'S TEMPLE

MY TESTIMONY

In my early years, my prayer life was transformed as I learned to engage God as a Person with my spiritual eyes. The principle of interacting with God with my spiritual senses became foundational, and it became a fountain of encounter from which worship gushed out. As a fruit of consistently meditating on the throne room in Revelation 4, my imagination quickly pictures Him and engages with Him whenever I spend time with Him. When I close my eyes, I see, hear, and feel the whispers of that room and God's splendor as though I'm really there.

This has been a powerful way to connect to Him as a real person, a helpful way to stay focused and engaged in my mind, and a place to experience awe and fascination with God. Most people struggle in prayer because of distracted thinking and because they don't have anything to focus their minds on. I've found that the prayer posture of gazing on God addresses the issue of a distracted mind and exercises more of our spiritual senses. Not only does it heal distraction, gazing on God supernaturally connects us to our heavenly position in Jesus and causes us to live from the throne room in every area of our lives.

SETTING OUR MINDS ON GOD

If then you were raised with Christ, seek those things which are above, where Christ is, sitting at the right hand of God. Set your mind on things above, not on things on the earth. For you died, and your life is hidden with Christ in God. When Christ who is our life appears, then you also will appear with Him in glory. Therefore put to death your members which are on the earth: fornication, uncleanness, passion, evil desire, and covetousness, which is idolatry.—Colossians 3:1-5

In Colossians 3, Paul calls believers to come into God's throne room to gaze on His beauty as a part of our inheritance in Christ. I love how he begins this chapter, "If then you were raised with Christ." If God raised our spirits with Christ into heaven, the logical response is to access and live from our position and experience in heaven. This passage screams of our identity in Christ and the benefits God has for us through His Son.

Initially, you might not see the throne room language in these verses, but Paul is clearly talking about the heavenly throne room. He uses different words to describe heaven, such as being "raised" with Christ, seeking those things which are "above," "where Christ is sitting at the right hand of God," and setting your mind on things "above" rather than the things on earth. Our spirits have access to heaven, but our members (bodies) are "on the earth." All these phrases are pointing to the throne room in heaven where Jesus and the Father are sitting.

PAUL'S INSIGHT

Paul invites us to enter the throne room in these verses and then tells us how to enter. He says to "set your mind on things above" as the pathway of spiritually accessing the throne room where God dwells. Paul is saying that believers can enter into and perceive the spiritual realm by setting their thoughts on God. We gaze on God and pursue experiences with Him in His throne room by setting our minds on Bible verses that describe Him and the throne room. Engaging our minds in Biblical meditation is a crucial spiritual principle!

What does it mean to set your mind on something? Setting your mind refers to choosing to think about a Biblical truth during meditation. You have to decide to focus your attention on God; otherwise, your mind will gravitate towards other things. Choosing to bring our thoughts into focus on God to experience Him, rather than focusing on the desires of the flesh, was one of Paul's main teaching points throughout his letters.[1] In context to the throne room, we set our minds by thinking about and praying about the Biblical descriptions of God's throne room.

The second aspect of setting our minds is to focus our thoughts on God's image. Our imaginations are from God, and they are our spiritual eyes with which we can behold God's faint image. In Ephesians 1, Paul calls them the "eyes of your understanding." Closing our eyes, and picturing God in the way that the Bible describes is a significant part of setting our mind on things above.

THE POWER OF SETTING OUR MINDS

God has given us a mind with a holy spiritual movie screen called the imagination or our spiritual eyes. On this same screen, God communicates things to us in the

---

1   Romans 8:5, 6:6, 11; Philippians 3:19.

form of prophecy, but also His physical beauty in the heavenly realm. We step into and experience spiritual realities as we set our minds on God. Meditation is more than just thinking about God and being inspired. Meditation connects the rest of our being with the spiritual reality that our spirit-man experiences all the time. I truly believe that our thoughts and imagination are God's ordained doorway into the spiritual realm, and if given enough time to be focused on Him, it will transform us.[2]

> *But we all, with unveiled face, beholding as in a mirror the glory of the Lord, are being transformed in the same image from glory to glory, just as by the Spirit of the Lord.*—2 Corinthians 3:18

When you close your eyes to picture God, a faint image will begin to form based on the Biblical descriptions you're meditating on. In 2 Corinthians 3:18, Paul talks about beholding the glory of God with our imaginations. One of his points in this verse is that we can behold God's glory but mostly in faint impressions, as in a reflection of an ancient mirror. In Paul's day, mirrors gave a dim and general reflection instead of the clear and detailed reflections we see in our mirrors today.

This same verse highlights another point that what we think about and what we picture in our minds releases spiritual light or darkness into our emotions, desires, and bodies. Our inner life is transformed as it receives God's light in the place where we behold and meditate on Him. In Matthew 6:22, Jesus said, *"If your eye is good then your whole body will be full of light, and if your eye is bad then your whole body is full of darkness."* This verse has many applications, but one is that what we look at with our spiritual eyes imparts spiritual power to our entire being.

---

2   Romans 12:1-2; Ephesians 4:23.

I picture our spiritual eyes as being doorways in the spiritual realm that let in whatever they look at whether that be God's light or demonic darkness. When we close our eyes and behold God's faint image, His light and glory supernaturally fill our spiritual eyes and go into the rest of our being to bring light and life. When we behold specific aspects of His presence, that presence illuminates the rest of our being.

In the same vein, our beings can be infected with darkness if we look at darkness with our eyes or behold darkness with our imaginations. In context to Matthew 6, areas of darkness include imagining immorality, money, and anger. When you view or imagine immoral images, imagine wealth, or imagine playing out anger towards others, they stir up all kinds of sinful passions inside. Imagining sinful activities also gives demons legal access to your inner man and body.

SEATED IN THE THRONE ROOM

Or do you not know that as many of us as were baptized into Christ Jesus were baptized into His death? Therefore we were buried with Him through baptism into death, that just as Christ was raised from the dead by the glory of the Father, even so we also should walk in newness of life.—Romans 6:3-4

Even when we were dead in trespasses, made us alive together with Christ (by grace you have been saved), and raised us up together, and made us sit together in the heavenly places in Christ Jesus.—Ephesians 2:5-6

For through Him we both have access by one Spirit to the Father. —Ephesians 2:18

Our spirits have been given literal access to God's throne room and seated on thrones with Him. We can gaze on God in His throne room and experience Him because our spirit-man has direct access there through our union with Jesus. In a spiritual sense, we have been joined to Him in His death, burial, resurrection, ascension, and enthronement in heaven.[3] In Ephesians 2:5-6, Paul says our spirit-man has been raised up or brought up to heaven with Jesus and made to sit together with Him in the throne room. In fact, we are already citizens of heaven, and our names have already been registered in the city's book.[4] Our bodies will experience the fullness of these realities at Jesus' second coming, but our spirit-man is already experiencing the benefits.

These verses and these spiritual realities have incredible implications on our identities in Christ and our partnership with Him in prayer, but my main point in this section is that we have access to gaze on God's manifest beauty with the eyes of our spirit. This is the good news of the gospel. Jesus has brought us into the beauty realm of God to be stunned and amazed as we look on and behold the uncreated God in all His splendor! He wants to fascinate us and satisfy us as we drink from the holy river of His indescribable glory!

LITERAL TEMPLE AND THRONE ROOM

There is a literal temple in heaven where Jesus and the Father sit enthroned. This is the temple that Jesus has given us access to through His blood. Temple and throne room are synonymous in God's perspective. The Old Testament priests needed the blood of a sacrifice to have access to God's presence in the Holy of

---

3   Romans 6:3-5.

4   Hebrews 12:22-23; Philippians 3:20.

holies. Likewise, we needed Jesus' blood to make a way into God's presence. But Jesus' blood was superior to the blood of animals. His blood didn't cleanse a human-made temple on the earth; it cleansed a temple that God made in heaven and reconciled us to God's manifest presence in that place.

> *Therefore it was necessary that the copies of the things in the heavens should be purified with these, but the heavenly things themselves with better sacrifices than these. For Christ has not entered the holy places made with hands, which are copies of the true, but into heaven itself, now to appear in the presence of God for us.—Hebrews 9:23-24*

> *But Christ came as a High Priest of the good things to come, with the greater and more perfect tabernacle not made with hands, that is, not of this creation. —Hebrews 9:11*

Hebrews highlights the reality that the earthly temples were only copies of the temple in heaven from God's perspective.[5] God showed Moses and King David the heavenly temples and instructed them to make divine copies on the earth. This means the earthly temples replicated parts of the heavenly temple, and that there is in fact a literal temple in heaven. Just as the High Priests sprinkled blood and entered God's presence in the earthly temple, Jesus entered into "heaven itself, now to appear in the presence of God for us." Jesus is the High Priest of a temple "not made with hands, that is, not of this creation." The earthly temples were copies of a "greater and more perfect tabernacle."

---

5 Hebrews 8:5.

Therefore brethren, having boldness to enter the holiest by the blood of Jesus, by a new and living way which He consecrated for us, through the veil, that is, His flesh. —Hebrews 10:19-20

Not with the blood of goats and calves, but with His own blood He entered the Most Holy Place once and for all, having obtained eternal redemption. —Hebrews 9:12

Jesus has made a way for us to literally come into the Holy of holies in His heavenly temple to live in the manifest presence of the Father. None of this is symbolic. His blood was real, and the heavenly temple is real. His manifest presence in that temple and our access is real. Jesus ministers as a Priest in this temple, and He beckons us to enter in with Him.

When we close our eyes and set our minds on things above, we access this temple and interact with God. Our spirit-man lives in this temple through our union with Jesus. When we set our minds on this room, our thoughts and emotions connect with the heavenly atmosphere that our spirit-man experiences. I believe we can see, feel, and hear the whispers of what heaven is like when we set our minds on the descriptions of the throne room and God's beauty with the Spirit.

THE BEAUTY OF BEAUTIES

God is beautiful in two different ways that are deeply connected: His visible physical presence and His personality. I believe King David beheld God's beauty in both ways all the days of his life.[6] God has revealed both areas to us in the

---

6   Psalm 27:4.

Bible, and they both speak into each other. God's physical presence is detailed and glorious, and it's a direct extension of God's personality because it is part of His being. The exterior glory reveals God's thoughts and emotions, because like other artists, the painting displays the inner workings of the painter.

His inward beauty is connected to His outer beauty and is released and experienced through the outer beauty. The glorious light that radiates from God comes from within Him and carries with it the experiential revelation of His personality. God reveals the hidden things of His heart in the visible glory around Him. The two expressions of beauty are one reality in God.

The throne room is the most beautiful and pleasure-filled place in the entire universe. All of creation reflects God's beauty and flows from His creativity. However, in the throne room, God's raw, uncreated, unveiled beauty dwells in fullness. All of creation is an expression of His artwork and displays Him. But there is a difference when the beauty is God Himself, not an extension or representation or reflection of Him. God has reserved the fullness of creativity and beauty for His dwelling place. It is the climax of heaven and the pinnacle of all beauty, joy, and pleasure. Life, breath, color, fragrance, power, and satisfaction pour out of His being. There is no place like this room, and there is no higher experience than God!

This next idea may sound strange at first, but God loves beauty and pleasure, and He loves to experience them. He invented the idea of beauty in the beginning, and things are only beautiful because He fashioned them. God is the master artist who divinely painted the vast galaxies and sunsets down to the colors and designs of the flowers that capture our attention. He loves beauty, and it flows out of Him like a mighty river. If God has displayed such beauty in creation, which is tainted by sin right now but still causes us to marvel, how much more His throne room and His actual presence? How much more detailed, and creative, and expressive would God be when creating His very own dwelling place.

Not only does He love beauty, but He also puts a longing for beauty within us. Everybody longs to see beauty and can identify beauty, and everybody experiences a sense of satisfaction when seeing it. This is only true because God has designed us to experience it and be the most satisfied in that experience. God has wired us to long for fascination in Him, and He has given us the capacity to gaze on Him now and in eternity.

This topic is foundational and essential to your prayer life because prayer is meant to be a discovery of the person of God that leads to encounter and fascination. And if God has revealed Himself the most in the throne room, that should be the starting place of discovering God.

WEEKLY ASSIGNMENT

Your assignment this week is to familiarize yourself with the main verses that describe God's throne room (Revelation 4; Exodus 19:18-20; Ezekiel 1:4-28; Isaiah 6:1-4; Daniel 7:9-10). Spend time reading through them, and then briefly read and pray out phrases from Revelation 4 as it's the main chapter the next chapters will build on. As you pray out phrases, try to picture the descriptions, and watch the Holy Spirit make the throne room more real.

29

GOD'S THRONE & GLORIOUS COLORS

INTRODUCTION

These next three chapters will equip you to understand the various passages that describe God's throne room. Each description will have a short explanation, verse references, an example of how I would picture it, and examples of how I would meditate on it. These chapters go verse by verse through Revelation chapter 4 and tie in the other foundational chapters.

There are a lot of descriptions of the throne room, so don't be overwhelmed. This module is only an introduction to the topic. The main purpose of reading through the throne room verses and picturing them in meditation is to begin your journey of seeing God in the Spirit. As you start to incorporate gazing on God in your everyday times with Him, you will probably only focus on one or two descriptions at a time. Over months of doing this, the Holy Spirit will help you begin to see multiple descriptions come together at the same time to see a fuller picture and experience of what's happening around the throne. Your role is to cultivate eyes that see God by setting your mind on one description at a time in meditation. His role is to bring you into an encounter so that what you set your mind on becomes a supernatural impression, and you end up just gazing in awe and wonder.

ENGAGING A PERSON

Focusing on God will lead you to a greater sense of intimacy with Him in prayer. I have experienced this, and I hear this testimony repeatedly from those around me. When you picture God right in front of you, it transforms prayer! When the throne room scene becomes more real, your sense of talking to a real Person will greatly increase. Prayer is so much more enjoyable and tangible when God feels like a living Person who is fully present. It will also produce sobriety and faith that He hears everything you say to Him and that the mighty One on the throne has the power to accomplish His purposes.

When I connect to God visually, everything about my time with Him in that moment completely changes. He's no longer distant and far off in heaven or vague and invisible, which makes my heart disconnect in unbelief. Initially, visualizing Him may take a lot of conscious effort, but taking time to picture God next to you or in the throne room will make your times with Him far more intimate.

IN THE SPIRIT (REVELATION 4:2)

John entered into the spiritual realm, which is where God and all the angels dwell. God is Spirit, and we must enter the spiritual realm to interact with Him.

It is a literal realm that is not seen by the physical eye. John had an open vision, which God may have for you at some point, but even the impression level, seeing in our imagination, is supernatural. We need the Holy Spirit to give us supernatural revelation as we gaze on God to experience it. We position our hearts in meditation and set our minds on the Biblical images and wait for the Spirit to make them alive in our hearts.[1]

BEHOLD (REVELATION 4:2)

The phrase, "I looked and behold," is used about seven different times in Revelation when John is seeing something significant in an open vision.[2] The Greek word for "behold" means to see with our eyes, see with our mind, perceive, become acquainted with by experience, and pay attention and respond.[3] John was gripped with fascination in seeing God as he experienced the throne room. His exhortation to us is to behold, pay great attention to this vision, slow down, and gaze upon God until we experience Him and are fascinated like John was.[4]

A THRONE SET IN HEAVEN (REVELATION 4:2)

The first thing John saw in heaven was the Father's throne. It is the center of the universe, and everything receives life and direction from this throne. It is the stability of creation. It is the place where God can rest. God's throne is highlighted about forty times in the book of Revelation because it reveals God's ultimate

---

1   Ephesians 1:17-19; John 16:13-14, 26; Ezekiel 11:24; 2 Kings 6:17.

2   Revelation 5:6, 7:9, 14:1, 14:14.

3   Strong's Greek #3708 - https://www.studylight.org/lexicons/greek/3708.html

4   Psalm 27:4; Revelation 5:6, 7:9, 14:14, 19:11.

leadership over the events of creation. John saw all the events of Revelation from the perspective of God being in control on the throne. John Wesley, the famous church leader in the 1700's, said that he was only fearful for a few moments during his life because he saw God ruling all things well on His throne.

God's throne speaks of His power, ownership, authority, involvement, and ultimate responsibility for creation. It also speaks of His wisdom, His ability to see all things and evaluate all things. It also speaks of His divine activity. The Father has all dominion over creation. Everything is His, and He has the right and power to bring to pass the things of His heart. God is King, and He governs from the throne. Every plan and decision is made and then decreed from the throne.

God's throne is set and established in heaven. It is immovable and unshakeable. It has been established and planted from eternity and nothing can overcome His power, "*The LORD has established His throne in the heavens, and His kingdom rules over all.*"[5] He is enthroned with power and rules righteously over all of creation, "*But the LORD sits enthroned forever; He has established His throne for justice, and He judges the world with righteousness; He judges the people with uprightness.*"[6]

FATHER'S THRONE

I watched till thrones were put in place, and the Ancient of Days was seated; His garment was white as snow, and the hair of His head was like pure wool. His throne was a fiery flame, its wheels a burning fire; a fiery stream issued and came forth from before Him.—Daniel 7:9-10

---

5 Psalm 103:19.

6 Psalm 9:7.

The Father's throne is a fiery flame. His throne is a raging fire with chariot-like wheels that are also on fire. The fire could speak of His all-consuming power, which burns up everything that hinders His kingdom and His absolute purity in all the things that He does. Revelation 20 describes the Father's throne as the great white throne on which He judges the dead. His throne is great in size, strength, and majesty, and it is a magnificent white color that radiates purity and light.

Out of the Father's throne comes forth a river of fire, which I believe is the river of life that comes out of God's throne, *"And he showed me a pure river of water of life, clear as crystal, proceeding from the throne of God and of the Lamb."*[7] This river flows from God as its source, and it brings God's life wherever it goes.

JESUS' THRONE

And above the firmament over their heads was the likeness of a throne, in appearance like a sapphire stone.—Ezekiel 1:27

Jesus' throne is next to the Father's throne.[8] Ezekiel saw Jesus' throne as a deep blue sapphire color, which is the same color and make-up as the sea of glass that makes up the floor in the throne room.[9] It's common to believe that the sapphire mentioned in the Bible is now called lapis lazuli. It has a true-blue color to it with reflective gold-like particles inside it.[10] I'm assuming it has a blue color to it like

---

7   Revelation 22:1.

8   Revelation 22:1; Hebrews 8:1; Psalm 110:1.

9   Exodus 24:10.

10 Hobart King, "Lapis Lazuli," Geology.com.
   https://geology.com/gemstones/lapis-lazuli/
   Joseph Jacobs and Immanuel Benzinger, "Sapphire," Jewish Encyclopedia online.
   http://www.jewishencyclopedia.com/articles/13190-sapphire

the sky, but with a supernatural clearness to it like crystal. His throne may be the same color as the sea of glass because it speaks of His involvement and connection to creation as a Man and His supremacy over creation as the King on the throne above the heavens.[11]

EXAMPLE IMAGES

I picture myself in front of Jesus' throne and the Father's throne, and I slowly picture their thrones' colors and qualities. Their thrones are majestic and stately and full of authority. I picture the Father on His fiery throne, and I see a vast bright bonfire. I visualize it, and then I listen to the sounds of the flames moving and burning. Next to the Father, I picture Jesus' throne with the deep but clear sapphire color with movement and supernatural clarity. I feel the weight and power of the Father's and Jesus' leadership over creation. They are the Creator and have all the rights to lead and the power to lead.

Then I picture the river of life surging out of their thrones. I picture myself standing in the middle of it to receive the life and fire of God. These thrones are the center of the universe and the source of all life.

EXAMPLE MEDITATION

Abba, You are sitting on Your throne. You are the center of the universe and the sustainer of all things. You have made all things, and You govern all things. This is the place where You rest and rule all things. You are the Creator, and all things are under Your control. Your throne will never be moved. It has been set and established

---

11 Other verse references for God's throne - Psalm 9:4-7, 11:4, 47:8, 89:14, 93:2, 97:2, 103:19; Job 26:9; Isaiah 6:1-4; 66:1; 1 Kings 22:19, 22.

in heaven above every other throne and power in the heavens and on the earth. The foundation of Your throne is justice and righteousness. Every decision You make is perfect in justice, and every command You make is righteous in its execution. You see all things, and I trust You to lead my life and to lead creation into the fullness of Your plans. Your throne is a fiery flame. You are the all-consuming fire sitting on the throne of fire. You designed Your throne, and it is majestic. There is no throne like Yours. You burn up everything that resists You and Your kingdom. You are filled with desire and zeal to fill the earth with Your glory, and nothing will stop You. I gaze at You on Your fiery throne, Father. Jesus, Your throne is the deep blue sapphire of the sky. Jesus, You are sitting on Your sapphire throne. You are the only Man that sits on God's throne. Your throne is beautiful as it flows into the sea of glass around You.

JASPER AND SARDIUS STONE (REVELATION 4:3)

Many people believe the jasper stone was a clear diamond-like color, while the sardius stone was a deep, red-colored stone. John saw the Father shining like a bright white and burning red diamond. The glory that comes from God's being has color to it.

JASPER - CLEAR DIAMOND

The jasper stone is mentioned three other times in Revelation to describe the wall around the New Jerusalem and the glorious light that comes from it, "*The great city, the holy Jerusalem, descending out of heaven from God, having the glory of God. Her light was like the most precious stone, like a jasper stone, clear as crystal.*"[12]

---

12 Revelation 21:10-11.

Who cover Yourself with light as with a garment, who stretch out the heavens like a curtain.—Psalm 104:2

Who alone has immortality, dwelling in unapproachable light, whom no man has seen or can see.—1 Timothy 6:16

There is a layer of bright light that comes from the Father and surrounds Him. Psalm 104 says that God has wrapped Himself with a garment of light. Uncreated light and splendor surround Him. His light is so glorious and so unique that it even outshines the brightest sun and overwhelms those around Him.[13] This brilliant white light could speak of His absolute purity and beauty.

SARDIUS - RED

The sardius stone color could speak of His burning desire. God is literally an all-consuming fire that is passionate and jealous for all of our love.[14] He burns on the inside of Himself for the ones that He loves, and His fiery love cannot be extinguished. The One on the throne is passionate and involved in the story of creation and He will bring His plans to completion. He is not disconnected from creation; instead, He is 100% emotionally involved and invested in bringing things to fullness.

God's fire and bright light are combined in other Biblical encounters. Ezekiel saw the combination of God's glory like bright light and burning fire, "*Also from the appearance of His waist and upward I saw as it were, the color of amber with the appearance of fire all around within it; and from the waist and downward I saw, as it*

---

13 Revelation 1:16, 21:23; Matthew 17:2; Isaiah 24:23, 60:19.

14 Hebrews 12:29; Deuteronomy 4:24.

were, the appearance of fire with brightness all around."[15] Daniel also saw the glory of God like brightness and fire, "*And the Ancient of Days was seated; His garment was white as snow, and the hair of His head was like pure wool, His throne was a fiery flame, its wheels a burning fire; a fiery stream issued and came forth from before Him.*"[16]

INTERNAL AND EXTERNAL BEAUTY

God's colorful light reveals Him in two different ways: it represents aspects of His heart, and it's a literal and visible expression of His heart. I believe His light has substance to it that releases an intimate experience with aspects of God's heart to those around Him. His light's substance is a tangible presence that can be felt, a fragrance that can be smelled, and revelation that can be experienced. The light of God's glory is the knowledge of God, which means that His light is the physical expression of His personality.[17] Waves of light pass over the millions of saints and angels and cause them to experience God and bow down in worship.

I think there are colors coming from God that have never been seen on the earth before, all of which express different aspects of His personality and release encounter with God. There may be one color that visibly express His humility, another His love, another His peace, another His joy, another His burning desire, and so on. From a scientific perspective, God has made our eyes to only see light. Light and colors are made up of energy waves, with every color having its own frequency. When light comes into our eyes, the energy's frequency gets processed, and then information is passed onto our minds as colors. Our eyes only perceive

---

15 Ezekiel 1:27.

16 Daniel 7:9.

17 2 Corinthians 4:6.

light, which I believe is another statement of how we were physically and spiritually made to gaze on God's beauty and experience Him.[18]

EXAMPLE IMAGES

First, I picture God as a giant bonfire with flames moving all around Him. Then I imagine progressive waves of glorious bright light coming off God to reveal Himself to those in the temple. The light would be blinding in the natural like the sun is on a clear day, but God's light is different. I picture those waves coming off Him and sweeping across the millions of angels and humans in the temple. As the light comes to them, they experience God supernaturally. I picture various colors flowing together in His glory, and I imagine the colors being alive with His life.

EXAMPLE MEDITATION

You are shining and filling heaven with all Your beauty. Light and life and burning desire break out from Your being and fill my heart with wonder. Your light is filled with life and revelation. Uncreated light. Uncreated beauty. My eyes were made to see You, God. Waves of Your marvelous light pass over again and again as I stand before You. Your colorful light is filled with the substance, and it releases encounters with Your heart. Your burning fire is Your burning passion for deep friendship with me. You love me with all Your heart, soul, mind, and strength, and You are jealous for all of me. You burn with a deep fiery passion. Uncontainable desire surges through Your being and comes out as fire.

---

18 Other verse references for God's light - Psalm 36:9; John 1:5; Colossians 1:12; 1 John 1:5.

A RAINBOW AROUND THE THRONE (REVELATION 4:3)

There is an emerald-green rainbow covering God's throne. The Greek word used for the rainbow in this verse gives the idea that the rainbow is more like a dome or halo than just a single strip of a rainbow.[19] John and Ezekiel both saw something like a rainbow over the throne of God, *"Like the appearance of a rainbow in a cloud on a rainy day, so was the appearance of the brightness all around it. This was the appearance of the likeness of the glory of the LORD."*[20]

And God said: "This is the sign of the covenant which I make between Me and you, and every living creature that is with you, for perpetual generations: I set My rainbow in the cloud, and it shall be for the sign of the covenant between Me and the earth. It shall be when I bring a cloud over the earth, that the rainbow shall be seen in the cloud; and I will remember My covenant which is between Me and you and every living creature of all flesh; the waters shall never again become a flood to destroy all flesh.—Genesis 9:12-15

The rainbow imagery is from the days of Noah, and it expresses God's sovereignty and His tender mercy. The rainbow is an everlasting sign of God's covenant with Noah and creation that He would be faithful to bring His covenant people through trouble. God sends a rainbow to the earth every time it rains to remind us that He will keep His promises. God looks at the earthly rainbows and thinks about His covenant with Noah. John saw the throne and the rainbow around God just before seeing the end-time flood of judgments, which implies God's mercy will still be evident amid wrath.

---

19 Strong's Greek #2943 - https://www.studylight.org/lexicons/eng/greek/2943.html
20 Ezekiel 1:28.

The rainbow speaks of God's desire to show mercy. The mercy rainbow covers the throne because everything God thinks and does is under the banner of mercy. In the Old Testament time frame, God's throne was in the Holy of holies in the temple as represented by the top of the ark of the covenant called the mercy seat. The blood of the sacrifice was sprinkled on the mercy seat to reconcile God and man.[21] The mercy seat was God's throne in the temple, which is powerful because His throne was called the place of mercy. Psalm 145:8-9 says that all that God does is under the banner of mercy. Even His judgments are filled with mercy because they are meant to awaken a love response and are progressively and methodically released.

EXAMPLE IMAGES

When I pray, I picture a beautiful, majestic, and huge dome-shaped rainbow standing clearly above God's glory on the throne. It has more colors than we know of on the earth. I picture all those on the sea of glass as being able to see this great and colorful structure surrounding God's glory. I thank Him for His mercy and for His eternal promise to honor the covenant with Noah and creation. I thank Him for His commitment to bringing creation into the fullness of what He has always planned.

EXAMPLE MEDITATION

There is a radiant rainbow around Your glory and Your throne. There is a shining emerald rainbow around You. Your rainbow is beautiful, Abba, all-encompassing and surrounding Your light with even more color. Your rainbow is extravagant in beauty

---

21 Leviticus 16:14.

and colors that amaze me. The colors are moving. The colors are vast and different than anything I've ever seen. I love to gaze on Your rainbow and remember Your mercy. You are slow to anger and great in mercy, and Your tender mercies cover all Your works. You remember Your commitments to Noah and creation, and the decisions You make on the throne are for mercy. Your throne decisions are under the banner of the mercy rainbow. Everything You think and do is within the covenants You have made and Your desire for mercy.

▌WEEKLY ASSIGNMENT

Your assignment this week is to take at least one prayer time to practice picturing the Biblical descriptions of God, His throne, and the rainbow around the throne. During your time, write down what you saw with your spiritual eyes, what you felt, and what you talked about with God. To get a rhythm in these descriptions, I encourage you to picture them during all your prayer and worship times this week. If you want to do an extra bonus, do a simple word study on the word "throne." Type the word in a Bible search website and read through every verse that references God's throne. Write down any information that is helpful to you.

DISCIPLESHIP MEETING GUIDE
MODULE 7: THRONE ROOM – CHAPTERS 28 & 29

MEETING FOCUS:

The purpose of this week's meeting is to discuss the spiritual principle of setting our minds on God's image in the throne room and to process the meditation assignment.

DISCUSSION QUESTIONS (IN ORDER OF IMPORTANCE):

1. *Spiritual Pursuits:*
   a. Practically, how is your prayer schedule going? How many days have you walked out your prayer schedule? Do you need to make small changes to your schedule? How are your daily prayer times going, and how is God impacting you through them?
   b. Briefly review your new *Spiritual Pursuits Document.*

2. *Chapter Questions:*
   a. Chapter 28 – Discuss any of your journaled thoughts and questions. What are your thoughts and questions on setting your mind on the throne room and having access to God's throne room by Jesus' blood?
   b. Chapter 29 – In-depth, share how your throne room meditation time went.

3. *Heart Issue:*
   a. Share how your heart issue has been going this past week. With heart issue discussions, process, confess, encourage, and pray together for God to release transformation. ***Pray in tongues together and ask God to release power to the heart issue.***

4. Briefly review the assignments for the next two weeks together.

MEETING NOTES:

_____

_____

_____

_____

_____

_____

_____

_____

_____

_____

30

GOD'S GLORY STORM

MY TESTIMONY

Gazing on God in the throne room has significantly impacted my relationship with God. For the first couple of years of pursuing God in prayer, I was hindered by a distracted mind, and I was disconnected from experiencing God as a present-tense person in my interactions with Him.

At some point, I began to engage my imagination by picturing myself praying in a valley near God's Mountain, and it made my experience more real. I used that image until I heard a teaching on God's throne room. I took a few months to study the Biblical descriptions and began to get a growing picture in my imagination of God's throne room. Little by little, I began to experience the living reality of the throne room in my times with God, and it changed my prayer life. The scene became real, and it became quick and easy to step into the scene whenever I engaged with God in any way.

In one specific season, a friend and I would pray around the truths of Revelation 4 a couple days a week for an hour. We would pray and sing in the spirit and then take turns speaking out the realities of the verses one phrase at a time, similar to a group meditation time. As we did that, we would experience the things we were focused on. The images would become a little more tangible. The sounds or colors or ideas would become alive to us, and sometimes it felt like the presence of that idea was manifested in our room, even if just a little. Sometimes God would touch our hearts in a clear way, and we would be filled with tears, joy, awe, and worship.

I've never had an open vision of heaven, but at the impression level, I can always see, hear, and feel things in God's throne room that I believe to be real in heaven. At times, I sense the faint sounds of the raging fire of the Father's throne or the choruses of the living creatures as they sing of God's beauty. Sometimes I feel the trembling power of the lightning and thunder around God or feel the glory of walking on the crystal sea mingled with fire as I pace in prayer.

I share all of this because I want you to know you can have a consistent supernatural (faint impressions) experience with God in context to His throne room. This consistent experience doesn't happen overnight, but if you see the truth of the scriptures and respond with time and meditation *until* you begin to experience it, you will be changed! This reality is for every believer, not just for elite prayer people, spiritually gifted seers, or certain personalities. It's for those that are hungry enough to say yes to the prayer process until they experience something more substantial.

Challenge the lie that an experience isn't available to you because it doesn't happen right away or because of the initial difficulties. God has brought you into the Holy of holies in heaven because He desires face-to-face communion with you. God has designed you with spiritual eyes and spiritual senses to engage with Him, and He will be faithful to shine His light on you as you draw near to Him.

GOD'S GLORY STORM (REVELATION 4:5)

This section includes the cloud of God's presence, lightning and thundering, and the voices that come from God. Around God's Being is the most awesome and terrifying storm. There is a swirling dark cloud that is a raging fire. Out of the cloud of fire, there are lightning, thunder, and voices. I believe all the components of God's storm speak of His power, divine activity, and intervention in the natural realm.

 # THE CLOUD OF GOD'S PRESENCE

THICK AND DARK CLOUD

Behold, I will come to you in the thick cloud.—Exodus 19:9

So the people stood afar off, but Moses drew near the thick darkness where God was.—Exodus 20:21

The LORD reigns; let the earth rejoice; let the multitude of isles be glad! Clouds and darkness surround Him; righteousness and justice are the foundation of His throne.—Psalm 97:1-2

God surrounds Himself with a thick and dark cloud of glory that is an extension of His being. To touch the cloud is to touch God and experience Him. It's moving and alive and releases an experience with God's heart in the midst of it. The cloud has enough divine substance and texture to it that God calls it thick. Earthly clouds are made of water droplets and dust, but God's cloud is tangible and is composed of His weighty substance so that people even fall in His presence. The cloud is dark in color, but it seems that even the darkness has substance because Moses called it thick darkness.

God consistently manifested Himself to Israel inside of His glory cloud through the books of Exodus, Leviticus, Numbers, and Deuteronomy. During the exodus from Egypt, God walked in front of Israel inside of a cloudy pillar during the day. Moses saw a thick and dark cloud cover Mt. Sinai. When God would meet with Moses in the tabernacle of meeting, He would descend through a cloudy pillar. The dark glory cloud filled Solomon's temple, The Father appeared to Jesus in a cloud on the Mount of Transfiguration, and Jesus said He would come back on the clouds of heaven with power and glory.[1]

FIERY CLOUD

Now Mount Sinai was completely in smoke, because the LORD descended upon it in fire. Its smoke ascended like the smoke of a furnace and the whole mountain quaked greatly.—Exodus 19:18

Then I looked, and behold, a whirlwind was coming out of the north, a great cloud with raging fire engulfing itself.—Ezekiel 1:4

The glory cloud has a supernatural dimension of fire that burns within it. God is an all-consuming fire of love, desire, and power, and a fire extends from His being within the cloud. The cloud that descended on Mt. Sinai was burning with an all-consuming fire that caused the mountain to smoke. Ezekiel saw the glory cloud of God like a whirlwind and saw a raging fire within the cloud.

---

1 Matthew 24:30.

490

RADIATING LIGHT

Then I looked, and behold, a whirlwind was coming out of the north, a great cloud with raging fire engulfing itself; and brightness was all around it and radiating out of its midst like the color of amber, out of the midst of the fire.
—Ezekiel 1:4

While He was still speaking, behold, a bright cloud overshadowed them; and suddenly a voice came out of the cloud, saying, "This is My beloved Son, in whom I am well pleased. Hear Him!—Matthew 19:7

The fiery cloud has a glorious light or brightness that is within and shines out of it. Ezekiel saw the raging fire with amber light radiating out of the midst of it. On the Mount of Transfiguration, the Father manifested to Jesus and the others in a cloud that had a brightness to it.

In summary, the cloud has several components. It's a dark cloud that also has brightness shining out of it. It is a cloud by itself, but there is a supernatural fire with smoke rising from the fire inside the cloud. The cloud has physical and spiritual substance because it's called God's glory, and at times people are unable to stand when the glory cloud is manifest.

EXAMPLE IMAGES

I picture a massive storm cloud that is on fire and swirling around God on His throne. I imagine a raging fire within the cloud, and I listen to the sounds of the flames burning. I picture the smoke of the fire rising higher and higher. Then

I imagine a brilliant light coming out of the cloud. I often have a sense of the majesty of God with this imagery. I stand outside the cloud to gaze on it, and then I enter into it to stand and experience His glory. I picture the brightness pervading the substance of the cloud, almost like bright sparkles within the darkness. I take time to feel the substance of the cloud as it is the extension of God Himself.

EXAMPLE MEDITATION

You dwell in a thick and dark cloud. You have a cloud that is made of supernatural substance. Your uncreated and raw power is within the mysterious cloud. Your cloud is Your glory. You cover the face of Your throne with Your cloud, and You make darkness Your hiding place. Who are You, God? Why do You dwell within the cloud? What is the cloud made from? What kind of substance is the cloud? It is Your glory. You are awesome in power, and I tremble before You. That swirling cloud of fire is all around You. That glorious and dark cloud is all around You. It is glorious with its heavenly light shining out. It is amazing with the light of Your face shining out. Oh, the majestic storm of God. The sight of Your glory is like a consuming fire within the cloud. You are a pillar of cloud and a pillar of fire with God as the source.

OTHER VERSE REFERENCES

Exodus 13:21, 14:24, 16:10, 24:16, 34:5, 40:35; Leviticus 16:2; Numbers 12:5; Deuteronomy 4:11, 33:26; 2 Samuel 22:12; 1 Kings 8:11; 2 Chronicles 5:13; Job 22:14, 26:9; Psalm 18:11, 68:4, 32-34, 104:3; Isaiah 4:5; 19:1; Ezekiel 10:4; Daniel 7:13; Nahum 1:3; Matthew 24:30, 26:64; Acts 1:9; 1 Thessalonians 4:17; Revelation 1:7, 14:14.

LIGHTNING AND THUNDERING

Then it came to pass on the third day, in the morning, that there were thunderings and lightnings, and a thick cloud on the mountain.—Exodus 19:16

At Your rebuke they fled; at the voice of Your thunder they hastened away. —Psalm 104:7

He sent out arrows and scattered them; lightning bolts, and He vanquished them.—2 Samuel 22:15

Lightning and thundering are within God's glory cloud. Throughout the book of Revelation in heaven, they are seen just before God moves in power to confront the darkness in the earthly realm.[2] Throughout Revelation and in many other passages, His lightning and thundering represent His divine activity and divine intervention in bringing justice. It's like He flexes His mighty arm by releasing raw power around the throne in the expression of lightning and thundering. I believe they release power encounters to those in the throne room as flashes of power break out from His being.

In the earthly realm, a lightning bolt is created by an incredible electrical charge in a storm cloud that can increase the air temperature by 50,000 degrees Fahrenheit, which is about five times hotter than the surface of the Sun. Thunder is the result of the air's heating and cooling around the lightning, which then

---

2 Revelation 4:5, 8:5, 11:19, 16:18.

creates sound waves that can be heard up to fifteen miles away.[3] In the heavenly realm, God is the source of the power that creates lightning and thunder. What kind of power is surging from Him in the throne room atmosphere if the earthly demonstration is so powerful?[4]

EXAMPLE IMAGES

I picture His lightning releasing overwhelming flashes of light all around the throne room, and I listen to His thunder shaking the atmosphere. Flashes of supernatural lightning break out from His being at different moments and fill the throne room with incredible ongoing streaks of light. I picture those streaks going over the masses of angels and saints on the sea of glass around the throne and striking them with raw power encounters with God. His thunder communicates who He is with a sound that has life and substance to it. His thunder overwhelms the senses in the best way. His glory storm is something to be absorbed in and lost in with the experience of awe, wonder, and fascination—and in humility when we know He is God, and we are but dust. His power isn't to be figured out and primarily analyzed, but first to be experienced and then be undone by, as we stand in awe before the infinite God Who is beyond our comprehension.

Picture yourself within the loudest and most powerful storm you've ever seen, and then multiply it by 100 to get a starting point for God's storm. I remember one storm years ago that was rumbling from miles away and filling the sky with

---

3 "Understanding Lightning Science." https://www.weather.gov/safety/lightning-science-overview

4   Other verse references for God's lightning and thunder - Exodus 9:23; 1 Samuel 2:10, 7:10; Psalm 18:13-14, 29:3, 77:18, 81:7, 97:4; Job 26:14, 36:32; Habakkuk 3:4; Zechariah 9:14.

ominous darkness. At the same time, unending massive streaks of lighting were breaking out and weaving in every direction in a way that lit up the sky. My friends and I were captivated by the power of the storm, so we went outside to experience it. As we stood outside, a bolt of lightning seemed to hit the ground in our area. The ground shook, and an incredible sound of thunder filled the atmosphere and shook us to the core. We all fell to the ground in fear and ran inside trembling. It was awesome! I imagine the atmosphere around God to be filled with this same vibrancy and electric life.

EXAMPLE MEDITATION

You are mighty within the storm. You are glorious and majestic and powerful. All power is Yours. The shaking power of lightning and thunder flows out of Your being. There is no external source, just the raw power of Your being. Flashes of lightning breaking out from the center of the universe, the throne of God. They break out and branch out in the upper atmosphere of the heavenly throne room. They flash from Your being and strike the masses of people on the sea of glass with the raw power of God. Saints and angels are falling under the power of God that is breaking out from the throne. I love the lightning of Your presence. I love the thunder of Your presence. You shake me to the core with the power and energy in Your thunder. I'm in awe of You, God. You are infinite and uncreated, and I am finite and created. You fascinate me with the levels of power that come from You, that same infinite power that created and now sustains every molecule of the universe. Who can understand the power of Your thunder? Who can understand the power that surges from You in the voice of Your thunder? You are mighty in heaven, and Your storm is the visible manifestation of the zeal that it is in Your heart to bring justice to the earth.

VOICES FROM THE THRONE

The LORD thundered from heaven, and the Most High uttered His voice.
—2 Samuel 22:14

Hear attentively the thunder of His voice, and the rumbling that comes from His mouth....After it a voice roars; He thunders with His majestic voice, And He does not restrain them when His voice is heard. God thunders marvelously with His voice; He does great things which we cannot comprehend.—Job 37:2

Now My soul is troubled, and what shall I say? "Father, save Me from this hour?" But for this purpose I came to this hour. Father, glorify Your name." Then a voice came from heaven, saying, "I have both glorified it and will glorify it again." Therefore the people who stood by and heard it said that it had thundered. Others said, "An angel has spoken to Him."—John 12:27-29

There are also voices coming out of the midst of the storm and proceeding from the throne of God. The voices must be God's voice because they're coming from His throne. In other Revelation passages, a voice comes from the midst of the four living creatures, the altar, the heavenly temple, or from heaven, which seem more general as to who is actually speaking. The Greek word for voices means a literal voice or a sound from an instrument or other inanimate objects.[5] This word is used about fifty times in Revelation alone. Most of the time, it refers to God's voice or an angel's voice, but several times it refers to the sound of an instrument

---

5   Strong's Greek #5456 - https://www.studylight.org/lexicons/greek/5456.html

or something moving. Some Bibles translate it as "rumblings" or "sounds" instead of "voices" to connect it to the sound of thunder.

I believe the voices are God's voice speaking, singing, and even the sound of music coming from Jesus, the Father, and the Spirit. His voice could sound like a trumpet, the flowing of many waters, and even sound like thunder.[6] I think it's also possible that the thunder that comes from His throne is an actual sound, but that it also carries with it the voice of God. In Revelation 10, seven thunders are personified and have voices that prophesy concerning the future. The seven thunders have voices and can articulate words, but they still have the sound of thunder.[7]

God's manifestation on Mount Sinai references trumpets blasting but doesn't explicitly say people heard God's voice, but Hebrews quotes the story and says it was God's voice that shook the earth.[8] It's possible that His voice was in the trumpet blast or that Exodus 19 just doesn't list His voice as shaking the earth. Because of the seven thunders having voices and because the trumpet on Mount Sinai possibly being connected to God's voice, I think it's possible that the thunder and His voice are connected in a way that seems impossible to us in the natural realm. It is significant to note that in the Bible God's voice is mostly compared to thunder.

EXAMPLE IMAGES

I picture myself standing before the glory storm of God, listening for various ways in which He might speak. I ask Him to talk to me about the things that are

---

6   Revelation 1:10, 15, 4:1, 14:2.

7   Other verse references for God's thunderous voice - Job 40:9; Psalm 18:13, 29:3, 77:18; Ezekiel 3:12.

8   Hebrews 12:18-19, 26.

on His heart so that I can know Him as a friend and so that I can partner with Him as a witness on the earth. Sometimes, at the impression level, I hear His voice like thunder in my heart, and sometimes I hear Him singing things to me and over me.

EXAMPLE MEDITATION

Here I am, Abba. Speak to me, sing to me, thunder over me. I open my heart to hear the majesty of Your voice. You are a real person with real thoughts and emotions that You want to communicate to me in words. You have a voice. God has a voice. Songs and melodies are flowing out of Your being. Voices are proceeding from the throne that those in heaven can hear—real voices from the Almighty. You are musical and filled with songs and declarations for Your people.

WEEKLY ASSIGNMENT

Your assignment this week is to take at least one prayer time to practice picturing the Biblical descriptions of God's glory storm. During your time, write down what you saw with your spiritual eyes, what you felt, and what you talked about with God. To get a rhythm in these descriptions, I encourage you to picture the throne room descriptions during all your prayer and worship times this week. If you want to do an extra assignment, do a simple word study on clouds, lighting, or thunder. Type these words in a Bible search website and read through every verse that references God's throne room or God's presence. Write down any information that is helpful to you.

31

AROUND GOD'S THRONE

HOLY FASCINATION

One thing I have desired of the Lord, that will I seek; that I may dwell in the house of the Lord all the days of my life, to behold the beauty of the LORD.
—Psalm 27:4

God wants to give His people a vision for encounter and fascination in Him that will awaken a wholehearted pursuit. King David had a vision to experience God's beauty, and that vision ruined him for anything less. Even as a king with many responsibilities and options for pleasure and entertainment, David had one primary life pursuit; to see God's beauty and experience fascination. David understood that God made him to experience His beauty and to overflow out of that place of encounter into the other areas of his life. David's chief longing through the day was to see God. Even in the midst of challenge and disappointment, which

Psalm 27 is about, David was anchored by this one thing. He knew what God made him for, and no circumstance or season could shake him and distract him from the place of encounter.

God has given you eyes to see, ears to hear, and a heart to perceive Him. God wants to fascinate you and satisfy the eternal longings for pleasure and beauty He has put within you as you gaze on Him. He is the joyful and overflowing Bridegroom God who loves to reveal Himself to your heart extravagantly. Stay in the bonfire of His presence, and He will show you more of Himself and begin to ruin you for any lesser pleasure that the earth, the world, or the devil can offer. Let Him wash away your dullness, distractions, and brokenness with the beauty of His holiness.

SEVEN LAMPS (REVELATION 4:5)

And you shall command the children of Israel that they bring you pure oil of pressed olives for the light, to cause the lamp to burn continually.—Exodus 27:20

Aaron will be in charge of it from evening until morning before the LORD continually; it shall be a statute forever in your generations. He shall be in charge of the lamps on the pure gold lampstand before the LORD continually. —Leviticus 24:3-4

Interestingly, the Holy Spirit manifests Himself as a burning lampstand before God instead of manifesting Himself as a person on a throne like the Father and Son. He is as much God as the Father and the Son. However, there is a reason in God's heart for the Spirit to manifest in this throne room scene as a lampstand.

The lamp image is a direct reference to the Jewish temples where one lampstand was put in the Holy Place right outside of the veil that led into the Holy of Holies. The lampstand was one large golden piece with six individual branches coming off the main branch, making a total of seven branches. At the end of each branch was a flame that was sustained with a wick and oil that was supposed to burn continually and be maintained by the priesthood. The Jewish temples were copies of the heavenly temple, so it is fair to assume this earthly lampstand was modeled after the Holy Spirit's lampstand in Revelation 4:5.

The lampstand in the earthly temples filled the dark holy place with continual light and represented God's presence, revelation, and truth to His people. It also represented His light and presence upon His covenant people to display His salvation to the nations. I believe these are the same foundational ideas of the heavenly lampstand of the Spirit. He is God's light, presence, and power, revealing the deep things of God to the human heart. The Father and Son are shining from the throne, but the Spirit is also burning and shining the light of the knowledge of God upon His people. He is active in ministering light and truth to God's people around the throne and on the earth.

And I looked, and behold, in the midst of the throne and of the four living creatures, and in the midst of the elders, stood a Lamb as though it had been slain, having seven horns and seven eyes, which are the seven Spirits of God sent out into all the earth.—Revelation 5:6

The lampstand of the Spirit is also the fullness of God's anointing resting upon Jesus as King of Kings. He anoints Jesus to bring salvation and healing to the nations as the Messiah. He is called the seven Spirits of God in relation to the lampstand because seven represents the fullness of His activity and power.[1] He is one Spirit with seven manifestations or expressions. Isaiah prophesied about this seven-fold anointing that would rest upon the Messiah.[2]

EXAMPLE IMAGES

I picture one large lamp, comparable to a tree trunk, with seven branches on it with a fire burning at each branch's end. The details of the lamp are not described, but I picture it as a beautiful clear gold fixture with fire moving through it to the end of the branches. Then I imagine large, powerful flames coming out of all seven branches that touch the bodies and hearts of those around the throne to impart power and the revelation of God. I ask the Spirit to reveal God to me and to be my divine escort into the beauty realm of God. Then I ask for His seven-fold anointing to rest upon me to bring His light and glory to those around me.

EXAMPLE MEDITATION

Seven lamps are burning in Your presence with a holy flame. The Spirit of God is burning in Your presence as lamps that never go out. You are the burning lampstand around the throne. You shine, and You burn, Holy Spirit. You are a servant who brings me into the revelation of the Father and the Son, thank you! Your lampstand shines with great glory and beauty. You are the seven-fold Spirit of God. Your ministry to me is complete. Seven Spirits of God. Seven-fold Spirit of God before the throne. I have the fullness of the Spirit available to me around the throne to bring me into the beauty of God's heart.

---

1   Revelation 1:4, 3:1, 5:6.

2   Isaiah 11:1-2.

SEA OF GLASS (REVELATION 4:6)

*And they saw the God of Israel. And there was under His feet as it were a paved work of sapphire stone, and it was like the very heavens in its clarity.
—Exodus 24:10*

The likeness of the firmament above the heads of the living creatures was like the color of an awesome crystal stretched out over their heads.—Ezekiel 1:22

And I saw something like a sea of glass mingled with fire and those who have the victory over the beast, over his image and over his mark and over the number of his name standing on the sea of glass having harps of God.—Revelation 15:2

The floor of the throne room consists of a beautiful transparent crystal. It's a vast floor for a vast throne room, and it goes as far as the eye can see. This floor is what the saints and angels gather on to worship God in heaven. In Revelation 15, John saw the sea of glass a second time, except this time, he saw fire moving inside the crystal. Moses and the elders saw God's throne and a sea of glass underneath it with a sapphire color. Ezekiel saw the sea of glass as an awesome crystal and called it a firmament or an expanse, which is the same language used for a specific layer of the sky in the creation account.

The sea of glass is part of the beauty of the throne room, and it is one of the ways God releases His glory to the people around Him. I believe the fire of God's being moves through the glass and touches the worshipers on it. As light radiates out of God's being, the crystal-like floor with sapphire (blue) color reflects the glorious light of God in every direction like a multifaceted diamond.

It is called the sea of glass because it is boundless like the sea so that you can't see the end of it in any direction. It is transparent like crystal yet has a sapphire blue color to it, which is the same as Jesus' throne in Ezekiel's vision. This connection to Jesus' throne makes it seem like the crystal is a direct extension of His throne.

Praise God in His sanctuary; praise Him in His mighty firmament.
—Psalm 150:1

The sea of glass could also represent God's position over all of creation and His deep involvement in the created order. In this representation, the sea of glass resembles the sky, or the firmament, that divides the heavens. God's throne is on top of the glass, speaking of His throne being over the circle of the earth.[3]

EXAMPLE IMAGES

I begin by picturing an endless crystal floor that goes in every direction. The crystal reflects and carries the glorious light of God to all those in the throne room. I imagine the light of God reflecting at different angles like light passing through a diamond. Then I picture fire from God's throne running through the glass and imparting God's life to His worshipers. When I'm sitting or walking in prayer, I visualize myself moving on the glass as if it's the floor I'm physically standing on in the moment.

EXAMPLE MEDITATION

Here I am, Abba, standing on the sea of glass mingled with the fire that comes from Your throne. I take my place on the glassy pavement and worship You with the

---

3 Genesis 1:8, 14-15.

host of heaven. Your glory radiates and reflects off the beautiful glass in every direction. There is a river of fire flowing inside the glass that imparts Your fire to my heart. I feel the fire and the substance of the floor as I walk and bow down before You! The crystal floor is alive with Your power and presence. Awesome crystal in every direction. Like the ocean in its length, width, and depth. There is no end in sight to this awesome pavement. It flows out of Your throne, God. It flows out of Your throne like an endless ocean.

ANGELS AND LIVING CREATURES (REVELATION 4:6)

But you have come to Mount Zion and to the city of the living God, the heavenly Jerusalem, to an innumerable company of angels.—Hebrews 12:22

Then I looked and I heard the voice of many angels around the throne, the living creatures, and the elders: The number of them was ten thousand times ten thousand and thousands of thousands saying with a loud voice, "Worthy is the lamb who was slain."—Revelation 5:11-12

There are countless angels of all rank, size, and glory around God. They work in the New Jerusalem and minister to those on the earth as "ministers of fire."[4] They also minister to God in worship. Daniel and John both saw an uncountable number of angels around the throne ministering to God. "Ten thousand times ten thousand" and "thousands of thousands" express an uncountable number. There could be hundreds of thousands or millions of angels in the throne room on the sea of glass at one time!

---

4   Hebrews 1:14.

A thousand thousands ministered to Him; ten thousand times ten thousand stood before Him.—Daniel 7:10

Angels praise, thank, and discover God in worship alongside their brethren, the saints. Like us, they get to peer into the depths of God's glory and respond in fascinated worship. Daniel specifically said they minister to God, a priestly term for friendship with God through worship and prayer. No doubt, their songs and dance fill the atmosphere in heaven as they pour out their love for God.

And in the midst of the throne, and around the throne, were four living creatures full of eyes in front and in back....The four living creatures each having six wings, were full of eyes around and within. And they do not rest day or night, saying, "Holy, holy, holy, Lord God Almighty, who was and is and is to come!"—Revelation 4:6, 8

Within the realm of angels, there is a specific rank called the living creatures. Many people believe these are the same creatures that Isaiah saw above Jesus' throne.[5] Isaiah called them seraphim, which means "burning ones."[6] These four angelic beings are the ones closest to God's throne, and they help lead the entire throne room in worship. As they worship God, it releases the revelation of God to the elders, saints, and other angels, who then are inspired to respond with their worship.[7]

The living creatures are unique in that they have six wings, and their bodies are filled with eyes. John mentions their eyes two times to express their significance.

---

5   Isaiah 6:2-4.

6   Strong's Hebrew #08314 - https://www.studylight.org/lexicons/eng/hebrew/08314.html

7   Revelation 4:9, 5:8, 5:14.

Their eyes are all around their bodies and wings, and even under their wings. God designed them to peer into His light with hundreds or thousands of eyes. They catch every angle of God's light as it hits them and moves in every direction around them in the room.

The worship of the creatures is unceasing. They gaze and proclaim without stopping, and they're never bored! Their worship is fueled by their ability to peer into the ocean of God's glory and experience fascination with all their eyes.

EXAMPLE IMAGES

I picture millions of angels standing on the sea of glass with me as I worship God. I imagine massive worship gatherings with celebratory music and dancing or massive prayer meetings with all those on the sea of glass singing prayers together. Then I picture tremendous waves of light spontaneously coming from God and passing through the masses of saints and angels in the throne room as they all respond with high praises or prostrate themselves on the sea of glass.

I picture large creatures flying around God's presence, gazing intently into His glory storm, and then singing out loud declarations of His beauty and His power. As I watch them, I listen to their loud proclamations of the beauty of God and watch the smoke of God's presence fill the room like in Isaiah's throne room scene. As they worship, I picture the room responding in worship from the inner circle working its way back in layers around the room.

EXAMPLE MEDITATION

Thousands upon thousands of angels on the sea of glass in Your presence! The place is filled with angels singing and dancing in Your glory. They minister to You in song.

I stand on the sea of glass with my brethren, the angels. I worship You with them by my side, Abba! Millions of saints and angels are singing and dancing in Your presence. They stand before You and minister to You in prayer and worship. This is the joyful gathering before the God of the whole earth. Four living creatures that are full of eyes to see Your depths, experience You, and respond to You. Abba, You have designed these angels and set them right in front of You for a reason. You love it when Your creation sees Your beauty and is filled with fascination. They do not rest day or night flying around Your glory, shaking the heavenly temple with the thunder of their praise. Their eyes are filled with Your light. They see to the depths of You and never stop looking for more! A thousand eyes night and day for thousands of years could not exhaust the depths of the knowledge of God! I can hear the echo of their songs even now, and I can see the sanctuary responding row by row as far as the eye can see.

ELDERS AND SAINTS (REVELATION 4:4)

To the general assembly and church of the firstborn who are registered in heaven.—Hebrews 12:23

Around the throne are the saints who have died throughout history and are now with the Lord. Hebrews calls them the "church of the firstborn who are registered in heaven." They live in the New Jerusalem and get to enter the throne room to worship God face to face with no hindrances! Similar to the number of angels, the number of saints must be countless. These are real people; some are even our friends and family that get to experience God's full glory! Hebrews 12 says we come to the "festal assembly and church of the firstborn," which means the church gathers for festive, joyful celebrations in heaven.

When He opened the fifth seal, I saw under the altar the souls of those who had been slain for the word of God and for the testimony which they held. And they cried with a loud voice, saying, "How long O Lord, holy and true, until you judge and avenge our blood on those who dwell on the earth?"—Revelation 6:9-10

After these things I looked, and behold, a great multitude, which no one could number, of all nations, tribes, peoples, and tongues, standing before the Lamb clothed with white robes with palm branches in their hands, and crying out with a loud voice, "Salvation belongs to our God who sits on the throne, and to the Lamb."—Revelation 7:9-10

They gather to worship God face to face, pray for the nations of the earth, and receive direction from God in their assignments. The saints, angels, and living creatures are connected by the Holy Spirit and respond to one another's worship. They are robed in holy garments and minister to God as priests.

Out of the masses of saints, twenty-four real people are sitting on their thrones around God's throne. John calls them elders because they have a governmental position with Jesus. I believe twenty-four specific people sit next to God as His governing council as a part of their eternal rewards. But I think that they also give us a picture of our kingly position with Jesus in prayer and worship. Every believer has been joined to Jesus and His throne and has the privilege of partnering with Him in ruling His kingdom.

These elders are close to God, which reveals His desire for an intimate partnership. Like the living creatures, they gaze at God's beauty and respond in worship.[8] They are robed with beautiful garments and glorious crowns as a complete picture of what it

---

8 Revelation 4:10, 5:8, 5:11, 5:14, 7:11, 11:16, 19:4.

looks like to be priestly kings. God's people rule and reign with Jesus by functioning as priests, including gazing on God, praying, and worshiping.

EXAMPLE IMAGES

I picture twenty-four men and women on these thrones with beautiful crowns on their heads and shining garments on their bodies. I picture their thrones encircling God's throne and facing Him. I imagine them looking into God's glory storm and falling on the ground in worship as the creatures praise Him. I listen for worship to go back and forth between the elders, saints, and angels, and I visualize them praying and agreeing with my prayers.

I set my mind on the throne room, and I picture myself in the same robe and crown on a governmental throne by God. I look at God face to face, and I speak my prayers and songs right to His heart. I take my place of governmental authority over the nations with Him on the elder's throne.

EXAMPLE MEDITATION

Twenty-four elders are sitting on twenty-four glorious thrones. God, You have ordained humanity to rule and reign with You for all of eternity. You set us right around Your throne to gaze on You and release Your power through prayer and worship. I sit on my throne on the sea of glass. I receive my robe and my crown, and I take my place of authority with You. I am a part of Your governing council. I get to make decisions with You in prayer and release Your plans in prayer.

WORSHIP IS A RESPONSE

Most believers want to experience genuine worship at the heart level and want to know how to cultivate it. To me, the key to growing in the heart of worship is seeing more of God. When we see more of God with our spiritual eyes, it naturally awakens wonder, praise, and thanksgiving. The living creatures have no problem flowing in worship at the heart level because they have eyes to see God and live from the place of discovery and fascination.

Worship can always be a choice when we're not feeling tender, but if worship is always only a choice, it's a sign of an unhealthy heart. True worship is a response to the revelation of God, and this is available to all of us. Stay before His bonfire, and genuine worship will continue to grow in your heart. Fascination will fill you and inspire songs and desire to flow like the living creatures.

WEEKLY ASSIGNMENT

Your first assignment this week is to take at least one prayer time to practice picturing the Biblical descriptions of God's glory storm. During your time, write down what you saw with your spiritual eyes, what you felt, and what you talked about with God. To get a rhythm in these descriptions, I encourage you to picture the throne room descriptions during all your prayer and worship times this week.

The second assignment is to participate in one 30-minute group tongues time this week. During this time, the group should focus on picturing and meditating on one throne room description while praying in tongues. Intermittently, take turns speaking or singing out truths from the throne room description as they come to you. This prayer time should feel like a group meditation time.

DISCIPLESHIP MEETING GUIDE
MODULE 7: THRONE ROOM – CHAPTERS 30 & 31

MEETING FOCUS:

The purpose of this week's meeting is to discuss the value of God's beauty and process the meditation assignments.

DISCUSSION QUESTIONS (IN ORDER OF IMPORTANCE):

1. ***Spiritual Pursuits:***
   a. Practically, how is your prayer schedule going? How many days have you walked out your prayer schedule? Do you need to make small changes to your schedule? How are your daily prayer times going, and how is God impacting you through them?
2. ***Chapter Questions:***
   a. Chapter 30 – In-depth, share how your meditation time went.
   b. Chapter 31 – What are your thoughts and questions about the "holy fascination" and "worship is a response" sections of the chapter? In-depth, share how your meditation time went.
3. ***Heart Issue:***
   a. Share how your heart issue has been going this past week. With heart issue discussions, process, confess, encourage, and pray together for God to release transformation. ***Pray in tongues together and ask God to release power to the heart issue.***
4. Briefly review the assignments for the next two weeks together. This is not necessary if you are having a group gathering to introduce the next module topic.

MEETING NOTES:

MODULE 8

FASTING

MODULE INTRODUCTION

For many people, the topic of fasting from food is either completely foreign, mystical, confusing, scary, or avoided. However, for those that long for God, fasting is a gift to bring them into the experience of His heart. In the physical weakness of fasting, there is an exponential tenderizing and awakening of desire for God that He then meets with the rivers of living waters.

When I got a vision for intimacy with God in college, I began weekly fasting and it grew the size of my heart. I began to touch God's heart, and those small experiences satisfied my growing thirst for more of Him. In each season where my desire is renewed or increased for nearness to God, I'm led to fast, and God satisfies me there.

Fasting is what your heart is longing for right now because your desire for Him has been increasing as you've been seeing His beauty and desire for you. He's been slowly awakening a longing for satisfaction and fascination in Him alone and fasting will soften your heart in a unique way. At some point, your desire will lead you to a place of wanting more of God, but you will feel like you've hit a plateau or spiritual wall. Fasting takes you past the wall and is the grace that escorts your heart into more intimacy with the Lord.

The purpose of this module is to give you a paradigm of fasting that is rooted in intimacy and longing for Jesus and equip you to fast weekly. The first chapter is focused on having a vision for intimacy with God in fasting. The last three chapters are geared towards preparing you in multiple ways for weekly fasting.

The assignments in this module will help you study and process the Biblical value of fasting and process your past experiences and perspectives on the topic. The practical assignments will help you think through what weekly fasting could look like for you, both now and in the future. There is no requirement to fast. Wherever you're at in your readiness or perspective on fasting, take this module to pray, study, and get more clarity on fasting to take one step forward.

As you begin this module on fasting, I need to give a clear disclaimer: I am not a doctor nor a nutritionist. My suggestions are coming from my experience and from fasting research I have done, but I encourage you to do more research and talk to your doctor and nutritionist in your own journey. Also, if you have struggled with body image issues and eating disorders, it would be wise to talk to your doctor and pastor to help discern if and when fasting could be healthy for you.

ASSIGNMENT OVERVIEW
MODULE 8 – FASTING

Schedule a 1-3 day fast during week 39 to include extra prayer times within the fast. The details and examples to this are at the end of chapter 33. There is an extra Discipleship meeting during the last week to discuss practical ways to transition out of the curriculum.

Week Thirty-six Assignments:

❑ Read Chapter 32 – "*Lovesick Fasting.*" Journal your thoughts and questions about the chapter.

❑ Journal about your excitement, fears, past experiences, concerns, possible wrong motivations, and any hindrances with fasting from your life. This week, talk to God about each one.

❑ Begin fasting if you're ready.

❑ Fill out a new *Spiritual Pursuits Document* for this module. The pursuits can stay the same or change but filling out the form monthly helps you refocus and develop a rhythm of intentionality.

Week Thirty-seven Assignments:

❏ Read Chapter 33 – "***Weekly Fasting Part 1.***" Journal your thoughts and questions about the chapter.

❏ Continue journaling, processing, and praying through any heart issues related to fasting.

❏ Write down a rough draft plan for weekly fasting.

❏ Fast according to your plan if you're ready.

❏ **Meet with your Discipleship Mentor.**

Week Thirty-eight Assignments:

❏ Read Chapter 34 – "***Weekly Fasting Part 2.***" Journal your thoughts and questions about the chapter.

❏ Continue journaling, processing, and praying through any heart issues related to fasting.

❏ Finalize your weekly fasting plan.

❏ Fast this week if you're ready.

❏ As a group, schedule and plan the details of a 1-3-day fast with extra prayer times for next week.

Week Thirty-nine Assignments:

❑ Read Chapter 35 – "*Weekly Fasting Part 3.*" Journal your thoughts and questions about the chapter.

❑ Continue journaling, processing, and praying through any heart issues related to fasting.

❑ Complete the 1–3-day group fast.

❑ **Meet with your Discipleship Mentor.**

Week Forty Assignments:

❑ Read Chapter 36 – *"Transition Week."* Journal your thoughts and questions about the chapter.

❑ Complete the *Transition Assignment* in preparation for your Discipleship Mentor meeting.

❑ Fast this week if you're ready.

❑ **Meet with your Discipleship Mentor.**

SPIRITUAL PURSUITS   *DATE:* _____

1. **Bible reading direction and plan**
   (Write down what you will read and when you will read it):

2. **Meditation verse** (Choose a verse that speaks truth into your heart issue):

3. **Sin/character issue from which to get freedom:**

4. **Lie from which to pursue deliverance:**

5. **Gifting to pursue** (Include simple ways you can pursue it):

6. **Weekly Prayer Schedule**—Write down your plan for the *specific times* you are committed to spending with God each day, and *what specifically you plan to do during those times*. Include what your study or meditation focus will be. Refer to the example schedule in Chapter Two. (e.g., Monday 6-6:30 am—Tongues, 6:30-7:30 am—Meditation on Song of Solomon 1:2)

Monday

Tuesday

Wednesday

Thursday

Friday

Saturday

Sunday

32

LOVESICK FASTING

▌ INTIMACY PARADIGM - MATTHEW 9

In Matthew 9:14-17, Jesus unveiled a new paradigm of fasting motivated out of longing for His nearness as the intimate Bridegroom. In context to these verses, Jesus knew He would be leaving His friends physically, and He knew that they would long for His nearness and friendship during His absence. Because of this, He gave them the gift of fasting as the doorway into the experience of His nearness in the Spirit. This intimacy paradigm, combined with the dynamic experience of God's heart in fasting, is the new wineskin that Jesus wanted His friends to grab onto as they formed the DNA of the early church.

The world, and some in the church, see fasting mostly as abstaining from food and legitimate pleasures, but Jesus sees fasting as feasting in the realm of the Spirit. Fasting is saying no to small and momentary pleasures unto drinking of the superior pleasures of God's heart. Fasting doesn't prove anything or earn anything from God, but it does posture our spirit, soul, and body to look for another source of life. When we posture our hearts towards Him instead of food in a prolonged way, something dynamic happens—God awakens longing inside us and satisfies us with His manifest presence.

JOHN'S DISCIPLES

Then the disciples of John came to Him, saying, "Why do we and the Pharisees fast often, but Your disciples do not fast?"—Matthew 9:14

Jesus' teaching begins as the disciples of John the Baptist come to Him to ask about fasting. They fasted often, and so did the Pharisees, which was probably two days a week.[1] Somehow, they knew that Jesus' disciples didn't fast, and they wanted to know why. It is significant that the people asking Jesus the question were John's disciples because we know that they agreed with John's values and that John had a revelation of God's value for fasting. So, we have to assume John and his disciples understood the dynamic role of fasting in God's kingdom.

John was the greatest prophet ever born and was extravagant in his fasting and intimacy with God. He was spiritually violent and aggressive in his pursuit of the Lord, and Jesus called him a "burning and shining lamp" that released God's light to his generation.[2] John exemplified the fasted lifestyle and its benefits by living in the wilderness away from the comforts and distractions of his day. Instead, he chose to feast on God in fasting, prayer, and meditation on the Word until the day of his appearing as a prophet.[3] In his season of ministry preparation,

---

1   Luke 18:12.

2   Matthew 9:11-14; John 5:35.

3   Luke 3:2.

John encountered the voice of Jesus as the passionate Bridegroom, and he was filled with all joy in his prayer times.[4] Needless to say, fasting was core to John's relationship with God, and the supernatural fruit was evident!

We see John's ministry, heart and how Jesus defined him in the scriptures, so when we read about his disciples, we must understand they owned and lived out John's values for fasting. They approached Jesus and asked about fasting because it was something John taught them to care about. Can you imagine the stories John shared with his disciples about fasting and encountering God? He had years of testimonies in the wilderness in preparation to be the sole person equipped to prepare Israel for God's coming in the flesh. John's testimonies inspired his disciples and caused them to follow him in the fasted lifestyle.

Undoubtedly, up until their meeting with Jesus, they had fasted with John and encountered God for themselves. I don't assume they were religious and legalistic in their approach. I believe they touched God's heart in fasting and did it often because John gave them a high vision for intimacy with God. John had an intense message for the nation, so anyone who would associate with him and follow him in his message and lifestyle would have been hungry and wholehearted in their relationship with God.

LONGING FOR THE BRIDEGROOM

And Jesus said to them, "Can the friends of the bridegroom mourn as long as the bridegroom is with them? But the days will come when the bridegroom will be taken away from them, and then they will fast.—Matthew 9:15

---

4   John 3:29.

John's disciples came to Jesus with their question because they cared deeply about fasting and intimacy with God. They were sincerely perplexed with the disciples' lack of fasting and wanted insight. Jesus responded to their spiritual hunger by giving them the greatest revelation of fasting He had ever taught, one which would reveal His core identity and desire.

Jesus revealed His identity as a Bridegroom who desired a bride. He is burning with eternal passion and longing for deep friendship and union with one that is made in His image. This is what He longed and burned for in the creation story. In Genesis 1, God saw that every creature had another one made in its likeness for friendship and fruitfulness, and He desired the same oneness with one made in His image. Jesus is a Bridegroom looking for a bride to lavish His love on and receive wholehearted love from. In this story, Jesus connected fasting with marital love and His desire to encounter us with love.

Jesus said that His disciples didn't need to fast because He was physically with them already. This reveals that the purpose of fasting is to experience God's manifest presence. In Jesus, the disciples had the fullness of God around them all the time. He experienced their friendship, and they experienced Him, so it wasn't necessary to fast for the sake of intimacy.

Then Jesus prophesied and said that a day was coming when He wouldn't be with His disciples anymore. In that day of physical absence, they would end up fasting often like John's disciples. In that day, they would come into the purpose of fasting, which is to experience deep friendship with God in His presence.

Jesus understood that His disciples would fast out of a lovesick desire for His nearness. Lovesickness is an emotion of love and passion for someone so strong that it makes you sick emotionally. There's a real pain and groaning with awakened yet unsatisfied longing. To be lovesick is to be fully surrendered to the longing for intimacy with Him to the point that you're taken over by longing and consumed until the longing is satisfied. Jesus knew His friends would be addicted to His presence after years of walking with Him. He knew their hearts would be ravished with love after experiencing such nearness and that they would do anything to feel that intimacy again during His physical absence.

Think about what they experienced in just a few years of walking with him. Their eyes saw the fullness of God's personality manifested in a human frame! They got to look at Jesus and see the details and color of His eyes, the curves and wrinkles of His cheeks, His facial expressions, and His mannerisms. Jesus is the happy God, so they also saw His smile, heard His unique laugh, and sang and danced with Him in worship. Daily, they talked to Him and listened to the subtle intonations and fluctuations of His voice. With their own ears, they heard Jesus say their names and say what He loved about them.

The disciples looked into the eyes of the Psalm 139 God who searched them, knew them, thought about them more than the sands of the sea, and burned with passion for them. They didn't just meditate on Psalm 139—they experienced it face to face with Jesus. How would you feel if God was standing next to you and knew every detail about your inner workings yet still probed you and searched out your heart in conversation? How understood, accepted, and enjoyed would you feel if He never left because of your sin and weakness but continually prophesied His love and your destiny over you? How content and satisfied would you be? This love is what His friends experienced for three years while walking with Him, and this is what ruined them for anything less.

While He was with them, He satisfied the God-given longings within each one of His friends. Then He gave them fasting as the means to experiencing that same presence by the Spirit in His absence. For the disciples, fasting became feasting on the presence of Jesus in their place of prayer. The One that they longed to hear, and see, and touch again was found in the time of fasting as God's gift to them.

NEW WINESKINS FOR HIS PRESENCE

Nor do they put new wine into old wineskins, or else the wineskins break, the wine is spilled, and the wineskins are ruined. But they put new wine into new wineskins and both are preserved.—Matthew 9:17

There are two pictures that Jesus gives to express what fasting does to the human heart. Both point to the renewing and tenderizing effect that fasting has on us. The first picture is of an unshrunk cloth being put on an old garment, and the second picture of new wine being poured into an old wineskin. In both scenarios, the new item isn't compatible with the old, and when they are put together, the old item is ruined.

When an unshrunk cloth is attached to an old garment that has been shrunk, it rips the fabric when it eventually shrinks. The idea is that the old garment isn't able to steward the new material. Likewise, the new wine wasn't compatible with old wineskins. New wine had to be put in a new skin because, over time, the wine would ferment, which would cause the skin to expand. Pouring new wine into an already expanded wineskin would cause it to stretch beyond its capacity, causing it to break open and pour out the wine.

Some commentators will say that Jesus used these pictures to say that His disciples shouldn't fast in the new covenant because it's unnecessary and people can't handle it. In this perspective, fasting is the old cloth and wineskin, which are incompatible with Jesus' disciples and those in the new covenant. I believe Jesus is saying the opposite. His point is that fasting with the intimacy perspective is the new wineskin lifestyle that can handle the new wine of His presence as the Bridegroom. Within this intimacy perspective, it's the fasted lifestyle that flows out of longing for God that tenderizes and expands the heart so that it can be a container for greater levels of God's manifest presence.

The fasted lifestyle and the expanded heart, combined with encountering Jesus as Bridegroom, is the spiritual infrastructure that Jesus wanted to sow into the early church. He sought to wound His friends with a deep and penetrating love so that they'd have a high vision for encounter through fasting during His absence and disciple others in the same vision. Jesus wanted the grace of fasting and the value of encountering Him as the Bridegroom God to saturate the church so that the first and greatest commandment would always be honored.

SUMMARY

Matthew 9 is the first time Jesus self-identifies as the Bridegroom, which is critical to understand. Jesus' identity and His desires are the central themes of this teaching. Why? Because He wants us to know that He is a Bridegroom God who has an infinite desire for friendship and union with His bride. God is burning for us! He created us out of a pure and burning longing and then died for us with the same heartbeat. Now He desires to share His thoughts and emotions with us as His bride through tangible encounters with His presence. God wants us to experience His heart and His nearness, and He wants to feel our love for Him. He is rich in love and pleasures, and His heart is to saturate our being with Him and display His glory to us![5] I believe that He desires to fascinate and satisfy us so that we live out of the overflow of fulfilled longings.

Though there may be a mountain of unbelief in some hearts regarding God's desire to encounter and satisfy, God's heart is to give us the fullness of His life.

---

5 John 17:24.

His invitation to abide in the vine of His love and joy and drink from the river of His presence is always open to those who thirst and desire for more of God. *"And let him who thirsts come. Whoever desires, let him take the water of life freely."*[6] God burns with desire for us to be rooted and grounded in the experience of His nearness and to be filled with the fullness of God as we encounter the depth, width, length, and height of His love for us.[7]

In God's heart, fasting is deeply knit to experiencing His love as the Bridegroom. It prepares the fabric of our hearts to encounter and then contain God's love. It supernaturally tenderizes us like a new wineskin and then expands the size of our hearts to experience Him even more. Fasting is a supernatural grace from God that transforms and prepares our hearts for a greater union with God as Bridegroom.

Friend, there is no withholding in God's kingdom; He is extravagant and willing to lavish His presence on us. The lack of being filled directly correlates to our lack of drawing near to drink from Him. He shows us the river and calls us to it, but we are the ones that have to choose to drink. Through the last few months, I believe God has been awakening your thirst and desire so that you can choose to draw near and drink from Him.

INTIMACY BENEFITS WITH FASTING

This section needs to be prefaced with the statement that every person will experience differing levels of these benefits during fasting. The differing factors are your history of fasting, amount of time fasting, amount of time spent with God on a fast, everyday lifestyle, and God's leadership. Overall, God is doing

---

6   Revelation 22:17; John 15:9-11.

7   Ephesians 3:16-19.

something personal in each person's life, so He knows what to release and what to delay in accordance with His long-term purpose in us.

History of fasting refers to someone's investment in fasting. If they've been fasting consistently, the benefits add up and the experience probably increases. The amount of time of fasting, whether it's one meal or two days, influences the experience in the same way that spending more time in prayer increases the experience. It's possible to fast without necessarily spending more time with God, so if you schedule more time with Him during fasting, more seeds will be sown in your heart. The last factor is lifestyle choices. What you sow into (flesh or spirit) as a lifestyle on non-fasting days will add to or detract from your fasting benefits. With this preface in mind, let the testimony of these benefits stir your heart with expectation!

LONGING FOR GOD

Fasting is an expression of longing for God, and it intensifies our longing for God. It's an expression of longing in that we choose to say no to legitimate needs and pleasures out of a desire for more of God. When we fast, we create more time and space for Him to be our source instead of other things. This is all birthed out of desire and longing for God.

While fasting, longing intensifies for two reasons. One is that when we're not eating, entertaining ourselves, or distracting ourselves, our longings are not pacified or wrongly satisfied. When they're not satisfied, they are allowed to grow and intensify like hunger pains that grow within us until we eat. Hunger pains are our bodies telling us what they need and motivating us to pursue food. Spiritual longings are like hunger pains, and they intensify to tell us to seek God until satisfied. Awakened longings motivate us to pursue God!

Longings also intensify while fasting because they are overwhelmingly satisfied in God's presence and begin to demand more of Him. Encounters with God's presence satisfy, and at the same time, they increase longing for more and more of Him. True intimacy with God births a deeper longing to be with and know Him in greater ways. *Longing and love are meant to grow.* Once we begin to experience more of God in fasting, satisfaction and longing will grow and motivate us to keep fasting. We choose to fast when there is a small amount of desire in us, but God will birth new levels of desire in us in the context of fasting and intimacy with Him.

TENDERNESS AND CONNECTEDNESS

Through fasting, the Holy Spirit transforms and prepares the fabric of hearts to be compatible with the new wine of God's presence. The main point from Jesus' fasting teaching is that those who prepare their hearts through fasting will experience His affections as the Bridegroom. This tenderizing effect results in a multiplied sensitivity to God's presence, a deeper sense of emotional connectedness to God, and flowing emotions of love. I want to be careful not to exaggerate or hype things up, but my experience and those I've run with prove that fasting multiplies our spiritual experience with God.

These experiences are real and change everything. This intimacy is the reward of fasting and validates the truth that God is the highest pleasure available to the human heart! Often, my emotions are awakened and overflow with gentle tears or weeping as I feel the love of God wash over me. During meditation, I experience gentle waves of His presence come upon my body. When I read the Bible and worship, my thoughts experience levels of fascination and excitement as the Spirit enlightens my eyes to His truths.

Last, the increased awareness of His presence in me produces a real sense of oneness and connectedness with God as a person. I would describe connectedness as a consistent flow of thoughts and emotions between God's heart and my heart. This connectedness is tangible.

EXPANDED HEART SIZE

Like the new wineskin imagery from Jesus' teaching, our hearts are containers for God's manifest presence, and they can expand and grow. Fasting and encounters with God work something in our hearts to increase their size. When our hearts grow, longing grows, pursuit grows, and the measure of His presence that we can experience grows. This means that your heart can steward more of God's glory in an encounter. The larger the wineskin, the greater the amount of wine it can contain at a time.

> *That He would grant you, according to the riches of His glory, to be strengthened with might through His Spirit in the inner man, that Christ may dwell in your hearts through faith; that you, being rooted and grounded in love, may be able to comprehend with all the saints what is the width and length and depth and height - to know the love of Christ which passes knowledge.*
> *—Ephesians 3:16-19*

Paul's prayer in Ephesians 3 tells us that our hearts can increase in their capacity to contain God's presence. First, he prays for the Holy Spirit to strengthen the inner man (the heart) with supernatural glory. When the Spirit strengthens our inner man with might, He enlarges our hearts' capacity to experience God's presence. The fruit of a strengthened heart is that Jesus' presence will increase and dwell there in a manifest way. As the Spirit enlarges our hearts with might and Jesus' manifest presence increases in us, we are prepared for greater experiences with the heights and depths of His love. Fasting positions our hearts to be strengthened and enlarged by the Spirit to experience the depths of God's love.

ASK FOR LOVESICKNESS

No matter where you're at in your experience and understanding of fasting, the most appropriate response to this chapter is to bow down at Jesus' feet and ask Him to touch you with holy longing. Pray for a longing to know His heart and affections as the Bridegroom in such a way that would cause you to fast out of lovesickness. God wants to renew your desire for Him and fasting, and He wants to heal any wrong perspectives, motivations, and bad experiences you've had. He wants to give you fresh hope that you can feel His affection for you in your thoughts and emotions through the tenderizing grace that fasting brings. I know that the topic of fasting can bring up a multitude of questions, fears, and hesitations, but be slow to disqualify yourself from the grace of fasting. When hope and desire take root, you will find your way in all of this—just start by inviting Him to move on your heart.

WEEKLY ASSIGNMENT

This week, take some time to journal your thoughts on fasting. Write down what excites you, what fears and concerns you have, what possible wrong motivations you've had, and any past experiences (positive or negative) you've had with fasting. While processing these things, talk to God about each one so that you're better prepared to practice fasting the next few weeks. If you know you're ready to fast or already fast consistently, begin considering what the next step in fasting might be for you.

33

WEEKLY FASTING PART ONE

MY JOURNEY

God has washed and transformed me in the place of fasting. I've been so impacted by my past seasons of consistent weekly fasting and specific extended fasts that I still look back on them when I need fresh hope and vision for intimacy with God. I'm almost twenty years into living out the fasted lifestyle, and I'm deeply convinced that fasting is available and critical for every believer to go deeper in God. From experience, I can say that it's a catalyst for God's activity in the human heart.

When I was twenty years old in college, my dad inspired me to go on a fast. My first fast ever, and I decided to do a 40-day fast! I had no clue what to do in the fast except to pray during my regular mealtimes so that God could be my sustenance. It was a "liquid" fast, which for me at that time meant instant breakfast shakes, milk, and juice. Not the healthiest way to fast, but it worked that time around. Needless to say, I broke my fast after seven days, but God met me, and it was sacred to me. I can still tell you the exact dates of that fast and all that God did to me. I experienced His presence in many of those alone times, which was newer for me. The Bible came alive, and I felt my desires for God increase in that one week. That's also when I received the infilling of the Holy Spirit, prayed in tongues, and began receiving prophetic impressions!

After that experience, I began fasting one day a week with two friends. Those fasting days were always special and set apart for more time with God, and what God did in that year set my spiritual foundation for the things to come. My milestone experiences with God happened the same year that I started fasting, and it helped me go as deep as I could in my early twenties.

My weekly fasting was strengthened when I went to Bible school, where fasting was taught and modeled right in front of me by leaders who had a long history of the fruitfulness of fasting. In my time there, I wanted to fast more often but was rarely able to until my third and fourth year in Bible school. Corey Russell led a program that many of my friends decided to join, including my future wife. In the program, we committed to fast together (1-3 days) weekly and share life daily in small groups and the prayer room. We touched a grace to fast that I had never experienced, and the interior fruit was undeniable.

During these two years, I first began to experience near-daily tears when reading the Bible and praying as God's presence touched me. On some days, just whispering one phrase from a verse would be enough for my heart to move and His presence to swirl inside of me. The exponential fruit of experiencing God in fasting in that two-year season convinced me that the inconveniences and challenges of fasting long-term were well worth it.

At various times, I draw back from fasting or break my weekly fast early because of a lack of vision, discouragement, dullness, an unhealthy dependency on food, or just physical weariness from life. But I quickly notice the diminished heart tenderness, and sign back up for fasting. Every time I say yes again, I'm surprised by how much He touches me and washes away dullness and discouragement.

FASTING DEFINED

By definition, fasting is abstaining from food in some way, whether limiting eating to certain foods or only taking in liquids. There are other legitimate and fruitful ways to fast, like turning off social media and entertainment for a time but abstaining from food is the core expression and type of fasting I encourage people to step into. Fasting is turning our attention away from our physical needs and appetites to focus on our spirit-man's needs and appetites. The purpose of fasting is to feast on superior and eternal pleasures instead of inferior and temporary pleasures.

WEAKNESS PERSPECTIVE

And He said to me, "My grace is sufficient for you, for My strength is made perfect in weakness." Therefore most gladly I will rather boast in my infirmities, that the power of Christ may rest upon me. Therefore I take pleasure in infirmities, in reproaches, in needs, in persecutions, in distresses, for Christ's sake. For when I am weak, then I am strong.—2 Corinthians 12:9-10

In God's kingdom, there is an unusual principle that Paul explains in 2 Corinthians 12. The principle is that God releases more supernatural power to believers when they are positioned in certain kinds of weakness. God's strength is made perfect in the midst of human weakness, and Jesus' power rests on those who choose the foolish and weak ways of the kingdom. Paul was weak in the sense that he was attacked by demons, persecuted, shipwrecked, hungry and sleepless at times, and in fastings often.[1] He had circumstances, and he made lifestyle decisions that put him at a disadvantage in the natural realm. Paul pleaded with Jesus to remove the thorn in his flesh in three different seasons before Jesus visited him and explained this principle.

After Jesus' visitation, Paul boasted in the circumstances and lifestyle choices that made him weak and dependent on God because he understood that the Spirit increased on him more in that posture. Paul knew that he was positioned to be made strong and mighty in the Spirit when he was weak. This principle completely contradicts the ways of the world!

Fasting is meant to be seen within this principle: it's a weakness that we choose in order to have God's Spirit rest on us. Paul had many weaknesses that were not voluntary, but he did choose to fast, and he often fasted to access God's power.

How is fasting a weakness? When you're not eating, you have less energy to accomplish things in your strength. When you can't accomplish what you need to, you should naturally end up with less money, less pleasure, and less of a reputation. And if you're fasting, you're probably spending more time in prayer, which makes it even worse. Time and energy are what we need to make our lives and our dreams work out, right? This is true in the marketplace but also in ministry. Suppose pastors give time and energy to fasting and prayer. In that case, they are choosing not to do things that would build up their ministries like counseling sessions, extra admin meetings, networking, developing skills, marketing, and evangelism.

When we fast food and give extra time to prayer, we are positioning ourselves in physical and mental weakness knowing that God's manifest strength will be

---

1   2 Corinthians 11:24-28, 12:7-10.

perfected in us and on us. His strength doesn't just mean the power to endure a fast. It refers to God's presence, encounters, supernatural tenderizing of our emotions, increased heart size, revelation in the Word, His activity through us in gifts of the Spirit, and Him making areas of our lives fruitful. God's power on us is multi-dimensional, and God more than makes up for "lost time" in fasting and prayer!

In the Sermon on the Mount, Jesus taught on the same principle. In Matthew 6, He highlighted five different postures of weakness that position us to receive more of His power. In context to the entire teaching of Matthew 5-7, His power breaks sin patterns and brings the human heart into the happiness of the beatitudes. The five areas of weakness are: serving others with good works, praying, forgiving and blessing our enemies, fasting, and giving money away. In his book, *The Rewards of Fasting*, Mike Bickle explains how each of the five expressions brings us into a place of natural weakness.

Jesus set forth these five activities as foundational to the Kingdom of God. By giving, we fast our money and financial strength. In serving and prayer, we are fasting our time and energy, investing it in others and in intercession. Blessing our enemies requires that we fast our words and reputation. In giving up food, we are fasting our physical and emotional strength.[2]

WEEKLY FASTING

My encouragement to you, no matter where you are in your journey, is to consider fasting weekly. Yes, long fasts are amazing and appear to be more radical

---

2 Bickle, Mike, and Dana Candler. 2005. *The Rewards of Fasting: Experiencing the Power and Affections of God* (Kansas City, MO: Forerunner Books), 71.

but think of a weekly lifestyle when you think of fasting. If you're newer to fasting, consider one meal or one day a week of some fast (liquid or partial) and a three-day fast every few months. If you're more experienced and have the desire, consider fasting one to two days a week and adding in a three-day fast every couple months. Some version of weekly fasting is doable and beneficial for every person in every season and creates a sustainable physical and spiritual rhythm.

I began my fasting journey in college by fasting one day a week, which lasted for a few years. Halfway through Bible school, I increased to two days a week while substituting in a three-day fast every month or two. At IHOP-KC, there is a corporate three-day fast every month on the first Monday through Wednesday that people worldwide join in on. Most times, I jumped into that corporate rhythm, and it really blessed me. My long-term vision is to make that three-day fast a part of my monthly rhythm before the Lord. The fast is called the Global Bridegroom Fast, and IHOP-KC hosts it every month. I encourage you to learn more about it to see if you'd like to participate in that.

PRACTICAL BENEFITS

There are many benefits to weekly fasting. First, it is doable and sustainable both physically and spiritually. I think most believers can do long fasts, but shorter weekly fasts are easier to say yes to and navigate. Second, weekly fasting helps develop a whole life rhythm of prayer, diet, and exercise. Fasting adds a unique but good pressure to think through how each area can flow together in harmony.

Simply put, you can't eat unhealthily and not exercise and expect to fast every week while feeling its benefits. If you only do long fasts, you change your life rhythm for a short window of time, but then, potentially, you revert to your old rhythms. Weekly fasts keep you in focus every week, and they allow your heart and body to adapt. In the same way that our bodies adapt and respond to regular exercise, our hearts and bodies adapt to fasting when it's done consistently. When I have a good fasting rhythm, I feel like my mind and body know my fasting days and kick into fasting mode.

The third benefit is that the small tenderizing effects of fasting days can carry over to the other days of the week. Paul said that God's power "rested" on him in His weakness. God's power will "rest" or remain on you on non-fasting days if you have a weekly posture of weakness. Along with the carry-over effect, the weekly tenderizing benefits will gradually build up month after month.

BIBLICAL AND HISTORICAL EXAMPLES

There is significant precedence for weekly fasting in the Bible and throughout church history, giving us courage and confidence. It was usual for some Pharisees in Jesus' day to voluntarily fast two days a week (Monday and Thursday).[3] Jesus didn't say their fasting was wrong, and He didn't rebuke every Pharisee. In one parable, He compared the potential self-righteous heart with an honest heart in Luke 18:12; this addresses the individual heart more than the act of fasting.

John's disciples fasted often and referenced the fasting of the Pharisees, which makes me think John and his disciples also fasted two days a week. Anna the prophetess, "Served God with fastings and prayers night and day."[4] The language of her fasting seems like it was consistent and even weekly for decades. You better believe Anna found a sustainable rhythm in fasting to be able to do it that long!

---

3   Julius Greenstone, Emil Hirsch, Hartwig Hirschfelf, "Fasting and Fasting Days." Jewish Encyclopedia online. https://www.jewishencyclopedia.com/articles/6033-fasting-and-fast-days

4   Luke 2:37.

The first-century Church adapted the Pharisee's rhythm and fasted on Wednesdays and Fridays.[5] The early church fasting rhythm shows that Jesus' disciples valued two days of fasting and reinforces the belief that John and his disciples did as well. Paul lived out the same fasting value by fasting for three days at his conversion, fasting with others for direction, fasting when commissioning new elders, and fasting "often" in his life.[6]

Revolutionary Church leaders modeled fasting throughout history. To mention a few, Martin Luther, John Knox, John Calvin, John Wesley, and Charles Finney were aggressive fasters. Martin Luther was against the false doctrines in the Catholic Church, but he understood fasting as a grace in God's kingdom and fasted so much that he was criticized by those who didn't understand grace. John Knox and John Calvin, both global revivalists after Luther, were mighty in spirit because of their commitment to fasting. It's said that Calvin fasted until the city of Geneva was in revival and that the Queen feared Knox's prayer and fasting more than enemy armies.[7]

John Wesley, a father of the 1st Great Awakening in America and Europe, fasted two days a week and only commissioned leaders who would fast two days a week and pray two hours a day like he did. Charles Finney shook America with preaching that pierced hearts in the 2nd Great Awakening, leading to hundreds of thousands coming to Jesus in radical ways. Frequently, he would fast Friday through

---

5   Thomas Turrants, "The Place of Fasting in the Christian Life," *Knowing and Doing Magazine,* Summer of 2018. https://www.cslewisinstitute.org/The_Place_of_Fasting_in_the_Christian_Life_FullArticle
Allen, George Cantrell, *The Didache* (London: Astolat Press, 1903) 8:1.

6   Acts 9:9, 13:2-3, 14:23; 2 Corinthians 6:5, 11:27.

7   Toni Cauchi, "Let's Put Fasting Back on the Table." https://www.revivallibrary.org/resources/revival_researchers/newsletter_articles/lets_put_fasting_back_on_menu.shtml

Sunday before preaching or fast for days when he felt the spirit of prayer decrease in his heart and the spirit of power decrease in his preaching.[8] Lest we have a low vision of what he called powerful preaching, it was common for unbelievers to groan and weep under the conviction of the Spirit during his preaching before they fully surrendered their hearts to God.

HOW TO FAST WEEKLY

This section is a basic introduction of things to think about or be aware of as you pray about fasting weekly. In the next chapter, we'll look at each of these areas in more detail. Thinking about these things will help you fast more consistently, and it will make your fasting times more intentional and sacred.

PLAN THE DETAILS

Begin preparing for weekly fasting by deciding what type of fast you'll be doing. Based on that, think through what you would need to buy or prepare ahead of time. There are four main types of weekly fasts to consider.[9] Each of them is doable for most people, but they offer different amounts of energy based on your health or life situation.

1. *Water fast* – This is limited to water or other liquids that do not provide calories or energy. Most people can do a water fast for part of a day or an entire day, but there is significantly less energy than the other fasts.

2. *Liquid fast* – This includes light fruit or vegetable juices (not blended smoothies) or other liquids that don't contain fats, proteins or require the stomach to work hard. The benefit of a liquid fast is that it allows the body

8 Ibid.

9 Bickle, *The Rewards of Fasting*, 77-78.

and digestive system to rest while still having a good amount of energy. The liquid fast is my "go-to" fast. It works with ministry responsibilities and the demands of young children, and I can determine my energy levels by how much juice I drink.

3. *Partial or Daniel fast* – This fast includes eating small portions of light foods like nuts and vegetables. Daniel mentions fasting on only vegetables in his early teenage years in Babylon.[10] In his elderly years, he mentions fasting twenty-one days with no pleasant foods, meats, or wine.[11] The Daniel fast is a legitimate fast! The idea is to eat small enough portions so that your body can still rest, and you can experience the strength of God while having enough energy for the day.

4. *Benedict fast* – Named after Saint Benedict, a leader in the monastic movement during the 6th century, this fast includes eating only one meal a day and water or liquids for the other meals. Like the Daniel fast, this is very sustainable yet touches the heart and benefits of fasting.

Next, choose your fasting day or days and what specific meals you plan on skipping. What time of the week works the best for you to have a little less energy? What days allow you to spend more time with the Lord while fasting? Do you have other weekly commitments you want to plan around?

CONSECRATION PLAN

To consecrate something means to make it sacred and set apart from ordinary life. How can you make your time sacred and different from the other days of

---

10 Daniel 1:8-21.

11 Daniel 10:2-3.

the week when you fast? Making it sacred could include planning extra prayer time and avoiding media, entertainment, recreational activities, unintentional hangouts, and other natural stimulants. You could also write down a vision sentence for your fasting times and write down any specific prayers you want to focus on consistently. As a sacred time with the Lord, prioritize fulfilling your fasting and prayer commitments, even when other things come up.

PHYSICAL PREPARATION

This will take a little time to research, and we'll get into more details in the next chapter, but you will need to think through how to prepare your body to go into and come out of your fasting times. Preparation mostly comes down to what you eat for one or two meals before and after a fasting day to acclimate your body. But this also includes learning how your body responds to fasting and establishing a healthy lifestyle of exercise and diet that help facilitate healthy long-term fasting.

CHALLENGES

There are many areas of challenge that go with the fasted lifestyle. Physically, there is a measure of detoxification, depending on your regular diet, that can make fasting uncomfortable or discouraging. You will have less energy, but you will have to push through to fulfill your life responsibilities. Emotionally, dullness and barrenness will be more exposed when other stimulants aren't an option. God will meet you in needy emotions, but there is a painful transition that will take time. Relationally, friends or family may not understand or support your decision to fast. Spiritually, the enemy will try to discourage you or distract you from fasting because he knows how powerful it is in the spiritual realm. You may even face the challenge of seeing your wrong motivations in fasting.

YOU CAN FAST!

Whether you have been fasting for years or this is the first time you've considered fasting, I want to declare that you can fast! Fasting is not for super Christians, and it's not for the "next season" that's hopefully easier, because that may or may not come. It's doable in this season, and God's powerful grace will touch you and tenderize you. There are real challenges, but God will help you conquer them like He's empowered you to overcome other things. Besides, all the challenges pale in comparison to the experience of the glory of God in fasting.

If you feel a lack of desire for God and fasting, continue to ask Him to give you the gift of desire until you feel it flowing in your emotions. If you want to fast but have fears or don't know how, start small like one meal a week, and go from there each week. God will lead you, and you'll overcome the fears that come with the unknown realities of fasting.

WEEKLY ASSIGNMENT

This week, take some time to write down your fasting desires and draft a realistic plan for weekly fasting. *Questions to answer: (1) What day/meal(s) will you fast? (2) What kind of fast will you do? (3) How long will it last? (4) When would you pray? (5) How will you prepare food-wise? (i.e., what will be your last meal, and what will you break your fast with?)*

You will refine your plans as an assignment for each chapter, so there is time to work them out.

If you're ready to fast according to your plan during this week, journal your thoughts, challenges (physical, emotional, etc.), and experiences from the fast. Reflecting will help you recognize any fasting benefits. It will also help you refine your fasting plans because you'll learn ways to steward your body and schedule from your experience.

There is no expectation as to how much you should fast. I suggest starting with a liquid or partial fast one day a week, but you could fast one to two meals if that's easier. There's no rush to fast more than what you're ready for. There's grace and lots of time, and you can be confident that if you take one more step into fasting, God will fill you and lead you into more grace for fasting long-term.

DISCIPLESHIP MEETING GUIDE
MODULE 8: FASTING – CHAPTERS 32 & 33

MEETING FOCUS:

The purpose of this meeting is to discuss your level of desire for fasting, process fears, and hindrances, and work on a weekly fasting plan.

DISCUSSION QUESTIONS: (IN ORDER OF IMPORTANCE)

1. ***Spiritual Pursuits:***
   a. Practically, how is your prayer schedule going? How many days have you walked out your prayer schedule? Do you need to make small changes to your schedule? How are your daily prayer times going, and how is God impacting you through them?
   b. Briefly review your new *Spiritual Pursuits Document*.

2. ***Chapter Questions:***
   a. Chapter 32 – Discuss any of your journaled thoughts and questions from the chapter. Have you had an intimacy paradigm of fasting before?
   b. Prayer Assignment - What are your experiences with fasting? What fears do you have concerning weekly fasting, and does anything excite you about it?
   c. Chapter 33 – Discuss any of your journaled thoughts and questions from the chapter. What are the most helpful practical questions you have about fasting? In-depth, discuss your rough draft fasting plans.

3. ***Heart Issue:***
   a. Share how your heart issue has been going this past week. With heart issue discussions, process, confess, encourage, and pray together for God to release transformation. ***Pray in tongues together and ask God to release power to the heart issue.***

4. Briefly review the assignments for the next two weeks together.

MEETING NOTES:

_____

_____

_____

_____

_____

_____

_____

_____

_____

_____

34

WEEKLY FASTING PART TWO

INTRODUCTION

In the previous chapter, I introduced an outline of things to be aware of and think through with weekly fasting. In this chapter, we're going to go much deeper into what fasting can look like and feel like to help prepare you for what you want to step into in this season. Thinking about these things will help you fast more consistently, because it will prepare you spiritually and physically, and it will help you to overcome fasting challenges when they come. Your fasting times will feel more intentional and sacred like you are "entering into" a holy fast each week. The more thought you put into your fasting times, the more ownership and commitment you will have.

I'm writing from my experience in fasting, what I've learned from others, and what I've gleaned in reading books on fasting. In saying that, your experiences or challenges with fasting might be different in some ways. You will need to journal your experiences and observe how your soul and body respond to fasting over the years to understand and steward fasting in your life.

I highly recommend reading fasting and nutrition books. They will help you better understand how your body responds to fasting and what diet and exercise should look like to best steward the fasted lifestyle. Example books to read are *The Miracle of Fasting* by Patricia and Paul Bragg, *The Complete Guide to Fasting* by Dr. Jason Fung and Jimmy Moore, and *Fasting God's Way* by Sam Quartey.

PLAN THE DETAILS

SCHEDULE FASTING TIMES

Begin planning the details of your weekly fast by picking the day of the week and the number of meals you want to skip. My suggestion is to consider fasting one entire day a week if you're newer to regular fasting. If you already have a good rhythm, look at fasting a day and a half or even two days a week. I started fasting one day a week in college without much equipping from others or experience in fasting, and it was doable, even with a full workload of school and work. Many people in my life have regularly fasted one day a week in every kind of life season, so I know it's doable and can be enjoyable for most people. Also, pray about joining the 3-day Global Bridegroom Fast that IHOP-KC hosts every month. Depending on your rhythm, joining in monthly or every few months could be very doable and impactful for you.

Be creative and strategic in how you schedule fasting times. Think through your week and pick the days and times that allow you to get as much time as possible with the Lord. Also, is there a day that works the best for you to have a little less energy? Do you have other weekly commitments you want to plan around, or can you move things around so that you have a whole day that has fewer commitments?

In my current life situation, I have a family with three young children that demand my energy in cooking, cleaning, feeding, and, most importantly, playtime! For me, creative scheduling looks like starting my fast after lunch on Mondays and ending at noon on Wednesdays. Beginning on Monday afternoon allows me to have enough energy to be with my family the rest of that day, and then Tuesday and Wednesday morning, I get extra prayer times. I eat a small lunch on Wednesday, and my energy levels increase to be fully present with my family the rest of the day after work. Because Tuesday is the only day that is potentially affected by my energy levels, we schedule easy meals for dinner that night and don't schedule hangouts to lighten the load of the evening.

If I need a nap or extra prayer time during dinner on Tuesdays, my wife gives me the freedom to do so. Otherwise, I spend that time with my family without eating. I've explained my reasons for fasting to my kids plenty of times in the past, but sometimes I remind them at dinner time. Now they understand it enough and hold me accountable if I start snacking on dinner!

FASTING TYPES

Research each of the four common types of fasting (water, liquid, partial/Daniel, Benedict), and decide which one you want to try consistently. You can be creative with this as well and combine them in different ways. An example is if you want to fast for two days, but you're not ready to do a liquid fast. You could fast with juices on one day and then do a Daniel fast on the second day as a way of transitioning into two days for a while and see how that goes for you.

I have two suggestions for choosing fasting types. The first one is to try liquid fasting. If you think your body isn't healthy enough to handle it, talk to your doctor and get a plan for what will work for you. If you're healthy but overwhelmed by the idea of fasting on only liquids, talk to God about it and address your fears. Ultimately, do the type of fasting that you're ready for and excited for, but be aware that the fear of not having food might be exaggerated until you try fasting one day. The second suggestion is to stick with your plan for several weeks before altering the fast type or the length of fasting. Doing this will allow you to get a sense of how your body and heart acclimate and respond to how you're fasting.

CONSECRATION PLAN

To consecrate something means to make it sacred and set apart from ordinary life. How can you make your fasting time holy? In what ways can you make it different from the other days of the week?

VISION

This vision category includes a written vision statement, written down fasting times (precisely when you're starting and ending), and a short prayer list for fasting days. In your journal, write down your weekly vision and desires for fasting, along with any specific prayer topics you want to pray into each week. Your prayer list could include long-term prayers and short-term prayers that could change on different weeks. The basic questions you're answering in your vision statement and prayer list are, "Why am I fasting this day each week, and what am I asking for in prayer?"

When I look at my vision statement on fasting days, my heart is aligned with purpose and consecration, and I recognize the holiness of what I'm stepping into. This makes the fast more enjoyable, strengthening my resolve when I'm tempted to break my fast early. The same thing is true when I pray through my short fasting prayer list. If I pray through it consistently over weeks, it becomes an instant source of life and connection to my fasting vision, and it increases my faith and resolve to keep fasting. If you pray them consistently through the fasting day, they become deep wells of life on future fasting days. This is especially true on a longer fast, but even on a 1-2 day fast, connecting to the vision and prayer points is powerful and necessary.

In the weak or mundane moments of fasting or the moments of subtle demonic discouragement, God will use your vision statement and prayer points to bring your heart back into alignment. Fasting is challenging by itself, but the demonic kingdom also wants to get you to believe your fasting doesn't matter so that you lose faith in the moment and break your fast. It's subtle, but it's real. If they can get you to believe that what you're doing isn't doing anything or isn't doing much in the spiritual realm, you'll be more tempted to give up.

EXTRA FEASTING TIME

When you're fasting from food, you are positioned to depend on, hunger for, and feast on the Lord's presence in a more tangible way. Deuteronomy 8 says we don't live on bread alone; but on every word that comes from God's mouth. This takes on an entirely new reality when you're literally not eating food to comfort or sustain yourself. In many ways, you will depend on experiencing God's presence and fellowshipping with Him, but it's more than just being "sustained" to get through the day. It's about having your spiritual longings satisfied in God in a unique and focused way. God wants to train your soul to "live" on His Word more than you live on food.

Fasting from food is feasting on God's presence. The goal on a fasting day isn't just to make it through the day by any means necessary. The goal is to feast on God with the extra time, space, and hunger. With this in mind, I suggest scheduling as much time with God as possible. You are going to have times of feeling tired, bored, and lazy. In those times, you're going to be tempted to fill or waste your time on things you're used to (YouTube, books, admin tasks, busyness, coffee hangouts) that don't directly connect you to Jesus. When we turn to these things, what we're really doing is distracting ourselves from physical hunger and spiritual boredom until we can eat food again. I have done this so many times, and it takes away from the true purpose of fasting.

Be creative and even stretch yourself to spend more time with Him than you think you can. Think outside the box of your regular schedule and find ways to get long chunks of time and even fifteen minutes at times throughout the day. Get some morning prayer, maybe an afternoon break, and then some time before bed. I didn't even know how to fast in college, but I spent hours in prayer outside of my classes and homework times. When I was single and working full-time, I prayed in the morning, prayed or napped during my lunch break, and spent the evening at my church prayer meeting. I've had friends in all kinds of family or workplace settings, and they've put the extra effort in to make fasting work. If a workday doesn't work for you, how about a weekend or a 24-hour slot from Friday until a Saturday lunch?

When you spend more time with Him, you'll experience His nearness and feast on His presence. That might sound crazy if you haven't done it before, but something in your soul will love the place of fasting if you consecrate your time to Him. How can you get more time in the morning, afternoon, and evening? How can you set your heart or arrange your atmosphere to engage with Him even while you're working or taking care of your kids?

SAYING NO

Consecrating your schedule to the Lord also means saying no to things that disrupt your fasting day. You have to decide for yourself what being flexible means, but my value is to say no ninety percent of the time to hangouts or responsibilities that would make me eat food on my fasting days or have less prayer time. Prioritizing fasting and prayer reflects your love and desire for God, so it's a holy thing to keep it!

FINISHING WELL

Set your heart to finish your fasts well without breaking early consistently. For most people, there's going to be tension between being too strict or too loose on finishing fasts. Growing in clarity and wisdom on how God feels about us breaking early versus us fulfilling our fasting commitment is a journey in Bible study and seeking the Lord's heart. As a starting point of discussion, I say try to finish your fasts as often as possible, even when it's a little challenging, or you feel like giving up. Yes, you're not proving anything to God by finishing, and He's ravished by our love no matter what, but I see lots of benefits to pushing through in the challenging moments and wrestling with beliefs in the process.

There will probably be wrong motivations for fasting coming to the surface, and that can be a temptation to stop fasting early, but I don't think that has to be the solution. Sometimes, the demonic kingdom gets us in a swirl about our motivations in a challenging moment of fasting. Then we break early and justify it by saying, "God still loves us, or it's not about us earning it anyway." Honestly, I've been too loose on breaking early. I've broken so many weekly fasts. Most of the time, I regret eating right after I do it, and I realize the food didn't really satisfy me in the way that I thought it would. The best way to address wrong motives is to talk to God about them while still fasting.

PHYSICAL PREPARATION

The topic of physical preparation for fasting is the area you need to spend more time researching. I'll share some helpful information in this section, but there is so much more understanding that you need to own for yourself as an investment into your fasting future. If you do it wisely, fasting can be very healthy for your body and doesn't have to be horrible. But if you don't it wisely, fasting will be more difficult and can negatively affect your body.

PREPARATION

In preparation for a 1-2 day fast, eat fruits and vegetables for your last 1-2 meals. A good ratio for short fasts is one transition meal per fasting day. This will help transition your digestive system, help your body ease into the detoxification that occurs during fasting, and it will help your mind enter into fasting mode. It's tempting to make your last meal a big tasty one because you know it will be a while before eating, but that will make your fast more difficult. I always regret doing a last big meal! If you start your fast well, you will end it well.

When I prepare like this for a weekly fast, it makes a significant difference on my fasting days. I've noticed that my hunger pains are minimal and go away quicker, and my stomach can rest and not digest a huge last meal. When I do it wrong, I feel my digestive system working all day, I experience hunger pains, and I feel tired and lethargic.

Prepare your body for fasting by monitoring how much you exercise or how much you do the last few hours before you begin your fast. It may not be wise to do a huge workout the day you begin a fast or the night before because your body may not be able to replenish its energy. I do my best to gauge my energy levels the half-day before I start my fast and do lighter workouts early in the day.

BREAKING

Breaking a fast is very similar to preparing to enter a fast. Take 1-2 meals to transition out of your weekly fast, about one transition meal per fasting day that you are doing. You can research and decide what's best for you to break on, but I like to eat cooked (steamed, baked, or in soup) veggies and watery fruit. If I fast for two days, I break by snacking on small portions throughout the day instead of eating full meals of fruits and veggies to let my body transition back into eating. If I overeat, even if it's healthy food, I feel tired and too full.

Breaking is almost as challenging as fasting itself. After abstaining from food for a day, you will probably be excited to eat, and eat, and eat! As you're breaking your fast, set your heart against your lusts and cravings, with the vision that the benefits of your fast will continue if you use self-control while breaking and easing back into eating.

I believe weekly fasting releases breakthroughs over all kinds of lusts and fleshly appetites. If you can continue the self-control and breakthrough in the transition process to eating, you're one step closer to living out the victory on the other days of the week. If you can sustain self-control with eating and your rhythms, you will feel more and more strengthened to complete each fast.

Ease back into exercise after you begin to eat by monitoring your energy levels and learning how much you can do right away. Initially, you might not be able to work out as much as on a typical day, but over time, your body might adapt enough to exercise more on a transition day. Ideally, my transition day exercise would be a short jog with a lot of stretching.

DURING THE FAST

Now imagine you're in the middle of your 1-2 day fast! What kinds of things do you need to be aware of? Begin by researching what types of liquids you want to drink. There are lots of nutritionist perspectives on what purified waters and juices to drink during a fast, so check out some other resources on that. As a starting point, drink purified water or buy a gallon of distilled water from your local grocery store. Drink water often throughout the day.

If you're drinking juices, water them down slightly and take in small amounts throughout the day to space out the nutrients and sugars. I have a juicer machine at my house that allows me to make fresh juice and control what goes in it. Seriously consider buying an affordable juicing machine for weekly fasting. Otherwise, buy quality bottled juice in the refrigerated fruit section at your store: pure fruit and vegetable juice, no added sugars, corn syrups, or anything else added to it. I drink 24-48 ounces of juice a day, depending on how I'm feeling. Monitor how you're feeling in your energy levels and resolve to continue fasting and take in juice if you are feeling weak, or as needed.

Know when to take breaks or when to slow down. If you're feeling physically weak, work sitting down or take a break altogether. If you try to push through the moment of weakness, it will probably get worse, and you'll have a hard time recovering your energy. If needed, and if you are able, take a short nap.

Regular exercise isn't usually suggested on a fasting day but walking and stretching are very realistic. I go for short walks outside and stretch at times, and it feels great. It increases my energy levels, clears my mind, and helps speed up the detoxification process.

On fasting days, I suggest avoiding being around food, your kitchen, and social events when possible. On a longer fast, this is important because small moments of being around food or social gatherings with food can weaken your vision and resolve for fasting. Just being around some of these things, smelling the food, and fantasizing about each bite that someone else takes has awakened hunger pains and physical appetites. It may not be as critical on a shorter fast, but it's most helpful when you're starting out or in a weak moment.

Even social events without food can decrease your vision and resolve for fasting. Why would social gatherings affect your fasting? If the hangout is casual and not focused on spiritual edification, it goes against the intensity and focus of your fasting for Jesus to be your food. When I'm at a casual gathering, the general atmosphere is everyday life and comfort, which isn't necessarily bad. But my mode on a fasting day is consecration and focused pursuit of Jesus. My vision and focus get blurry in casual hangouts.

LIFESTYLE

After reading through some of these fasting sections, you are probably getting a greater sense of how a fasting day impacts your lifestyle through the week. This is very true. Fasting puts a healthy pressure on us to adjust our lifestyle and weekly rhythm in several ways. I'm only going to comment on a few: exercise, diet, prayer, and life rhythm. A weekly routine of working out is healthy and will make fasting days easier and more sustainable. What you eat through the week needs to be thought through because your body will automatically start to rid itself of toxins on fasting days. If you're putting toxins in your body by eating unhealthy foods, you're going to pay the price on your fasting day. Detox symptoms (headaches, dry mouth, aches, nausea) will make you quit your fast. Continue to grow in your daily prayer rhythm because this will train your heart to receive life from the Lord on your fasting days.

The last area is life rhythm, which is your weekly schedule. If you haven't thought through a daily and weekly schedule for your life, your lack of rhythm in various areas will collide on your fasting days over time and negatively affect them. I encourage you to develop a written schedule for each day of the week that includes detailed things, but the major ones are diet, exercise, prayer, consistent sleep times, and what you're doing in your free time.

▍ WEEKLY ASSIGNMENT

This week, reflect on the fasting plans you created last week and refine them based on the content of this chapter. Answer the same questions but write down more detailed thoughts if you have them. *Questions to answer: (1) What day/meal(s) will you fast? (2) What kind of fast will you do? (3) How long will it last? (4) When would you pray? (5) How will you prepare food-wise? (i.e., what will be your last meal, and what will you break your fast with?)*

If you choose to fast according to your plan during this week, journal your thoughts, challenges (physical, emotional, etc.), and experiences from the fast. Reflecting will help you recognize any fasting benefits. It will also help you refine your fasting plans because you'll learn ways to steward your body and schedule from your experience.

35

WEEKLY FASTING PART THREE

FASTING CHALLENGES

PHYSICAL CHALLENGES

There are at least three different physical challenges involved with fasting. The obvious one is lower energy levels. Depending on the type of fasting, you will have varying amounts of decreased energy. The point of fasting is to have less energy and enter into the spiritual principle of weakness that Paul and Jesus preached. While it's a real challenge to be aware of, it's to be embraced with the revelation that God's power will increase.

Set your heart to be okay with less energy and less productivity on fasting days. You can monitor your juice or vegetable intake to maintain a sustainable, though lower, energy level. Honestly, it doesn't have to be too bad, but you have to be aware of it and embrace it to whatever level you fast. Water-only fasts are very challenging because of the lack of energy, but juice and Daniel fasts are very sustainable. I've done short and long juice and Daniel fasts consistently and have found them to be very doable for people in all kinds of situations. Don't let the fear of unknown energy levels hold you back from growing in weekly fasting or more extended fasting.

The second challenge on a fasting day is experiencing detoxification symptoms. During fasting, the body naturally begins to rid the body of toxins or things that are unhealthy. When this happens, there are headaches, dry mouth, bad breath, joint pain, tiredness, acne, and increased mucus. Some of the physical discomforts are also related to your body going without specific daily intakes such as caffeine and refined sugars.

One fear people have about fasting for the first time, or entering back into a lifestyle of weekly fasting, is that they will experience detox symptoms every week. Don't let that be your fear! There are lifestyle changes you can make to address potential detoxing. I've found taking walks outside, stretching, and drinking healthy juices help with any detoxing that may be happening on fasting days.

The last physical challenge is to change your lifestyle to promote enjoyable fasting. You can research ways to help with the detoxification symptoms, but the longer-term solution is to evaluate your lifestyle and make changes that decrease your toxin intake. Yes, begin and end your weekly fasts with intentionality, but eating healthy and intentionally most days will make fasting even easier. Regular exercise will also cleanse and strengthen your body during the week. We all know lifestyle changes are a challenge, but they are well worth the change. If you want to step into fasting, you will be faced with any unhealthy diet, exercise, and rhythms you have, so you might as well address some of them now.

My wife and I eat relatively healthy, and because of that, I don't experience the consistent detox symptoms I used to in my early days. We were radical and cut every source of refined sugar in our diet and recipes, and replaced them with honey, or stopped eating them altogether. During Bible school, I didn't eat healthily or drink healthy liquids on fasting days. I made fasting much harder than it needed to be! It is so much easier now that I'm eating healthier and transitioning in and out of fasts wisely, and the detox symptoms are usually only there if I ate badly the week before.

EMOTIONAL CHALLENGES

Emotional challenges include low emotional energy and unpacified emotions. I don't know the science behind this, but depending on how your body responds to fasting, you may have lower energy in your emotions. This is similar to having less physical energy.

Your emotions will be raw and unable to be pacified by everything that usually supports them. In my opinion, this is the most significant challenge of fasting! Think of all the things you might say no to on fasting days: movies, YouTube, social media, unintentional hangouts, books, drinking coffee, cooking, and eating food. Your emotions are stimulated, supported, or distracted by some of these things daily. These are probably the things you turn to when you feel sad, discouraged, bored, angry, confused, and overwhelmed. But on fasting days, they are all stripped away.

Emotional crutches are exposed in fasting. When this happens, the actual state of your heart will be revealed. In this place, you will hopefully see the areas of your heart where you are dull or broken in your relationship with the Lord. You might feel great and "connected" to God on Sundays when there's a coffee in your hand, loud music, and lunch right afterward. But how do you feel when there's no other stimulation, and it's just you, your Bible, and Jesus all day? What does your heart sound like when there's no white noise in the background?

I don't fully know what your journey will be like, but the exposure of emotional crutches will be a good thing. Realizing that there are areas of dullness and brokenness in your heart is the first step towards hungering and thirsting for God to be our source. You can't be hungry and thirsty for God if you're filling your soul with other things, and you won't encounter God as much without cultivating spiritual hunger.

The process of realizing spiritual dullness, unto awakening spiritual hunger for God, unto a more focused pursuit of God, cannot be bypassed. Spiritual hunger is always the prerequisite for something more in God. Jesus said that those who hunger and thirst would be filled, and David said, *"O God, You are my God; early will I seek You; my soul thirsts for You; my flesh longs for You in a dry and thirsty land where there is no water. So I have looked for You in the sanctuary, to see Your power and Your glory."*[1]

If you can say no to all the emotional band aids on fasting days, Jesus will heal them and become your source of life over time. Fasting and being stripped of all the crutches is the barren wilderness in which He wants to encounter you and transform your appetites. Just like the Israelites in the wilderness, God wants to remove all the emotional supports and train your soul to feast on Him alone.

RELATIONAL CHALLENGES

Relationship challenges sound like an odd difficulty, but they are real. King David and John the Baptist experienced challenges in their relationships because of fasting.[2] Fasting is a strange topic in itself, but it's a whole lot stranger to people

---

1   Matthew 5:6; Psalm 63:1-3.

2   Psalm 69:6-10; Matthew 11:18.

when fasting is a part of your lifestyle. Some of your family, friends, co-workers, and church friends might not know what to do with the topic or understand how to interact with you on fasting days. This is where the challenges lie.

There are ways to keep fasting days private so others don't even know you're doing it, but some people will figure it out, and others you'll want to tell at necessary times. So, what happens when people know you fast regularly or that you're on a longer fast? Some will be intrigued and ask questions, which is amazing! Some won't be sure what they can ask you because fasting is mainly seen as a private thing. This will leave them unsure of what to say or how to interact with you on fasting days. You might be the only person they've met that actually fasts. Others might inwardly or verbally disagree with fasting, either for perceived health concerns or because of their Biblical perspectives. Another group of people might feel challenged, convicted, and provoked by your fasting and assume you think they should be fasting as well, even if you never call them to it.

What can you do in these different situations? My first response is that you don't have to tell everyone you're fasting, and you can fast in ways that keep it hidden from a lot of people. As you fast weekly, you will figure out ways to keep it hidden. If it's going to be evident to certain ones, come up with a short explanation of why you fast. Bring them into a dialogue to ask questions or share concerns and help them understand how they can relate to you on fasting days, like if they should invite you for a meal, break time, or workout session. The awkwardness and confusion can be removed by good conversation.

If you are intentionally telling your Jesus-loving friends, have a Biblical explanation and a heart reason for fasting, and be ready to respond in love to all kinds of positive or negative responses. If they are close friends, the conversations could be very healthy and help them understand your heart and get a vision for fasting in their lives.

SPIRITUAL CHALLENGES

The two spiritual challenges that I have observed are demonic resistance and the awareness of wrong motivations. I'll comment on the wrong motivations later in this chapter. Whether felt or not, there will be some level of demonic resistance in your life if you pursue fasting. Resistance could look like an increased accusation in your thoughts, greater temptation to break a fast, increased lusts or opportunities to express sin, negative situations, hard prayer times, relational conflict, and demonic dreams. On the other hand, God's power will increase in your life in every area if you pursue fasting, and His power will be greater than the Devil's, so there's nothing to fear. Be aware that fasting is a spiritual threat and recognize that some challenges might be demonic and will have to be overcome through prayer and diligence.

FASTING BENEFITS

In the first fasting chapter, I highlighted a few benefits related to intimacy with God: a longing for God, tenderness, and expanded heart size. Below is a list of four more spiritual benefits. We have to recognize and celebrate the benefits of fasting to build a personal testimony that will encourage us in the fasted lifestyle.

VULNERABILITY TO TRUTH

Fasting breaks down our defenses and makes us vulnerable so that God's truths can go deep in a quick way. If you compare the heart to the soil in a garden, then a fasting heart is soft, wet, fertilized soil compared to hard, dry, and malnourished soil. The fasting process is like pouring water on hard ground, breaking the soil into small pieces, and then mixing fertilizer into it until it's a perfect environment for seeds to enter and grow. The seeds of God's Word are then released into the soil and easily penetrate it and go deep. Then they bear much fruit! Fasting prepares the soil of our hearts to receive and nourish the seed of God's Word. Mark 4 describes our heart conditions and directly relates the fruit of God's Word in us to the condition of the soil.

CLARITY

I liken the clarity that comes through fasting to someone getting their head above the clouds on a dreary day or to a blinding fog evaporating. In both cases, darkness or something was hindering clear sight, but in the process of fasting, the hindrances are removed to see clearly. I experience substantial clarity in thoughts and emotions in fasting, and I get a renewed vision for my life. Detoxing during a fast can hinder clarity, but if there is minimal detoxing, or if I'm 1-2 days into a short fast, my mind becomes more alert and able to think about the Lord. My emotions feel clear and more connected to truth, and I feel spiritual clarity and discernment in other areas of my life. Lies I have been believing become more apparent and easier to address in prayer. Sinful patterns are clearer to me and easier to turn from in confession and repentance. Accusations or any other oppression that I've been under become more apparent and easier to address.

These are a result of the complete silencing and stilling of the body and soul during fasting. Anxieties, fears, confusion, lusts, and physical appetites diminish, creating a unique quietness that makes everything clearer. God's whispers are easier to hear, and processing thoughts and emotions are significantly easier. Every time I experience this, I'm somewhat shocked by the quietness and the grace to process life in an organized way. This could be the exact opposite of what you experience as you begin to fast, but as you continue in fasting this stillness is your portion!

HEART POSTURED TOWARDS GOD

Our hearts are postured towards something or someone for satisfaction all the time. Fasting postures our hearts towards God for life through the day as opposed to other natural sources. On fasting days, I become more aware of the earthly things my heart is postured towards. When I'm aware of this, I can choose to turn or set my heart on God in the moment. Because of posturing my heart towards Him repeatedly during my prayer times, my heart begins to look to God more naturally throughout the week.

"So He humbled you, allowed you to hunger, and fed you with manna which you did not know nor did your fathers know, that He might make you know that man shall not live by bread alone, but man lives by every word that proceeds from the mouth of the LORD."—Deuteronomy 8:3

In Deuteronomy 8, God brought Israel into the wilderness to change the orientation of their hearts from external and temporal to internal and eternal. The wilderness caused them to be aware of what they looked to for life through the day so that they could address it and turn to God for life. As we fast from food and other sources of life, God wants our hearts to learn that the intimate Words of His mouth are the real source of life. In this process, our hearts turn to God as the source of life, impacting the heart on non-fasting days. It's like a chiropractic adjustment for our soul, which rightly aligns it towards God. This process trains the soul to look to God through the day and transforms your internal appetites to desire God.

HEART AGREEMENT

The "yes and amen" in our hearts grows stronger and deeper as a result of fasting. Whether it be a 1-day fast or a 40-day fast, God strengthens our wills to agree with His values and commandments. We are supposed to agree and say yes to His values in everyday life, but there can be a resounding and sustained "yes" within fasting. This could pertain to His promises over our lives, His love for us, or conviction in an area of righteousness. In the tenderness of fasting, our hearts can dynamically grab onto the truth.

WRONG MOTIVATIONS?

Will you have wrong motivations in fasting, like losing a few pounds, impressing others, or trying to earn something from God? Yes, you probably will! You might not be aware of them right away, but they will likely come to the surface after more fasting. Are these your entire motivation for fasting? You'll have to ask the Lord about that, but there's a good chance you're fasting out of a sincere desire for God, and these other motivations are mixed in to different degrees.

I counsel people to respond to wrong motivations by repenting before the Lord, confessing to friends, and not quitting their fast. Why not quit the fast if the motives are not 100% pure? Because fasting is part of what positioned you to see your motivations clearer and fasting will be what positions you to receive breakthroughs from the wrong motivations. Compare wrong motivations in fasting with wrong motivations in prayer or Bible study. Would you stop praying or reading your Bible if you became aware of wrong motivations? No, prayer and the Word are the sources of deliverance and clarity. They are the means by which God will remove wrong motives!

Clarity is a sign of God's work of wisdom and revelation, so praise God you see clearly. If there are mixed motivations in fasting, the same mixed motivations are with every other spiritual activity. If this is true, God is probably addressing a root issue affecting your entire approach to relating to Him.

When you're aware of the wrong motivation, take a minute and talk to God about it and address it by repenting of it. God might encounter you with the truth if you tell him your motivations and talk it through with Him. As often as the motivation comes to the surface, repent of it and bring it up to your close friends for prayer and accountability.

In more extreme situations with body image struggles and eating disorders, you should stop fasting. If you or a friend struggle with either of these issues in fasting, bring them up to your trusted church leaders for counsel.

WHAT IF I BREAK EARLY?

How does God feel if you break a fast, and what should you do when it happens? I think God can speak into individual situations to give His full perspective, but in general, He's deeply moved by our desire and attempts to fast. God's heart is easily overcome with love by the movements of our hearts towards Him. He sees the slightest movements of love and desire that get you to fast and spend time with Him, and it ravishes His heart![1] God is not discouraged or disappointed in you for breaking, and He's not calling it a sin. God is blessed by you, celebrates your attempt, and He sees where you're going in fasting in the long-term journey of it all. God is a proud Father over your life!

God isn't an angry father who has unrealistic expectations of His children, who isn't willing to go through the process of training them in something. He's

---

1 Song of Songs 4:9.

gentle and patient, and He's with you in the journey of fasting, just like every other area of your life. God is a Father who leads you by inviting you into things, encouraging you, directing you, and then laboring with you for maturity and consistency. He does this in every area of your life, including fasting. If you are newer to fasting or stepping out in new ways, God is holding your fingers through it like a father helping his child learn how to walk.

PUSH DELETE

When you break a fast early, you have the choice to jump back into your fast with a happy heart or to start up again the next week. I love what Mike Bickle always says, "Push delete and get back in." If you have the resolve in your heart to fast, jump back in with no shame or guilt before God! If you don't have the determination to fast, decide to end and get ready for next week's fasting time.

MATURING IN FASTING

I believe God wants us to be free from shame and guilt in breaking early, but He also wants us to mature and be able to persevere through tempting moments. If you notice you regularly break your fasts, re-evaluate your fasting commitment or talk to the Lord about why you're struggling. You have to walk free from shame in breaking early and carry the sobriety of wanting to sow in the Spirit in fasting and being diligent. At times, I've gotten into patterns of breaking early consistently, and I've found that I have to re-consecrate my fasting times to the Lord. When I make the shift in my heart to take it more seriously, I connect to the power of fasting, and I walk out fasting with more vision and diligence.

If you consider the sowing and reaping principle or the weakness principle, fulfilling your fast does matter. Again, fasting doesn't prove anything to God, but it does soften your heart and position you to receive more. If you're consistently breaking early, you're going to miss out on some levels of the fasting benefits. It's the same with prayer; if you always spend less time in prayer, your heart will experience less.

If you are having a hard day with fasting, you can talk to the Lord about it and see what He says, but I don't think you have to ask His permission to break early. If you don't want to fast that day and don't have the resolve to ask Him for help and persevere, don't feel bad about breaking.

WEEKLY ASSIGNMENT

This week, reflect on any fasting days you've done during the module and refine and adjust your fasting plans as needed. For some of you, you might be ready to plan for more fasting, and for others, refining may only include small adjustments. Answer the same questions but write down more detailed thoughts if you have them. *Questions to answer: (1) What day/meal(s) will you fast? (2) What kind of fast will you do? (3) How long will it last? (4) When would you pray? (5) How will you prepare food-wise? (i.e., what will be your last meal, and what will you break your fast with?)* If you choose to fast according to your plan during this week, journal your thoughts, challenges, and experience from the fast. Reflecting on your fast will help your heart and help you refine your plans.

To end this program, schedule a 1-3-day fast with your group. Schedule how long it will be and what days are best. Then plan when the individual and group prayer times will be. I've led people that were newer in fasting into 1–3-day group fasts and it was a great experience for them, though stretching. These fasts started on a Friday morning and ended on a Sunday evening with group prayer times every morning and evening. A group fast is beneficial during this module because it helps bring the group into the next step of fasting with the grace that comes in doing things together. It also stretches people to taste long prayer hours three days in a row, which can tenderize hearts quickly and get people longing for longer hours moving forward.

DISCIPLESHIP MEETING GUIDE
MODULE 8: FASTING – CHAPTERS 34 & 35

MEETING FOCUS:

The purpose of this meeting is to continue to process the prayer assignment (fears, hindrances, and what excites you concerning fasting), process how fasting is going, and work on a weekly fasting plan.

DISCUSSION QUESTIONS (IN ORDER OF IMPORTANCE):

1. *Spiritual pursuits*:
   a. Practically, how is your prayer schedule going? How many days have you walked out your prayer schedule? Do you need to make small changes to your schedule? How are your daily prayer times going, and how is God impacting you through them?

2. *Chapter questions*:
   a. Chapter 34 – Discuss any journaled thoughts and questions from the chapter. What are the most helpful practical questions you have? What were your thoughts on the Consecration Plan section in the chapter?
   b. Discuss your finalized weekly fasting plan. If you're fasting, how is it going for you? Do you have more you need to process and pray through regarding fasting experiences, fears, hindrances, wrong motivations, or things that excite you about it?
   c. Chapter 35 – Discuss any journaled thoughts and questions from the chapter. Which fasting challenge and fasting benefit impacted you the most?
   d. Talk through what the 1-3-day fast could look like for you this week.

3. *Heart Issue*:
   a. Share how your heart issue has been going this past week. With heart issue discussions, process, confess, encourage, and pray together for God to release transformation. ***Pray in tongues together and ask God to release power to the heart issue.***

4. Briefly review next week's homework together.

MEETING NOTES:

_____

_____

_____

_____

_____

_____

_____

_____

_____

_____

36
TRANSITION WEEK

▌ CONGRATULATIONS!

You did it! This is the last chapter of the discipleship program! I am so blessed by your diligence to stay in the place of prayer through all the challenges, circumstances, new topics, new rhythms, and allowing leaders and your church community to call you higher. ***This week marks 40 weeks of pursuing daily prayer.*** As you read this, I pray you have developed God's perspective on your pursuit over the 40 weeks and are encouraged by how much you've grown and how much you've sown that will be reaped in this next year.

▌ CONTINUING YOUR RHYTHM

This last week is an important transition for you. You've had a lot of structure and support around you for 40 weeks, and now you must think about how life looks without the formal training experience and expectations of the program.

The goal of this program was for you to learn a lifestyle of prayer and have the support you need to grow into a rhythm of prayer. If you can transition well, you will maintain your new rhythms and values and continue to grow!

Your experiences with God in each module and the daily prayer rhythm you've grown in are priceless. In a prayer-less generation, what you've cultivated so far is a huge gift, not only for you but for those that you will disciple. Therefore, I strongly encourage you to steward your new prayer life by continuing in daily prayer and focusing on growing in each prayer expression. These 40 weeks have served to strengthen your foundation, but now you can keep building and grow upon it.

Deep daily intimacy with God through prayer is why you exist, and it's the only thing that will continue to satisfy and transform you. As I said in the beginning, the structure of this program is likened to the wooden forms and braces that keep wet cement in place until dry and in perfect shape. I'm confident that the cement of your prayer life has been formed and hardened in place, so now you can continue to build on your prayer life.

I realize that coming out of a structure with assignments and expectations it can be natural to "take a break" from such pursuit of God. Part of this is okay because you've been stretched, you've grown your rhythms, and you've had book reading and prayer assignments on top of normal life. So yes, take a couple of weeks off from assignments, but don't take a break from your prayer rhythm; that's where you're experiencing God's life. Satan would love nothing more than for you to stop or slow down in prayer for a month so that he can get you back into a spiritual rut.

TRANSITION OPTIONS

By design, most of the components of this curriculum can be continued within your local church long-term. There isn't a lot of mystery as to how you can continue growing in prayer with structure and community because everything you've been doing can be normal to continue within discipleship and your friendships at church. You don't have to grow in prayer alone! God has ordained strength for you through living in a church community. Below are the main components of the curriculum that can be continued.

MAIN COMPONENTS

1. **Daily Prayer** – You can continue your commitment of 1-2 hours of daily prayer. When you are ready, grow into longer prayer times each day.

2. **Spiritual Pursuits** – You can continue to fill out a new Spiritual Pursuits document every couple of months to maintain your spiritual clarity. This document was designed to be used long-term, and we use it as a part of our lifestyle. For every season of your life, this includes having Bible direction and plans, a heart issue to pursue breakthrough in, and a part of your calling to grow in, as well as having a detailed weekly prayer schedule.

3. **Discipleship Mentor Meetings** – Within God's plans for the local church, it should be normal to be discipled and to disciple others. Therefore, God wants to encourage, strengthen, and challenge you by meeting with a Discipleship Mentor regularly. We never have to graduate from being discipled! As a helpful guide, you could continue to center your conversations around your Spiritual Pursuits.

4. **Prayer Room** – If you started a prayer room or joined an existing one, keep it going each week. God designed you to grow in prayer and friendship with others by praying and reading the Bible together. Get a long-term vision for growing your prayer room and bring others into it so they can taste the glory of praying together. Investing time and energy into

bringing people together will be worth it because God is worthy of more worship, and because prayer rooms are invaluable to discipling people in prayer.

5. **Learning Prayer Expressions** – When you're ready to focus on learning more about the prayer expressions from the curriculum, go through one module at a time at your own pace. You will glean more from each chapter the more times you go through them and apply the principles and practical tips. You could also go through other books that are focused on training people in meditation, tongues, worship, fasting, etc.

6. **Group Gatherings** – Within your local church, it should be normal to have Bible study groups or prayer accountability groups. You can continue to grow in your prayer life and share your life in God with others in regular gatherings. This could also include extended group prayer days on a regular basis.

STRUCTURE IDEAS

There are several relationship and structure options that you can transition into to walk out your prayer life. Each option provides the structure and support necessary to help you grow in prayer. If this is something you're desiring, consider which one or two options you would want to create or join if your church already has them operating.

1. **Prayer partners** – With this option, you could gather one or more peers to meet every one-two weeks to talk through your Spiritual Pursuits. In these times, you could share what God is doing in your times in prayer and the Word, confess sins and testify related to your areas of transformation, discuss your desired areas of growth, pray for each other, and hold each

other accountable to your Spiritual Pursuits. Also, you could focus on slowly reading one module at a time.

2. **Be discipled using the Spiritual Pursuits** – You could continue to meet with a Discipleship Mentor at your church with the Spiritual Pursuits topics as your main conversation. Within this option, there are lots of directions you could go based on what you want to focus on growing in (prayer expressions, dealing with heart issues, growing in aspects of your calling, or going through Bible teachings together).

3. **Disciple someone with the curriculum** – You could choose to disciple someone else through this same curriculum. Doing this would help you go through the content and assignments again to strengthen your rhythm. It would also cause you to grow in prayer and own the values more because you would be calling others into the lifestyle and modeling the way.

4. **Be discipled through the curriculum again** – If you feel the need to go through the entire content and structure of the curriculum again, I encourage you to do it. Your prayer life will be strengthened, your heart issues will be addressed more fully, and you'll glean more from the chapter contents every time you go through them.

WEEKLY ASSIGNMENT

For your last assignment, respond to the questions on the Transition Assignment document. This document will walk you through the practical questions you need to think through to transition well, so take your time so you feel clear about your next steps. Also, some of the questions are reflective of the last 40 weeks to help you see what God has done in you based on your initial Consecration Assignment responses from week one.

TRANSITION ASSIGNMENT
CONSECRATION ASSIGNMENT REFLECTIONS

1. Read through your Consecration Assignment answers from *Week One* of the program. To celebrate growth and victory, reflect on them, and write down which ones were answered by God to some measure.

2. Ask God the following questions and write down what you sense Him saying to you. How do You feel about my pursuit of You during this program? What did You do in my life and heart during these 40 weeks? What encouragements do You have for me as I end these 40 weeks?

3. Do you feel any measure of weariness from the structure and assignments of the program? How does the idea of continuing in daily prayer and group accountability (discipleship or prayer partners) sound to you? If you feel weary, take some time to ask God to wash you with His thoughts, and for Him to renew your desires and strengthen your heart from being stretched in your prayer rhythms and lifestyle.

PRACTICAL TRANSITION QUESTIONS

4. Ask God how He wants you to consecrate yourself to Him in this next season.

5. Which module impacted you the most and why? Which module topic would you like to study and grow in after the program?

6. What specific components of the curriculum do you want to continue using (refer to the "Main Components" section in the chapter reading)?

7. If any, what relationship structure would you like to participate in, and when would you want to begin (refer to the "Structure Ideas" section in the chapter reading)? Write down why you want that specific structure.

8. Write down action items of what you need to do and who you need to talk to based on your answers to questions 5, 6, and 7.

DISCIPLESHIP MEETING GUIDE
LAST MEETING: TRANSITION PLAN – CHAPTER 36

MEETING FOCUS:

The purpose of this week's meeting is to review your *Transition Assignment* and to decide how to transition out of the program well.

DISCUSSION QUESTIONS:

1. *Transition Assignment*
   a. Share what you wrote down for each of the questions in the Transition Assignment that were related to reflecting on your *Consecration Assignment* from Week 1.
   b. Share what you wrote down for each of the questions in the Transition Assignment about what next steps you want to take. Finalize a plan together.
   c. Take time to thank God for the past 40 weeks together, encourage one another, and pray over the next few weeks of transition.

Made in the USA
Columbia, SC
05 December 2023

27794289R00322